HUMAN AGGRESSION AND CONFLICT

Prentice-Hall Psychology Series
Richard S. Lazarus, *editor*

HUMAN AGGRESSION AND CONFLICT

interdisciplinary perspectives

KLAUS R. SCHERER / *University of Giessen, Germany*

RONALD P. ABELES / *Social Science Research Council, New York*

CLAUDE S. FISCHER / *University of California, Berkeley*

Prentice-Hall, Inc., Englewood Cliffs, New Jersey

Library of Congress Cataloging in Publication Data

SCHERER, KLAUS RAINER.
    Human aggression and conflict.

    (Prentice-Hall psychology series)
    Bibliography: p. 296
    Includes index.
    1. Aggressiveness (Psychology) 2. Social conflict.
I. Abeles, Ronald P.,   joint author.
II. Fischer, Claude S.,   joint author.
III. Title.
BF575.A3S3   155.2′4   74-23131
ISBN   0-13-444620-8 pbk.

Prentice-Hall International, Inc., *London*
Prentice-Hall of Australia, Pty. Ltd., *Sydney*
Prentice-Hall of Canada, Ltd., *Toronto*
Prentice-Hall of India Private Limited, *New Delhi*
Prentice-Hall of Japan, Inc., *Tokyo*

To the Harvard Department of Social Relations,
as we knew it.

contents

preface

Remember the parable of the three blind men and the elephant? The first blind man felt its coarse, hairy tail and believed the elephant was a thick rope. The second one examined its flexible trunk and thought he had hold of a hose. Finally, the third blind man bumped into its massive legs and declared the beast to be a grove of trees. Each examined a part of the same animal, but from his own limited perspective, and each arrived at an inadequate description of the whole animal.

The parable of the three blind men parallels in many ways the study of conflict, violence, and aggression. There are many learned volumes on the psychology or sociology or anthropology or biology of violence. Each unique approach contributes to our understanding, but each alone can provide but a partial description of the total phenomenon. Taken and integrated together, however, these various perspectives can more fully illuminate the causes of human aggression.

One goal of this book is to investigate conflict and aggression from two of these perspectives: psychology and sociology. In each chapter we emphasize somewhat different causes of conflict and aggression. We hope that by focusing on the unique aspects of the physiological, motivational, interactional, social structural, and social systemic origins of aggression within the framework of a single text, the reader will gain a better appreciation of the contributions and shortcomings of each discipline and learn that all are necessary to gain a more complete understanding.

As well as studying violence specifically, this book has a second purpose: to demonstrate the nature of social scientific thinking. Each chapter attempts to present concepts and approaches that go beyond the particular topic of aggression and to impart a basic knowledge and understanding of selected areas of psychology and sociology. By focusing on aggression, we hope the reader will comprehend how social science progresses through the development of theories and hypotheses, the collection of facts, the testing of theories against data, and the gradual accumulation of substantiated propositions concerning the nature of a social phenomenon. Though the chapters present different approaches to the question of what causes violence and introduce different concepts, they all demonstrate the basic process of the scientific search into human behavior.

Given the dual nature of the book, it may be used in a variety of ways. First, it may serve as the main textbook for a course on conflict and aggression as given in many psychology, sociology, or political science departments. Here it may be supplemented by other more detailed theoretical and empirical materials stressing particular aspects of the topic. As a main textbook, it attempts to present a general overview to the field of conflict and aggression. While the instructor may emphasize the contributions of his own discipline through supplementary readings, he may also use the text to expose his students to the host of other variables involved in understanding the complexities of human conflict (and of human behavior in general).

Second, the text may be used as supplementary readings to introductory and middle-level courses in psychology and sociology. The text offers an opportunity to show how social science can be relevant to understanding "real world" events. By frequent references to both scientific investigations and actual events, the text presents and applies social science concepts in a systematic fashion. In conjunction with a general social science text, it offers the reader a grounding in basic concepts.

In addition, we feel that the discussion offers the general reader a not too technical, though scientifically valid, overview of some social scientific explanations of aggression. We attempt to make clear that the popularized "nature-nurture" controversy in the aggression literature (e.g., R. Ardrey's *The Territorial Imperative*) is but a single issue in the study of aggression. We hope that the book will give the reader some insight into the complexities of social conflict and thereby inoculate him against simple solutions to social problems.

Before moving on to the substance of our discussion, we would like to express our sincere appreciation to the many people who aided us in this seemingly endless project. Margaret V. Sachs helped research and prepare materials for a few chapters. Various chapters have benefited greatly from the comments, suggestions, and criticisms of Anna Harrison Abeles, Robert Apsler, Diane Barthel, Herbert Blumer, Ted Gurr, J. Roy Hopkins, Jeanne Messer, Mary Morton, L. Anne Peplau, Ursula Scherer, Arthur Stinchcombe, and four anonymous reviewers. We would also like to acknowledge the secretarial assistance of Elizabeth E. Burnham and Camille Buda along with the bibliographic assistance of Elaine Friedman.

Finally, just a few words about the division of labor. The original idea and impetus for this book came from Klaus Scherer. Together the three of us selected a list of topics and took individual and joint responsibility for the various chapters. Klaus Scherer, a social psychologist, wrote Chapters 1–3, which deal heavily with psychological topics. Ronald Abeles, also a social psychologist but with some sociological inclinations, was responsible for Chapter 6 and for Chapters 1, 4, and 5 with Scherer. Claude Fischer, a sociologist, prepared the last two chapters. Finally, Abeles had responsibility for the overall coordination and editing of our efforts. Of course, we each benefited from the reviews and comments of our coauthors, colleagues, and friends.

K. R. S.
R. P. A.
C. S. F.

INTRODUCTION

YOUTHS DRENCH WOMAN WITH GASOLINE, TORCH HER TO DEATH

SENATOR SHOT AND ROBBED

THREE SLAIN IN VIRGIN ISLANDS

ARAB TERRORISTS BOMB AMSTERDAM EL AL OFFICE

WILDCAT STRIKE CLOSES STEEL MILL

BLACKS WHITES CLASH AT HIGH SCHOOL

CHILEAN ARMY TOPPLES MARXIST GOVT

POLISH DOCK WORKERS RIOT

MARTIN LUTHER KING ASSASSINATED

Our newspapers tell us in large letters that conflict, violence, and aggression are daily events in the lives of millions of people the world over. Most Americans believe that church bombings, sit-ins, protests, riots, wars, assassinations, muggings, rapes, and mass murders have marked the past decade as one of extraordinary violence. While it is difficult to know whether the last ten years really were more violent than preceding decades,[1] Americans are certainly more concerned about violence today. For example, 42 percent of the people questioned in a December 1972 Gallup poll felt afraid to walk alone at night in their own neighborhoods. Just four years earlier, less than one out of three Americans had similar fears. This same poll showed that residents of big

1

cities were particularly worried about crime, and their concern was seven times greater in 1972 than in 1948. In 1972 crime was cited as their city's worst problem by 21 percent of big-city dwellers as compared to 3 percent in 1948.[2]

Partly reflecting the man-in-the-street's concern, the federal government has spent millions of dollars on commissions to study the origins of conflict, violence, and crime and to make recommendations for their prevention.[3] Local, state, and federal governments have spent even more money bolstering police forces. New anticrime laws have been passed with severe penalties (including attempts to bypass the Supreme Court's ruling against capital punishment), and "Crime in the Streets" and "Law and Order" have become decisive campaign issues. Regardless of whether the last ten years were more violent than previous years, Americans believe these to be particularly dangerous times and wonder about the causes and potential cures for war, crime, and civil unrest.

Given this concern and the actual magnitude of the problem, aggression and violence certainly deserve the careful attention of laymen and scientists. Obviously, any attempts at diminishing the amount of mayhem among our fellow men should be based on sound knowledge. In order to solve a problem, we need to know what its causes are. As we shall see, conflict, violence, and aggression are complex phenomena demanding equally complex methods for reducing their occurrence.

WHAT IS AGGRESSION?

An initial step in the scientific investigation of any subject is to define and delimit the topic of concern. We shall do this by trying to define aggression, which we see as differing only in degree from violence and as a potential outcome of social conflict. But can we really define aggression? At first glance, this seems like a simple task. We all know aggression when we see it. Or do we? Is a lion killing its prey aggression? What about a soldier shooting the enemy? A boy dreaming of hurting his baby sister? A surgeon operating on a cancer victim? A man accidentally striking another person? A white women thinking evil thoughts about a Negro? Or a junior executive pushing his way to the top?

Some of us might call all of these examples instances of aggression, while others might pick out just a few. Social scientists are also not unanimous in deciding when a behavior is aggressive. However, most definitions of aggression equate it with behavior that is intended to harm another member of the same species. Let's look at this definition in some detail.[4]

First, the definition rules out predation or cross-species killing as aggression. The lion's killing an antelope is no more aggressive than our buying a steak at the supermarket. This limitation is included mainly to simplify the problem and in recognition that there may be differences in the origins of interspecies and intraspecies behaviors. Since we are more concerned with why men kill other men than with why men kill cattle, we shall limit our discussion and definition to intraspecies behaviors.

Second, our definition focuses on the person's intention or the goals of his behavior. Consequently, accidentally harming someone is not considered to be an instance of aggression. Similarly, the surgeon's inflicting pain in order to save his patient's life is not a case of aggression. True, he intends to cause pain, but the primary goal of his behavior is not to harm another. It is often problematic, however, whether a person intends to harm another or not, as those of us who suspect dentists of being oral sadists well know! As we observe someone's behavior, we often find it difficult to know the person's true goal or intention. And, as Freud pointed out, even the person himself may not be aware of his underlying motives. Thus, an ambiguity is built into our definition. We cannot rely upon the observation of a behavior alone to determine whether it is aggression. We have to tap the person's psychological state at the time he initiated the behavior.

This ambiguity has led some social scientists to concentrate only on the person's behavior.[5] They argue that we can never truly know a person's intentions, so we should define aggression purely in terms of a behavior's effects upon another person: "Did he hurt him or not?" Unfortunately, this behavioral definition creates new problems. For example, accidents become aggression, and inept attempts at harming another person are now not aggression. According to this definition, a "hit man" who misses his mark has not been aggressive! Since this conflicts with common sense, we shall stick with defining aggression in terms of the actor's intentions.

Another complication arises if we distinguish "intentions" from "desires." A person may intend to harm another, but not desire to do so. A soldier may not want to kill, but fires his rifle anyway. In shooting his enemy, the soldier certainly intends to harm him, even though he may not desire to do it or like what he is doing. Do we want to call such behaviors aggressive? According to our definition, harming someone at the command of another is aggression. Since this behavior occurs quite frequently and is commonly assumed to be aggression, we shall also include it under the topic of aggression.

Besides harming someone on command, people often feel compelled to harm others because they see it as a means to achieving some other goal. Their end goal is not to hurt someone else, but aggression is a means to a desired end. For example, war often is not pursued as an end in itself, but as a means of obtaining other goals such as natural resources. Governments may resort to war when other nonviolent or less aggressive means fail. We shall consider such acts of "instrumental" aggression as part of aggression in general and we shall return to this in some detail in later chapters.

Finally, we have to specify what we mean by "harming" another person. Is just thinking nasty thoughts about someone an act of aggression? Sometimes we engage in vivid fantasies where we inflict severe punishments upon our enemies, but we never act out our dreams. At other times we may verbally attack another, but not engage in a physical attack. For our purposes, we shall consider such thoughts and verbalizations as aggression. A person may desire to physically harm another, but for a variety of reasons (e.g., the other guy is bigger and stronger) he may feel inhibited from acting upon his intentions. We shall want to look at those factors that serve to instigate aggressive tendencies and at those that facilitate or inhibit their translation into overt behavior. As for verbalizations, we can consider them as just one type of overt behavior. In addition, our own experience tells us that they can be as harmful and painful as physical attacks, or even more so.

The difficulties in simply defining the term "aggression" suggest that we are dealing with a very complex issue. Perhaps there is no single, generic behavior pattern that corresponds to the term aggression. There may be many human behaviors that we casually call aggression, but that are in fact different from each other. We may incorrectly group them under a single term and thereby mistakenly suggest that they have a common origin. It might be useful to recognize the nonunitary nature of aggression and to conceive of there being several different types of aggression. These different "aggressions" may or may not have similar causes. If we are dealing with a multifaceted phenomenon, we should not seek out a single cause to explain aggression. On the contrary, we should look at a wide spectrum of variables, keeping in mind that each may play a role in causing the various types of aggression.[6]

While we are not ready at this time to set forth a new definition of aggression or to list the varieties of aggression, we plan in the following pages to discuss some of the possible causes of aggression. We shall, in fact, use the terms "aggression" and "violence" rather casually and interchangeably in accordance with common, everyday usage. However, we do have in mind a definition restricting the terms to behavior whose intent is the harm (physical or nonphysical) of another individual. The main thrust of our discussion is towards investigating the many psychological and sociological factors underlying aggression.

OUR GOALS

In discussing conflict and aggression we have two goals in mind. First, for those interested in understanding aggression, we hope to demonstrate how different psychological and sociological perspectives can shed light on the topic. Second, for those new to social science, we hope to inform them about the nature of social-scientific concepts, analyses, and evidence through their application to one topical issue.

We hope that each chapter will demonstrate the nature of social-scientific thinking. We attempt to show how hypotheses are developed, data collected, and theories tested, and how new and revised hypotheses are generated. Though each chapter presents a different approach to the question of what causes violence, each embodies the basic process of the scientific search into human behavior.[7]

At the same time, the chapters represent different perspectives on the origins of aggression. We shall explore several different areas of psychology and sociology and thereby emphasize somewhat different causes of conflict and aggression. By fully comprehending the unique aspects of the various approaches, we should gain a better appreciation of what each specific one can contribute to our total understanding. At the same time, we may gain insights into each one's deficiencies. Perhaps by combining the many perspectives, we can arrive at a more satisfactory understanding of aggression than we could ever obtain from the narrow viewpoint of any one perspective.

We forthrightly admit the limitations of our cross-disciplinary survey. Except for the occasional da Vinci or Goethe, few persons can master more than one or two trades. Expecially in the present age of specialization, the alternative of being "a jack of all and a master of none" is not viable for scientist, teacher, or layman. Consequently, we can convey adequately only a small portion of the spectrum of potential approaches to investigating aggression. We shall deal mainly with the psychological, social-psychological, and sociological perspectives because these are our areas of relative expertise. Even within those fields, some important approaches will be missing or given less than their due. For example, we devote little space to the role of personality in conflict and violence.[8] Greatest of all in our omissions is the perspective of anthropology. This is unfortunate, since anthropology enables us to place the particular experience of our own society within the context of the many human societies. Much of what we consider "natural" or even "human" turns out to be nothing of the sort. "Human nature" varies tremendously across the globe, and anthropological evidence would help us greatly in understanding this topic.[9]

However, some limits must be placed upon our discussion. We have tried to select topics and concepts that we believe are important and reasonably within our competence. This does not imply that omitted concepts and perspectives are without merit. On the contrary, we hope that our discussion stimulates people to pursue those omitted disciplines in order to more fully round out their understanding of aggression. We hope that the reader, either new to social science or to the topic of aggression, will share the excitement we feel with regard to an interdisciplinary approach. We are convinced that progress in understanding human behavior will occur when a topic is pursued across disciplinary boundaries. This faith grew in each of us through our experience together as graduate students at Harvard University's Department of Social Relations. The presence of students from psychology, sociology, anthropology, and social psychology created a unique and exciting intellectual atmosphere. Although the Department of Social Relations was recently disbanded, we believe that the insights possible through interdisciplinary work are not diminished. We hope that multidisciplinary departments will reappear on the academic scene.

AN OVERVIEW

Rather than continuing to proselytize, we shall now turn to a brief overview of our discussion. In a sense, the topics covered in the following chapters move upward and outward from the individual person. We start with a discussion of human physiology and end with a discussion of human society. Our first chapter raises the issue of the *physiological* origin of aggression and whether aggression is the result of a malfunction in the brain. We discuss a few neural centers that seem to mediate aggression and whether abnormalities in these centers or other organs might be responsible for aggression.

In Chapter 2 we continue searching for the origins of violence in "human nature" by asking what forces *drive* or *motivate* aggression. According to Freudian and ethological *instinct theories,* mankind is doomed to eternal strife because he is saddled with primeval aggressive drives that demand satisfaction. Man must kill to live just as he must eat to survive. Instinct theories claim that mankind is aggressive because the blood of "killer apes" still flows through our veins. Besides surveying instinct theories, we also discuss the popular *frustration-aggression theory* in some detail. Chapter 2 ends by considering the role of emotional reactions to frustration as the impetus to aggression.

We pursue the underlying motivation for aggression further in Chapter 3 by exploring concepts from *learning theory.* Rather than seeing aggression as the consequence of innate drives or reactions to frustrations, learning theorists perceive it as no different from any other complex human behavior. Thus whether a person aggresses against another depends upon his past experience of being rewarded or punished for aggression. We end this chapter by considering factors that may diminish aggressive drives (regardless of their origin). In particular, we discuss the impact of television violence. Does watching violent TV shows teach us to be aggressive or does it serve as a "safety valve" for our violent impulses?

The first three chapters focus mainly upon factors within individuals that may result in aggression. These chapters rely upon concepts from physiology and psychology in explaining aggression. In the following two chapters, we take into account the fact that human beings are social animals. Our question is whether other people influence our behavior in such a way as to make aggression more or less likely. Chapters 4 and 5 deal with the importance of the social environment as it acts through social perception, stereotypes, attitudes, conformity, cooperation and competition, social roles, etc. Here we are concerned with *social psychological* processes and their effects on aggression.

In Chapter 6 we start to move away from conceptions about individuals (i.e., what makes a particular person tick) to conceptions about societies. Not only do people interact with many other people, but they interact with them in the context of highly structured social systems. Possibly the very nature of human *society* may create pressures towards both interpersonal and intergroup violence. Chapter 6 argues that this is indeed possible and sees the origins of violence not in individuals, but in their social world.

Our sociological analysis continues in Chapter 7 by considering the role of *ecology* (i.e., the structure of our physical environment) in aggression. Many social philosophers have seen the downfall of humanity in the rise of cities. To them, cities corrupt the "true nature" of mankind. We pursue this possibility by asking whether there is something about urban life *per se* that is "corrupting" and brings out the beast in human nature. Chapter 7 focuses on ecological factors that may or may not account for the high crime rates of American cities.

Finally, in Chapter 8 we depart somewhat from the level of the preceding discussions. This chapter is more advanced and abstract than the first seven in that it covers a theoretical approach to conflict called *systems theory.* Systems theory attempts to understand conflict, and aggression as a part of conflict, as a process commonly and naturally arising out of the operation of societies and groups within society, independently of the individuals within them. It is presented partly as a challenge to earlier perspectives and as a summary of our discussion as a whole.

FOOTNOTES

[1] Levy (1969); R. M. Brown (1969).

[2] Gallup (1973).

[3] Eisenhower (1968); Kerner (1968).

[4] The following discussion is based heavily on Kaufmann (1970), pp. 1–11, and Johnson (1972), pp. 1–8.

[5] Buss (1961).

[6] Johnson (1972), pp. 7–8.

[7] See Homans (1967) and Madge (1965).

[8] For an overview of personality and aggression, see Olweus (1973).

[9] For an introduction to fields not covered in this book, particularly anthropology, see Bramson and Goethals (1968), Bohanan (1967), Fried, Harris, and Murphy (1967), Graham and Gurr (1969), Hartup (1974), McNeil (1965), Mead (1961), Pruitt and Snyder (1969), and Swingle (1970).

1 / IS AGGRESSION PATHOLOGICAL?

physiological factors

FOCUS
Have You Taken Your Noaggressatol Pill Today?

"WASHINGTON, Jan. 1, 2000. The National Commission on the Psychotechnological Control of Violence announced today that its program of controlling violence through biochemical and psychosurgical intervention has been a complete success. Violent crimes, police brutality, urban riots, industrial strikes, and capital punishment have all become things of the past, since the Antiviolence Law of 1984 made it mandatory for all government officials and private citizens to take daily dosages of the aggression-reducing drug Noaggressatol and for all violent criminals to undergo psychosurgical implantation of remote-control units in their brains. With the adoption of their program on a worldwide basis in 1991, the Commission noted that an unprecedented era of world peace has dawned. Now that the world's political and military leaders' aggressive tendencies are restrained through the miracles of modern science, the world no longer seems doomed to nuclear destruction because of man's naturally violent nature."

Science fiction? Certainly these events have not yet occurred, but there is little to suggest that they could not happen in the near future. The psychotechnology is already available to some extent and is already being used. Tranquilizers are routinely administered in mental hospitals and in some public schools to curb the aggressive tendencies of hyperactive and hyperirritable patients and students. Brain surgery is sometimes performed to control the most severe cases of pathological antisocial hostility in psychotics,[1] and, at a few advanced research centers, scientists are attempting to control their patients' aggression through the electrical stimulation of certain brain centers.[2] Recently, Kenneth Clark, a past president of the American Psychological Association, advocated that these technologies be employed to control aggression in the very terms described in our fictitious news report.[3] Even though a number of prominent psychologists denounced such a "quick technological fix" for society's ills as incompatible with the bulk of scientific knowledge concerning the causes of aggression, the notion of "curing" a world beset by violence and destructiveness through drugs and surgery has a powerful appeal to laymen and scientists alike.

Although the desirability of such a brave, new world with daily Noaggressatol rations is still a matter of debate, some scientists believe such a society is possible. These scientists foresee a time in the future when we shall take a pill whenever we feel the irrational desire to kick our cat, yell at our friends, or take a pot shot at a total stranger. Just as we now take an aspirin for headaches, we might some day swallow Noaggressatol for aggression. To Kenneth Clark, aggression is a disease for which we are now developing medical treatments: "All medicines are drugs—and all drugs used therapeutically are forms of intervention to influence and control the natural processes of disease. Selective and appropriate medication to assure psychological health and moral integrity is now imperative for the survival of human society."[4]

Obviously, an important assumption behind the demand for the psychotechnological control of aggression is that aggression is a disease and that any individual or society manifesting aggressive "symptoms" needs medical attention. But is aggression a disease? And who is ill? Individuals, societies, or the whole human race? When we say that we are sick, we are saying that some bodily organs or systems are not functioning normally. The abnormality or symptom is readily seen or felt and diagnosed. Is this true for aggression?

This medical analogy suggests that aggression is "abnormal" behavior. But how do we define "abnormal behavior"? We could define it as rare or unusual behavior (i.e., statistically infrequent), but it is obvious from the front page of any newspaper that aggression is anything but rare and unusual. Indeed, some claim that aggression is as "American as apple pie." Perhaps we should define abnormal behavior as illegal or criminal behavior. But many acts of aggression are legal (e.g., capital punishment) or are carried out by authorized agents of the government (e.g., police, army) in the name of the law. Maybe we should just ask people which behaviors they consider aggressive and which not aggressive, and use this public consensus as our definition of abnormality. The only problem with this is that people do not agree. Some people consider the ghetto disorders of the 1960s as criminally violent acts, while others consider the same behaviors to be political protests and, therefore, do not call them violent. (See pp. 121–22.)

Since we have no good definitions of abnormality, we cannot decide the question of the pathology of aggression on the basis of the symptom (i.e., aggressive behavior) alone. Frequently we resort to an investigation of the motivation underlying a certain behavior in order to decide whether that behavior is pathological or not. If a policeman shoots a bank robber in an exchange of gunfire, we find his aggressive behavior reasonable and understandable. However, when we hear of a mass murder of victims seemingly chosen at random, we find these acts utterly irrational and, therefore, pathological: "The murderer must be mentally ill."

Unfortunately, by explaining aggression in terms of mental illness, we raise new and equally difficult questions about the nature of mental illness. Are we justified in calling a person mentally ill when he does something incomprehensible to us? How do we know what is mentally healthy and what is mentally ill? Psychologists and psychiatrists are still debating whether there is such a thing as "mental illness" and the criteria for proclaiming someone mentally ill. For example, the psychiatrist Thomas Szasz argues that mental illness is a myth or a quasi-religious concept that we use to rationalize the institutionalization of people whom we believe to be dangerous, or who irritate and bother us because of their characteristics and habits. In the past we justified our treatment of such people by evoking religious concepts (e.g., possession by an evil spirit); today we rely upon medical concepts. Szasz maintains that our present usage of the term "mental illness" is really just a label for "deviance" (i.e., behavior that is socially defined as unacceptable). Calling a person mentally ill does not tell us much about what is wrong with him, except that his behavior is different from that of others. In terms of diagnostic benefits, Szasz insists that we would be better to talk about an illness or disease in only those cases where the symptoms can be traced to definite organic causes.[5]

Thus, it seems to be extremely difficult to define aggression as pathology or abnormality. Perhaps we should reject the "medical model's" assumption that aggression is an illness, but retain its suggestion that aggression has physiological roots. This means that we should investigate the organic bases of aggression. Since aggressive behavior, like any other complex behavior, is initiated and coordinated by the nervous system, we shall turn our attention to the role of the brain in aggression. The question that we shall bear in mind is whether or not most aggressive behavior is a consequence of malfunctions and deformations of definite structures in the central nervous system, thus suggesting surgery or medication as cures, or whether aggressive behavior can be the result of perfectly normal processes in a well-functioning nervous system.

AGGRESSION AND THE BRAIN

Since virtually all of human behavior is initiated and coordinated by the brain (except for simple reflexes), we would expect that brain functions play an important role in the mediation of aggressive behavior. In fact, some people have argued that because all behavior "filters" through the central nervous system, studying the relationship between the brain and aggression is the best way to understand aggression.[6] We shall return to this assertion at the end of this chapter, for it is closely related to the argument that if our knowledge of neurophysiology were complete, we would not need such imprecise disciplines as psychology and sociology to understand human behavior. Since this is only the first chapter of this book, you would be right in guessing that we do not share this opinion!

With the help of microelectrodes that probe electrical activity deep within the brain, we now know a great deal about the areas of the brain that mediate sensory, motor, and cognitive processes and about the motivational functions of certain brain centers (e.g., so-called "pain" and "pleasure" centers). However, it is much more difficult to find "aggression centers" in the brain than it is to locate projection areas for visual perception. The difficulty stems from aggression being a complex behavior pattern, which requires the interplay of a variety of brain functions. For example, when Bobby hits his little brother because he popped Bobby's balloon, Bobby's brain has to perform a chain of different processes. It has to receive the visual and auditory input concerning the fate of his balloon; it has to evaluate the significance of this input in regard to his brother's behavior; it has to initiate an aggressive impulse, to cope with inhibitory influences, to coordinate the motor act of hitting, and to process internal and external feedback from this act. Obviously, there are many brain functions involved in an aggressive sequence such as this one. Therefore, the question becomes whether there are any specific neural mechanisms that mediate the facilitation and inhibition of aggressive impulses. Is there an "aggression center" in the brain?

Structure of the Brain

Before we can turn to a discussion of this important question, we must first quickly survey the major subdivisions of the brain in terms of their structure and function. Since many physiological studies have been done with lower animals, we have to keep in mind the evolutionary continuity of brain structures and functions in infrahuman animals and human beings. Furthermore, it is a common view that aggression is part of our "animal nature." This suggests that the physiological origins of ag-

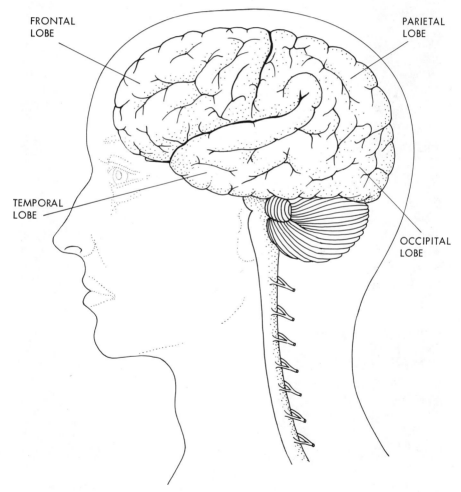

Figure 1-1 A side view of the human brain showing the location of the brain lobes.

gression lie in the phylogenetically older and more primitive parts of the human brain, which we share with many species of animals.

When life evolved from unicellular to multicellular forms, in which different cells specialized to perform different functions, primitive nerve

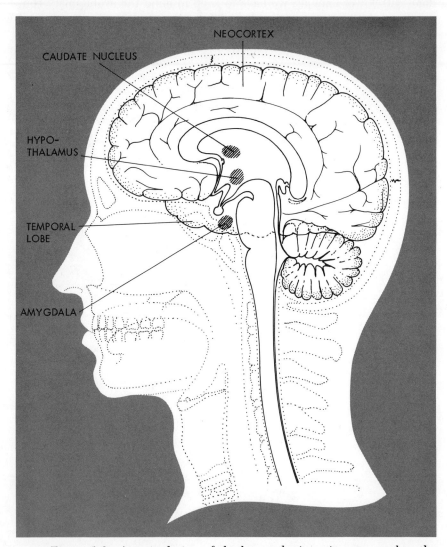

Figure 1-2 A sagittal view of the human brain as it appears when the brain is sliced in the midline to separate the left and right hemispheres. The areas indicated have been found to be important in the mediation of aggression.

fibers developed to transmit information and coordinate bodily functions. As life became more and more complex, these nerve fibers became more and more concentrated and centralized into a single system. The main direction in the evolution of the central nervous system is *encephalization* or the tendency of brain structures to grow and overlay older structures at the front or head-end of the organism. Thus, the older, lower parts of the brain, which developed early in the course of evolution and which regulate vital activities like respiration, have remained intact. However, newer structures, which serve increasingly complex functions of "reasoning," were added and superimposed on these older structures. Consequently, we find that phylogenetically ancient parts of the brain (e.g., the brain stem) are similar in structure and function in human and subhuman animals.

The *hypothalamus* is one particularly ancient part of the brain. It controls autonomic processes (e.g., respiration, heartbeat, body temperature), hormones, and many emotional and motivational processes. As we shall see, the hypothalamus and the *amygdala*, which are part of the *limbic system*, are closely associated with the mediation of aggressive behavior.

In many lower animals, such as reptiles, the brain consists mainly of phylogenetically ancient structures, whereas in most mammals there is the additional development of the *neocortex*. The neocortex controls and integrates the functions of the phylogenetically older regions of the brain and makes possible "the higher functions" of cognitive activity such as reasoning and symbolic representation. The neocortex is divided into two hemispheres by a longitudinal fissure, and, with a few exceptions, the hemispheres duplicate each other in terms of their functions. Anatomists divide the neocortex somewhat arbitrarily into four lobes (i.e., frontal, occipital, parietal, and temporal), which serve as a rough guide to indicate the location of many specialized regions within the neocortex.

Needless to say, the organization of the brain is much more complex than we have presented it. There are many specialized structures and interconnecting neural pathways that have not been mentioned.[7] However, given our concern with the physiology of aggression, we shall focus our attention mainly on two small, but enormously complex structures in the ancient lower layers of the brain: the hypothalamus and the amygdala.

Cerebral "Aggression Centers"

Although experimental lesions or electrical stimulation have been rarely performed in the human hypothalamus, evidence from a few human studies and many animal studies suggests that the *hypothalamus* plays an important role in mediating the aggressive behaviors of attack, defense, and flight in most species, including man. For example, the physiologist W. R. Hess and his collaborators have shown through patient point-by-point electrical stimulation of certain parts of the hypothalamus (using implanted microelectrodes) in freely moving cats that there are definite aggression areas.[8] In addition, Hess found that stimulating different hypothalamic sites produced different types of aggressive behavior (defense versus attack behaviors). Finally, stimulation of another area produced escape or "flight" behavior, which resulted in aggression whenever the cat's escape route was blocked. This last type of aggression ("fear-induced aggression") suggests that whether aggression follows stimulation of hypothalamic areas depends not only on the specific area stimulated, but also on the environment (e.g., whether the cat is cornered or not).[9] Other studies show that the destruction of certain areas in the hypothalamus leads to marked reductions in aggressiveness and, in many cases, to a complete loss of emotional reactivity.[10]

Another source of evidence concerning the role of the hypothalamus in aggression comes from studies involving the surgical removal of the entire neocortex. This brain operation is frequently used to investigate the degree of coordination and integration that the neocortex performs in organizing an animal's behavior. Physiologists have used this technique to study whether animals can still engage in aggressive behavior without their neocortex. Studies performed around the turn of the century showed that *decorticate* animals (i.e., animals without a neocortex) respond aggressively to stimuli that normally do not elicit violent reactions (e.g., gentle petting).[11] Physiologists call this phenomenon *sham rage*, because they believe it to lack true emotional nature and because of its lack of coordination (i.e., the decorticate animal will strike at anything), increased intensity, and short duration as compared to rage responses in normal animals. Sham rage is thought to result from releasing the hypothalamus from the normal inhibition of the neocortex. That is, in normal animals the neocortex serves to inhibit or moderate the aggression "centers" of the hypothalamus. When the neocortex is removed, then the hypothalamus is no longer restrained, and aggressive responses occur more easily.

Instead of removing the entire neocortex as in decorticate animals, one can remove or destroy smaller parts and observe the consequences on the animal's behavior. A pioneering study of this kind was performed by KlueX and Bucy in 1935. They showed that the removal of the *temporal lobes* of the neocortex and the adjoining *amygdala* of the limbic

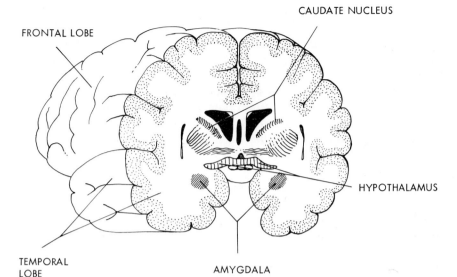

CAUDATE NUCLEUS

FRONTAL LOBE

HYPOTHALAMUS

TEMPORAL
LOBE

AMYGDALA

Figure 1-3 A view of the human brain with the posterior (back) portion removed, showing an anterior (frontal) cross section. Note that the amygdaloid nuclei are located in the temporal lobes.

system in rhesus monkeys made these generally vicious animals more tame and placid. In addition to a reduction in aggression, the monkeys also developed orality (i.e., an extraordinary tendency to put everything they encountered into their mouth) and hypersexuality (i.e., they mounted other animals and even objects indiscriminately and continuously).[12]

In spite of these severe side effects, which also included an inability to interpret visual stimuli and a change from vegetarianism to meat-eating, the efficacy of temporal lobotomy (i.e., removal of the temporal lobes) in taming aggressive monkeys led some brain surgeons to attempt the same operation on violent mental patients. As in the rhesus monkeys, this operation resulted in a marked decrease in general hostility and the frequency of violent behavior. Previously violent patients became quiet and docile. However, the patients showed many of the same side effects that the monkeys experienced, including hypersexuality, the inability to recognize familiar persons, and memory deficiencies.

Although the taming effects of such operations are well demonstrated, it is unclear exactly which structures' removal is responsible for the reduction in aggression, since temporal lobotomy involves the surgical removal of extensive areas of brain tissue. Other research suggests that the *amygdala,* which is almost contiguous with the temporal lobe and is usually removed in temporal lobotomy, is mainly responsible for aggression. Bilateral amygdalectomy (i.e., the removal of the amygdala from both brain hemispheres) tends to reduce aggression.[13] The amygdala not only mediates aggression in such laboratory animals as cats, rats, and monkeys, but also in human beings. Lesions placed in the amygdala of hostile, hyperirritable mental patients have generally resulted in a normalization of their social behavior and, in some cases, a release from the mental hospital or a transfer from solitary confinement to open wards.[14]

Since the insertion of electrodes into the amygdala allows both the recording of electrical activity as well as the destruction of brain tissue around the tips of the electrode by applying a stronger current, it is possible to first monitor the electrical activity of the amygdala in mental patients to determine where the site of abnormal activity is located. Once the site is located, it can be destroyed. Two brain surgeons at the Harvard Medical School, Mark and Ervin, have used this technique with some success.

FOCUS
Julia

Julia, a mental patient frequently afflicted by epileptic seizures, approached the duty nurse on her ward, who was busy writing a report, and said, "I feel another spell coming on, please help me." The nurse replied, "I'll be with you in just one minute." With sudden rage, Julia grabbed a pair of scissors and stabbed the nurse in the chest without warning.

For Julia this was just one of many violent attacks that she had committed. In another incident she almost killed a girl in a movie theater with a knife that she carried with her. Attempts at treating her epileptic seizures and her violent tendencies had been made at many institutions using a variety of antiseizure drugs, electroshock, and other treatments without success.

After a detailed neurological examination, Drs. Vernon H. Mark and Frank R. Ervin decided to place electrodes in both of Julia's amygdalas. Recordings from these electrodes showed characteristic electrical epileptic seizure patterns, and, through stimulation of either amygdala, the symptoms indicative of seizures could be produced. Since the amygdala in the left brain hemisphere seemed to be mainly responsible for this abnormal electrical behavior, Mark and Ervin made a destructive lesion in the left amygdala and removed the electrodes.

However, Julia's behavior did not change much. She continued to have seizures as well as violent outbursts. At this point, Mark and Ervin used a remote brain stimulation and recording apparatus that had been developed by José Delgado of Yale University. This apparatus consists of a radio transmitter that is stationary and a very small receiver that is attached to the electrode implanted in the patient's head. The apparatus also includes a miniature FM-amplifier-transmitter combination that transmits the recorded brain signals to brain-wave analyzing equipment. Since no external wires are required for either recording or stimulation, the patient is free to engage in normal activities.

The electrodes connected to a miniature receiver-transmitter were implanted in Julia's right temporal lobe and amygdala. While recordings were made from these electrodes, Mark and Ervin carefully monitored Julia's behavior. It soon became apparent that seizures and rage attacks occurred during periods of abnormal brain-wave activity in Julia's right amygdala. Julia was then told that her right amygdala would be stimulated from time to time. However, she was not told when the stimulation would occur. After the onset of the stimulation, the brain-wave pattern characteristic of the beginning of seizure activity occurred. Shortly after these brain-wave patterns began, Julia's behavior became violent. One time her amygdala was stimulated while Julia was playing her guitar. At first, the stimulation seemed to have no effect. But then, Julia suddenly swung the guitar at her psychiatrist's head—barely missing him!

These stimulation sequences established the exact location of the abnormal electrical activity in the amygdala that preceded her seizures or rage attacks. Consequently, Drs. Mark and Ervin made a destructive lesion in Julia's right amygdala. Although they consider it still too early to make a final assessment of this operation, they report that Julia showed only two mild rage episodes in the first postoperative year and none in the second.[15]

So far we have only mentioned *excitatory* areas that produce aggression upon stimulation or whose removal results in decreased aggression. In addition to these excitatory areas, there are *inhibitory* areas for aggression. Stimulation of these areas reduces aggressiveness and their removal increases it. For example, J. M. R. Delgado has demonstrated dramatically the influence of inhibitory centers by stopping a charging bull in midattack by the remote-control stimulation of the bull's brain.[16]

FOCUS
Aggression Control by Radio Stimulation

Remember the school bully who always went out of his way to be mean? Didn't you wish at times you had a little button you could push that would stop him in his tracks? Many of us as adults probably still wish for such a magical button that we could use against domineering bosses, irritable spouses, and other aggressive fellows. While for us this must remain a dream, it became a reality for a subordinate monkey in one of José Delgado's experiments.

This poor monkey was constantly harassed by the boss monkey of the colony's dominance hierarchy. The subordinate's life became much more bearable when he learned to use a lever installed in the cage. This lever activated a radio stimulator that transmitted impulses to a little receiver strapped to the boss monkey's back. From there the impulses travelled to the boss monkey's *caudate nucleus,* a small subcortical brain structure. To the subordinate's great relief, the stimulation of this area had an immediate taming effect on the boss monkey. If the subordinate monkey pressed the lever after the boss threatened him, then the boss would not back up his threat with an attack. If the subordinate pulled the lever during an attack, the boss monkey would suddenly abandon the chase. Needless to say, the little monkey got along quite nicely with his boss after the installation of the "magic" button!

Delgado has shown in other experiments that stimulation of "aggression inhibiting brain centers," mainly the caudate nucleus, can change the social organization in a monkey colony. If the dominant animal receives inhibitory stimulation and is consequently less aggressive, his territory is reduced. The other animals, who normally avoid him, now move around freely without making their usual submissive gestures to him. However, there is no permanent taming effect. If the current is turned off, the animal becomes just as aggressive as before. Just as the stimulation of some areas momentarily makes animals more aggressive, the stimulation of inhibitory "centers" makes them momentarily less aggressive.[17]

The Dyscontrol Syndrome

What happens if these inhibitory areas of the brain are inoperative or impaired? We would expect that individuals with such brain dysfunctions would be abnormally violent. Perhaps the slightest touch would send them into a rage. Almost any stimulus might serve as a catalyst for

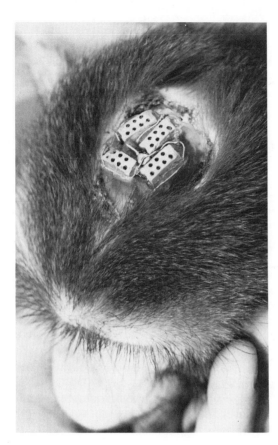

Figure 1-4 Four "chemitrodes" (chemical cannula and electrode combinations) implanted into the brain of a rhesus monkey. The chemitrodes are surrounded by a stainless steel grounding wire and a matrix of acrylic dental cement. Courtesy of Daniel R. Snyder, Ph.D., Neurobehavioral Laboratory, Yale University School of Medicine.

aggressive behavior without the moderating effects of the aggression inhibiting centers. Mark and Ervin suggest that dysfunctions in the limbic system, which relays impulses from neocortical inhibitory areas, may account for the extremely violent behavior of some individuals.

Mark and Ervin note that the lack of inhibition, among hospitalized patients characterized by "poor impulse control," is not limited to a single behavioral domain. Instead, it extends to a number of behavioral patterns. In their investigation, they compared the case histories of their violent patients, with known limbic brain disease, to violent patients in other hospitals (i.e., people hospitalized for other reasons than limbic disorders) and to violent prisoners in a large penitentiary.[18] Mark and Ervin found that their violent patients with limbic dysfunctions usually shared four characteristic symptoms that distinguished them from the other groups of violent patients and prisoners: (1) a history of physical

Figure 1-5 An example of aggressive behavior between rhesus monkeys elicited by electrical stimulation of the brain. The monkey on the right is wearing a transmitter-receiver apparatus on his back. The stimulated monkey displays all the components of spontaneous threat: erect tail, pilo-erection, head thrust forward, mouth open, ears flattened, and direct stare. Note the head and eye aversion and submissive posture of the other monkey. Courtesy of Daniel R. Snyder, Ph.D., Neurobehavioral Laboratory, Yale University School of Medicine.

assault, especially wife and child beating, (2) pathological intoxication (i.e., drinking even a small amount of alcohol triggers violent acts), (3) a history of impulsive sexual behavior, at times including rape, and (4) a history of many traffic violations and serious car accidents. Taken together these symptoms make up what Mark and Ervin have called the *dyscontrol syndrome*.

Now, Mark and Ervin do not claim that all people who show this syndrome are suffering from brain damage, nor do they imply that all violence results from "sick brains." They suggest, however, that people showing this syndrome have a good chance of having some brain pathology and that it may be worthwhile to thoroughly investigate this possibility. If brain disorders are found, then it may be possible to medically treat the individual in order to reduce his violent tendencies (as in the example of Julia, presented above).

"It Ain't Necessarily So"

The evidence presented so far suggests that the subcortical areas of the hypothalamus and amygdaloid areas are important excitatory "centers" and the caudate nucleus is an important inhibitory "center" for aggression. Electrical stimulation of the excitatory areas can result in aggressive responses, while their destruction usually renders aggressive animals into placid and docile creatures. Of course, just the opposite is true for inhibitory areas. In addition, other evidence (e.g., the removal of the neocortex and sham rage) indicates that neocortical areas can act as inhibitory "centers" for aggression, moderating the subcortical aggression "centers."

But the picture is not as clear-cut as we have represented it. The very existence of such excitatory and inhibitory aggression "centers" is surrounded by controversy. There is much disagreement among researchers about the functions of the amygdala, hypothalamus, and caudate nucleus; but there is agreement that more is unknown than known about the neural control of aggression. As we shall see, it is premature to claim that we have located particular aggression "centers" and that we need only to refine our technology before ushering in a "brave new world." The critics of aggression "center" research point to three major problem areas: methodology, reliability, and validity.[19]

Methodology.   To the uninitiated, the sophisticated technology of brain research gives it an aura of scientific exactitude. In actuality, however, the research abounds in ambiguities. First, unless an autopsy is performed, brain researchers cannot be absolutely sure where they have implanted an electrode. Thus, they cannot positively identify which brain structures they have stimulated or destroyed. While general "road maps" can be made to guide the placement of electrodes, they can only be approximations because brains differ greatly from individual to individual just as faces do. This variation means that the psychosurgeon is working in the dark, so to speak, and can make only sophisticated guesses about where particular brain sites are located. In short, unless the patient or animal dies and his brain is examined, there is no way to know exactly which neural structures were stimulated or destroyed by the placement of microelectrodes. Of course, this makes it difficult to specify which areas are mediating particular behaviors.

Second, it is almost impossible (with our present technology) to activate exactly the same group of neurons in different individuals. Not only is it difficult to accurately implant electrodes, but the neural circuits are so complex and intermeshed that the slightest difference in placement may result in the stimulation or destruction of different neural structures. In addition, electrodes are likely to stimulate or destroy more than just a single neural structure or system. Similarly, natural pathologies like tumors may affect several neural systems and structures making it nearly impossibe to specify which damaged areas are responsible for behavioral abnormalities.

Third, there is a limit to the number of electrodes that can be placed in any part of a person's brain. Consequently, if the behavior is controlled by many different neural structures, which is highly likely, it is easy to miss important sites. That is, the researcher may base his conclusions on only partial information about the total neural system mediating a complex behavior such as aggression.

Finally, there are shortcomings in the evaluation and reporting of experimental results. The evaluation of the patient's postoperative behavior is frequently highly subjective and imprecise. For example, the surgeon who performed the operation is often the person who evaluates its effectiveness. Of course, this opens up the possibility of so-called "experimenter biases." Knowing what the results of the operation should be, the surgeon-evaluator may be biased towards "seeing" certain behaviors when they do not actually exist. This does not imply that the researcher consciously fakes his data, but that he may unconsciously miscategorize the patient's ambiguous and complex behaviors. Similarly, these studies often suffer from the lack of experimental control groups (e.g., patients with similar behavior and/or pathologies who are not operated on). Without a control group, it is difficult to establish that the operation is responsible for any behavioral changes. Perhaps the patient's behavior would have changed "naturally" without the surgical treatment. In addition, the evaluations of the patient's behavior are often in terms of gross and unstandardized descriptions that make it difficult to know exactly what changes, if any, have occurred. Also, the evaluators frequently fail to look for other changes in the patient's behavior besides the one they are concerned with. Consequently, they may overlook such "side effects" as changes in intellectual performance or emotional reactivity that may account for changes in the patient's aggressive behaviors. Lastly, the evidence in favor of particular pathological origins of aggression is selectively reported. That is, the cases cited are usually positive instances of, say, a tumor being associated with aggression. But the negative instances of both tumors without aggression and aggression without tumors are not cited. Because autopsies in search of particular pathologies are not always performed, it is hard for us to know the relative frequencies of such positive and negative instances.

Reliability. Another problem is an inconsistency in results from one study to the next. Electrodes implanted in the same place in different animals often result in different behaviors, and electrodes placed in different sites in the same animal frequently result in the same behavior. For example, not all hypothalamic and amygdaloid area lesions result in reduced aggression. In some animal studies, amygdalectomy has led to increases in the frequency and ferocity of aggressive behavior.[20] Of course, this inconsistency may reflect the methodological problems we just finished discussing. However, other more theoretically important factors may be involved.

FOCUS
Brain Stimulation and the Social Environment

There is some evidence that environmental factors partially determine the outcomes of these operations. This is dramatically demonstrated in M. E. Rosvold, A. F. Mirsky, and K. H. Pribram's study of the effects of amygdalectomy on the dominance hierarchies of monkeys. In one study, the top monkeys in the hierarchy, Dave and Zeke, became docile and nonaggressive after amygdalectomy and consequently fell to the bottom of the dominance hierarchy. After Dave and Zeke's operation, the originally No. 3 monkey (Riva) became the king monkey. But when Riva underwent an amygdalectomy, he became more aggressive and retained his "throne."[21] Pribram explains this by noting that Riva was aggressive to begin with and constantly challenged Dave and Zeke's supremacy before any of them underwent amygdalectomy. After their operations, Dave and Zeke were faced with an aggressive rival and they lost their superior position. But, after Riva's operation, he had no serious challenger, since the new No. 2 monkey, Herby, was placid and unaggressive.[22]

In a similar study, Delgado found that electrical stimulation of one monkey's aggression "centers" does not lead to indiscriminate attacks against all other monkeys. In his colony of free-ranging monkeys implanted with remote-control devices, the stimulation of the boss monkey's aggression "centers" evoked well-organized attacks against all other animals except against the boss's special friend, the No. 2 monkey. Generally, monkeys under stimulation do not attack other monkeys with whom they are friends. However, they readily attack those animals with whom they are on bad terms. In fact, they become so vicious that they literally drive their victims "up the wall," leaving them hanging from the ceiling or hiding in the corner.[23]

These experiments suggest that such factors as the length of time that a stable dominance hierarchy has existed, the habitual behavioral patterns of other monkeys in the hierarchy, and the past relationships between monkeys may help determine the behavioral consequences of physiological changes (e.g., electrical stimulation or amygdalectomy).

Further evidence for the importance of environmental factors comes from the study of cats. For example, the stimulation of a defense or an attack area is more likely to produce aggression if an appropriate stimulus is available (i.e., a live as opposed to a dead mouse).[24] In another investigation, cats with amygdaloid-area lesions were more aggressive when they were in their "home territory" (i.e., inside their cage) than on "foreign territory" (i.e., outside their cage).[25] In short, environmental cues may be important in determining whether aggressive or nonaggressive responses result from brain lesions or stimulation. In fact, one investigator argues that different kinds of aggression, such as predatory, intermale, fear-induced, territorial, maternal, and instrumental, are produced by different classes of external stimuli or situations and may be mediated by different physiological systems.[26]

Unfortunately, we do not understand the physiological mechanisms mediating these environmental effects. But we do know that stimuli are recognized and interpreted by the cognitive areas of the neocortex. The sensory input from environmental stimuli are not directly and only fed to the subcortical aggression "centers." Part of the processing of sensory input involves the interpretative functions of the neocortex. Depending on how stimuli are interpreted, cortical centers may inhibit excitatory aggression areas via subcortical relay stations. For our purposes, the important point is that stimuli are perceived, evaluated, and interpreted by the cognitive areas of the neocortex, which may exert inhibitory influences over the subcortical aggression "centers."

In addition to environmental factors, the individual's personality, rather than the location of the electrode, may determine the outcome of electrical stimulation. For example, the stimulation of aggressive rats makes them more aggressive, but the stimulation of the same hypothalamic areas in passive rats does not make them aggressive.[27] Similarly, in human beings, amygdaloid-area stimulation may result in aggression for previously violent patients, but not in previously nonviolent patients.[28] Responses to amygdaloid stimulation seem to be highly individualized and to reflect the patient's personality. The roles of personality and environment in determining the outcome of the electrical stimulation of aggression "centers" cast a large shadow of doubt on any inevitable relationships between particular neural sites and aggression.

Validity. To call a neural structure an "aggression center" implies (1) that it mediates only aggression and not other behaviors or functions, and (2) that it is the source of aggressive impulses. On the basis of existing evidence, no neural areas meet these criteria for an "aggression center." First, the amygdala is composed of several nuclear groups (i.e., clusters of cell bodies) with diverse functions both in respect to type of influence (excitatory versus inhibitory) and in respect to type of behavior (e.g., feeding, reproductive, aggressive, pituitary regulatory). Similarly, the caudate nucleus has many general functions regarding the sensory and motoric control of complex behaviors. In fact, there are few, if any, areas of the brain that control only one behavior. A single brain area usually performs a wide variety of functions and influences many different behaviors. Thus, it is unlikely that the so-called "aggression centers" mediate only aggressive behaviors.

Second, it is not clear that any of the neural areas discussed are the source of aggressive impulses. The causal relationship between the stimulation of subcortical areas and aggression is open to a variety of interpretations. For example, Delgado's demonstration of stopping a charging bull in midattack may not be what it seems to be. Delgado claims that stimulation of the caudate nucleus inhibited the bull's aggressive impulses. However, Elliot Valenstein, a physiological psychologist at the University of Michigan, suggests that Delgado merely stimulated a motor system that interfered with the bull's attack. True, the bull stopped his attack after stimulation, turning in circles so long as the stimulation occurred. After the current was turned off, he resumed his attack, only to be zapped again and to turn in circles. After charging several times and being forced to turn in circles, the poor frustrated and confused animal probably just gave up attacking Delgado![29]

Now this is a far cry from saying that the bull's aggressive impulses were reduced by stimulating the caudate nucleus. Rather it seems that stimulation made it impossible for the bull to carry out his "aggressive intentions." A similar interpretation can be given to Delgado's experiment with monkeys (discussed above). The caudate nucleus plays an important role in controlling muscular movements. The stimulation of the caudate nucleus often produces an "arrest reaction" that stops any on-going behavior, be it eating or fighting! Thus, the boss monkey may have stopped his attack on the subordinate monkey because of this arrest reaction and not because he felt less aggressive.

Similarly, the reduction in aggression following amygdalectomy may reflect a generalized decrease in emotional responsiveness. Amygdalectomy interferes with the interpretation and relation of visual information to past experience. Thus, the reduction in aggression may result from a deficit in the animal's ability to function correctly. Rather than aggressiveness being reduced, there is a generalized lowered responsiveness to most stimuli that produce emotional responses of any sort.[30] The amygdalectomized animal may be just as aggressive as before, but not recognize those stimuli that previously provoked his aggression.

Another alternative interpretation is that the stimulation of neural areas results in pain, fear, confusion, and/or unfamiliar sensations, and that these emotional reactions cause the animal's aggressive behavior. This argument suggests that the correlation between the stimulation of any particular neural area and aggression may be spurious, since the cause of aggression may lie in the resulting emotional reaction. These alternative explanations, combined with the methodology and reliability problems, argue against jumping to any conclusions about the existence of "aggression centers." All in all, there is as yet no convincing evidence for neural "centers" whose stimulation inevitably leads to aggression. The lack of evidence for so-called "aggression centers," however, should not blind us to the possibility that complex neural systems mediate aggressive behaviors and that physical pathologies may cause some instances and types of aggression. Therefore, we shall now turn to a short survey of possible causes of brain damage in human beings.

BORN TO RAISE HELL

Early in the nineteenth century, the Italian criminologist Cesare Lombroso set forth one of the earliest theories of the origins of criminal violence. Lombroso held that criminals were evolutionary misfits with faulty genetic makeup. Lombroso deduced the "genetic abnormality" of criminals not only from their deviant behavior, but also from analyses of their physiognomies and body types, which he believed differed from those of normal people.[31] Although Lombroso's theory of innate criminal tendencies has long been rejected and replaced with environmental explanations for crime, scientists found what seemed to be belated evidence for his theory in the early 1950s. These investigators found a statistical relationship between certain abnormalities in chromosomes and the violent tendencies of some criminals. This discovery had such a powerful public impact that it was used by two lawyers to get more lenient sentences for their clients accused of murder and afflicted by the so-called XYY syndrome.[32]

This "supermale syndrome" is produced by an abnormality in the number of sex chromosomes that a person inherits. Ordinarily males have one X and one Y chromosome (XY), and females have two X chromosomes (XX). However, in rare instances, individuals who are morphologically male inherit an additional sex chromosome. Early studies showed that the occurrence of XXY or XYY syndromes (i.e., males with either an extra "female chromosome," X, or an extra "male chromosome," Y) was greater among males imprisoned for violent crimes than among males in the general population. That is, these chromosome abnormalities were associated with histories of violent behavior. This suggested that the XXY or XYY syndrome might be an inherited, genetic predisposition toward aggression.

However, recent studies with better investigatory techniques have cast doubt upon this hypothesis. One recent overview of this research area concludes, for example, that there is no convincing evidence for a relationship between these chromosome syndromes and aggressive behavior.[33] In addition, whatever relationship that does exist cannot be automatically ascribed to innate or inherited aggressive tendencies. Interpreting any relationship between these genetic abnormalities and aggression is complicated by the fact that the syndromes result in such morphological characteristics as above-average height. Perhaps this unusual tallness contributes to the individual's aggressiveness. He may be treated differently by others or he may feel less fear to be aggressive because of his height.[34] In other words, there may not be direct links between genetic abnormalities and aggression, in the sense of a genetic predisposition towards aggression.

Although there seems to be no direct relationship between specific genetic abnormalities and violent behavior, it is unlikely that there are no genetic influences at all. It is a well-known fact that we can create aggressive breeds of animals such as fighting bulls and Siamese fighting fish through selective mating. Genetic factors may enhance or reduce the potential for aggression among human beings. Unfortunately, these processes are not well understood at the present time, and this is especially true in respect to brain functioning. While it is possible that genetic abnormalities could cause brain damage, our meager knowledge precludes our even speculating on this regarding aggressive behavior. However, our lack of understanding in this area may not be very harmful. These two chromosome abnormalities seem to be rare events occurring in about three out of every 1,000 people. In addition, while the abnormalities have been found to be fifteen times more frequent in criminal populations than in newborn males and normal adults, they occurred in less than 6 percent of the prison inmates.[35] Thus, for all practical purposes, we can disregard such genetic abnormalities as major causes of brain damage and/or aggression.

There are many other potential causes of brain damage, which can occur at any time in the development of the fetus into an adult. Inadequate prenatal care, which is frequently found in big-city slums and poor rural areas, can severely affect the normal development of an infant. Inadequate oxygen supply to the brain during birth is known to cause the death of brain cells and can lead to mental deficiency or epilepsy. Such children sometimes become "hyperkinetic" (i.e., they are constantly and compulsively on the move) and engage in antisocial activities. Malnutrition, the lack of important vitamins and minerals, and viral infections can also cause severe brain damage. A familiar case in point is rabies, which is a viral infection of the central nervous system and which leads to violent behavior of "mad dogs."

In addition, abnormal cell growths such as tumors can occur in vital parts of the brain and can lead to a variety of dysfunctions and in some cases to violent behavior. For example, the infamous Texas Tower sniper, Charles Whitman, who shot thirty-eight people without provocation in 1966, was found to have a large tumor in the amygdaloid area.[36] Finally, physical accidents of many kinds can cause brain damage (e.g., industrial accidents, war wounds, automobile accidents, blows to the head). Thus, there are many potential causes of brain damage that can occur either at or before birth or during the maturation process. Except for a few spectacular cases like Charles Whitman, however, there is little evidence that they play an important role in most violent incidents or individuals. (However, this may reflect the fact that such pathologies are not always looked for.)

Finally, the causal relationship between brain damage and aggression is not always clear-cut. Most of the time the evidence is merely correlational; it does not prove, for example, that Whitman's tumor caused his shooting spree. All that we know is that Whitman had a tumor and that he shot thirty-eight people. The causal relation is even more suspect when brain damage is the result of some physical injury (e.g., a blow to the head). Unless we know that the physical injury preceded the person's aggressive nature, we cannot tell anything about its causal relationship to his aggressive behavior. His brain damage may be a result of earlier aggressive incidents and, therefore, not be the cause of his current aggressive behavior (e.g., prize fighters).

THE DRUG SCENE

Until now we have concentrated on the potential causes of permanent brain malfunctions such as structural brain damage. In addition to these long-term dysfunctions there are short-term, temporary dysfunctions that occur when the subtle chemical processes in the nervous system are thrown off balance by drugs (e.g., narcotics or alcohol). A normal, healthy brain's ability to appraise environmental information and to direct behavioral responses may be temporarily impaired. Many drugs, especially alcohol, act in particular upon the executive centers of the brain and thereby interfere with the normal functioning of the "reasoning" and inhibitory centers. Consequently, individuals may incorrectly interpret stimuli and, due to reduced inhibition, be more prone to react violently to these stimuli.

FOCUS
The Pep Pill Murder Case—A Rare Event

After a 1,600-mile nonstop trip, during which he took repeated doses of amphetamines, a twenty-seven-year-old truck driver was arrested when he reported to the police that narcotics had been planted on his truck. While in jail, he constantly feared being gassed to death. Once released into the custody of his boss, he became convinced that his life was in danger when he "smelled poison gas" in his boss's car. In fear for his life, he panicked and shot his boss to death.

Actually, however, he was never in danger of being gassed by the police or his boss. This is one of about a dozen cases described by Dr. Everett Ellinwood, a psychiatrist at the Duke University Medical Center, in which amphetamine abuse was closely associated with violent crimes. Specifically, heavy dosages of the drug, which is a stimulant, seem to foster delusional thinking that frequently leads to paranoia. When these feelings of persecution are coupled with an impaired ability to test the reality of one's thoughts, then the individual may react violently to protect himself from his "tormentors."[37]

However, drugs do not drive people to acts of violence. In most of the cases studied by Dr. Ellinwood, other facts in addition to drug abuse contributed to the violent incidents. In many cases predisposing personality traits such as aggressiveness, impulsiveness, and general emotional instability were associated with drug abuse and violence. Consequently, there is **no** evidence that the drugs per se cause violence. In fact, some studies directly contradict claims of a causal relationship between amphetamines and violence.[38] Large doses can produce paranoia, which, when combined with the often violent life-style of amphetamine users, may predispose a person towards aggression. But this is different from saying that amphetamines create an urge to kill. Amphetamines, and other drugs, seem to "set the stage" for violence in people already predisposed to violence.

In fact, drugs have few associations with violence.[39] Depressant drugs such as the opiates (i.e., morphine, codeine, heroin) usually relieve tension and anxiety, diminish sexual urges, and result in drowsiness, apathy, lessened physical activity, and in an inability to concentrate. These symptoms are not usually conducive to aggression. Similarly, studies of the effects of marijuana, another depressant, suggest that it may even reduce aggression. While hallucinogens or psychedelic drugs such as LSD and mescaline produce a variety of distortions in perceptual, cognitive, and motoric functioning, there is again no evidence that they lead to violence. After a careful review of the drug literature, a staff report to the National Commission on the Causes and Prevention of Violence concluded that:

> there is no evidence to support the suggestion that there is a causal relationship between the use of drugs and narcotics and the commission of

crime and violent acts. It is the person and not the drug who performs the act. What the drug will do depends upon the person, the circumstances under which it is taken ("the setting") and the user's expectations ("the set"). It seems unlikely that a well-adjusted individual would become violent under the influence of drugs or narcotics; on the other hand, those narcotics users who have criminal tendencies to begin with are more likely to engage in drug-facilitated violence.[40]

While there is little evidence for an association between the abuse of narcotics and violence, a much stronger case can be made for the role of alcohol in violence. Alcohol acts rapidly on the central nervous system and removes some of the "controls" that generally operate on individuals. It first impairs the person's ability to make judgments and perform complicated motoric tasks, then interferes with semiautomatic motor skills, and finally it may even disrupt such survival mechanisms as the respiratory system. In general, alcohol seems to operate on the controlling and inhibiting centers of the brain.[41]

As in the case of narcotics, alcohol does not drive people to commit acts of violence. However, a staff report to the National Commission on the Causes and Prevention of Violence noted that "No other psychoactive substance is more frequently associated with violent crimes, suicide, and automobile accidents than alcohol." For example, in a large study of homicide in Philadelphia, alcohol was involved in 64 percent of the homicides. In 44 percent of the homicides both the victim and the offender had been drinking.[42] This does not mean that alcohol caused the murders. The relationship between alcohol and violence is highly complex and involves many psychological and social factors as well as the pharmacological effects of alcohol. While alcohol seems to contribute to the likelihood of violence by removing many inhibitions (both physiological and social), it is unlikely that it creates aggressive urges.

HORMONAL BALANCE: SEX AND STRESS

Hormones are chemicals secreted by the endocrine glands that perform important regulatory functions (e.g., metabolism, menstrual cycle) in conjunction with the nervous system. One of the important functions of some hormones seems to be preparing animals for seasonal functions such as reproduction, hibernation, and migration. These cyclical activities are regulated by a complex interrelationship between physiological events (e.g., secretion of hormones) and environmental stimulation. For example, the secretion of estrogens from the female ring dove's sexual organs seems to stimulate nest building by the female ring dove. In addition, however, the male dove's courtship behavior speeds up the female's nest-building activities. Similarly, an isolated female dove usually will not lay eggs unless there are other doves present.

Since the endocrine glands and the nervous system are interconnected through a complicated feedback system (e.g., pituitary gland and the hypothalamus), some hormones may arouse the aggression areas or "deaden" the inhibitory areas of the nervous system. Although the exact mechanisms through which hormones affect aggression are not well understood, there is ample evidence that changes in the hormonal balance of an organism can lead to increased or reduced aggressiveness.[43]

It has been known for many centuries that the castration of males, which reduces the secretion of male hormones (i.e., *androgens*), results in a marked reduction in aggressive tendencies. Castration has been used frequently to tame animals, such as roosters and bulls, and occasionally to curb human aggressiveness. In countries and states where castration has been employed as part of the penal system, it has resulted in less aggression among inmates jailed for violent sex crimes.[44] Effects similar to castration can be achieved through the administration of antiandrogenic chemicals or female hormones (i.e., *estrogens*).[45]

When we think of aggression, we frequently think of it as a male phenomenon. Indeed, as we shall see in later chapters, males commit more aggressive crimes than females. However, women can and do display violent behavior. More interestingly, they seem to do it more often at a particular time in their menstrual cycle that is commonly referred to as premenstrual tension. For example, females are more likely to commit crimes during this part of their menstrual cycle.[46] Again, the exact physiological basis for this is not clearly known and is probably highly complex. It is even questionable whether physiological factors are primarily the cause of the psychological and physical symptoms associated with premenstrual tension.[47] One possibility is that specific hormones, which normally have an effect on the sites mediating the inhibition of aggression, reach a low level during this period. Consequently, the excitatory areas are given a relatively freer reign.[48]

In males and females, aggressive behavior is affected by some of the hormones secreted by the adrenal glands, which prepare the body for action in emergency situations. The adrenal glands secrete *adrenalin* in situations calling for aggressive defense or flight and *noradrenalin* in situations characterized by tension and stress. While these hormones may not directly cause aggression, they may prepare the mediating nervous centers to increase the body's readiness for appropriate aggressive action in specific situations.[49] In any event, the adrenal hormones are closely associated with the physiological changes accompanying the emotions of fear and anger, which often precede aggression.

An interesting illustration of the complex interrelationship between endocrine glands, the environment, and aggressive behavior is the effect of overcrowding on the adrenal glands. In many species of animals, overcrowding leads to a breakdown of the normal social organization of the animal community. Ordinarily the social organization of such animals as chickens and baboons consists of a dominance hierarchy or a "pecking order." Once a dominance hierarchy is established, the degree of fighting within the group is minimized. In overcrowding, however, the status relationships between animals are no longer clearly determined, and frequent fights erupt in attempts to establish a dominance hierarchy. The constant readiness for fighting leads to continuous stress. In order to deal with this chronic emergency, more adrenal hormones are needed to keep the animal in a constant state of alert for defense, offense, or retreat. The adrenal glands become abnormally large to meet the increased demands placed upon them, and this results in changes within the organism that ultimately reduce its chances of survival! The abnormal growth of the adrenal glands impairs body growth, impairs the development of antibodies and reduces resistance to diseases, and impairs the reproductive organs. These impairments increase the number of deaths in the overcrowded community and thereby reduce its size. Thus, the severity of overcrowding is diminished. The relationship among adrenal secretions, aggression, and population density forms a homeostatic system for population control.[50]

THE CASE AGAINST BRAIN CONTROL

We have pointed out in our brief survey of possible physiological sources of aggression that there are identifiable areas in the human brain that may play a role in the arousal and control of aggressive behavior. Given the limited scope of our discussion, we have focused our attention on two areas of the brain: the hypothalamus and the amygdala. However, there are probably many smaller structures and regions of the brain that may mediate aggressive behavior. In addition, these regions and structures are not isolated from each other, but are connected via a large and incredibly complex network of nerve fibers. Aggressive impulses can travel in an ascending fashion (i.e., from the brain stem up towards the neocortex), in a descending direction, or even in complex feedback loops.

In the normal course of an aggressive reaction (e.g., a cat's rage on seeing a dog), the aggressive impulse is triggered by the perception of an external stimulus, which has to be processed by a large number of neural centers. These centers evaluate and interpret the incoming sensory information before passing along impulses to motoric centers that direct physical reactions to the stimulus. Some of these neural relay stations have excitatory functions, while others serve to inhibit the aggressive impulse and do not allow its passage to the command centers for motor responses.

In short, there are definite physiological mechanisms that mediate aggressive behaviors. We have raised the possibility that abnormalities (e.g., tumors or brain damage) may interfere with normal brain functioning and thereby "short-circuit" the system. Abnormalities may make some individuals unusually violent (e.g., the Texas Tower murderer), while other "malfunctions" (e.g., marijuana-induced effects) may make people less aggressive. However, the mechanisms mediating aggression seem to be "normal and natural" parts of our animal physiology. In this sense, aggression cannot be considered to be a "disease" or "abnormality." Unless we can point to specific dysfunctions in aggression "centers," we should not speak of aggression in terms of pathology. Indeed, the documented instances of aggression resulting from pathology are relatively rare in comparison to the total number of violent incidents in our society.

We started this chapter with a futuristic account of the physiological control of aggression through artificial techniques. While our present level of technology is only suggestive of what the future might bring, in a few decades we may be capable of controlling the complex physiological processes of large numbers of people. But our brief discussion of aggression and the brain suggests that an exclusively physiological and pathological view of the origins of aggression is insufficient. Under these circumstances, can the physiological control of aggression be successful?

We readily concede that physiological techniques may be very effective in controlling aggression whenever biological dysfunctions are at the root of the violent behavior. But in other instances the argument for physiological intervention is more dubious. Dr. Clark's "modest proposal" (p. 10) raises at least three immediate problems. First, who controls the brain controllers? Recent events in the U.S.S.R. show clearly how medicine and psychiatry may be abused to stifle political dissidents.[51] Second, physiological control may interfere with the beneficial consequences of aggression or aggression-related behaviors. Perhaps physiological intervention might disrupt such normal and socially desirable human motives as defense, achievement motivation, curiosity, and emotions, which may be tied up with aggression. In short, intervention might have consequences that we cannot anticipate.

Finally, pleasant dreams of peaceful human societies without violence may be premature for it is not clear that even intensive programs of physiological control could stamp out all aggression. The evidence for the effectiveness of physiological controls comes from studies of "emotional" aggression, usually related to anger or rage.[52] What about cold-blooded murder (i.e., instrumental aggression)? Perhaps physiological intervention could eliminate crimes of passion, which occur without premeditation and make up the bulk of individual criminal violence. However, aggression may result from a "rational" consideration of the various and most effective means available for obtaining a desired goal, rather than from hasty emotional reactions. "Noaggressatol" might prevent politicians and generals from rashly "pushing the button," but it might not stop them from calmly deciding to wage war (e.g., President Johnson's bombing of North Vietnam).

The brain is not a place where we can simply turn aggression on and off like an electric light bulb. It is a highly complex piece of machinery located inside of an extremely complex organism. And the organism operates within a complicated social and physical environment, where it interacts with other similar and complex organisms. Consequently, we must go beyond the physiological bases of aggression to understand it more fully and to control it.

One of our most important concerns is the problem of motivation or the energizing force that lies behind behavior. What "forces" fuel the physiological machinery and impel it to behave in a particular manner? Is human nature tainted with an innate biological urge towards violence?

SUMMARY

Is it possible for medical science to eradicate the "plague of violence" just as it did the "black plague"? Right now many people, laymen and scientists alike, foresee a future where violence could be controlled through biochemical and psychosurgical techniques like many other diseases. Of course, this view is based on the assumption that human aggression is a pathology just like cancer. Unfortunately, there are many difficulties in deciding whether a behavior like aggression is pathological or normal. Such a "medical model" does suggest, however, that we look to possible physiological processes for the origins of human aggression.

Since most human behavior is controlled to some degree by the central nervous system, especially the brain, many researchers have looked to the brain for the physiological wellsprings of aggression. Specifically, they raise the question of whether there are definite "aggression centers" that cause aggression. The evidence from such techniques as electrostimulation and ablation (i.e., removal of neural tissues through surgery) points to some subcortical areas as excitatory (e.g., amygdala, hypothalamus) or inhibitory areas (e.g., caudate nucleus) for aggression.

However, there is little evidence that these areas are "aggression centers" in the sense that (1) they mediate only aggression and not other behaviors and (2) they are the sole or major sources of aggressive impulses. Studies claiming to have located "aggression centers" suffer from a variety of methodological, reliability, and validity problems that cast doubt upon the existence of "aggression centers." Most important, there are alternative physiological explanations that account for the results attributed to "aggression centers." However, this does not mean that there are no physiological roots to aggression. Rather, it suggests that aggression is a complex behavior mediated by many neural areas and that aggression is part of the normal (i.e., nonpathological) functioning of the human organism.

Of course the evidence does not rule out the possibility that aggression may sometimes have pathological origins. A brief survey of possible causes of brain damage (e.g., tumors, genetics, drugs, hormonal imbalance) suggests that documented instances of pathologically based aggression are rare. It seems instead that physiological effects, both normal and pathological, are often moderated or directed by preexisting personality factors and/or social environmental forces. In short, there is little reason to believe that aggression can be turned on and off like a light bulb through psychosurgical or biochemical intervention.

FOOTNOTES

[1] See Moyer (1971) for a good overview.

[2] See the work of Mark and Ervin (1970), which is summarized on pp. 18–22.

[3] Clark (1971).

[4] Clark (1971), p. 35.

[5] Szasz (1961).

[6] Mark and Ervin (1970), p. 2.

[7] More detailed, yet relatively nontechnical discussions of brain structure and evolution can be found in Isaacson et al. (1971).

[8] Summarized in Kaada (1967).

[9] Summarized in Kaada (1967).

[10] The relevant studies are summarized in Kaada (1967) and Moyer (1971).

[11] Milner (1970), pp. 359–64.

[12] Kluever and Bucy (1937).

[13] Kaada (1967); Moyer (1968).

[14] Moyer (1971), p. 71.

[15] Paraphrased from pp. 97–108 in *Violence and the Brain* by Vernon H. Mark and Frank R. Ervin. Copyright © 1970 by Harper & Row, Publishers, Inc. By permission of the publisher.

[16] Delgado (1967).

[17] J. M. R. Delgado. Cerebral heterostimulation in a monkey colony. *Science* 141 (12 July 1963): 161–63. Copyright 1963 by the American Association for the Advancement of Science. Paraphrased by permission.

[18] Mark and Ervin (1970), pp. 125–35.

[19] Valenstein (1973).

[20] Goddard (1964). In addition, stimulation of the amygdala sometimes produces fear-motivated flight behavior, which inhibits aggression.

[21] Rosvold, Mirsky, and Pribram (1954).

[22] Pribram (1962).

[23] Delgado (1963).

[24] Moyer (1968), p. 66.

[25] Green, Clemente, and DeGroot (1957).

[26] Moyer (1968).

[27] Panksepp (1971).

[28] Kim and Umbach (1972).

[29] Valenstein (1973), pp. 98–104.

[30] Valenstein (1973), pp. 136–39.

[31] Lombroso (1911).

[32] Boelkins and Heiser (1970), p. 24.

[33] Kessler and Moos (1969).

[34] Jarvik, Klodin, and Matsuyama (1973).

[35] Jarvik, Klodin, and Matsuyama (1973), pp. 677–79.

[36] Sweet, Ervin, and Mark (1969).

[37] Ellinwood (1971).

[38] Mulvihill and Tumin (1969), pp. 669–70.

[39] Mulvihill and Tumin (1969), pp. 639–95.

[40] Mulvihill and Tumin (1969), p. 667.

[41] Mulvihill and Tumin (1969), pp. 641–49.

[42] Wolfgang (1966), p. 136.

[43] Davis (1964); Moyer (1971); Boelkins and Heiser (1971).

[44] LeMaire (1956); Hawke (1950).

[45] Moyer (1971), pp. 75–78.

[46] Dalton (1964).

[47] Paige (1973); Parlee (1973).

[48] Moyer (1971), pp. 77–78

[49] Davis (1964), pp. 64–65.

[50] Christian and Davis (1964).

[51] Medvedev and Medvedev (1971); Chorover (1973, 1974), Trotter (1974).

[52] Many animal studies deal with predatory aggression, which is not emotional. Obviously, physiological intervention that eliminated this type of aggression might have disastrous consequences for these animals. Physiological studies of human beings seem to deal more with emotional aggression (e.g., Julia, pp. 18–19).

2 / THE URGE TO ATTACK

motivational factors

THE NATURE OF MOTIVATION

In this chapter we move beyond the intricacies of the human nervous system to the forces that energize and direct the "human machine." By focusing on human *motivation,* we move from the realm of more directly observable and measurable systems and processes of "hard-nosed" physiologists and neurosurgeons to that of the less observable and measurable concepts of relatively "soft-nosed" psychologists. We have to concern ourselves with a much higher level of abstraction and to work with inferred or hypothetical constructs that defy direct observation and analysis. Although the area of human motivation is central to understanding the "causes" of human actions, it is sadly an under-developed region in the science of human behavior. This is scarcely due to neglect of the topic. In fact, speculations about the nature of human motives lie at the root of almost all philosophical and psychological theories.[1]

However, the concept of motivation is highly conjectural. We observe a piece of behavior and then speculate on the causes that led the person to behave in such a way. In this speculation, we take into account a number of factors external to the person, such as situational influences or past events, as well as internal factors including personality, emotion, values, desires, etc. (see the discussion of attribution in Chapter 4). Although we may have a very thorough first-hand knowledge of the external factors, we have to infer how they have affected the person and why they may have been instrumental in bringing about the action. Internal factors are even more difficult to get at, since we have to extrapolate from a person's past behavior, rely on his self-reports (which may or may not be accurate), or ask a psychiatrist to make an educated guess about these internal factors. In the classic detective story, the search for an internal factor, the motive, is the most important and most subjective part of the sleuth's job. Did the victim accidentally stumble across the scene of another crime and thus have "to be taken care of" (an external motivating factor), or was he the victim of a psychopathic killer craving for blood (an internal motivating factor)? Short of a confession, the motive has to be reconstructed from circumstantial evidence. In short, motives are hypothetical in nature, difficult to link to behavior, and hard to test empirically.

The motive has been particularly difficult to prove in the scientific analysis of aggressive behavior. Is aggressive behavior due to powerful "built-in" aggressive drives or instincts that are part of "human nature" and inherited from our infrahuman forefathers? Or is aggression due to external environmental factors, such as frustration and learning, that affect the organism from the outside and produce certain reactions? These two questions reflect the views of the scientific doctrines of "nativism" and "environmentalism."[2] In this chapter, we shall survey the various theories advanced by the proponents of these doctrines and evaluate the evidence presented for each point of view. We shall begin with the nativist *action theories,* as we shall call them. These theories argue that aggressive behavior is the result of innate driving forces that energize the "action." We shall then turn to *reaction theories* that require an environmental instigation in order to call forth an aggressive "reaction." After we have examined the similarities and differences between these two types of theories we shall attempt to use the concepts of emotion and coping behavior to provide a bridge between them.

Occam's Razor

Before embarking on this survey, we have to arm ourselves with a tool for evaluating the various theories. If motivation is inferred and cannot be directly observed, how will we judge the merits of each theory, and what evidence are we willing to accept? We shall use "Occam's razor," the principle of parsimony and simplicity of scientific explanation proposed by William Occam, a fourteenth-century philosopher. We shall attempt to find the theory that needs the fewest, simplest, and most testable assumptions to account for all of our behavioral observations and experimental outcomes. For example, before we accept telepathy as an explanation for a strange event, we shall first make sure that other more mundane possibilities (including cheating or chance) are ruled out.

A further criterion for the acceptability or usefulness of a theory is its conduciveness to empirical testing. Does the theory allow us to make predictions that can be shown to be true or false by objective observational methods that can be repeated at will by different scientists? This demand of a positivist-oriented philosophy of science implies that the concepts, even though they may be hypothetical constructs (i.e., not directly observable themselves), must be related to observable and measurable phenomena. One specific issue that we shall repeatedly raise in this context is the nature of the specific recommendations and predictions a theory advances for the control of human aggression. This will be a useful device in demonstrating the important basic differences between theories.

Finally, we shall reject a theory if it is plainly contradicted by established empirical facts and findings in its own area or even neighboring areas. Thus, we cannot accept a psychological theory of motivation that seems to be totally out of line with physiological research on the arousal processes in the central nervous system.

Arouse, Sustain, and Direct

Let us now consider what we want a theory of motivation to explain. Remember the white-hatted cowboy of western movie fame who chased a black-hatted cowboy across the Great American West to avenge his friend's death? Our theory should explain why the good guy is aroused or instigated to set out on his "search-and-destroy" mission. It should further specify the nature of the energy that sustains his activity in spite of all adversities. Finally, it should account for the directedness or purposiveness of the aggressive action, the dogged determination of our hero that leads up to the inevitable shoot-out in Dodge City. Our theory must deal with those forces that *arouse, sustain,* and *direct* aggressive behavior.[3] Let us illustrate what we mean by these three aspects of motivation by using a rather mundane type of human motivation: hunger.

Hunger is considered to be one of the most primary, biologically based motives in animals and is consequently one of the best-researched areas in motivation. The processes connected with the hunger drive and the resulting behavior can be roughly described as follows: A deviation from an optimal amount of nutrient material in the bloodstream (and possibly muscular contractions in an empty stomach) give rise to signals, transmitted to so-called "feeding centers" in the brain. These processes can lead to a subjective experience of hunger (at least in human beings) and to food-seeking behavior that is concluded by a consummatory act (i.e., eating and digestion). Even though animals cannot report hunger feelings, a large number of experiments have made it quite clear that stimulation of the feeding center in the brain leads to food-seeking behavior. The same effect can be produced by food deprivation for various periods of time. Consequently, although the motive "hunger" cannot be directly observed or measured (except by self-report in human beings), the source, energy, and goal of the hypothesized motivational state or drive can be identified. The *source* of the drive is the imbalance between an existing and an optimal metabolic state of the organism. This imbalance creates a tension that provides the *energy* for activities designed to reduce this tension by reestablishing the optimal state. The *goal* or purpose of the drive is the consummation of nutritive material, which, upon digestion, enters the bloodstream and signals restoration of the optimal state. Thus, the system is a homeostatic (self-regulative) feedback process (see Chapter 8).

Although this discussion is much simplified,[4] it helps to point out the essential features of innate, biologically organized drives. The source of the drive or the instigation for specific drive-related activities can be found in internal stimulation, independent of specific external environmental influences. Even if we could not use the tools of the physiologist to pinpoint the specific sources of the hunger drive, we could assert the drive character of hunger by showing that a person will report hunger after a period of starvation independent of any environmental changes.[5]

How does all this relate to the motivation behind aggression? We have implicitly set down a number of criteria that aggressive behavior should meet, if we were to postulate the existence of an innate aggressive drive. First, aggressive behavior should be spontaneous (i.e., triggered by internal impulses rather than outside provocation). Second, aggressive energy should be present and should accumulate until the organism "discharges" the energy by engaging in an aggressive action. There should be little or no energy left for further aggression after such a discharge. Finally, there should be specific aggression goals or targets, which can serve to reduce aggressive energy. Does aggressive behavior meet these criteria? This is the complex question that we shall now tackle in discussing and contrasting action and reaction theories of aggression.

ACTION THEORIES OF AGGRESSION

Psychoanalytic Notions of Aggressive Energy

FOCUS
Why War? And How to Avoid It.

In the aftermath of World War I and one year before Hitler came to power in Germany, Albert Einstein wrote an open letter to Sigmund Freud. Why, Einstein asked, can the ruling classes incite the masses to mad fury and self-sacrifice in wars where only the masses bear the suffering? Is it possible to influence the psychological development of mankind to make men more able to resist the lust for hatred and destruction?

Freud's answer was very pessimistic: "There is no use in trying to get rid of man's aggressive inclinations." Freud went on to outline his

Figure 2-1 Shortly after World War I Albert Einstein, *left,* wrote an open letter to Sigmund Freud, *right,* asking whether psychoanalytic theory had any suggestions for preventing future wars. Freud's answer was pessimistic in that he saw the origin of war in human nature itself. Wide World Photos.

most recent theory on the existence of a fundamental human drive towards aggression and destruction. He postulated that this drive, which he called the death instinct, represented a basic striving of all organic living matter to return to an inorganic state. If unchecked, the death instinct would lead to self-destruction and the death of the organism. However, as Love opposes Hate, the destructive death instinct (Thanatos) is opposed by Eros, the life-preserving instinct representing attraction and love. In order to prevent the organism from self-destruction, the life instinct redirects the thrust of the death instinct towards the outside world. To avoid destroying ourselves, we have to drain our destructive impulses by engaging in violent acts directed at others.

This postulate was not the only ground for Freud's pessimism concerning the chances for eternal peace. Just as love is often found in a curious coexistence with hate, the death instinct can be found in an unholy alliance with erotic instincts. Various mixtures of destructive and erotic instincts are possible, from cruel punishment in the name of idealistic motives to sexual satisfaction arising from sadistic aggression. Because of this mixture of instinct, Freud argued that maybe one of the reasons why humans are easily incited to war is that it is easy to justify aggression in the name of noble motives, thus conveniently forgetting baser ones.

Does the nature of human motivation condemn the species to constant aggression and eternal war? Freud mentioned two indirect methods for combating war. First, it would be necessary to redirect the aggressive impulses so that they would not find expression in war. One possibility is to establish strong positive emotional ties of a nonsexual nature between people, since such ties would be incompatible with aggressive behavior. Second, he suggested educating the ruling classes, which he regarded as the inevitable authority in each society, so as to direct the dependent masses in a peaceful and nonaggressive direction.

Freud ended his letter to Einstein on a more optimistic note by arguing that only cultural development can tame the primitive instinctual appetites of people by internalizing in them prohibitions against violence in the form of a superego or conscience. Thus, Freud saw hope for the development of a "constitutional intolerance" for war in the process of further cultural evolution.[6]

More than forty years since Freud's letter to Einstein, we are still asking the same question: Why war? Clearly, Freud's modest proposals have not been followed. We do not seem to love each other more, nor have our elites undergone a metamorphosis into a more enlightened state. Culture does not seem to have progressed to the point of our obtaining a "constitutional intolerance" to war. Obviously the causes of war and aggression are enormously complex. But for now, we shall take up only Freud's notion of the death instinct as the innate driving force behind human aggression.

Aggression plays only a minor role in Freud's earlier psychoanalytic theory. It is seen as originating from a "loss of love" or from frustrations of the libido. His early theory was concerned mostly with infantile sexuality, the id, ego, and superego, and the etiology of psychological abnormalities. However, a combination of events led Freud to postulate a major role for aggression in the human psyche. First, Freud was deeply affected by the massive destruction and human suffering of World War I. Second, Freud found it difficult to account for a number of phenomena by relying solely on his concepts of libido and the pleasure principle (i.e., the organism's consistent striving for pleasurable experiences). For example, some of his patients suffering from war neuroses kept having dreams in which they constantly relived the traumatic events that led to their neuroses. This "repetition compulsion" was very difficult to explain by the pleasure principle, since the dreams were obviously anything but pleasurable. Similarly, patients tended to repeat infantile actions, which had led to their psychological difficulties, in their inter- action with the analyst.

These events led Freud to conclude that the essential nature of human motivation is "conservative." By this Freud meant that drives represent an urge to return to a prior state of the organism. However, the very first state of the organism was inanimate, since lifelessness precedes life. Consequently, Freud argued, death is the goal of all life. Thus, he postulated a death instinct to parallel the life instinct.

What are the source, energy, and goal of Freud's death instinct, the force behind human aggressiveness? Its *source* is the divergence of the organism's life condition from an inorganic state or death. This divergence results in tension or energy that sustains activities directed at the *goal* of returning the organism to an inorganic state. However, just as the energy provided by Eros, the sexual and life instinct, can be neutralized and used to pursue other goals, the energy of the death instinct can be put to different uses and redirected at different goals. In fact, it has to be redirected totally, or to a large degree, because it would otherwise destroy the organism. Consequently, the proper goal of the death instinct, the self, is frequently substituted for by outside targets. In Freud's view, men must aggress against others and inanimate objects in order to avoid self-destruction.

In summary, Freud's position was that aggression against the self and against environmental objects (both animate and inanimate) is the result of an innate, biologically rooted drive. How can we evaluate this theory in terms of the criteria we outlined earlier? Since Freud's assumption of a death instinct was based mainly on biological speculations, we should first look at modern biological evidence. Although it is a biological fact that all organisms age and die, there is no evidence for an energy source for self-destruction as postulated by Freud.[7]

Our second criterion for a "good theory" was that it be empirically testable. However, one major problem with psychoanalytic theorizing is the difficulty of establishing clear-cut operational definitions for essential concepts. For example, is the concept of psychic energy to be thought of as obeying the laws of physical energy? In much of psychoanalytic thinking there is a confusion of jargons. Concepts for persons (e.g., self) are mixed with concepts from hydrodynamics, biology, and physiology.[8] This vagueness and indeterminacy of concepts have made it difficult, if not impossible, to empirically test psychoanalytic theories.

Even though physiologists have failed to find evidence for a constantly operative biological system underlying an aggressive drive and even though empirical tests of psychoanalytic concepts seem impossible, we might argue that we need to retain the idea of an innate aggressive drive as a hypothetical construct in order to explain much of human behavior. Most modern psychoanalysts reject Freud's notion of a death instinct, but retain the concept of a primarily innate, aggressive drive as the dualistic antagonist to Eros.[9] They argue that it is a useful concept and should be retained. Before wielding Occam's razor and excising the concept of an innate aggressive drive from the body of psychological theorizing, we should first examine other theories that make fewer and less-speculative assumptions than psychoanalysis. Only then can we decide on the merits of postulating an innate aggressive drive as a hypothetical construct.

At this point, we might wonder why worry about whether the drive exists or not. Let us get along with the pressing business of preventing aggression and violence. Why engage in sterile arguments about hypothetical drives? Unfortunately, it is exactly the question of controlling violence that forces us to consider the likelihood of an innate aggressive drive.

If the action theories of aggression are correct and if there is a constant flow of aggressive energy that must find a suitable outlet, we have to provide safe outlets. We had better open the floodgates before the dam bursts. Many theorists, who subscribe to the notion of an aggressive instinct, prescribe this as a cure for aggression. Here are a few examples:

> Rural life before farming was mechanized offered the child at least a chance for vicarious discharge of violence. In my native Austria slaugh-

tering the pig was a distinct highlight in the lives of peasant children. But so were chopping wood and other forms of aggressive manipulation of nature which at least provided outlets that were socially useful and contributed to the well being of the family.[10]

When deprived of an outlet for our aggressions, we become upset. White Americans ought to be thankful to the Negro for providing, since the earliest days of slavery, handy targets for their hostile aggressions.[11]

While some early forms of sport, like the jousting of medieval knights, may have had an appreciable influence on sexual selection, the main function of sport today lies in the cathartic discharge of aggressive urges; besides that, of course, it is of the greatest importance in keeping people healthy.[12]

As we shall see later, psychologists leaning towards reaction theories of aggression, especially learned aggression, argue that such mildly aggressive substitutes for violence, such as competitive sports, are dangerous, because they may arouse and instigate a person towards more severe violence or habituate him to aggressive behavior in general (see Chapter 3). According to these theorists, mild substitutes for violence increase the likelihood of aggression rather than decrease it. Consequently, the actions we take to prevent violence depend upon whether we believe its origins to lie in an innate aggressive drive or not. Therefore, it is imperative for us to continue assessing the concept of an innate aggressive drive.

Aggression as Instinct: The Ethologist's View

Psychoanalysts have not been the sole champions of the biological nature and origin of aggressive behavior. Ethologists, working from radically different theories and data, have reached similar conclusions. The work of ethologists such as the Nobel laureate Konrad Lorenz, whose book *On Aggression* was a bestseller, has revitalized instinctual theories of aggression and made them respectable once again.[13] Although ethologists have studied mainly the behavior of infrahuman animals, their work is relevant to a discussion of human aggression because of their attempts to clearly define the concept of instinct, to specify the evolutionary significance of aggression, and to provide empirical evidence for the existence of instinctive aggressive behavior patterns.

The bulk of their research has been concerned with such routine behaviors as the way fish rhythmically move their fins, chickens peck for grain, and male dogs lift their hindlegs. The important contribution of these studies is that many of these movements occur in very standard, stereotyped manners (hence they are called *fixed action patterns*) and seem to be motivated by their own internal drive (or *central excitatory potential* in ethologists' jargon). In other words, they are not merely re-flexes that occur only after some external environmental stimulation has evoked them, but possibly result from internal stimulation generated by the nervous system.

However, this does not mean that the performance of fixed action patterns is completely independent of environmental influences. Before the central excitatory potential can lead to the occurrence of a behavior pattern, it needs to be released by an innate releasing mechanism that is triggered by an external "key" stimulus. Just as a key opens a lock, this releasing stimulus activates a mechanism that removes inhibitions that have prevented the internal drive from releasing its energy. Without the inhibitions and appropriate key stimuli, the constantly produced central excitatory potential would lead to dysfunctional and wasted behavior. Chickens would be pecking for grain even though there was no grain in sight. The presence of a key stimulus (e.g., grain) appropriate to the release of a particular instinctive impulse (e.g., pecking) guarantees that behavior is purposive and functional.

The trouble is that there might not always be grain for our chicken to peck. This is troublesome for reasons other than potential starvation, since the "pecking" excitatory potential or drive accumulates if it is not released regularly. According to instinctual theorists, the energy-produc-ing source in the central nervous system is automatic and constantly operative. This is the reason for describing such theories as "hydraulic." They are based on the analogy of water flowing into a reservoir behind a dam. The water continues to accumulate and will overflow the dam un-less it is periodically drained off.

Let us return to our chicken who has no grain to peck. As time goes by he will show restless behavior as if he were searching for an appro-priate key stimulus to release the dammed-up energy. As the energy builds, the threshold for releaser stimuli becomes lower. Weaker or substitute stimuli, which would not ordinarily release pecking behavior, now do. For example, Lorenz describes an early experiment in which a male dove was deprived of a female partner for various periods of time. Depending on the length of the "mateless" period, the dove courted first a stuffed pigeon, then a rolled-up cloth, and finally bowed and cooed in front of an empty corner.[14]

What happens if not even a substitute stimulus can be found to unlock the floodgates? One possibility is displacement—the flowing over of a dammed-up instinctive impulse into the action patterns of another instinct. The water is diverted into another basin, so to speak. Tinbergen, another famous ethologist and Nobel laureate, found that a sexually aroused stickleback fish will engage in nest-ventilating behavior (i.e., fan-ning water over the still-empty nest) if a female does not respond to his courtship dance. The energy of the sexual drive is diverted to nesting behavior.[15] Similarly, if aggressive motivation is instinctual, it too could be displaced into some other activity. Of course, this mechanism reminds us very much of Freud's notion of the rechanneling of aggressive and

Figure 2-2 Displacement of aggression, but this time with a just ending. © *Punch,* London.

libidinal energy into culturally acceptable activities, which he called sublimation, or of the redirection of the death instinct from inward to outward channels.

There is another possibility besides displacement. Consider a dam and its reservoir. As the reservoir fills and the water rises, the dam will either burst or be breached unless the floodgates are opened to drain off the accumulating water. The floodgates act as safety valves.

Now let us apply this analogy. The rising water is the steadily accumulating internal energy and the safety valves are the releaser stimuli that "drain off water" with increasingly lower thresholds as the pressure increases. But what if all of the "floodgates are jammed," if not even remotely adequate releaser stimuli can be found? The dam will burst and our chicken will suddenly, and possibly explosively, show *vacuum activity*. Our chicken will peck even though his pecking has not been triggered in any specifiable way by an external key stimulus. The organism engages in motor behavior that closely corresponds to the action-specific energy that had accumulated, but which has not been released. Lorenz gives the example of a hand-reared starling (a bird) that had never caught insects before, but all of a sudden performed the full routine of catching, killing, and swallowing an insect. Lorenz assures us that there could not have been prey of that kind in the room or, at least, that he could not find any *afterwards,* even by climbing a ladder and examining the ceiling.[16] Lorenz claimed the starling engaged in vacuum behavior. Of course, the trouble with this anecdote is that the starling just might have swallowed the evidence! However, other ethologists assure us that similar types of vacuum behavior have been observed in other species.[17] The existence of vacuum behavior is important evidence for instinctual drives that must release their energy.

Now that we have become familiar with the terms and concepts employed by ethologists, do similar instinctual mechanisms motivate aggressive behavior? There is not much agreement on an answer to this question even among ethologists.[18] However, the most influential opinion has been strongly affirmative. Lorenz, for example, claims that "aggression, the effects of which are frequently equated to those of the death wish, is an instinct like any other and in natural conditions it helps just as much as any other to ensure the survival of the individual and the species."[19] Lorenz postulates an aggression-specific internal excitatory potential or energy source with its own fixed action pattern, innate releasing mechanism, and key stimuli. If the aggressive energy is not released by appropriate releasing stimuli leading to the appropriate aggressive patterns, the aggressive energy will accumulate. This leads to a lowering of the threshold for acceptable releaser stimuli, and if the damming continues without suitable release, the pent-up pressure will explode into an aggressive act (i.e., vacuum activity) that is unrelated to any environmental provocation. In Lorenz's eyes, as in Freud's, aggression is inevitable.

How convincing are the ethological arguments advanced by Lorenz and others? Let us use Occam's razor on this theory and see whether we need the notion of an aggressive instinct to explain aggressive behavior.

One important point in this respect is the *functionality* of aggression in evolutionary terms. In terms of self-preservation, an internally fueled motivation towards interspecific aggression would be a good evolutionary mechanism to keep animals fighting for food. But this is not the kind of aggression that Lorenz has in mind. He is concerned with intraspecific aggression: fighting between members of the same species. Does an instinct toward fighting with one's family make evolutionary sense?

Lorenz believes that such an instinct fulfills four important functions.[20] First, it provides for the even distribution of animals over an inhabitable area. This is a consequence of territoriality or the struggle for possession of feeding and breeding space. It insures that the stronger animals will have the better conditions for survival and breeding. Second, it operates in sexual selection by insuring that only the best and strongest animals mate. This not only helps keep up the quality of the species' gene pool, but it also provides strong and aggressive protectors for offspring. Third, it is involved in brood defense against members of the same species. In some species, only the brood-protecting sex shows intraspecific aggression. Finally, aggression provides motivational energy for activities that seem to be outwardly quite unrelated to aggression. One example is the establishment and maintenance of ranking orders or "pecking hierarchies" in animal societies, which stabilize the interactions between animals and prevent recurrent and chaotic fights. Lorenz even deduces a behavior rather antithetical to aggression from this motivational function of aggression: love. "Undoubtedly," Lorenz states, "the personal bond developed at that phase of evolution when, in aggressive animals, the cooperation of two or more animals was necessary for a species-preserving purpose, usually brood tending. Doubtless the personal bond, love, arose in many cases from intraspecific aggression, by way of ritualization of a redirected attack or threatening."[21]

We have to agree that aggressive behavior towards one's own kind can serve useful functions. Of course, this does not necessarily mean that it originates in an innate aggressive drive. In addition, an innate ever-accumulating aggressive energy has its dysfunctional side. It is like having a self-destruction device built into the organism. Unless it is properly dealt with, it constantly threatens to explode. How is this obviously dysfunctional aspect neutralized before it destroys the species?

Lorenz offers a rather dialectical explanation for this problem. He argues that the "two great constructors of evolution" (mutation and selection) solve the problem in the following manner: ". . . the generally useful, indispensable drive remains unaltered, but for the particular case in which it might prove harmful, a very special inhibitive mechanism is constructed ad hoc."[22] He points to a large number of examples of this principle in the fighting behavior of animals, where dominance struggles between rivals are often settled by the most impressive threat display rather than a fight-to-the-death. If fighting does occur, it is often a rather harmless nature, like a tug-of-war. In most cases when things get rough, the losing animal engages in appeasement rites that inhibit the winning animal's aggressive behavior. For example, a baboon losing an argument will present its behind for mounting by the winner and thus prevent further attacks. Lorenz claims that there is a direct relationship between the effectiveness of the weapons of a species and the reliability and strength of such inhibiting mechanisms. In short, when dysfunctional consequences are likely to result from the generally functional aggressive drive, special inhibitory mechanisms act to "turn off" the aggression.

Why do not such inhibitions check man's aggressiveness and prevent him from killing his neighbors? Why are human beings different from baboons in this respect? Lorenz argues that during the early stages

Figure 2-3 The dominance hierarchy in a baboon troop is in part maintained by the exchange of aggressive threats and appeasement gestures. An adult male baboon, *left,* is threatening another baboon by showing his canine teeth and the whites of his eyelids. In the accompanying photograph, *right,* a male baboon who is being threatened by another male presents his hindquarters to be mounted by his tormentor. This is an act of appeasement that lowers the level of aggression in the group. Irven DeVore/Anthro-Photo.

of human evolution such inhibitions must have been operative and effective, particularly since human beings did not naturally possess very effective weapons. However, the invention of artificial weapons destroyed the balance between aggression and its innate inhibitors. Lorenz believes that weapons, particularly long-distance (e.g., guns) or remote-control weapons (e.g., guided missiles), "screen the killer against the stimulus situation which would otherwise activate his killing inhibitions."[23]

Of course, this hypothesis is highly speculative and untestable without a time-machine. It is certainly possible and even likely that seeing the consequences of one's aggressive acts, such as the victim's pain, may inhibit further aggression (see p. 142). But it is also likely that they would encourage greater aggression by informing the assailant of his attack's success. In addition, it is hard to justify the weight that Lorenz places upon the invention of weapons in explaining human aggression. The invention of weapons was probably accompanied, if not preceded, by many other dramatic changes in human evolution, particularly the development of language and cognition. These capacities enabled human beings to transcend the here-and-now, to plan, to expect, and to predict. Such abilities may have been much more influential in determining the nature and frequency of human aggression in the course of human evolution and may be primarily responsible for the differences between human and animal aggression.

This is not to deny the role of inhibitions in human aggression and the possible effects of artificial weapons, but Lorenz's analysis of their influence does not convince us of the presence of a single dynamic instinct of aggression. In terms of scientific theorizing, it does not seem very parsimonious to postulate a particular mechanism just because there are corrective factors (e.g., inhibitions) that keep it from going wrong. For example, we do not justify our car's acceleration by the fact that there are brakes. Inhibitory mechanisms would be necessary even if we assumed that aggressive behavior is motivated by not one instinct of combat, but by several *subinstincts of aggression*. In this view, aggression is not a general instinct in its own right, but rather a part of more general instincts such as reproduction, feeding, or defense.

Consider the following example. An inexperienced turkey hen, guarding her first brood, will attack any object of reasonable size moving near her nest. She would even kill her own chicks if it were not for an inhibitory mechanism that is elicited by the "distress cries" of the chicks. However, deafened hens will peck at and kill their own brood.[24]

How can we account for this phenomenon? It seems functional that parents are particularly aggressive during that period of time when their young are unable to defend themselves. We all know of stories about human or animal mothers showing desperate bravery in fighting powerful enemies whom they would normally never attack. In such situations, "unusual" targets for aggression are attacked. That is, the targets usually evoke flight rather than fight reactions. Consequently, it seems impossible and dysfunctional to have built-in recognition mechanisms for all possible enemies that ordinarily elicit fear and flight. However, if a general readiness to attack is represented by a subinstinct of the general parental instinct, then a special inhibitory mechanism must be present to protect those for whose safety the special aggressive drive was originally intended. In this instance, aggression and its inhibitory mechanism are similarly parts of the general parental instinct.

This example shows that it seems more reasonable to assume aggressive subinstincts in the service of important species-preserving instincts than to posit a general aggressive instinct, whose consequences would be dysfunctional during much of the individual's life span. The notion of aggressive subinstinct would also answer two important questions: (1) Why is aggressive behavior, in many animals, more frequent during certain seasons (e.g., the mating season) than in others, and (2) Where does the energy or excitatory potential originate?

In an authoritative survey of animal behavior, Hinde pointed out that territorial fighting (which is often used as evidence for a single dynamic instinct of aggression) occurs in many species mainly during the mating season. A number of observations show that cyclical physiological processes cause the gonads to release sex hormones into the bloodstream during that season, which in turn, as we have seen in the last chapter, have a strong influence on aggressive behavior.[25] Again, it seems reasonable to have an extra supply of aggressive energy available at a time when fights for sexual partners and territory are likely. The existence of such a well-timed and directed increase in aggression as part of the reproductive instinct makes us even less likely to accept the idea of a single, always active, instinct of aggression.

Hinde has further questioned the emphasis that Lorenz puts on the internal motivation to aggress. Specifically, he attacks the notion of the damming up of aggressive energy, which leads to threshold lowering and vacuum activities. Hinde stresses the importance of social release stimuli and argues that the influence of the internal condition of an organism, such as the hormonal balance, lies not so much in its effects on the intensity of behavior, but on the evaluation of external stimuli.[26] For example, the mother turkey hen will consider as relevant targets for attack many moving objects that she would normally ignore or flee. Particular internal processes (e.g., hormonal changes) lead to an increased attention and responsiveness to external stimuli. This idea also helps explain the phenomenon of threshold lowering. The fact that animals attack real enemies more ferociously than they do dummies suggests that the internal drive state does not influence the intensity of aggressive behavior.[27] This directly contradicts Lorenz's hydraulic theory. If the aggressive energy has been dammed up to the point where the dummy can serve as a releaser (through threshold lowering), more rather than less aggression should be discharged.

We have to conclude that there is little evidence for Lorenz's hydraulic theory of a spontaneous aggressive instinct because many of his examples can be reinterpreted into different theoretical frameworks and because many of his anecdotal observations are contradicted or qualified by other students of animal behavior.[28] If the evidence for a spontaneous aggressive instinct is slim in the case of animals, it is virtually nonexistent in the case of man. Critics have frequently accused Lorenz of drawing inappropriate analogies from animals to humans by overemphasizing the evolutionary continuities between infrahuman animals and humans and by neglecting the importance of learning and cultural developments.[29] The development of cognitive and communicative abilities has freed man greatly from the control of rigid instincts and has enabled him to plan his behavior by taking into account the contingencies of the situation. Because of this important discontinuity in the evolution of man compared to the evolution of other animals, we are extremely hesitant to accept data on animal behavior as conclusive evidence for instincts in human beings.

The special nature of the "human condition" in terms of violence was nicely expressed by an eminent aggression "researcher" whose theories are all too often neglected these days. The seventeenth-century philosopher Thomas Hobbes described some eminently human proclivities for violence:

FOCUS
". . . and the life of man, solitary, poor, nasty, brutish, and short."

"From this equality of ability, ariseth equality of hope in the attaining of our ends. And therefore if any two men desire the same thing, which nevertheless they cannot both enjoy, they become enemies; and in the way to their end, which is principally their own conservation, and sometimes their delectation only, endeavor to destroy, or subdue one another. And from hence it comes to pass, that where an invader hath no more to fear, than another man's single power; if one plant, sow, build, or possess a convenient seat, others may probably be expected to come prepared with forces united, to dispossess, and deprive him, not only of the fruit of his labour, but also of his life, or liberty. And the invader again is in the like danger of another.

"And from this diffidence of one another, there is no way for any man to secure himself, so reasonable, as anticipation; that is, by force, or wiles, to master the persons of all men he can, so long, till he see no other power great enough to endanger him: and this is no more than his own conservation requireth, and is generally allowed. . . .

"So that in the nature of man, we find three principal causes of quarrel. First, competition; second, diffidence; thirdly, glory.

"The first, maketh men invade for gain; the second, for safety; and the third, for reputation."[30]

Since there seem to be no reports of animals stealthily slaying potential enemies through anticipation of future danger or massacring other herds for the greater glory of themselves and their own herd, there must be some specific human factors involved. Such considerations greatly reduce our confidence in simple analogies from animal behavior to human behavior.

This is not to say that the ethological approach to aggression has to be rejected altogether. Many animal species, and possibly even man, may possess *some* unlearned, instinctive fixed-action patterns for aggression as well as innate releasing mechanisms or inhibitory mechanisms for aggression.[31]

However, we have to doubt that what is "released" in aggressive acts is accumulated aggressive energy from a reservoir fed by a constant source. Since no conclusive proof is reported anywhere in the literature that aggressive behavior can occur spontaneously, it is more parsimonious to postulate that aggression is *reactive*. In other words, the motivation to aggress is not always present, waiting to be called upon, but is produced by external stimulation. We could say that aggression is an *emergency* reaction of the organism and not a *maintenance* action. From this point of view, a constant aggressive driving force would be counterproductive since there is no homeostatic equilibrium to be maintained, as in the case of hunger. Instead, there is only adequate coping with environmental emergencies. We shall now turn to reactive theories of aggression and to an examination of the evidence supporting them.

REACTION THEORIES OF AGGRESSION

What situations lead to the emergency reaction of aggression? Some psychologists have argued that almost all of the ethologists' examples of aggression in animals are reactive in nature and can help us determine the characteristics of aggression-eliciting stimuli.[32] These *instigating* stimuli are almost always interferences with an organism's "interests" or on-going goal-directed activities. For example, the appearance of a rival interferes with the staking out of territory or with mating; the appearance of a predator endangers the well-being of the animal's offspring. If we were dealing with human beings, we would say that there are conflicts of interest between rivals and between predator and prey. In the language of behavioristic psychology, we might say that *reinforcing* stimulus conditions are in the animal's "interest" and are sought out, while *aversive* stimulus conditions are not in its "interest" and are avoided. Our question now is do animals react with aggression to aversive stimuli that they cannot avoid?

Pain is a well-known aversive stimulus that both animals and humans (except for masochists) try to avoid. It is also a very potent elicitor of aggression in many species of animals. The psychologist Nathan Azrin and his collaborators have shown in a series of experiments with rats, monkeys, hamsters, and many other species that painful electric shock will induce aggression against both animate and inanimate objects.[33] Besides pain, the withholding of expected positive reinforcements is also aversive and can lead to aggression.[34] In one experiment, Azrin taught a pigeon to peck a lever by reinforcing each peck with some food. After the pecking response was well established, the experimenters stopped rewarding the pecking response and also placed another pigeon in the cage. This second pigeon was restrained so that it could not defend itself. When the first pigeon no longer received food for pecking the lever, it viciously pecked at the innocent bystander.[35] The thwarted pigeon's response is not unfamiliar and is all too parallel to human behavior in similarly frustrating circumstances. The common observation that frustration often leads to aggression lies at the root of one of the earliest and most influential psychological theories of aggression: *the frustration-aggression hypothesis.*

Frustration and Aggression

The popularity of the frustration-aggression theory is easily explained by the pervasiveness of the phenomenon it describes. In fact, each and every one of us might have "discovered" this explanation for human aggression by systematic analysis of his own aggressive reactions. At least among psychologists, the theory has been around for quite a while. William McDougall, a pioneer social psychologist at the turn of the century, held that the "instinct of pugnacity" was instigated by the frustration of other instinctive impulses.[36] As we mentioned earlier,

Freud at first postulated that aggression is the result of a blocking of the libidinal instinct: a frustration of pleasure-seeking or pain-avoiding impulses.[37] But the frustration-aggression hypotheses (F-A for short) really got off the ground in 1939 when a group of young psychologists at Yale University published a monograph entitled, naturally, "Frustration and Aggression."[38] These psychologists, J. Dollard, L. Doob, N. E. Miller, O. H. Mowrer, and R. R. Sears, although acknowledging an intellectual debt to Freud, were strongly rooted in the behaviorist tradition. Distrusting nativist instinct notions, they posited a purely reactive theory of aggression, attempted a more precise definition of the concepts involved, and proceeded to postulate a number of testable hypotheses. Because of the strong and lasting influence of this approach and the many research areas it has opened up, we shall devote a Focus to its essential formulations.

FOCUS
The Case of the Cheating Soda Machine

It has been a long, hot, and hard day at the office. You feel instigated to initiate a behavior sequence leading to the goal-response of drinking a deliciously cold can of your favorite soda from the vending machine around the corner. You run through all parts of the behavior sequence of getting up, asking colleagues for change, marching to the machine, depositing your quarter, listening to the whirring and burring inside the machine, and waiting for the climax, the can. And then— nothing. The machine cheated. It interfered with the occurrence of your thirst-instigated goal-response of drinking at its proper time in the behavior sequence. This is exactly how the Yale psychologists have defined frustration.[39] The inevitable reaction to such a frustration, they theorized, is aggression, which they defined as any "sequence of behaving, the goal response to which is the injury of the person to whom it is directed."[40] This aggression can take a variety of forms from thoughts to words to deeds, and it may even be displaced from the frustrating agent to an innocent bystander or an inanimate object. Our cheating soda machine, in a way, is all of these things, and we shall most certainly kick it after it has frustrated us.

The frustration-aggression theory in its earliest form held- that all aggressions were a consequence of frustration and that each frustration inevitably leads to some kind of aggression. But what about the non-frustrated professional soda machine "muggers" who commit aggression against the machines in the process of robbing them? The Yale psychologists specifically excluded such cases of "instrumental aggression," in which a learned form of aggression is used actively and deliberately—not reactively and emotionally—to some further end.

However, the distinction between frustration-induced and instrumental aggression is not an easy one to make. If we define instrumental activity by its functional, goal-directed nature, we have a hard time excluding those cases of frustration-induced aggression that serve the function of removing or destroying the obstacle blocking our goal-response. Our kicking and battering the cheating soda machine may be motivated to some extent by our desire to get the machine moving again in order to get our drink. In such cases it would be very hard to sort out to what extent aggressive action is sheer reaction to frustration and to what extent it is employed (deliberately or not) in an instrumental way. Trying to use the notion of the intentionality of instrumental aggression as a criterion for the distinction does not really get us anywhere either, since psychologists dealing with the problem of aggression have really grappled in vain with the question of how to empirically define and measure intentional versus unintentional aggression (see Introduction).

To make the distinction between instrumental and frustration-induced aggression dependent on whether the aggressive behavior seems to be learned or not is equally problematic, since it cannot be excluded that, at least to some extent, aggression is a learned reaction to frustration. For example, early critics of the F-A hypothesis pointed out that aggression does not seem to be a typical response to frustration in all cultures and that this hypothesized relationship could be a result of culture-specific learning.[41] It is equally possible of course that aggression is the "natural" response to frustration and people in some cultures are taught to use alternative response modes. However, it is hard to deny that many of the specific types of aggressive responses to frustration must have been acquired in some learning process, as in the case of using obscene gestures!

Consequently, since it is very hard to determine to what extent a specific aggressive act is learned or not, and to what extent it serves some ulterior function or instrumental purpose, the distinction between frustration-induced and instrumental aggression seems almost futile. Obviously, this problem greatly reduces the usefulness of the F-A hypothesis since it is, by definition, only applicable to purely frustration-induced aggression.

Similarly problematic has been the original hypothesis that aggression necessarily follows frustration. Many critics have pointed out that this is not so.[42] Frustration could lead to helpless resignation or fear instead, or aggression could be absent because one has learned to deal rationally with frustrations. We may not kick the soda machine because someone is watching us and we are afraid of making a fool of ourselves or because we are afraid of hurting our foot! As early as two years after its formulation, one of the original authors of the theory, Neal Miller, acknowledged that aggression is only one of many possible responses to frustration.[43] This again greatly reduced the usefulness of the theory since now many additional assumptions about the circumstances that *do* lead to aggression are necessary.

What about the second part of the hypothesis? Is aggression, when it occurs, always preceded by frustration? The notion that all noninstrumental aggression is the reaction to a frustration has been more long-lived, but it also has been very difficult to prove experimentally. One problem has been the definition of frustration. Contrary to the original, narrow definition given above, a multitude of aversive stimuli have been termed frustration in the literature. Some authors, notably Arnold Buss,[44] have attempted to differentiate between noxious stimuli, such as pain and physical and psychological injury, and the blocking of goal-responses. Since both classes of aversive stimuli can lead to aggression[45] and since pain, for example, can be conceptualized as an interference with a desired state of well-being, this distinction has done little to clear up the confusion. A further problem is that the severity of a frustration can vary tremendously depending on how the interference with the goal-response is perceived. If the soda machine flashes a little red sign reading "EMPTY" and returns our quarter, we may feel much less frustrated than in the case of cheating. Perhaps nonarbitrary and/or expected frustrations are much less likely to arouse aggression than arbitrary, unexpected ones, although our goal-oriented behavior may cease if we expect it to be thwarted, thus theoretically excluding the possibility of frustration. In general the role of expectations seems to be very important.[46] There is evidence that the nonfulfillment of expectations (technically called the *nonconsummation of anticipatory goal-responses*) increases the likelihood of aggression. Indeed, as we shall see, this is the stuff that revolutions are made of.[47]

Before we conclude this Focus on the frustration-aggression theory, we should mention a number of specific hypotheses put forward by the Yale psychologists. They argued that the strength of the instigation to aggress depends on the severity of the frustration, which is a function of (1) the strength of the instigation to the thwarted response, (2) the degree of interference with the frustrated response, and (3) the number of frustrated response-sequences.[48] In other words, the more thirsty we are, the less soda we get in the end, and the more often we have been thwarted before, the harder we shall kick the machine.

What if we stand the chance of being arrested for vandalism in this case? "The strength of inhibition of any act of aggression varies positively with the amount of punishment anticipated to be a consequence of that act,"[49] wrote the Yale psychologists. But this does not preclude aggression altogether. Although it is assumed that "the strongest aggressive tendencies aroused by a frustration would be directed against the frustrating object,"[50] these tendencies can be displaced towards persons or things more or less similar to the frustrating agent. If we are afraid to kick the soda machine because of our fragile toes we might kick a plastic wastepaper basket instead. This should strike a familiar chord since the idea of displacement is part of Lorenz's ethological theory and Freud's psychoanalytic theory. The parallels to these theories become even more obvious in the Yale psychologists' final hypothesis which postulates that aggressive acts reduce the strength of the instigation to further aggression, in other words, have a cathartic function. Since these hypotheses are relevant for other aspects of aggression, we shall discuss the empirical evidence relating to these hypotheses in later chapters.[51]

At this point we might start wondering about the differences among Freud, Lorenz, and Yale behaviorism. Actually there are many important differences. For example, Lorenz argues that aggressive energy accumulates and is discharged fully when triggered by a substitute stimulus as in threshold lowering. However, Miller holds that the strength of the instigation to aggress declines with increasing dissimilarity of the substitute person or object to the frustrating agent.[52] Most importantly, of course, we have the differences between an active, constantly operative drive and a reactive instigation to aggress, which can be increased in strength only by further frustrations.

The question of whether aggression is active or reactive determines our approach to both causes and cures for violence in society. If Lorenz's notion were correct we could have stopped our discussion a long time ago and just considered the most harmless substitute types of aggression to drain the reservoir. If we adopt a reactive theory of aggression, we have to go on to study the antecedents of frustration as well as other sources of learned aggression as specified in the learning theories of aggression (see the following chapter).

Before we can do this, we have to further analyze the motivational underpinnings of the frustration-aggression hypothesis. There is little doubt that frustration can and, at times, does lead to aggression. But what is the source and nature of the motivation underlying the relationship between frustration and aggression? Is aggression just a learned response to frustration or does frustration have a motivational dynamic of its own? The Yale psychologists were never quite clear on this issue and they simply postulated a universal causal relationship between frustration and aggression. They acknowledged that learning might be an origin or a modifying influence on the relationship, but they never denied the possibility of a built-in innate basis for the relationship. Leonard Berkowitz, a psychologist at the University of Wisconsin and a major adherent to a modified F-A theory, points to animal experiments in which aggressive behavior followed frustration without any prior learning experience (e.g., our earlier pigeon example). Therefore, Berkowitz believes that "the frustration-aggression relationship may be learnable without being entirely learned."[53] He assumes that the motivational energy that powers aggression is provided by an *emotional state* (e.g., rage or anger), which he believes to be a primary inborn reaction to frustration. Furthermore, "aggression may be the innately determined response to anger but the exact form of this aggression, and perhaps even its vigor and intensity, may be affected if not molded entirely by past experiences."[54] In sum, Berkowitz suggests that frustration results in emotional reactions that, in turn, facilitate or energize aggression. Thus, emotion is seen as an intervening variable between frustration and aggression.

Summary

Since things are starting to get complicated, we want to pause here and consider what we have said so far and map out what lies ahead. In dealing with the motivating forces behind aggression we have first considered the view that aggression is an *instinct* with its own *action-specific* energy which *accumulates* unless discharged regularly and thus can occur *spontaneously* without provocation. This "active" view of aggressive motivation as held by Freud and particularly by Lorenz and his followers was found wanting on both theoretical as well as empirical grounds, particularly in its application to human beings.

In turning to *"reactive"* theories of aggressive motivation we examined the possibility that, rather than being self-generated, aggressive behavior is an organism's *response* to an outside provocation such as a *frustration*. For many years this notion was firmly held by a large number of psychologists subscribing to the *frustration-aggression hypothesis*. Although we did not have enough space for a detailed criticism of the theory, we found that the *definition* of "frustration" is so vague as to be almost synonymous with *"aversive experience."* Further problems arise through the difficult differentiation between frustration-induced and *instrumental* aggression. It also became quickly apparent that *many types of responses* other than aggression can result from frustrating experiences. Finally, in order to specify the nature of the aggressive motivation, the F-A hypothesis was modified by the assumption that an *emo-*

tional state such as rage or anger serves as the motivational link between frustration and aggression.

Greatly simplified, we could summarize the present state of affairs by the following statement: "Aversive experiences *can* lead to emotional arousal that *can* give rise to aggressive behavior." Although this statement roughly fits the views held by many prominent aggression researchers today, it is certainly much too vague to be useful in analyzing, predicting, and controlling aggressive behavior. We would like to know, for example, under which conditions anger will lead to aggressive behavior rather than to some other type of activity. Obviously, past and/or expected rewards or punishments may play a decisive role here. The tremendous importance of *learning* as a controlling factor of aggressive behavior will be discussed in the next chapter. In the remainder of this chapter we want to discuss the nature of aversive experiences, which we shall find heavily dependent on *cognitive appraisal,* and the nature of aggression-inducing emotional arousal. As we shall see, one important issue in our present context is the question of whether emotions are innate responses to environmental stimulation or whether they are the outcome of cognitive labeling of nonspecific arousal. We shall discuss two opposing theories and their respective shortcomings and then turn to the notion of emotional reactions as coping mechanisms in adapting to environmental contingencies as an integrative concept. We shall end the chapter with a general evaluation of the adaptive and maladaptive functions of aggressive and violent behavior in coping or failing to cope with the "struggle for existence."

The Role of Emotional Arousal

How does the concept of emotion differ from a drive? Even though a drive may not be constantly active, it is governed through the homeostatic mechanism described earlier and is consequently self-perpetuating. However, emotion can be described as an emergency reaction to an unforeseen environmental event. Since we shall stress the importance of emotional arousal as an "energizer" of aggressive behavior, we shall look at the nature of emotional arousal in some detail. Before we can discuss whether emotion is an innate, predetermined response of the organism to some environmental stimulation (emotion as a sort of reactive instinct) or whether emotion is, at least in humans, heavily influenced by cognitive appraisal of the situation, we shall assert that emotional arousal has a motivating effect (i.e., it can arouse, sustain, and direct specific behaviors).

The motivational character of emotions has not always been acknowledged in psychology. For quite a while it was treated as a disorganized state of the organism in which an overwhelming affective reaction to some environmental emergency prevents rational cognitive problem-solving and adaptation to changing situations.[55] Indeed, it has been found experimentally that too much affective arousal can be quite a handicap for effectively organized behavior. For example, if someone is "mad with fear" as in a movie theater blaze, he is unlikely to have many brilliant ideas for escape. More likely he will panic or just freeze, making things worse. On the other hand, too little arousal can be just as dysfunctional for effective behavior. Relaxing in a comfortable armchair on a quiet Sunday afternoon, dozing off every now and then, is not very conducive to innovative and creative thoughts. When we are drowsy or sleepy we tend to be very clumsy, too. Psychologists have found out that we need just the right amount of arousal—an optimal middle level. Such a theory maintains that the motivating function of arousal depends on the degree of physiological activation of the organism. Adherents to such an activation theory have argued that the concepts of different emotions and differences in felt or experienced affect are largely introspective and subjective matters unworthy of a strictly empirical and behavioristic science.[56] The claim that only physiological activation can be objectively observed and measured is further supported by the fact that physiologists have had a remarkably hard time in finding differences in physiological indices for widely different emotions.

Emotion as innate response. Yet the indisputable fact that even psychologists experience the whole gamut of emotional experiences such as anger, joy, sorrow, and sometimes fear in interacting with colleagues, friends, family, and dogs has kept the concept of different emotions alive and well. This is all the more so because our subjective emotional experience is externalized in a prominent place—our face. We find emotional expression in movements of our body, in our facial expression, and in our tone of voice. Furthermore, there are remarkable parallels to similar expressions in animals. This parallel led Charles Darwin to speculate that the expression of emotion in man and animals was innate and that it consisted largely of remnants of "serviceable functions" (i.e., actions designed to cope with the environmental situation that created the affect).[57] If we watch a threat display between two dogs on the brink of a fight, we see that they bare their teeth, flatten their ears, bristle their manes, and make other similar preparation for actual biting. We would say that the dogs look "angry"; and it seems clear that this "anger" is expressed by actions that are preparations for or part of coping behavior in this situation. The innateness of specific emotions and their bodily expressions would then consist in those typical physiological and behavioral patterns a particular species adopts to cope with various contingencies.

Figure 2-4   Left, terror from a photograph by Dr. Duchenne. *Right,* dog approaching another dog with hostile intentions, by Mr. Riviere. Drawings from Charles Darwin's *The Expression of the Emotions in Man and Animals.* Copyright, 1965, University of Chicago Press.

R. Plutchik, a psychologist, has suggested such a "functional" theory of emotion. He attempts to represent the basic dimensions of emotions as prototypical behavior patterns that have developed as adaptive devices to secure the organism's survival.[58] The two emotions that interest us most in this context, rage and anger, are based on the prototypical behavior pattern of "destruction." This kind of behavior, which is essentially aggression, of course, is said to occur "when the organism contacts a barrier to the satisfaction of some need, and consists essentially in an attempt to destroy the barrier."[59]

This theory seems to be a blend of a reactive concept of aggression, as in the frustration-aggression theory, and of evolutionary, functional concepts, as in Lorenz's instinct theory of aggression (although no active drive character of aggression is assumed). Yet this marriage between adaptive, evolutionary thinking and reactive, behavioristic thinking does not make us entirely happy. One reason is that the role of emotion is quite unclear. Plutchik conceptualizes emotion as "overall behavior," in terms of total body reactions, which is one prerequisite for being able to base emotions on primitive, prototypical behavior patterns. Thus, he makes no differentiation between (1) the physiological components of emotions, which may prepare the organism for action, (2) the subjective introspective experience of affect, which accompanies emotion at least in humans, and (3) the actual adaptive reaction to the stimulus producing the emotion. This makes it very hard to separate anger from aggression, since one always would have to find behavioral evidence for anger. However, we all have at times "swallowed" our anger and behaved as if everything was just fine. Frequently, open aggression as a consequence of anger is inhibited because we are afraid of the consequences or because of social norms, while the emotional experience of anger is quite strong.

To account for the fact that aggressive behavior does not always follow anger, the psychologist Seymour Feshbach has suggested differentiating between "aggressive drive" leading to behavior intended to hurt someone, on the one hand, and "innate aggressive reactions" to certain stimuli and "expressive aggression," on the other hand. The latter two are mediated through the innate emotional reaction of anger. Feshbach argues that:

> The anger response is characterized by autonomic changes and heightened motoric activity. Biologically, its primary adaptive function is expressive, serving as a warning signal to other organisms. It also energizes the musculature, and, in addition, as both Freud and Darwin have suggested, the excited physical activity serves as a means of tension regulation and discharge. As part of the process of socialization, one learns to inhibit the expression of affect, and, in this regard, we can speak of a need for expressive activity when the affect is aroused. When anger is elicited in the young child, he has a drive to hit rather than hurt. Although by maturity anger has become closely associated with the motive to inflict injury, these response modes can still occur independently.[60]

The trouble with this analysis is twofold. First, it reintroduces the serious problem of having to differentiate between intentional and unintentional and between instrumental and reactive aggression to isolate "aggressive drive" from "innate aggressive reactions." This, as we have seen (pp. 2–4), seems to be an enormously complex if not impossible task. Second, the implicit notion that innate aggressive reactions are automatically evoked by certain stressful stimuli is certainly not self-evident.

There is little doubt that man is not preprogrammed by instinct mechanisms to recognize and deal with a restricted set of environmental situations in a rather narrow life space. On the contrary, we often boast about our cognitive information-processing abilities, or to put it more simply, our ability to evaluate relevant stimuli in our environment and think about them and their implications. This must obviously be very important for the way in which our emotions are patterned. Although we may share the emotion of anger with our dog (of course, we do not know whether he "feels" anything like what we call anger), it is quite likely that the processes through which we become angry are very different. We assume these differences lie in the degree to which *cognitive processing* plays a role in experiencing emotions.

Cognitive labeling of feeling states. Some psychologists have argued that cognition is the key to emotion. A prominent spokesman for this position has been Stanley Schachter, a social psychologist at Columbia University. Together with psychologist Jerome Singer, Schachter conducted an experiment to assess the role of cognition in emotional arousal.

FOCUS
Cognitive Contagion of Joy and Anger

The subjects in the experiment believed that they were serving in a study designed to test the effects of a new drug with which they had been injected upon arrival in the laboratory. Some subjects, who were to serve as controls, had actually been injected with a placebo: a simple saline solution that usually does not have any physiological effects. However, the experimental subjects had received epinephrine, a stimulant that produces heart pounding, tremor, and a flushed face. Some of the subjects were told to expect these effects, and others were not told anything. A third group was misinformed about the types of symptoms to expect. The investigators wanted to see how the subjects were going to make sense of the feelings of physiological arousal that would set in after the drug took effect. Their interest focused particularly on those subjects who had no idea or the wrong idea about what to expect.

To have some control over the kind of interpretation the subjects would give, Schachter and Singer provided a "controlled environment." Supposedly while waiting for the drug to take effect, the subjects waited in a small room together with one of the most indispensable ploys of all social-psychological experiments: a stooge. For half of the subjects the stooge, an actor hired by Schachter and Singer, was in a very euphoric mood. He jumped around the room shooting baskets with paper balls and flying paper airplanes. While for the other half of the subjects, he acted very angrily by swearing and tearing up copies of a highly personal and insulting questionnaire that he and the subjects were supposed to fill out.

The question is: Were the emotions displayed by the stooge contagious? Did they influence the interpretations the subjects gave to their own feeling state? The crux of the experimental findings was that those subjects who had received the real drug and had not been told the nature of the effects were most strongly affected by the stooge's mood. They rated themselves as having been more euphoric or angry, depending on the condition they were in. They had used the situation they were in to interpret the nature of the arousal they were experiencing at that moment. They used the stooge's perceived emotion to define their own ambiguous feelings.

Based on these and similar findings, Schachter has argued that there may be only one rather undifferentiated type of physiological arousal or activation that is interpreted as different emotions depending on the nature of the cognitions one has about the social situation and his own past experiences. Cognitions serve a "steering function" and help us label our physiological arousal in accordance with our perception of the situation around us and our role in it.[61]

Why have we dealt with this strongly social-psychological view in so much detail? If the emotion of anger predisposes us towards aggression and if anger is produced mainly by our cognitions about situations as justifying anger, then we would have to follow rather different paths in inquiring about causes and cures of aggression. We could not be satisfied with the simple notion that frustration produces anger, and that this in turn leads to aggression. It would be most important to study those situational cues that are cognitively interpreted as warranting anger (i.e., to define frustration in terms of those situational characteristics that lead to the cognitive labeling as "anger").

Facilitation of aggression by emotional arousal. Furthermore, the notion that the arousal is nonspecific (i.e., that there are no separate physiological reactions to different emotions) opens a rather interesting set of possibilities. One intriguing aspect is the possibility that arousal due to one kind of situational instigation, such as sexual stimuli, can be reinterpreted as a different emotion, possibly anger, if the situation changes and requires a "relabeling" of the arousal to fit the new situational cues. We shall devote our next Focus to an interesting study designed to explore this possibility.

FOCUS
Sex and Aggression

Before we can get into the nitty-gritty of any aggression research program, we have to become acquainted with two indispensable gadgets of any accomplished aggression researcher: the obnoxious and/or insulting experimenter and the "aggression machine."[62] The latter is a shock generator usually housed in a cabinet with professional and impressive-looking lights, pushbuttons, levers, and caution signs. In a large percentage of laboratory aggression experiments this device is used to provide the subjects with an instrument to "aggress" against some other "subject," usually a confederate. Usually, the impressive buttons are not wired to a shock generator at all, but to an event recorder that measures the intensity and the duration of the "shock" administered by the subject. All this is often done in the guise of a learning experiment in which the subject-aggressor has to punish his victim for "mistakes" that have been carefully planned in advance. Thus the aggression machine provides the experiment with a convenient *dependent variable* to measure aggression.[63]

The obnoxious experimenter or confederate comes into the act right after the unsuspecting subject walks into the lab. His task is to "frustrate" the subject by insulting or hurting him in order to make him angry and to raise his level of arousal. Anger arousal tends to increase aggressive motivation, as we shall see.

In an experiment by D. Zillman, the tormenting confederate is supposedly another subject for whom the real subject is supposed to serve as a teacher in a learning experiment.[64] In a preliminary "getting-to-know-each-other" period the confederate delivers a number of painful electric shocks to the subject, supposedly to express his disagreement with attitudes stated by the subject. This, of course, was designed to anger the subjects and to instigate them towards aggression against the confederate. They were then told that before they could begin the teaching period they were to see a short movie related to the task.

The nature of this film varied depending on which of three experimental groups the subject was in. In the "neutral" group, subjects saw an unexciting, if not boring, educational film about Marco Polo's travels. Subjects in the "aggressive" group saw "Body and Soul," a violent prize fight film, and subjects in the "erotic" group saw *The Couch,* a film showing some nude sexual encounters. In a pretest, a variety of physiological measures of arousal such as blood pressure, heart rate, and skin temperature showed that the erotic film was most arousing, the aggressive film was medium, and the neutral film least arousing. Zillman postulated that the physiological arousal produced by these movies would not disappear immediately after the last frame of the film, but would decay slowly. This would mean that if a lot of arousal had been induced, any activity occurring right after seeing the movies should be strengthened by transfer of this arousal.

In the present experiment, subjects had an opportunity to aggress against the confederate, who had shocked them earlier, by administering electric shocks of varying strengths and durations as punishment for mistakes in a learning task. As predicted, the subjects' aggressive behavior was facilitated by the arousal "left over" from viewing the film. The degree of facilitation varied with the strength of the prior arousal:

Subjects in the erotic group delivered the most intensive shocks, the neutral-film subjects the least intensive, and the aggressive-film subjects were in between.

Although we may debate whether these shocks were aggression or "benevolent" punishment to achieve better learning, the results seem to support the notion that emotional arousal may be nonspecific and can be transferred to a new situation, in which any remaining residue of the original arousal can intensify the response in that situation.

The experiments by Schachter and Zillman have given us some important leads concerning the predominant role of cognitive cues in the genesis of anger and anger-induced aggression. These results strengthen the arguments advanced in Chapter 1 where we argued that the study of aggression-relevant physiological mechanisms is relatively useless unless we are able to specify the cognitive cues that trigger these mechanisms. We argued that we should turn our attention from internal to external environmental factors. In the course of the following chapters we shall continue to analyze a wide variety of social stimuli and social situations that make the occurrence of anger and aggression more likely.

The emphasis on cognitive factors in Schachter's theory of emotion is complemented by the assumption of nonspecific arousal. We saw how Zillman used this notion to explain how aggressive behavior can be "powered" by arousal produced by quite innocuous sources.[65] The psychologist Percy Tannenbaum, who has long worked with an arousal model, has experimentally demonstrated the importance of this view for the TV-violence debate. He argues that the emotional arousal resulting from watching televised fights, rather than the actual content of a show, may facilitate aggressive behavior.[66] In the view of a general arousal model, the nonspecific arousal, which is cognitively labeled as a subjective emotion, has motivating power only in the sense that there is more energy or vigor available for a given behavior. The organism seems like a multipurpose machine with more or less power available to it.

Yet another possible effect of general arousal is sensitizing a person to aggressive cues. Berkowitz has argued that arousal will increase the likelihood that a person will respond aggressively when exposed to cues that have been previously associated with violence.[67] One laboratory study showed that college students exposed to violent cues in an aggressive boxing film gave more painful shocks to an experimental accomplice when they had been aroused by auditory stimulation (white noise).[68] Of course, the "aggression machine" itself, like any weapon, is an aggression-related cue.[69] Therefore, one might suppose that an aroused person will use an available weapon more readily than will a nonaroused person.

The trouble with this assumption is the difficulty of distinguishing between (1) whether arousal sensitizes a person to aggressive cues and thus instigates aggression, or (2) whether its effect lies mainly in removing inhibitions against aggression. For example, emotional arousal may impair one's judgment and thereby lead to impulsive acts. We shall return to this point later. Here we can conclude that general nonspecific arousal may both sensitize a person to aggressive cues and thus make an aggressive response more likely and may serve to increase the strength of aggressive behavior.

Limitations of the cognitive labeling approach. At this point we may wonder what became of the special relationship between anger and aggression that we had postulated earlier and that we had explained in functional, evolutionary terms as an adaptational response to interferences with an organism's plans or desires. Remember that this approach views emotion as an *intervening variable* between environmental contingency and the organism's response. The extremely cognitively oriented theories of emotion (e.g., Schachter) seem to lose sight of the fact that specific emotions facilitate and render more likely the occurrence of specific actions. Schachter and Zillman seem to deal mainly with self-attribution, with labeling, in an introspective sense rather than with behavioral consequences. Their approach is mainly applicable to those cases where we feel aroused, but do not know or do not remember the cause of this arousal. Since all humans have an urge to understand the causes of their behavior and feelings, we feel compelled to attribute our arousal to specific characteristics of our social situation. In order to make sense of this self-attribution and to further justify our feelings, we may well behave in line with what we consider the situational demands.[70]

Consider the case of the Schachterian subject, epinephrine-aroused, waiting with the angry stooge. He feels aroused, needs to explain this arousal, labels his feelings anger (most likely because he perceives the stooge to be angry), and attributes his anger to the fact that he (and the stooge) has to fill out an insulting questionnaire. He may very well proceed to act in an angry, aggressive manner as well (e.g., tearing up the questionnaire, insulting the experimenter) to justify the strong feelings of arousal, which he now experiences as anger. The violent quarrels of lovers can be nicely explained in similar terms: Heightened arousal due to the closeness of the relationship is attributed by each party to stem from anger. This in turn will escalate the quarrel.

Cognitive appraisal as the basis of emotional arousal. We have to acknowledge, however, that cases in which arousal is produced by drugs with unknown effects or fast-changing situations that make it hard to keep track of the sources of arousal are quite rare and possibly, as in the case of Schachter's experiment, quite artificial. In most cases we are angry for very good reasons and we know it. Often we will follow up our feelings with the appropriate action. In the normal case, then, there may well be a specific set of releasing or instigating stimuli, with appropriate cognitions about these, leading to concomitant physiological reactions that prepare specific behavior patterns as responses. This does not deny the importance of cognitive processes, but merely stresses the important steering function of emotions for the organism's adaptational responses. This has been particularly emphasized by a Berkeley psychologist, Richard Lazarus.

Like most other recent theories of emotion, Lazarus's contribution[71] stresses the significance of emotion in the cognitive appraisal processes which help man to evaluate and cope with environmental stimuli. Lazarus argues that every emotion flows from the appraisal of the adaptive significance of various stimuli. In line with a classical tradition in psychology,[72] Lazarus differentiates two classes of appraisals: benign appraisal and threat appraisal. A stimulus or situation appraised as threatening obviously endangers the well-being or even the existence of the organism. Lazarus assumes that the primary appraisal of threat is followed by a secondary appraisal in which possible ways of coping with the threatening situation are evaluated. This secondary appraisal determines which emotion and which corresponding action tendencies are aroused. For example, whether we feel fear and flight impulses or anger and attack impulses depends on our assessment of the nature of the threat and our potential ability to cope with it. If you are the frail academic type and if you are mugged by an unarmed bandit, you will probably be fearful and inclined to run. But you may get very angry and hit the guy if you are the world's heavyweight boxing champion. In addition, if you feel very much in control of the situation, there may not even be an appraisal of threat and an anger response, but rather a benign appraisal (e.g., such as if a five-year-old tried to mug you). The absence of threat appraisal and anger does not preclude the occurrence of aggression, however. Lazarus assumes that one type of response to benign appraisal is an "automized" response to a potential danger with which one can deal very easily. Obviously, the notion of instrumental aggression (i.e., the nonaffective type of aggression used as a rationally planned means toward some desired end) would fit this possibility very well.

We have dealt in some detail with Lazarus's notions of emotion because they provide us with the necessary link between the functional, adaptational view of anger and aggression (as espoused by most ethologists and also, to some extent, in Berkowitz's reformulation of the frustration-aggression hypothesis) and the importance of cognitive processes for human aggression (to which Lorenz and others fail to give proper weight). Lazarus's theory also stresses the motivational and behavior-steering aspects of emotions such as anger by arguing that there are direct action tendencies or impulses for every emotion.

Aggression and Survival

In Lazarus's contribution, the role of emotion (and aggression) as coping mechanisms in adaptation and adjustment to the physical and social environment is stressed. As we pointed out before, we shall use the concept of coping to integrate the diverse motivational states that have been postulated as underlying aggressive behavior—instincts, drives, frustrations, and emotions. The functional aspects of aggression and violence in terms of coping and adaptation have been present, at least implicitly, in all the theories that we have discussed. However, we have faulted many of these theories for not taking into account that, in the course of evolution, human beings have developed other coping mechanisms than innate instincts, preprogrammed drives, or automatically reactive emotions. As our argument has unfolded we have seen more and more clearly that we have to take into account *cognitive processing of environmental events*.

In coping with environmental emergencies, man can cognitively evaluate and appraise the external and internal stimuli relevant to his plans and goals. He can do so in a time perspective by using memory and past experiences as evaluative standards and by expectations and extrapolation into the future. Rather than respond in a preprogrammed way man can weigh various behavioral alternatives and rationally decide on the most desirable one. Yet, in spite of these advances in cognitive processing capacity, man is not the ultimate rational being: He is not a computer. Emotion clearly plays a role in man's coping behavior. If we are to fully understand the nature of human aggressive behavior, we have to know more about coping and adaptation and the role of aggression in these processes.[73] A major attempt to look at violence in this perspective has been made recently by a group of psychologists and psychiatrists at the Stanford University School of Medicine.

FOCUS
Violence and the Struggle for Existence[74]

The day after Robert Kennedy was slain by an assassin's bullet, members of the Department of Psychiatry at Stanford University, who felt outraged, confused, shocked, and saddened by what had happened, formed a Committee on Violence. Attempting to contribute the skills and insights of behavioral scientists to the problems posed by the contemporary "crisis of violence," these scholars reviewed and evaluated the major theories on the causes of aggression and violence, examined a variety of current issues of violence in the United States, and drew up a number of recommendations on how to control and reduce the amount of violence in society.

The group decided to view violence in the context of man's struggle to adapt to his environment. In a way, all of the theories on aggression covered (also reviewed in this text) can and must be viewed in the context of coping with or adapting to the environment, although the theories differ on whether the motivational basis for the adaptive behavior is seen as innate instinct, reactive drive, emotional reaction, or learned behavior.

Two members of the Stanford Committee, F. T. Melges and R. F. Harris, presented one of the most pervasive reformulations of the role of anger and aggression in man's attempt to cope with his environment. Their view is summarized as follows:

> . . . The process of emotion arises when a plan of action is interrupted. The function of emotion is to change or reinstate goals in light of (1) the subjective probabilities of reaching the goals and (2) the value of specific goals. The affects that reflect these processes alert the person to the possible need for changing goals and plans. A given appraisal of outcomes, signalled by an affect, helps one change his motives or intentions so that subsequent action will produce the most favorable outcome in the situation.[75]

From the flavor of this quote, we can see how the emphasis has changed from behavior (as in the frustration-aggression theory) to cognition about goals, their values, and, most importantly, to the perceived subjective probabilities of reaching the goals. Just as Lazarus does, Melges and Harris stress the cognitive appraisal of outcomes of behavior (i.e., our expectations about possible consequences of behavior). They define anger as a subjective signal of an *unexpected* interruption of an action toward a valued goal by an interference *specific enough* to be attacked. In other words, anger sets in when we do not expect to be thwarted and if we think we are enough in control of the situation to be able to do something about it. "Dashed hopes" and "unfulfilled expectations" often lead to anger and aggression (see Chapter 6, pp. 209–10).

Another very frequent source of anger is the feeling that certain individuals or groups are antagonistic towards our goals or values, creating a situation of *conflict*.[76] We shall have a lot more to say about the situations and the social factors that lead to conflict. In fact, we shall even use this concept to systematize many issues of aggression and violence in concluding this book (see Chapter 8). The Stanford Committee on Violence was aware of the central role of conflict. They argued: "The concept of coping is crucial in understanding violence and in pursuing alternatives to violence, since violent behavior represents an effort to resolve conflicts."[77]

There seems to be little doubt that we often resort to aggression and violence to solve problems and conflicts. Since there are many other possible ways of coping with such emergencies, we have to ask why it is that we often prefer violence. There seem to be three major possibilities: (1) aggression is our "natural," innate reaction to conflict, (2) aggression is used as a last resort when all other coping strategies fail or are unavailable, and (3) we have learned to react aggressively to conflict because it has paid off in the past and is rewarded by society.[78]

As often is true with explanations in the social and behavioral sciences, all of these explanations may be true to some extent. The view that aggression is a sort of evolutionary liability from our past is a popular one. Konrad Lorenz and others have argued that the invention of weapons catapulted human aggressiveness far beyond its functional and adaptational purposes. Following from this, Lorenz argued that we should give people innocuous opportunities to aggress in order to siphon off this archaic residue. Richard Lazarus also sees emotions and aggression as residues from the past, although he argues somewhat differently than Lorenz:

> One of the phylogenetic contexts in which emotions may be maladaptive is that we no longer live in the physical environment from which we evolved as a species, because the explosion of culture and civilization (cultural evolution) has far outrun biological evolution. Therefore, what may have been positively adaptive, emotionally charged reactions in early man in the forest or cave may not be necessarily adaptive in us city dwellers, although we keep on reacting biologically in essentially the same way. One may think here of all the anger-arousing situations in modern life in which one cannot fight, or fear-arousing situations which one cannot flee.[79]

The Stanford Committee on Violence devoted much effort to the second possibility that violence reflects a failure to resolve conflicts through nonviolent means. In their conclusion to the Committee's report, D. N. Daniels and M. F. Gilula identify three facts that frequently produce aggression as a coping response to conflict.[80] One factor is the lack of actual or perceived alternative and attainable goals or means to goals. For example, some have argued that ghetto riots may represent

this type of coping. Since no other avenues for social change and better-
ment seemed available or met with success, some ghetto residents felt
"trapped" and responded with violence as a means of protest.

A second factor is concerned with time. People differ in terms of
how much time they allow to successfully cope with a problem. The
feeling that time is running out for one's chances to reach a goal may
easily prompt violence as a last resort—a factor which may underlie
some cases of juvenile delinquency. "Taking only the present view,"
without considering alternatives and future consequences, is a frequent
by-product of strong anger which may account for some of the relationship between anger and aggression.

The third factor that will often induce violence as a means of
coping is stress. As we have seen before, we do not function very well
under conditions of too low or too high emotional arousal. This is why
we are often advised "to sleep on it" before making a decision on how
to behave when we are infuriated, anxious, or under other kinds of
stress. Daniels and Gilula argue that coping also functions in a curvi-
linear function: Up to a point increasing arousal facilitates coping behavior, but after a breaking point, if arousal increases further, coping
skills are reduced and may break down, leading to violence.

The Stanford Committee on Violence has not overlooked the fact
that aggression is not always reactive, is not always emotionally determined or the result of a breakdown of other coping strategies. As
many other behavioral scientists, they point to the fact that aggression
is often the primary coping strategy used, coldly and rationally. The
reason is that violence often "pays." As a generation of learning theorists
in psychology has convincingly demonstrated, any organism, from cock-
roaches to Harvard undergraduates, will tend to repeat behaviors that
have been rewarded in the past. Learning is one of the most powerful
strategies for long-range coping and adaptation, and man (through
culture) relies most heavily on learning to survive. It is obvious, therefore, that learning plays a major part in the origin and control of aggressive behavior. In the next chapter we shall examine the laws of learning
that govern violent behavior.

SUMMARY

Motivation refers to the psychological and/or physiological forces that
arouse, sustain, and direct behavior. However, unlike physiological structures, motivation cannot be directly observed and must be inferred from

the organism's behavior. Consequently, it is extremely difficult to specify the nature of the motivation behind aggression. The controversy surrounding aggression motivation centers on whether it is basically active or reactive. *Active* theories are based on the premise that aggression is the result of innate driving forces, while *reactive* theories are grounded on the assumption that aggression is called forth by environmental instigations. Both theories have in common the belief that the motivation is based on aversive tensions. Active theories see the aversive tensions as resulting from internal drives, while reactive theories see the origin in frustrations. The distinction between active and reactive theories is more than just an academic argument. The course of action we take to control or reduce aggression will depend to a great degree on the motivational sources of aggression.

For aggression motivation to be active, three criteria must be met: (1) Aggressive behavior should be spontaneous; (2) aggressive energy should be present and accumulate until the organism "discharges" it through aggression; and (3) there should be specific aggressive goals or targets that can serve to reduce aggressive energy. *Psychoanalytic theory* was an early active theory and postulated that aggression results from a "death instinct." According to classical psychoanalytic thought, aggression is a redirection of the death instinct away from oneself onto others. While psychoanalytic theories are now generally treated with skepticism, a more recent active theory, *ethological theory,* has revived the notion of innate aggressive drives.

However, it seems unlikely that a general aggression instinct exists, especially in human beings. If aggression is at all innate, it probably is not a general instinct but rather a subinstinct of such general instincts as mating or brood-tending. In any event, it is questionable whether we can safely generalize from the animal studies, upon which ethological theories are based, to human beings. The development of cognitive and communicative abilities has freed human beings from the control of rigid instincts. This is not to say that the ethological approach is without merit. Many animals, possibly even humans, may possess some unlearned, instinctive fixed-action patterns for aggression. However, we have to doubt that what is "released" in aggressive acts is an accumulated aggressive energy fed by a constant source.

Rather than seeing aggression as a maintenance function, the reactive theories perceive it as an emergency reaction to environmental events. *Frustration-aggression theory* postulates that aggression results from environmental interferences in the organism's goal-achievement. While early statements of F-A theory saw frustration as lying behind all instances of aggression, later versions attempted to limit the theory to instances of "emotional" as opposed to "instrumental" aggression. Another revision recognized that aggression was not the only possible outcome of frustration. While making the theory more plausible, these revisions have raised a host of still other unresolved problems.

One major problem with F-A theory is where the energy for aggression comes from. How does frustration energize behavior? One possibility is that frustration results in an emotional (i.e., physiological) arousal such as anger, which, in turn, energizes aggressive behavior. But there is little evidence for specific physiological arousal patterns that correspond to particular emotions. More likely, there is a general non-specific arousal state that is interpreted as different emotions depending upon a cognitive appraisal of the environment. Whether we feel fear and flight impulses or anger and attack impulses depends on our assessment of the nature of the threat (i.e., frustration) and of our potential ability to cope with it.

In sum, a revised F-A theory postulates environmental frustrations that lead to emotional arousal that, in turn, energizes aggressive behaviors. The forces that arouse, sustain, and direct aggression are reactions to the environment.

FOOTNOTES

[1] Cofer and Appley (1964), pp. 19–55.

[2] The controversy as to how much of human behavior can be attributed to instinctive, innate, or hereditary factors and how much is due purely to environmental or learned factors has not been restricted to the field of aggression. The issue is far from being totally forgotten even today. Most recently the controversy has surfaced surrounding the genetic basis of intelligence. See Dobzhansky (1973), Herrnstein (1973), and Jensen (1973).

[3] A detailed discussion of these three aspects of motivation can be found in Madsen (1959).

[4] A more detailed and highly readable discussion of the hunger drive can be found in Teitelbaum (1967).

[5] Even a drive as clear-cut as hunger apparently can be strongly influenced by the environment. It looks like obese people, for example, are much more influenced by external factors such as the proper eating time than by internal factors. See Schachter (1971).

[6] "Why War?" in *Collected Papers of Sigmund Freud*, edited by Ernest Jones, M.D., Vol. V. Published by Basic Books, Inc. by arrangement with The Hogarth Press Ltd. and The Institute of Psycho-Analysis, London, 1959. Paraphrased by permission.

[7] Peterfreund and Schwartz (1972).

[8] Peterfreund and Schwartz (1972).

[9] Berkowitz (1962), Chapter 1; Hartmann, Kris, and Lowenstein (1949).

[10] Bettelheim (1966), pp. 55–56.

[11] Abrahamsen (1970), p. 245.

[12] Lorenz (1966), p. 271.

[13] Lorenz (1966). Tinbergen (1969), Hinde (1970), and Eibl-Eibesfeld (1970) provide comprehensive overviews of the development and current state of ethological theory and research. Our discussion of ethology is largely based on these books.

[14] Lorenz (1966), pp. 48–49. See Wallace (1918).

[15] Tinbergen (1969), p. 116.

[16] Lorenz (1966), pp. 49–50.

[17] Eibl-Eibesfeld (1970), pp. 53–55.

[18] Eibl-Eibesfeld (1970), p. 326; Hinde (1970).

[19] Lorenz (1966), p. x.

[20] Lorenz (1966), pp. 20–45.

[21] Lorenz (1966), p. 209.

[22] Lorenz (1966), p. 105.

[23] Lorenz (1966), p. 234.

[24] Lorenz (1966), pp. 111–13.

[25] Hinde (1970).

[26] Hinde (1970).

[27] Hinde (1970).

[28] Hinde (1970); Scott (1958).

[29] Montagu (1968).

[30] Hobbes (1967), pp. 95–96.

[31] One possible innate inhibiting stimulus in man might be eye contact with the victim. See pp. 139–42.

[32] Feshbach (1970), p. 177.

[33] Azrin (1967); Azrin, Hutchinson, and Hake (1967). See Ulrich (1966).

[34] Further examples are cited by Hinde (1970).

[35] Azrin, Hutchinson, and Hake (1966).

[36] McDougall (1960), p. 51.

[37] Freud (1959).

[38] Dollard et al. (1939).

[39] Dollard et al. (1939), p. 7.

[40] Dollard et al. (1939), p. 9.

[41] Bateson (1941).

[42] These arguments are well summarized in Berkowitz (1962, 1969).

[43] Miller (1941).

[44] Buss (1961).

[45] See discussion of Azrin's animal research on p. 57.

[46] Berkowitz (1969).

[47] Cf. pp. 209–10.

[48] Dollard et al. (1939).

[49] Dollard et al. (1939), p. 33.

[50] Dollard et al. (1939), p. 39.

[51] For the role of punishment, see Chapter 3, pp. 92–93; for displacement and scapegoating, see Chapter 5, pp. 163–64; for catharsis, see Chapter 3, pp. 94–104.

[52] Miller (1941).

[53] Berkowitz (1969).

[54] Berkowitz (1969).

[55] Arnold (1970).

[56] See Duffy (1962).

[57] Darwin (1872).

[58] Plutchik (1962).

[59] Plutchik (1962), p. 285.

[60] Feshbach (1971).

[61] Schachter and Singer (1962).

[62] See Buss (1961).

[63] In studies using the "teacher-learner" paradigm, it is unfortunately not always possible to tell whether the teacher wants to hurt or help the learner. The latter can be expected particularly if the teacher uses more shock since he attributes task-competence to the learner. See Rule and Hewitt (1971).

[64] Zillman (1971).

[65] The relationship between sex and aggression is, of course, much more complex. See Feshbach (1973).

[66] Tannenbaum (1972).

[67] Berkowitz (1969, 1974); Berkowitz and Buck (1967).

[68] Geen and O'Neal (1969). A problem with this study is that the bursts of white noise, which can sound quite noxious at certain loudnesses, induced anger rather than general arousal in the subjects (even though the authors claim that the noise was arousing but not aversive). Thus, we really have a further demonstration for anger-induced aggression rather than evidence for sensitization to aggressive cues by general arousal.

[69] One experiment (Berkowitz and LePage [1967]) suggests that the mere presence of weapons in the experiment room increased the number and severity of shocks delivered by the subjects to the experimental accomplice. However, this study has been severely criticized on methodological grounds. See Page and Scheidt (1971), Schuck and Pisor (1974).

[70] The human need for understanding causes in the environment is the basis for a new and growing area of research in social psychology: attribution theory. See Chapter 4, pp. 128–37.

[71] Lazarus (1968). See Geen, Stonner, and Kelley (1974).

[72] See Arnold (1970).

[73] A survey of relevant material can be found in Coelho, Hamburg, and Adams (in press). Also see Hamburg (1970).

[74] Daniels, Gilula, and Ochberg (1970).

[75] Melges and Harris (1970), p. 103.

[76] Hobbes clearly recognized the importance of this factor: "But the most frequent reason why men desire to hurt each other, ariseth hence, that many men at the same time have an appetite to the same thing; which yet very often they can neither enjoy in common, nor yet divide it; whence it follows that the strongest must have it, and who is strongest must be decided by the sword."

[77] Daniels and Gilula (1970), p. 414.

[78] Buss (1971).

[79] Lazarus (1968), pp. 210–11.

[80] Daniels and Gilula (1970).

3 / THE LEARNING
OF AGGRESSION

<hr>

reward-cost factors

In this chapter we shall continue to deal with the motivational under-pinnings of aggressive behavior. However, we are shifting our focus away from the "reactive" coping processes of the previous chapter to "proactive" coping processes that are motivated by anticipated consequences of particular behaviors. Until now we have spoken of the motivation for aggression as arising either from an aggressive drive or from frustrations. In either case, the motivation was directed towards the removal of some *aversive* tension (i.e., internal drive tensions or frustration tensions). Now we shall consider the possibility that people are motivated to be aggressive because they anticipate receiving *benefits* as a result of aggression. A leading proponent of social learning theory, Albert Bandura, has characterized this change in focus in the following manner: "In the social learning analysis of motivation, incentives also constitute important impellers of action. A great deal of aggression is prompted by its anticipated benefits. Here the instigator is the pull of expected success rather than the push of aversive treatment."[1]

The "pull of expected success" is not a new concept in psychology, for philosophers have turned to it in one form or another in analyzing human behavior. The ancient premises of Greek hedonism, as a description of human nature, also underlie the modern theories of learning. In fact, some learning theorists claim that the science of human behavior *is* the analysis of how rewards and punishments shape our behavior.[2] However, most modern learning theorists include a host of other variables besides stimuli and responses (so-called S-R psychology), particularly cognitive variables, in their analysis of human behavior.[3] Since we cannot possibly deal with all aspects of learning in relation to aggression, we shall restrict our discussion to two important questions: (1) How do people acquire *new* aggressive behaviors (i.e., types of aggression that they have not engaged in previously), and (2) what types of reinforcement or rewards motivate people to aggress?

In answering these questions, we shall describe two types of learning that together account for a wide variety of learned behavior, including aggression: (1) the shaping of behavior through selective reinforcement, and (2) learning through the observation and imitation of models. These two mechanisms do not exclude each other, even though their respective theorists tend to overemphasize one at the expense of the other. In fact, the two complement each other. For example, observational learning theorists can easily account for the acquisition of new behavior patterns, whereas reinforcement theorists are hard put to explain how complex behavior patterns are learned quickly through such processes as trial-and-error. Conversely, reinforcement theorists can explain why the occurrence of successful behavior patterns becomes more and more likely, which is something that modeling theorists find difficult to account for. Just how interlocking these processes can be is demonstrated by child rearing. Parents influence the behavior of their child by serving as models for "correct" behavior and by administering rewards and punishments to control their child's behavior. Since these learning processes are so prevalent and powerful in general socialization, we would expect them to be equally influential in the learning of aggressive responses. Obviously, there is no lack of models for aggression in our society. In fact, aggression is often rewarded while pacifism is often punished.

LEARNING TO AGGRESS

Exposure to Aggressive Models

FOCUS
Sock It to the Bobo Doll

In a series of experiments widely know as the "Bobo Doll Experiments," Albert Bandura and his colleagues at Stanford University have attempted to support their theory that the mere observation of a behavior is sufficient for learning the behavior. They argue that the observation of a behavior leads to a cognitive representation of it in the mind of the observer and to vicarious reinforcement. Although mere exposure to a behavior is sufficient to enable the observer to perform the behavior himself, this does not necessarily mean that he will do so. The behavior learned through observation may be performed at a later time or never at all, if there are strong factors inhibiting its occurrence.[4]

In one experiment Bandura and his associates showed that children tend to imitate an adult model's aggressive responses toward a toy in a game. Using three groups of nursery school children, the investigators had one group watch an adult model vigorously kicking, pummeling, and insulting an inflated Bobo doll; the second group observed the same model in quiet, nonaggressive play with tinker toys. The third group did not see the model at all. After some slight frustration, the children were then taken to a different room with a variety of toys, including a Bobo doll, and left to play. As predicted, the children who had observed the aggressive model not only imitated the physical and verbal attacks against the doll, but also engaged in more nonimitative aggressive play with other toys than any of the other groups. Clearly, the children learned by observation not only some novel techniques for manhandling a Bobo doll, but also became more ready to engage in aggressive behavior.[5]

Bandura and his colleagues next compared the effects of real-life models and of filmed models.[6] Children in three experimental groups saw, respectively, a real-life adult in person, a filmed human adult, or a filmed adult dressed up as a cartoon-cat, all aggressing against the Bobo doll. Again the behavior of these children in a play situation was compared to the behavior of the control group children who had not seen a model. In all three experimental conditions, the children exhibited a great deal of imitation of aggression compared to the control group. The most effective model in terms of producing most imitative and particularly nonimitative aggression was the filmed human model.

In the next experiment, Bandura and his associates manipulated the consequences of the aggressive acts of filmed models to see whether this factor would make imitation more or less likely.[7] In one film, the adult male model was subsequently punished for his treatment of the Bobo doll, whereas in the other film he was rewarded for his aggression. Two different groups of nursery school children were exposed to these films and compared to two control groups, one group seeing a nonaggressive yet vigorously playing model and one seeing no model. The results indicated that the children exposed to the rewarded aggressive model showed more aggression than any of the other groups. Thus, perceived success of the model increases the probability that the observed behavior will be imitated.[8]

For obvious reasons these findings of the Bandura group have frequently made the headlines. They seem to provide strong arguments for those who maintain that media violence corrupts our children and fosters aggression. Media executives have countered by arguing that the Bandura experiments are nothing but a bunch of sterile, artificial laboratory exercises without much relevance to real television viewing or real aggression.[9] We shall evaluate this controversy in more detail later on. Here we can conclude that, in spite of the fact that these studies were done in the laboratory, they provide us with important insights on the effects of model learning in the area of aggressive behavior.

The importance of imitative learning outside of the laboratory is suggested by the rash of aggressive behaviors that often occur following the report in the mass media of some unusually violent aggressive act. For example, there is some statistical evidence that President Kennedy's assassination and the Speck and Whitman mass murders were followed by unusual increases in the number of violent crimes reported by the police.[10] More recently, the Boston police chief and others blamed the murder by burning of a young woman in Boston on a particularly brutal TV film, which featured similar murders and which was on TV the night before the crime. Such "contagion" of criminal violence also seems to occur for burglaries or even murder strategies. Following the broadcast of unusual strategies, there is often a rash of crimes employing imitations of the media crimes. A good example of this is the surge of airplane hijackings and bombings that followed the reporting of the first initially successful attempts by extortionists and terrorists.[11]

Although we can readily understand that various new and clever ways of hurting our fellow human beings can be taught by models, we still need to explain why observers tend to imitate these models and perform the behaviors learned through symbolic means (i.e., by watching or reading about such behaviors). Bandura mentions several processes through which modeling may enhance the expression of previously learned aggressive responses: *response facilitation* (imitation of prestigeful models usually leads to reinforcement), *strengthening or weakening inhibitions* (depending on the consequences of the models' actions and the degree to which these actions seem legitimate), *stimulus enhancing effects* (for example, directing attention to ways in which tools or weapons can be used), and *emotional arousal* (watching a fight seems to have an arousal effect that may increase the strength of aggressive responses).[12]

At this point, we might object that we do not run around wielding a knife every time we see a murder mystery on TV. Of course, the

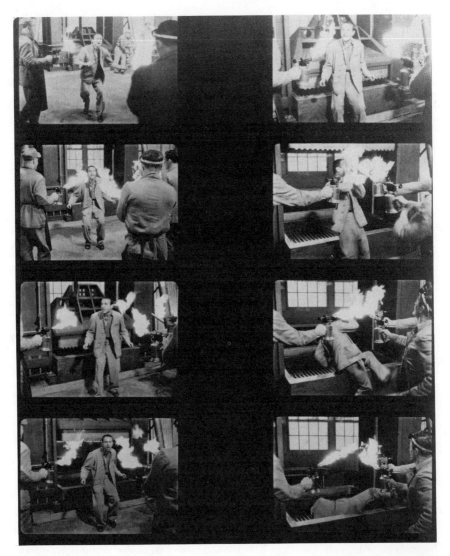

Figure 3-1 Research by social learning theorists suggests that viewing aggressive films increases aggression by children and adults. Copyright 1947, Universal Pictures, Inc.; photo courtesy of Mark A. Binn.

impact of aggressive models on a person's aggressive behavior is not a one-shot deal and is not the same for everyone. Important individual differences in this respect are produced by differential experiences with aggressive models, for example, in one's family and subculture. We mentioned earlier that the punishing father is an impressive aggressive model for a child. This is all the more so since he is a prestigeful model and his aggression is never punished. His prestige and the success of his aggression combine to make him an impressive model in the child's eyes. Although the empirical data are not as clear-cut as we might hope, children from families where physical punishment is used tend to be more aggressive than children disciplined by "psychological" methods (e.g., love withdrawal). This is particularly so when the physically punishing parents also encourage aggressive behavior on the part of their child.[13]

In addition to experiences with aggressive models, another important factor in aggression training is how often a person has been reinforced or punished for his own aggressive behavior. Whether or not a person will put into practice the novel forms of aggression that he has learned through imitation depends upon whether his aggression is rewarded or not. For aggression, like all other learned behaviors, follows the *law of effect:* Any organism will tend to repeat a behavior that has been reinforced in the past.

The Reinforcement of Aggression

To understand how aggression might be reinforced, we first have to ask the difficult question about how behaviors in general are reinforced. Unfortunately, learning theorists have found it very hard to pin down exactly which events constitute a reinforcement or reward. While some theorists have defined reinforcement rather circularly as anything that can be shown to reinforce behavior (i.e., make its occurrence more probable), one school of psychologists, centered around the work of the late Yale psychologist Clark Hull, linked reinforcement to the reduction of tensions produced by an imbalance in an organism's need states.[14] A satisfaction of the organism's wants, needs, or drives restores balance, reduces tension, and is experienced as rewarding. Food, for example, is rewarding because it reduces the tension arising from an imbalance (i.e., lack) of nutrients in the bloodstream.

Thus, aggressive behavior would be rewarding in itself if it reduces tension produced by emotional arousal such as anger, as the catharsis hypothesis suggests (see pp. 94–104). Such a tension reduction effect could be due to either the physiological exhaustion of the activation produced by anger or the removal of a frustrating agent or object, which had been blocking the satisfaction of a need or the completion of a goal-response. In the latter case, aggression would be instrumental in achieving one's goals and thus rewarding.

Of course, aggression is found to be instrumental and rewarding even more frequently in planned nonemotional goal-directed behavior. The successful mugger has learned that street aggression "pays." Such instrumental use of aggression is particularly frequent when only limited resources for need satisfaction are available and there is competition over the possession of such resources. This is true for conflict between individuals and conflicts between groups, classes, or societies, as we shall see in later chapters. The important role of aggression as a way to decide conflicts in one's own interest is often played down in discussions of aggressive motivation, especially in psychoanalytic and ethological viewpoints. However, there is little doubt that if all other means fail to attain a goal or to solve a conflict, aggression is often an effective means to achieve one's aims, at least in the short run. Because of its effectiveness as a means to need satisfaction, aggression is often not turned to as the last resort, but as the first.

Aggression is helpful not only in obtaining material resources and rewards, but also in satisfying immaterial needs. The need for security and protection, for example, is satisfied if we use aggressive behavior to cope with a threat or to defend ourselves from an attack. The tension reduction experienced after a successful repulsion of an enemy will also serve to reward and reinforce the aggressive behavior employed to this aim.

Still other needs may be satisfied by aggressive behavior. For example, aggression may bolster one's self-esteem, especially if notions of manliness, vigor, power, and the like are involved. The excessive violence observed in boys' gangs in city slums can be explained in terms of its function for sex role definition as a "man" and for gaining status in the gang.[15] Since we are all somewhat motivated to compare ourselves to others and to be "one up," successful aggression can well be rewarding in terms of satisfying ego-enhancement and status needs.

We also seem to have a need for social approval, to receive praise for our activities from significant others around us. Almost any behavior can be reinforced by social approval in the form of applause, assent, or even very subtle headnods or "hmms." That aggression seems to be no exception is shown by laboratory experiments conducted by the psychologist Russell Geen and his collaborators at the University of Missouri.[16] These researchers rewarded subjects for delivering electroshocks to the experimenter's confederate in the guise of an experiment on the effects of punishment. Each time the members of the experimental group pushed one of ten shock level levers on the aggression machine, they were rewarded by the experimenter with comments such as "That's good," or "You're doing fine." Control group subjects were not reinforced for shocks. It turned out that the reinforced subjects not only strongly increased the intensity of the shocks they delivered following the reinforcements but also subsequently, and without further reinforcements, delivered stronger shocks in response to aggressive verbal cues.

Even though aggression and violence are officially shunned, many types of violent behavior are overtly or covertly rewarded in our society. In addition, there seems to be a lot of social approval for aggressive acts in some American subcultures[17] and particularly at certain stages of the socialization process. Parents often admonish their male children not to be sissies and openly or covertly reward their offspring for aggression on the playground. Of course, one's peers are also a potent source of social approval for aggression.[18]

A beautiful example of how aggressive behavior is reinforced during the socialization process and how it can become a dominant response in a person's behavior repertoire is provided by a naturalistic field study in several nursery schools.[19] G. Patterson, R. Littman, and W. Bricker observed the interactions between three- to four-year-old children in two middle-class nursery schools. Over a period of twenty-six weeks they recorded aggressive acts initiated by children and the victims' responses and behavior. In addition, children were rated as to their general activity level and the intensity of their verbal and motor behavior. In line with learning theory premises, the authors hypothesized that if a child-aggressor was rewarded by his victim with positive consequences (i.e., crying, running away, relinquishing toys or candy, etc.), then the likelihood of further aggressive acts against this victim would be increased, while negative consequences, such as counterattack by the victim or censure by the teacher, would result in at least a temporary suppression of aggressive acts. It was found that the positive consequences of aggressive acts far outweighed the negative consequences in the nursery schools. In other words, the aggressors were very often rewarded for their act by the victim's behavior. These results imply that the nursery school setting provides a training ground for aggression, especially for active children who interacted a lot with other children. Those who came to the nursery school with pronounced aggressive tendencies remained highly aggressive. Those who came to the nursery school with few aggressive tendencies strikingly increased their frequency of aggressive responses because of their mostly positive experiences with the consequences of aggression against other children.

This study shows very clearly how aggressive behavior can become an end in itself (a functionally autonomous motive)[20] if it occurs regularly and is reinforced often enough. In other words, for some children the aggressive behavior was no longer a consequence of an emotional reaction (e.g., anger) to being victimized nor an instrument for obtaining some other goal (e.g., self-defense). The reinforcement that followed aggression became a goal in itself and led to the initiation of aggressive behavior for its own sake. Such aggressive habits can help us account for many so-called "senseless" acts of aggression in which the aggression seems to serve no particular purpose or where the level of brutality used bears no relationship to the amount of force required. The "excesses" of violence during war may result from aggression becoming a goal in its own right. The torturing of enemy soldiers could be rationalized as an instrumental act to obtain information, but the slaughter of unarmed civilians can hardly be justified in this manner. Perhaps this brutal behavior of soldiers results from their having been consistently reinforced for acts of killing and torture.

We might object that these soldiers probably had been trained to kill armed enemy soldiers, but had not been reinforced for the murder of innocent women and children. At this point, we have to introduce two additional aspects of the learning process that facilitate the spread of learned behavior to new targets and that make the appearance of new responses likely: stimulus and response generalization.

Generalizing targets for aggression. Most (operant) behavior is under the control of a so-called *discriminative stimulus.* For example, if a rat is reinforced with a food pellet for pressing a lever only when a buzzer is sounded, the onset of this buzzer will serve as a discriminative stimulus. The rat, after a while, will press the bar only when the buzzer is on. Similarly, aggressive behavior requires a specific target as a discriminative stimulus. American soldiers in Vietnam probably were trained and reinforced to shoot another soldier only if he was a Vietcong or a North Vietnamese, not if he was another American. The discriminative stimuli in this learning situation may have been small stature, brownish skin color, and a particular type of uniform. Just as a rat will tend to bar press for a bell if it is sounded instead of a buzzer, the American soldiers may have gone through stimulus generalization in the process of attacking people meeting some but not all of the criteria of the original discriminative stimulus. The aggression may have generalized to women and children who were also of small stature, brown-skinned, and considered "gooks." Of course, the occurrence of stimulus generalization is dependent on the similarity of the stimuli involved. It will not occur if a new stimulus is too dissimilar from the original discriminative stimulus.

The generalization of aggressive responses from one situation to another is probably a rather frequent phenomenon in the course of human development. A famous study by the psychologists R. Walters and M. Brown showed how children generalize aggressive responses from fantasy objects to interpersonal encounters.[21] Children were rewarded with a marble each time they struck a Bobo doll. Afterwards they engaged in competitive games with other children. These children were consistently more aggressive towards their playmates than other children who had not seen a Bobo doll at all or who had not been reinforced for striking it.

Figure 3-2 The process of stimulus generalization explains how aggressive acts are transferred from one target to another. *Left*, American troops learning to use the bayonet. United Press International Photo. *Right*, Mukti Bahini soldiers executing collaborators during the Pakistan civil war, December 1971. Wide World Photos.

We can easily see how the process of stimulus generalization furthers the development of aggressive habits. The more stimuli provoke aggressive behavior, the more often will aggression occur (if it is consistently reinforced), and the more stable the behavior will become. The only process that can check the generalization of aggressive behavior to more and more stimuli with less and less similarity to the original aggression-provoking stimulus is *stimulus discrimination*. This can occur when aggression against a multitude of stimuli is reinforced only in some cases and remains unrewarded or gets punished in the other cases. Under these circumstances the aggressor will discriminate among targets and choose only those for which he expects successful aggression. For example, if the American soldiers had been severely punished each time they had hurt anyone other than an enemy soldier, they might have shown better discrimination in picking their targets.

The trouble with discrimination learning is that it is very hard to *consistently* punish or prevent reinforcement for generalized behavior to unwanted stimuli. The problem is that the controller is not always at hand to monitor and possibly punish the undesirable behavior. Many of the gruesome acts of war may never have gotten to the attention of the commanding officers or, if they did, they were not punished. The events that became publicly known, such as the My Lai massacre, and that were brought to trial, were few interruptions in a consistent series of no punishments or even reinforcements.

This last example suggests that the consistency with which a behavior is rewarded or punished is important in determining whether it will be learned. If a child is only rewarded from time to time for aggressive acts, we might expect him to be less aggressive than another child who is always rewarded. However, this is *not* the case, but rather the opposite is true. One of the strongest and most reliable "laws" of learning theory is that *intermittent* reinforcement is far superior to *continuous* reinforcement, both in terms of the stability of the learned behavior and in terms of resistance to extinction (i.e., the gradual disappearance of a learned behavior when it is no longer reinforced). Thus, contrary to common sense, the child who is rewarded for aggression from time to time is *more* aggressive than the child who is always rewarded!

This surprising claim is supported by the work of P. Cowan and R. Walters in which they used three different reinforcement schedules to reward the aggressive behavior of children.[22] One group of children received a marble each time they struck the Bobo doll (100 percent reinforcement), another group was rewarded every third time they struck the doll (fixed ratio reinforcement on a three-trial interval), and a last experimental group had to strike the doll six times in a row before receiving a marble as reward (fixed ratio on a six-trial interval). Both normal and emotionally disturbed, institutionalized children were used in all three groups. After the aggressive behavior pattern of striking the Bobo doll was well established in the reinforcement session, the experimenters started the extinction period. That is, no more marbles were given to the children regardless of how often and how viciously they struck the Bobo doll. As expected, the children who had received a marble each time they struck the Bobo doll caught on very quickly that it now was a waste of energy to hit the Bobo doll and stopped. However, those who had received a marble only every sixth time stubbornly clung to their aggressive behavior and took a much longer time to "extinguish" (i.e., to drop the behavior that was no longer reinforced) than the other two groups. The three-trial fixed ratio group was second slowest.

If we are accustomed to having to wait for our rewards, we do not give up very quickly if they seem to be a little slower in coming, and it will take a while before we shall give up hope entirely. Thus, aggressive behavior does not have to be reinforced every single time to become a firmly established part of an individual's behavioral repertoire. On the contrary, intermittent reinforcement, especially if it occurs irregularly (i.e., on a *variable* ratio between rewarded and unrewarded trials), tends to produce a more stable and persistent habit of aggression.

Generalization of aggressive responses. It may seem a little far-fetched to talk about horrible massacres in Vietnam and childish blows at a Bobo doll in one breath. We might feel that one has nothing to do with the other and it is hard to see how, for example, hitting a Bobo doll, or shooting at dummies in training camps, can lead to the killing of innocent women and children. Learning theorists have shown, however, that we generalize not only from one stimulus or target to another (from Bobo doll to playmate, or from dummy to enemy soldier), but also from one response to another. *Response generalization* refers to the fact that if we have found one type of aggressive behavior to be successful and reinforcing, we tend to try out other similar aggressive behaviors.

One particularly interesting instance is the generalization from verbal to physical aggression. Are we more likely to hurt our opponents physically if we have been previously rewarded for verbally insulting them? A study done with children supports the notion that successful verbal aggression can facilitate physical aggression.[23] O. Lövaas reinforced one group of nursery children for verbal aggression directed against a doll figure ("bad doll," "doll should be spanked"), whereas a comparable group was rewarded for nonaggressive verbal responses. Afterwards, all children had a choice of playing with either an aggressive toy (depressing a lever leading to one doll striking another) or a nonaggressive toy (flipping a ball inside a cage with a lever-mechanism). It turned out that the children who had received a reward for verbally aggressive responses played much more frequently with the aggressive toy than the control group. This suggests that verbal aggression may lead to physical aggression through the mechanism of response generalization.

Inhibition and punishment of aggression. How can these disquieting tendencies toward an ever-expanding readiness towards violence based on stimulus and response generalization and reinforcement of aggressive behavior be checked? Until now we have talked just about reinforcement; what about *punishment* of aggressive behavior? Might not this be just as effective a learning mechanism serving to control aggression? Psychologists, interested in learning and child development, have carefully studied the effects of punishment on aggressive behavior. Unfortunately, they conclude that punishment has limited usefulness as a device for stamping out aggression. Punishment generally has only *inhibitive* effects. That is, it can serve to suppress an undesirable behavior through the threat of further punishment, but it does not remove the undesirable behavior from the person's behavioral repertoire. Thus, it does not guarantee that the aggressive response will not occur in the future, especially if no further punishment ensues. For punishment to be an effective inhibitor, the person's aggression has to be constantly, consistently, and immediately punished. This means the effects of punishment are contingent upon the presence of a punishing agent who is constantly monitoring the individual's behavior. However, punishment may be somewhat effective because it can lead to anxiety (i.e., fear of future punishment), which will inhibit the undesirable response regardless of the controlling agent's presence.

Bandura points out that the effectiveness of the threat of punishment in deterring aggressive behavior is very much dependent on the strength of the instigation towards aggression and on the level of reward resulting from the aggressive act as well as the alternative means available for achieving such rewards.[24] For example, a drug addict may be much less deterred from robbing a rich shopkeeper by fear of being punished than a nonaddict would be. The potential rewards (i.e., securing his drug supply) are extremely high for the addict, and he may not see any other means for attaining the needed money. In addition, the consequences of punishment may be less severe for someone who is disadvantaged to begin with: He has less to lose in terms of money and status than some higher-status person.

However, the main disadvantage to punishment is that it has strong aggressive components to it, especially when physical punishment is used. As we pointed out earlier, a punishing father can serve as an aggressive model for a child.[25] In addition, the pain involved in physical punishment may lead to anger and increase the likelihood of emotional aggression. Although many factors may be involved, many studies show that parental punishment is positively related to the amount of aggressive behavior children display. Thus, punishment may in fact foster aggressive behavior instead of inhibiting it.

We can now summarize the ways in which learning processes may provide motivational mechanisms that increase the likelihood of aggressive behavior. *Aggressive models* can serve to foster the acquisition of novel aggressive behavior patterns through *cognitive learning* and may lead to a high probability of actual *imitation* of such behaviors through *vicarious reinforcement,* when the observer sees the model rewarded for its aggressive acts. *Direct reinforcement* for aggressive acts increases the likelihood of further occurrence of such acts, especially if the *reinforcement* schedule has been *intermittent.* In such cases the aggressive behavior becomes a very *stable* behavior pattern and is difficult to extinguish. Through *stimulus generalization* aggressive acts may be directed at similar targets. Through *response generalization* one type or mode of aggression can facilitate the occurrence of other possibly more severe types of aggression. *Punishment* may *inhibit* or suppress aggressive behaviors, but it cannot remove them from the behavioral repertoire or encourage more prosocial behaviors. On the contrary, through modeling effects, anger arousal, and other mechanisms, punishment seems to encourage aggression in the socialization process.

Up to this point we have been concerned with possible mechanisms serving to *increase* aggressive motivation. We have considered the notions of an innate drive or instinct of aggression, of a reactive emotional arousal leading to aggression, and finally of an increasing tendency towards aggressive behavior via learning processes. We have repeatedly stressed that these mechanisms are all believed to create or increase the organism's readiness to aggress but do not determine whether or not a particular act of aggression will occur in a specific situation. In later chapters we shall turn to a number of factors that are involved in the facilitation or inhibition of an overt, aggressive act once aggressive tendencies are aroused.

DECREASING AGGRESSIVE MOTIVATION

Before we leave the level of motivational analysis, we should consider some mechanisms that may *decrease* aggressive motivation. Such mechanisms are usually described as *cathartic*, which stems from Aristotle's idea of catharsis in his theory of tragedy. Aristotle believed that drama helped "purify" emotions by allowing people to express them. Social scientists have studied two major classes of cathartic effects on aggressive behavior. The major premise is that aggressive motivation is "drained off" (1) through an overt act of aggression directed against a frustrator or a substitute person or object, or (2) through vicarious experience or observation of aggression in the "real world" or in the make-believe world of the movies, literature, or fantasy. After a cathartic experience, the individual's aggressive energy is supposed to have been released and, therefore, he is no longer motivated to be aggressive. Since the concept of a release of pent-up energy is a very intuitive one, the catharsis hypothesis has been popular among scientists and laymen alike.

Catharsis and Overt Aggression

But what is the evidence? Let us first investigate the cathartic effects of overtly aggressive acts. Since the type of "draining" or decrease in aggressive acts may depend on the nature of the underlying motivation we should assess separately the cathartic effects for drive-, emotion-, and learning-generated aggressive tendencies.

Catharsis and drive- or instinct-generated aggression. In our discussion of the action theories of aggression we have already quoted (pp.

46–47) some statements of drive theorists arguing for the importance of substitute activities such as competitive sports, outdoor activities, etc. to keep the level of aggressive energy down. One simple test of this notion would be to see whether athletes in competitive or aggressive sports or outdoors-men are more peaceful fellows than office employees. There are not many of these studies, but a review of the available evidence indicates that most people do *not* have either (1) weaker aggressive inclinations or (2) less concern about their hostile tendencies after engaging in socially sanctioned aggressive sports.[26]

The idea that combative sports drain off aggressive energy might lead us to expect that cultures with aggressive sports would be less warlike. That is, aggressive sports might redirect aggressive impulses away from such physically aggressive activities such as war and murder. An anthropologist, Richard Sipes, recently tested this hypothesis by sampling various cultures around the world and coding them in terms of (1) whether they had aggressive or nonaggressive games and (2) whether they engaged frequently or infrequently in wars. Contrary to the catharsis hypothesis, those cultures which engaged in wars also had aggressive sports. Thus, this cross-cultural study casts doubt upon the efficacy of aggressive sports and games as a means for reducing aggression.[27]

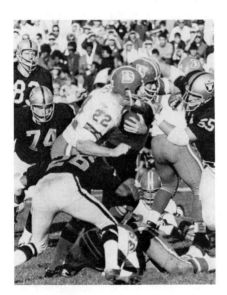 

Figure 3-3 The catharis theory of aggression suggests that watching or engaging in aggressive sports like football should make aggression in general less likely. However, this does not seem to be the case. Societies with aggressive sports tend to have many wars. Wide World Photos.

Although there are very few naturalistic field studies testing the catharsis hypothesis, there are many laboratory studies of it. Most of these experiments were designed so that the experimental subjects were induced to engage in some aggressive activity while the control subjects did not have that opportunity. After that, both groups of subjects were given further opportunity to aggress verbally or physically against persons or objects. Unfortunately, the results from these studies are contradictory. In some studies aggressive activities led to a decrease in subsequent aggressive action, while in others they led to no difference or even an increase in aggressive tendencies. For example, the psychologist Seymour Feshbach found, on the one hand, that boys given an opportunity to engage in aggressive play with toys were rated as *more* aggressive in their interactions with other children than boys that played with neutral toys. On the other hand, in a study with college undergraduates, Feshbach found that angered students who had had an opportunity for fantasy aggression showed *less* hostility on a final questionnaire than a neutral control group. Reviewing these and similar contradictory findings, Feshbach suggests, "the apparent inconsistency can be resolved if it is assumed that aggressive drive must be elicited at the time of vicarious or direct aggressive behavior if the aggressive act is to have a drive-reducing effect."[28] Since Feshbach is one of the few experimental psychologists inclined to support even a modified version of the catharsis hypothesis, we can take his assumptions as an indication that there is no consistent evidence for cathartic drainage of pent-up aggressive energy *without* prior reactive arousal. This supports our general evaluation in the last chapter that a drive or instinct conception of aggression seems theoretically and empirically untenable at this point.

Catharsis of emotion-induced aggression. Feshbach has argued that catharsis can occur when emotional arousal is present in the form of anger. We conceptualized anger as a signal of a cognitively evaluated conflict between one's on-going plans of action and environmental frustrations, leading to dashed expectations. We argued that the physiological arousal accompanying the subjective feeling of anger prepares the organism for instrumental action to remove the frustration and makes aggression more likely because of distortions of cognitive processes. How could these factors be affected by catharsis through overt aggression? There are three possibilities: (1) the reduction of arousal through tension reduction, (2) the removal of a frustration, and (3) the "completion" or goal attainment of an aggressive response sequence.

Since anger-arousal supposedly "energizes" the organism for aggressive action, it should be "used up" if aggression actually occurs. Again, this is a kind of "draining" concept that differs from the instinct notion in that the energy boost is of a reactive nature and constitutes a short-run phenomenon. Since only some kind of physical action should be necessary to "drain" the physiological arousal, it should not matter whether a frustrator or a substitute person or object are the targets of aggression. In fact, aggression may not even be necessary—any vigorous activity should do to get the physiological arousal "out of the system" (unless it is kept stimulated by cognitive processes). Since this argument is rather on the physiological side, we shall now focus on a series of studies by the psychologist Jack Hokanson and his collaborators at Florida State University.

FOCUS
The Learning of Catharsis[29]

Meet again the old ploys of experimental aggression research: Subjects are insulted by an obnoxious experimenter and then get a chance to get back at him via the "aggression machine," delivering electric shocks as punishments in a "learning experiment." In studies of possible cathartic effects of aggression, the obnoxious experimenter's angering of the subjects is a most important aspect. As we have seen, Feshbach argued that catharsis can only occur if some aggressive *arousal* is present.

The first experiment in Hokanson's laboratory showed that the standardized harassment-insult procedure produced a physiologically demonstrable increase in arousal: the subjects' blood pressure went up. The question then was whether an act of physical aggression on the part of the subjects would bring the blood pressure down to normal, that is, would have a cathartic, arousal-reducing effect. Therefore, the same subjects were given an opportunity for socially sanctioned aggression against their frustrator by being able to "shock" him in a simulated learning experiment. As predicted by the catharsis hypothesis, blood pressure went down for this group of subjects, while it stayed up for the control group subjects.[30] Although this looked like strong support for the catharsis hypothesis, some further studies along this line suggested that aggressive acts may have arousal-reducing effects only under very specific conditions. No such effects were observed for fantasy aggression, for displaced aggression towards a target unrelated to the source of frustration, or with aggression towards a higher-status frustrator.

This made Hokanson and his collaborators wonder whether or not nonaggressive counter-responses to provocations might have a cathartic effect as well. They devised a new experimental setup in which the subject could receive a painful shock or a token reward from an imaginary "fellow subject" in an interpersonal game. The experimental subject could also respond with either of these two possibilities. As predicted, the subjects' blood pressure went up upon receipt of a shock from their partner. Did it go down again when the subjects responded with counter-shock? Yes—but only for male subjects! For females, a friendly response to a shock was much more tension-reducing than an aggressive response!

Hokanson and his co-workers suggested a learning model to account for these results: they argued that "any response that serves to terminate, reduce, or avoid noxious stimulation from others will acquire cathartic-like properties." In other words, if we have found some behavior instrumental in warding off aggression directed against us, such behavior will be reinforced, since it was successful. And it will be accompanied by "anticipatory signs of relief," since it helped to reduce tension in the past. This does not mean that this behavior must still be functional or instrumental. Even though it may have become useless or dangerous, it may, at least for a while, retain its tension-reducing properties based on its past instrumentality. In terms of the results reported above, this would mean that the males had learned as part of the male role that aggression would be an instrumental response to threat, while the females had found friendliness more effective in dealing with threats. Thus the sexes experienced different tension-reduction effects from aggressive behavior.

Hokanson and his collaborators could support their model by manipulating their subjects' learning experience in terms of the instrumentality of aggression or friendliness in turning off their "fellow subjects' " shock in the interpersonal game situation. Thus, male subjects could be "reconditioned" in a short period of time to experience arousal reduction through friendly responses to shocks. This demonstrates that the "learned instrumentality of the counter behavior . . . may be the critical factor in the elicitation of arousal reducing reactions."[31]

This research points out that aggression may be tension-reducing, but only if it has been learned as an instrumental response. Aggression per se, unrelated to the respective frustration situation and the learned instrumentality, does not necessarily have cathartic effects.

While discussing Hokanson's research we have already implied that aggression may have cathartic effects when it removes a frustration (i.e., an interference with an on-going plan). Obviously, in functional terms, the arousal needed to cope with the interference will not be needed any longer and may dissipate. This is most clearly seen in children. If a frustration occurs (e.g., a toy is taken away, no money for ice cream, etc.), the child will become angry and possibly physically attack the frustrator. But as soon as the frustration is removed (e.g., the toy is handed back), calm and peace will return instantly.

Can we conclude from this that the mere removal of a frustration, independent of whether it has been brought about by acts of aggression or not, has cathartic effects upon aggressive motivation? Unfortunately not. The psychologist Leonard Berkowitz has argued that there may be a "completion tendency" as part of an activated aggressive response sequence which is only satisfied if the goal of the sequence (i.e., injury of the frustrator) is achieved.[32] In other words, no matter whether a frustration continues or not, once we have been angered by someone and are motivated to hurt him, we shall not stop until we have reached this aim. Obviously, there are motives other than reactive emotional arousal in response to frustration that support this notion of "revenge" or "getting even." Unfortunately, there is very little in the way of theorizing and research on the possibility of a *motivational shift* as a response to a frustration. It could be that the original goal, which was frustrated, is no longer important and that a new goal, to punish the frustrator, now takes first priority. This may be based on some naive conception of justice that requires that our frustrator be punished before we can rest[33] (see discussion of "face-saving" in Chapter 5).

It may be sufficient for us to observe our frustrator's and enemy's plight, even if it is not by our own hands, to achieve catharsis and to refrain from further aggression. A study by psychologists D. Bramel, B. Taub, and B. Blum suggests that this is so. Their subjects were angered by an obnoxious experimenter whom some subjects later observed to suffer painfully while others saw him euphoric. After this, those subjects who saw him suffer were significantly less hostile towards the experimenter than those who saw him euphoric. The investigators suggest that "catharsis appears most clearly when there is unambiguous feedback that the enemy is hurt, guilt is absent, and there are no factors encouraging imitation of aggression or the releasing of inhibitions of aggression."[34]

To summarize, overt aggressive acts may have cathartic, arousal-reducing functions if they actually remove a frustration, or have been instrumental in the past, or if they satisfy the motive of "getting back" at the frustrator by seeing him harmed.

Catharsis from a learning theory perspective. Learning theory predicts that any act followed by a reinforcement will be more likely to occur in the future. Since tension reduction is usually considered to be a reinforcer, a cathartic effect of an overtly aggressive act will actually reinforce this behavior. Thus, according to learning theory, catharsis may decrease aggressive motivation in the short run, but actually increase it in the long run. Catharsis may result in the learning of aggressive habits through reinforcement.

On the whole, the case for catharsis as a means of controlling or alleviating aggression is rather weak. Catharsis through overtly aggressive behavior seems to occur only if aggressive motivation is already aroused, if the aggressive act is or has been instrumental in removing a frustrator or coping with a threat, and/or if the frustrator gets hurt. We have very little evidence that substitute activities or displaced aggression against harmless objects have cathartic effects and that they can be used to "drain" the aggressive energy. Even if catharsis has positive short-run benefits, it will boost aggressive tendencies in the long run.[35]

Catharsis through Vicarious Experience of Aggression

The question of whether fictional or symbolic aggression can have cathartic effects has been one of the most hotly debated issues of recent years. Far from being an academic problem, this issue is a public controversy because of the possible effects of violence in the mass media. What effect, if any, does watching violence on TV have on the millions of children who spend hours a day in front of their TV sets? Few deny that there is an ample supply of violence in our mass media and that it is accessible to children.[36] Opinions are divided, however, on whether the effects of exposure to media violence are harmful, inconsequential, or even beneficial. Media spokesmen have argued that media violence may have an important input to moral development because the good guys always clobber the bad guys and the law always wins out in the end. Another proviolence argument is that the fantasy violence provided on TV can serve as an outlet for the children's aggressive tendencies and thus have cathartic functions. The overwhelming majority of psychologists and psychiatrists hotly contradict this notion on the basis of extensive empirical experiments and case studies. Since an enormous number of publications on this topic have found their way into both professional journals and the popular press we cannot possibly review even a small part of that literature in this overview. We shall have to restrict ourselves to a short discussion of the major approaches in this area and a summary of the results.

Laboratory studies. A large number of investigators have tried to study the effects of the vicarious experience of violence under controlled conditions in the laboratory. The standard procedure generally consists of first arousing the subjects via insult and frustration, showing an aggressive movie to the experimental group and a peaceful one to the control group, and then giving each group of subjects an opportunity to aggress.

The results have been quite consistent in all of these studies. Rather than decreasing aggression, exposure to an aggressive movie increases it.[37] Several explanations have been adduced for these results. We have already discussed the role of social learning and imitation in this context. As we saw in an earlier Focus, Bandura has shown convincingly that children learn aggressive behavior patterns from mere observation and tend to imitate these behaviors, particularly if the model has been reinforced for its behavior. On TV, at least, the good guys are almost always reinforced for beating, shooting, or maiming the bad guys.

Additional factors have been pointed out and experimentally demonstrated by one long-time aggression researcher, Leonard Berkowitz. Berkowitz argues that the portrayal of violence in the media may serve to release or lessen the inhibitions against aggressive behavior. Such disinhibiting effects are particularly probable if the violent behavior is depicted as legitimate and morally proper. In several experiments Berkowitz and his co-workers manipulated the perceived legitimacy of the violence in the movies they showed to their subjects. When exposed to *justified* aggression in a movie, subjects administered more severe shocks to a person who had angered them earlier. Another process, suggested by Berkowitz, is the cue-value of aggressive material. Aggressive material may serve as a *cue* to stimulate latent aggressive ideas, feelings, or behavior patterns in a person who has been angered and aroused. Berkowitz assumes that if aggression-related stimuli depicted in the media have been repeatedly associated with aggressive acts in the past, they will be able to elicit aggression in the future, if the person is instigated or motivated towards aggressive behavior.[38] One class of strong aggressive cues is weapons and it would be consistent with the above argument that the sight of a weapon in a movie or in real life should stimulate aggressive tendencies. Some experiments by Berkowitz and his group imply that this may be so.[39] If such findings can be substantiated, questions arise about the value of toy guns for children or the open display of guns by policemen.

Media spokesmen, as well as critical social scientists, have objected that the rather artificial laboratory setting does not allow a generalization of these results to the effect of real-life media exposure.[40] Clearly, what has been loosely called "aggression" or "violence" in these studies can hardly be compared to more realistic acts of violence such as physically beating or shooting another person. A further problem is that exposure to experimental material such as movies or videotapes is always a one-shot deal, and a very short one, too. Even though effects of up to six months have been reported for aggressive media imitation in one experiment,[41] it is difficult to argue that fundamental behavior changes will occur as a consequence of one-shot exposure. The argument that if one exposure has slight effects, repeated exposures to aggressive material in the daily TV fare must have very powerful effects is not quite cogent. Any type of experimentation is subject to the influence of methodological artifacts, particularly of "demand characteristics." This notion stresses the fact that an experiment is something out of the ordinary for the subject and the subject will try to guess what the experimenter wants him to do and tries to do it as best as he can. Thus, any manipulation, any design feature of an experiment can exert a "demand" to behave in a particular way, a power that this feature would not have outside of the artificial atmosphere of the laboratory.[42]

Yet these methodological problems *do not justify* statements to the effect that "if the mass media do stimulate and reinforce aggressive behavior, the effects are subtle and restricted to a small and probably disturbed segment of the population."[43] The fact that the laboratory results might not be conclusive does not mean that portrayal of mass media violence does not have any effects. It provides a challenge for further experimentation less subject to methodological artifacts and an attempt to study the effects of mass media violence in more real-life settings. To date only a few such field studies have been done.

Field studies. Since experimentation requires the differential manipulation and control of all or most essential variables in a situation, experimental field studies on the effect of mass communication are very difficult to conduct. Because of the very nature of the media everybody has access to them and it is hard to determine or even control who sees *what, where, when,* and to observe *with what effect.* Psychologists

Figure 3-4 "We moved out of the city so he wouldn't be exposed to all that crime, sex, and violence!" Reprinted by permission of NEA.

S. Feshbach and R. D. Singer had the rare opportunity to at least approximate that desirable state of affairs.[44] They were able to randomly assign aggressive or nonaggressive television fare to boys in institutional settings (private schools and boys' homes). The boys could watch as much TV as they wanted to, but were restricted in their choice to the "diet" prescribed for them (i.e., either a list of aggressive programs like westerns and mysteries, or a list of nonviolent programs like soap operas, talk shows, and the like). In addition to having the boys take a large number of tests and questionnaires measuring their aggressive tendencies, their supervisors were asked to record the frequency of aggressive incidents for each of the boys. The investigators found no increase in the frequency of aggressive behavior in the group of boys restricted to an aggressive TV diet for six weeks. On the contrary, they found that some boys, who were exposed to aggressive material, manifested less verbal and physical aggression towards peers and authority figures than did the control group boys, who were exposed to nonaggressive materials. This was particularly true for boys from low socioeconomic backgrounds and with high initial levels of aggressiveness. The authors concluded that exposure to aggressive content in television does not lead to an increase in aggressive behavior and that exposure may reduce or control the expression of aggression in aggressive boys from low socioeconomic backgrounds.

Should we advocate that aggressive boys watch a lot of violent TV shows? Feshbach acknowledges that this would be inappropriate, since a single experiment is not definitive and alternative interpretations of the data are possible. In addition, there are a number of rather severe methodological shortcomings to the study.[45] For example, some of the boys were forced to take part in the study and they, as well as some volunteers, might have resented the prohibition against viewing their favorite violent programs. Because of this, some boys from the nonaggressive program control group occasionally were even allowed to watch violent programs to minimize frustration! Such frustration might have led to anger and aggression. Furthermore, although the supervisors, who had to rate the boys' aggressive behavior, were deceived about the real purpose, they might have guessed and might have systematically biased their ratings or might have been stricter with those boys exposed to the violent programs to keep them from "getting out of hand." The most severe reservation against the Feshbach and Singer conclusion is that not only a large body of laboratory research flatly contradicts it, but that also a number of correlational field studies come to different conclusions.

In 1960, the psychologist Leonard Eron studied the TV viewing habits of 875 third-grade children. He found that children who preferred violent TV programs were more aggressive in school as rated by peers than children preferring less violent programs.[46] Ten years later, Eron and his collaborators did a follow-up study on about half of their original subjects. The results showed that children who had preferred violent programs ten years ago still behaved much more aggressively towards their peers than subjects who had earlier preferred nonviolent programming. This study, because of its longitudinal aspects, is somewhat more reassuring about the *causal* impact of media violence on aggressive behavior than other correlational studies in which similar relationships between violence viewing habits and aggressive behavior were found. The authors conclude that "the weight of evidence from this study when coupled with previous laboratory studies supports the theory that during a critical period in a boy's development, regular viewing and liking of violent television leads to the formation of a more aggressive life-style."[47]

On the whole, we have to be very skeptical about the possibility of the cathartic effects of vicariously experienced violence. There is almost no empirical corroboration for such effects. In addition, it is hard, theoretically, to see why there should be catharsis. Even Feshbach and Singer prefer to account for their findings by a "cognitive support" hypothesis claiming "that the boy who does not or cannot engage in self-generated aggressive fantasy needs the external support provided by the vicarious fantasy experience of watching violence on television."[48] However, the theory that exposure to violent programs stimulates and fosters aggressive behavior can muster more and much stronger support than cathartic notions. Yet even here, the evidence is not conclusive. One important point, made by Feshbach and Singer, is that there are different types of violence and that these may have differential effects. They argue that children are able to differentiate between fictional violence, as in plays or cartoons, and real violence, as in the news, and that the latter is much more likely to reinforce, stimulate, or elicit aggressive responses.[49] Clearly, we shall need much further research before this issue will be settled. Yet it may be premature to predict that the catharsis hypothesis will fade away soon. It just sounds right to too many people.

CONCLUSION

At this point we want to step back and take stock of our long and tortuous journey through the vicissitudes of aggressive motivation. We have attempted to show which intrapersonal processes make the occurrence of aggressive behavior more or less *likely*. We concluded that these processes are mainly *reactive* in nature. Cognitive and emotional processes lead to an increased readiness to aggress because of conflicts

between the organism's needs, wants, or plans and environmental interferences (frustrations) or because of an expectation of reinforcement for
an aggressive act (based on a past history of reinforcement for instrumental aggression or observation of a successful model). We also have
seen that such motivational tendencies toward aggression can be
"drained" only by removing the condition that led to their arousal
(abolishing frustration) or by engaging in the behavior toward which
the motivational tendency is aimed (e.g., hurting some designated person
or object).

Even though there are many loose ends, we might conclude that
the motivational aspects that we have to look out for are the following:
First, the emotional arousal of anger predisposes us toward aggressive
action that may be easily elicited by aggressive cues in the situation.
Second, anger may interfere with the cognitive functions of evaluating
all relevant variables in a situation and with the proper assessment of
the consequences of various behavioral alternatives. Third, if we observe
violent behavior to be successful or experience reinforcements for such
behavior ourselves, the likelihood of further aggression increases.

Perhaps there should be even more aggression in the world than
we observe today if all these motivational processes are operative. However, we have repeatedly pointed out that these processes make aggression more *likely* but do not determine its occurrence. Many other factors
are important and help determine whether aggression occurs. For
example, some potential influences are the nature of social interaction,
the groups we belong to (including social structural units like class or
race), and ecological factors. We shall turn to these variables in the
chapters to come.

SUMMARY

In this chapter we continued to pursue the motivational forces behind
aggression by discussing how aggression may be learned. In contrast to
the previous chapter, which emphasized the "push" towards aggression
by aversive tensions, this chapter highlighted the "pull" towards aggression by anticipated rewards. A learning theory analysis of aggression
raises two basic questions: (1) How are new aggressive behaviors
acquired? and (2) What types of rewards motivate aggression?

New aggressive behaviors may be learned through the *observation
and imitation* of another person's behavior. Observation teaches a person
not only how to be aggressive, but also what the possible outcomes of
aggression are. In short, observation teaches people how and when to
be aggressive.

However, whether the person actually puts the new aggressive behaviors into practice depends on the *direct reinforcement* of those behaviors. By definition, behaviors that are rewarded tend to be repeated. Aggression is often rewarding because it (1) reduces emotional arousal, (2) leads to the attainment of goals, (3) bolsters self-esteem, especially if notions of manliness are involved, (4) leads to social approval, and (5) becomes an autonomous motive or an end in itself. Through the process of *stimulus generalization,* people may act aggressively in situations other than the original learning situation; through the process of *response generalization,* people may employ many different types of aggressive behavior in the same situation. Thus, unless *selective reinforcement* and *punishment* are employed, aggressive behaviors tend to spread to new situations and to new forms of aggression. However, punishment by itself is not an effective means of preventing aggression. This is partly so because punishment serves as a model of successful aggression and is frustrating.

In the second half of this chapter we considered some *cathartic* mechanisms that may decrease aggressive motivation. The major premise is that aggressive motivation may be "drained off" (1) through an *overt act* of aggression directed against a frustrator or a substitute person or object, or (2) through *vicarious experience* of aggression in the "real world" or in the make-believe world of movies, literature, or fantasy.

On the whole, *overt* aggressive acts may have some cathartic reducing effects, if specific preconditions are met (e.g., the aggression actually removes the source of frustration). However, the case for catharsis through overt aggressive acts as a means for decreasing aggression is rather weak. In addition, there is very little evidence that substitute activities (e.g., sports) or displaced aggression against harmless objects (e.g., chopping wood) have cathartic effects.

Similarly, the evidence for general cathartic effects through the *vicarious experience* of aggression (e.g., watching violent TV shows) is weak. The existing laboratory and field studies suggest, in fact, that vicarious experience is likely to increase aggressive behavior. However, the last word is not in yet, and the issue is still being hotly debated.

FOOTNOTES

[1] Bandura (1973), p. 57.
[2] Skinner (1953, 1971).
[3] Bandura (1973).
[4] This theory is spelled out in detail in Bandura and Walters (1964) and in Bandura (1973).

[5] Bandura, Ross, and Ross (1963*b*).

[6] Bandura, Ross, and Ross (1963*a*).

[7] Bandura, Ross, and Ross (1963*b*).

[8] Cf. Bandura (1965).

[9] This view is summarized in Klapper (1968) and in Liebert, Neale, and Davidson (1973).

[10] Berkowitz and Macaulay (1971).

[11] Bandura (1973), pp. 101–7.

[12] Bandura (1973), pp. 127–39.

[13] Feshbach (1970) and Bandura (1973), pp. 93–94 and 225–27.

[14] Hilgard (1948).

[15] Cohen (1955); Short (1968). See Chapter 6, pp. 197–98.

[16] Geen and Pigg (1970); Geen and Stonner (1971).

[17] See pp. 199–203.

[18] Bandura (1973), pp. 93–101.

[19] Patterson, Littman, and Bricker (1967).

[20] Cofer and Appley (1964), pp. 571–72.

[21] Walters and Brown (1963).

[22] Cowan and Walters (1963).

[23] Lövaas (1961).

[24] Bandura (1973), pp. 222–24.

[25] Bandura (1973), p. 226.

[26] Berkowitz (1962), p. 205.

[27] Sipes (1973).

[28] Feshbach (1970), p. 236.

[29] Adaptation of "Psychophysiological Evaluation of the Catharsis Hypothesis" by Jack E. Hokanson, in *The Dynamics of Aggression,* edited by Edwin I. Megargee and Jack E. Hokanson. Copyright © 1970 by Edwin I. Megargee and Jack E. Hokanson. By permission of Harper & Row, Publishers, Inc.

[30] More recently, Baker and Schaie (1969) also found that overt aggression can lead to a decrease in physiological arousal (blood pressure changes).

[31] Hokanson (1970), p. 83.

[32] Berkowitz (1962), pp. 220–26. See Staub (1971).

[33] Feshbach (n.d.) talks about a "moral" basis for aggression in this context.

[34] Bramel, Taub, and Blum (1968).

[35] Berkowitz (1973).

[36] See Larsen (1968); Gerbner (1972).

[37] See Feshbach (1970), The Surgeon General's Scientific Advisory Committee on Television and Social Behavior (1972), Singer (1971), and Bandura (1973).

[38] Berkowitz (1971).

[39] See n. 69, Chap. 2.

[40] Klapper (1968).

[41] Hicks (1965).

[42] Orne (1969); but see the critique of demand characteristics in Bandura (1973), pp. 138–39.

[43] Feshbach (1970), p. 239.

[44] Feshbach and Singer (1971).

[45] Methodological criticisms are summarized in Bandura (1973), pp. 134–42.

[46] Eron (1963).

[47] Eron et al. (1972).

[48] Feshbach and Singer (1971), p. 155.

[49] Feshbach and Singer (1971), pp. 158–59. See critique by Bandura (1973), p. 142.

4 / IN THE EYE OF THE BEHOLDER

cognitive factors

FOCUS
"My God! They're Killing Us!"

May Day, 1970: South Vietnamese and American soldiers crossed into Cambodia escalating the Vietnam war to new heights. Half a world away, thousands of American college students went on strike in protest. At first, the protests at Kent State University were no different from those at scores of other college campuses. Peaceful protest rallies were held on campus, and not-so-peaceful confrontations with the local police occurred in the streets of Kent, Ohio. On May 3, the twenty-nine-man Kent police force arrested twelve students during a "trashing" spree, which erupted when the police attempted to clear the streets. The following night's events became more heated when a crowd of students burned down the ROTC building. With the town in an uproar over the two nights of student demonstrations, Mayor Leroy Satrom called upon Governor James Rhodes to activate the National Guard. To the citizens of Kent, Armageddon was upon them: "If these anarchists get away with it here, no campus in the country is safe."

The governor quickly ordered 6,000 Guardsmen to the campus, declared martial law, and announced that the students were ". . . worse

Figure 4-1 Ohio National Guardsmen stand between student demonstrators and the burnt-out ROTC building at the Kent State University campus on May 5, 1970. Behind the buildings at the upper left is where four students were shot by National Guardsmen. Wide World Photos.

than the 'brownshirt' and the Communist element and also the night-riders in the vigilantes . . . the worst type of people that we harbor in America. We are going to eradicate the problem. . . . It's over with in Ohio."

On the following day, May 4, rock-throwing students confronted tear-gas-shooting National Guardsmen. At one point, a detachment of about forty troopers was sent to clear students from the football field and parking lot. As the students retreated before the advancing troops, they continued to hurl epithets and stones, and the soldiers fired volleys of gas. Then, the soldiers ran out of gas grenades and started to retrace their steps back to the main body of troops. Several times they pointed their loaded rifles at the following crowd in apparent attempts to frighten the students. Suddenly, without warning, they fired. In eleven seconds over fifty-four shots were fired by twenty-nine soldiers, four students were killed, and nine others were wounded. The order to cease fire had to be repeated several times, and some Guardsmen had to be physically restrained from continuing to fire.

Most of the dead and wounded were over seventy-five feet from the soldiers and all but four were shot in the backs or the sides. According to an FBI report, six of the victims were not even active participants in the confrontation. They were shot on their way to class. Two of the dead and three of the wounded were in front of the crowd taunting the troops and two other wounded may have been encouraging other students to throw stones.

The Guardsmen claimed that they had shot in self-defense after being fired upon by a sniper. (An FBI report failed to find evidence of a sniper.) However, more recent evidence suggests that a shot actually may have been fired, which precipitated the National Guard's shooting. The Guard insisted that the students were a large mob that was about to surround and overrun them. The troops feared they would be disarmed by the students. (On the basis of photographs, the FBI investigation concluded that the troops were not surrounded and that only a few students actually confronted the Guard.) General Canterbury, commander of the Ohio National Guard, claimed that ". . . these troops felt that their lives were in danger. I felt I could have been killed out there." The general concluded that, since Ohio National Guard regulations permit each individual soldier to shoot without an officer's orders whenever he feels that his life is endangered, the shootings were justified and legal.[1]

Figure 4-2 Masked National Guardsmen fire barrages of tear gas into a crowd of student demonstrators at Kent State University. Note the many aggressive cues in the form of uniforms and weapons and that the Guardsmen are deindividuated by their gas masks.

How can we account for the complicated events at Kent State that culminated in the violent deaths of four students? In previous chapters we saw that although physiological and motivational processes can strongly affect the occurrence of aggressive behavior in men and animals, they clearly do not deserve the exclusive attention that much of the psychology of aggression has paid them. Aggression seems to be very much determined by events in the *social environment* that *instigate* motivational and physiological processes leading up to aggressive behavior or *trigger* such behavior, if the instigation is already present. We have noted that the emotion of anger, which seems to be a common precursor to aggression, has motivational properties and is accompanied by physiological reactions. Although it is important to know about the motivational and physiological aspects of anger and aggression, it may be more essential to learn about the kinds of social stimuli that evoke anger and aggression.

Consequently, to understand violence more fully, we have to shift our attention to the *interpersonal level* of analysis. The deaths at Kent State were part of a complicated interaction between many people acting as individuals and as members of groups. Each person's behavior was affected by the people he was interacting with. In this chapter and the following one, our question is what are the factors in human interaction that lead to aggression? In tackling this question, we shall depart slightly from the approach of the previous chapters. Instead of focusing on research dealing directly with aggression, we shall focus on the processes of social interaction and try to isolate those most likely to foster or inhibit aggression. We shall give particular attention to the processes that lead to anger and hostility and to the stimuli that may contribute to the transformation of anger into aggression.

In this chapter, we shall focus upon *intra*personal factors such as perception, cognition, stereotypes, attribution of intentions and emotions, and attitudes. Thus, we are concerned with the psychological processes of receiving, interpreting, and reacting to environmental stimuli. These are processes that occur within the minds of single individuals. But we are concerned with them to the extent that they are influenced by and have consequences for the person's social interactions. In the following chapter, we shall turn to more strictly *inter*personal factors, for example, social influence and conformity.

Perception and Cognition

Much of human behavior deals with trying to cope with environmental contingencies in order to carry out our plans, satisfy our needs, or just to survive. Obviously, we need to receive information about the physical and social environment in order to cope with it. The term *perception* refers to those processes by which we *become aware* of environmental information, while *cognition* denotes the mental processes that *evaluate* and *utilize* this information. The human "data-gathering machine" is not a perfectly veridical or unbiased apparatus. Social and psychological factors influence perception and cognition and, consequently, affect our information about the environment. Some of these biases may distort information in such a way as to make aggressive behavior more or less likely. We shall deal with five aspects of perception and cognition that may have such consequences for human aggression: (1) attention to and recognition of social stimuli (social perception), (2) categorization and the role of stereotypes, (3) making inferences about causation and intention, (4) perception of emotions, and (5) social evaluations (attitudes and prejudice).

SOCIAL PERCEPTION

In order to obtain information about a stimulus—a thing, person, or event—we have to be exposed to it, pay attention to it, and recognize or identify it in terms of the class or category of stimuli to which it belongs. For example, to "perceive" a burglar breaking into our house, we have to hear the noise of his breaking in, we have to pay attention to this noise rather than to our stereo, and we have to categorize it as the sounds of a burglar rather than the innocuous murmur of the wind in the trees. Obviously, the perceiver is not just a passive recipient of information in this process. He can prevent exposure to the noise by putting on his muffling stereo headphones; he can focus all of his attention on the flute solo in the concerto he is listening to and disregard the sound of shattering glass; and, he can categorize the noise as "accidental noises produced by pets and children, to be disregarded." Many different factors might influence his exposure, attention, and categorization of sounds. If he is a Caspar Milquetoast who is afraid of his own shadow or if he just finished reading Poe's "Tell-tale Heart," he might be particularly sensitive to the slightest rustle and quickly interpret it as an all-out attack by bloodthirsty Mafiosi upon his life and property. In addition, the fear of becoming a burglary-murder statistic may be sufficiently great so that he even imagines suspicious sounds where none actually exist. In such a case, emotional and motivational factors not only affect the perceptual process in terms of directing exposure, attention, and categorization, but actually produce images in the person's mind.

In short, human perception is not like a tape recorder that passively records all sounds to which it is sensitive. Human perception is *selective*.[2] Of all the sights, sounds, and smells that are capable of firing neurons in our eyes, ears, and nose only a small percentage reach awareness. This is partially due to the human sensory system's filtering of stimuli. For example, we can consciously select some stimuli while ignoring others, as when we selectively tune into different conversations at a party.

Besides being selective, perception is also *organized*.[3] The stimulus world is not perceived as random entities or as a chaos of sights and sounds. On the contrary, stimuli are perceived as perceptual wholes or units. For example, the words on this page are seen as distinct units and stand out as figures on the white background of the paper. To some extent, perceptual organization seems to be inherent in the nature of our perceptual apparatus. However, past experience and learning also play an important role in determining how stimuli are perceptually organized.

Learning is probably most important in the process of *categorization*.[4] Part of perception is learning to classify stimuli on the basis of perceptual cues. We learn that a particular configuration of stimuli is a "man," while another set is a "woman." Categories allow us to focus on the most important aspects or attributes of a thing, person, or event and help us store information about stimuli and make decisions about responding to the stimuli. The categories, which we learn through actual or vicarious experience, may also influence the actual perception of stimuli. People may more readily or easily perceive objects that "fit" existing perceptual categories, and they may misperceive or distort stimuli so that they are seen as corresponding to their categories. Categories increase the likelihood of our perceiving an object and our interpreting it in a particular way. This process is called *perceptual readiness*.[5] If we have adequate categories available for our use, we are able to sort, identify, evaluate, and remember stimuli much more readily than without such categories.

Therefore, perception depends partly on the categories available to a person, and the factors that influence the availability of perceptual categories are particularly important in understanding social perception. One way of organizing these factors is to distinguish between response disposition and response salience.[6] *Response disposition* refers to the person's past experience with stimuli or perceptual categories. The more frequently a person has been exposed to a stimulus in the past, the more readily he will respond to it when it is presented in the future. For example, when words are flashed on a screen at low illumination, familiar words are more easily seen than unfamiliar words. Because of prior perceptual experience or familiarity, stimuli are easily categorized and categories are easily employed. That is, people develop perceptual "habits" through frequent exposure and use.

Response salience refers to contemporary conditions (as opposed to past conditions) that predispose a person to respond in a particular manner. Given equal familiarity with stimuli, contemporary or momentary factors may make it easier for a person to perceive one stimulus rather than another. For example, a hungry man is more likely to perceive pictures of food than of nonfood objects when both are flashed on a screen at equal intensity. The person's momentary "set" may influence his perception and categorization of stimuli.

Now that we have defined a few terms and briefly described some aspects of perception, let us turn to the issue of social perception and aggression by first looking at factors that work through response salience.

Response Salience and Aggression

We have all heard of the thirsty desert traveller who "sees" an oasis where none exists. This poor fellow is often cited as an example of how motivation may affect perception. The person is so strongly motivated towards a goal that he tries to satisfy his needs through "wishful thinking." Although it is often enjoyable to dream about having the good things in life, it would be quite dysfunctional to indulge consistently in wishful thinking. We might delude ourselves to the point of hurting our chances of realistically adapting to the circumstances at hand. However, it would be functional if our needs and emotions directed our attention to those stimuli that are relevant to our needs. That is, our needs and emotions may increase the response saliency of particular perceptual categories and make us "vigilant" for those stimuli. The extent to which our perceptions are guided or even governed by our motivational states has been the concern of the so-called "New Look" approach to the psychology of perception.[7] One particularly interesting hypothesis is that we *project* our needs and emotions onto the stimuli that we perceive, particularly in cases where the stimuli are ambiguous. Our stranded desert traveller is thought of as projecting his need for life-saving water onto the images of immense sand dunes. The "New Look" psychologists have tried to produce such "mirages" in the experimental laboratory.

In one study, after being deprived of food for various periods of time, subjects were shown pictures of various objects, including food, through a piece of ground glass, which distorted the pictures and made it difficult to recognize the photographs. As expected, hungry subjects more frequently reported seeing food objects. In a similar study, submarine trainees were deprived of food for different time periods and were asked to tell stories about several ambiguous pictures. Again, the hungrier subjects included more food-related items in their stories. These studies suggest that the subjects were projecting their needs into their imagery. Although there have been many criticisms of these and similar studies, it is safe to conclude that a person's momentary need-states do affect his perception by heightening his awareness of and attention to stimuli that may satisfy his needs.[8] How could such tendencies of projection work in the case of anger and aggression?

Just as the need for food can make us more alert for food-related stimuli, so the emotion of anger may selectively increase our attention to aggressive cues and to potential victims for our aggression. Thus, we may become more alert to the availability of potential weapons. In the previous chapter, we referred to one study in which the mere presence of weapons in the experimental room led angered subjects to electroshock a victim more frequently than when no weapons were present.[9] It is possible that the emotional state of anger might sensitize people to the presence of weapons and to the aggressive actions associated with them. The heightened sensitivity and awareness of such aggressive cues may lead to an increased readiness to aggress.

In addition to sensitizing a person to possible weapons, the effects of anger may include the perception and categorization of other people as instigators of the feelings of anger (i.e., frustrators) and/or as potential victims for an aggressive act. Obviously, the search for a potential victim is most intense when an attack on the frustrator himself is impossible or inadvisable. The angered person may be sensitized to any cues that would mark someone else as a substitute target. Rather than randomly expressing his aggression, a person often waits until he finds some reason, however trivial, to justify his attack on a scapegoat. In such cases, people seem to be particularly eager to find a legitimate reason for aggression that allows them to be punitive and self-righteous. In terms of social perception, the emotion of anger sensitizes the frustrated person to any cues that might allow him to act out his aggression.

Complementary projection is one mechanism that could be important in this process. Unfortunately, there are no empirical studies illustrating this process for the emotion of anger, but there is a good one for the emotion of fear. In a famous 1933 study, the Harvard psychologist Henry Murray played the "murder game" with a number of children at a child's birthday party. The murder game, played in a darkened house, proved to be pretty scary for the children. Before the game started, Murray asked the children to judge the maliciousness of several men shown in photographs. When asked to make these judgments again after the frightening game, the children rated the men as much more malicious than before.[10] These results suggest that the children had to justify their fear to themselves, and, by seeing maliciousness in the photographs, they found good reason for their fear. Complementary projection is a tendency to justify our felt emotions by attributing a particular personality trait, intention, or motivation to some other person.

We can easily see how complementary projection might operate in situations of anger arousal. If we attribute to another person intentions or actions that are hostile or frustrating to us, we can justify the presence of anger. Such complementary projections have the additional advantage of providing us with a convenient outlet (target) for our anger-induced aggression. We shall return to the role of attribution of hostile intentions in aggression later in this chapter.

Does all this tell us anything about Kent State? At the time of their arrival, the troops were already tired and tense after serving five days in Cleveland during a wildcat Teamster strike. They were angered and frustrated by having their tour of duty extended and not being able to return to their normal civilian lives. And, they blamed the students for their additional duty. Of course, the men were surrounded by aggressive cues in the shape of rifles, military vehicles, and uniformed men. These cues along with their anger and frustration heightened their sensitivity to any stimuli that could trigger aggression, and the students supplied them with plenty of stimuli by verbally and physically abusing the troops.

At the time of the shooting, the small isolated band of soldiers became particularly sensitive to the number and physical location of the students (i.e., they felt they were about to be surrounded and overrun). Their fear and anger probably led them to categorize all students as potential aggressors; in addition, their fear was heightened when they ran out of tear gas and were forced to retreat. Perhaps through the mechanism of complementary projection, they perceived the students to be particularly hostile, dangerous, and intent on overpowering the soldiers in order to obtain firearms. At this point, they were probably particularly vigilant for any signs of attack by the students. Then, an unexplained shot rang out, and the troops quickly categorized it as sniper fire. In their panic, they "returned" fire. In short, their momentary state of anger, fear, and frustration made the troops alert for aggressive targets and, through complementary projection, they perceived the students as a dangerous, hostile, and menacing mob. (Of course, there was some reality to their perception, since the students were throwing stones. However, none of the soldiers was seriously hurt throughout the entire confrontation. The perceptual processes, in this case, operated to exaggerate the perceived danger of their situation.)

Response Disposition and Aggression

In addition to momentary motivational states, more enduring psychological factors are also important in social perception. Earlier we stated in passing that people perceive familiar stimuli more readily than unfamiliar stimuli. For example, people are more likely to perceive stimuli that are part of their cultural complex and of their daily lives than stimuli that are from a foreign culture. In one study, Mexican and American subjects were shown photographs of various social events, such as weddings or sporting games. For each event there were pictures of both the Mexican and American versions. For instance, there were pictures of both American and Mexican weddings and of American baseball games and Mexican bullfights. The subjects were shown the photographs in a device similar to the old stereoscopes, which were popular around the turn of the century. The subjects looked through a lens system so that their right eye saw one photograph while their left eye saw another and different picture. (This is called "binocular rivalry.") The photographs were shown so that one eye saw a Mexican picture and the other an American picture for one minute. Under these conditions, the subjects reported seeing only one image, not two conflicting pictures, and they saw the picture of the event with which they were more familiar. Mexicans reported seeing a bullfight, and Americans saw a baseball game.[11] The more familiar event dominated the less familiar event in their perception.

Extrapolating to aggressive behavior, we would expect that the more frequently a person has been exposed to aggression-related stimuli, the more readily he would perceive them and the more likely he would react aggressively, especially when emotionally aroused. One study tests part of this hypothesis by using the binocular rivalry technique. Instead of exposing subjects to conflicting pictures of cultural stimuli, subjects were shown violent and nonviolent images (e.g., a drawing of a man pointing a gun at another man versus one of a man plowing a field). In this study, advanced police administration students were more likely than a control group of psychology students to see the violent images. This does not seem to represent the more aggressive nature of police administration students, since "rookies" in the program were less likely than advanced students and just as likely as psychology students to see the violent images. The study suggests that the police administration program imparted more than knowledge about police practices. It also exposed students to violence and made them more perceptually alert to aggression-related stimuli[12] (cf. National Guardsmen). Similarly, we might expect that exposure to violence in the mass media would make people sensitive to aggressive cues as would living in a high-crime area. In short, the more exposure a person has to aggression-related stimuli through his culture or his own experience, the more readily he will perceive them and, therefore, the more likely he will behave aggressively.

Of course, other factors than mere exposure are involved. If a person is exposed to aggressive stimuli, but punished each time, we might expect him to be less likely to perceive these stimuli in the future. He might block them from awareness. (This is a phenomenon known as "perceptual defense.")[13] Consequently, the pairing of punishment with aggression-related stimuli might have inhibitory effects by reducing the probability of observing the instigating stimuli. However, the opposite might happen if the aggression-related stimuli were paired with rewards. For example, the police administration students were probably rewarded whenever they reported seeing aggressive incidents. This would increase their vigilance for such stimuli. Although there are no studies on the effects of rewards and punishments on the perception of aggression-related stimuli, there are some showing that the principle is generally reasonable.[14]

Just as a person's needs make him momentarily sensitive to need-related stimuli, so may his *values* and *attitudes* make him permanently sensitive to appropriate stimuli. If a person is interested in politics, we might expect him to perceive political slogans more readily than religious quotations. Values and attitudes may "tune" the person to receive particular stimuli. In a now-classic experiment, the psychologists L. Postman, J. Bruner, and E. McGinnies tested this hypothesis by first measuring the strength of their subjects' interest in six value domains: theoretical, economic, aesthetic, social, political, and religious. Then, they flashed words from these value domains on a screen with an apparatus similar to a slide projector. As expected, the more interested a person was in a value domain, the more easily he perceived words representing that value.[15] Now, we might suspect that this is true because people are more familiar with words that represent their values. They probably have been exposed to them more frequently. However, subsequent studies have controlled for familiarity, and they have continued to find that the person's values sensitize him to value-related stimuli.[16]

Consequently, we would expect a person's attitudes towards other people to influence his perception of them. This may be particularly true when we are dealing with strong attitudes like hate or prejudice. The social psychologist Gordon Allport argued that "it is important to the prejudiced person to learn the cues whereby he may identify his enemy."[17] Allport suggested that hatred and prejudice may lead to an increased sensitivity among the prejudiced to cues such as gestures, speech, physiognomic features, etc. that can serve to identify a person as belonging to the outgroup. This phenomenon has been investigated quite extensively by social psychologists, particularly in terms of whether anti-Semites have an edge in distinguishing Jews from Gentiles.

As in many areas of psychology, there is conflicting evidence as to the accuracy of anti-Semites in recognizing Jews on the basis of physiognomic features. However, there seems to be little doubt that anti-Semitic persons show a strong bias in applying ethnic labels to other people on the basis of minimal cues. In most of these studies, the prejudiced subjects tended to apply the label "Jew" much more frequently to the people they judged than did nonprejudiced persons. As a consequence, the prejudiced persons labeled more Jews as "Jewish" than did the nonprejudiced. However, they also labeled more Gentiles as "Jewish" than did the nonprejudiced subjects. The anti-Semites' increased sensitivity to physiognomic cues and their readiness to label a suspect are quite important regardless of their accuracy. The prejudiced are constantly vigilant for potential victims (their "enemies") and, in their vigilance, they condemn many "innocent" people along with the "guilty." They see a Jew, a communist, or a "nigger" behind every bush and beneath every bed.[18]

These studies of prejudice suggest that attitudes and values influence social perception through categorization of stimuli. Besides being sensitive to identifying cues, prejudiced individuals are also quick to categorize someone as a member of the outgroup. For example, the troops at Kent State probably categorized all students as "dangerous radicals." This is important because how we categorize a stimulus helps to determine how we react to it. In general, if we dislike a person or a group we tend to classify their behavior as "bad," "threatening," or "harmful." No matter what they do, we are suspicious of their motivation and perceive them as being up to no good. In other words, two people may perceive the same stimulus, but they may categorize it as "good" or "bad" depending upon their attitudes. This is rather well exemplified by the public's perception of recent student and black protests and of violence in general.

FOCUS
In the Eye of the Beholder

Do you think of looting as violence? What about burning a draft card? Is student protest violence? Do you think of police shooting a looter as violence? Researchers at the Institute for Social Research of the University of Michigan asked about 1,400 American men these and other questions in order to study how men thought about violence and what determined their attitudes and perceptions of violence.[19] Table 4-1 shows how these men answered the questions in 1969. The data suggest that many American men consider dissent per se as violence, but they do not classify the acts of the police as violence. Also, when given a list of bipolar adjectives (e.g., good-bad), most men feel that violence is bad, fierce, strong, unnecessary, and avoidable.

Of course, it comes as no great surprise that their attitudes towards social protest are reflected in their appraisal of protest as violence. Men who are hostile to student and black protestors are likely to classify protests as violence, but are unlikely to categorize police behaviors as violence. In addition, such general values as *humanism* (i.e., valuing equality, freedom, and human dignity over respect for property, respect for law, and financial security), *retributive justice* (e.g., " 'An eye for an eye and a tooth for a tooth' is a good rule for living"), *giving priority to people over property* (e.g., "Some people say that stealing or damaging property is as bad as hurting people. Others say that damaging property is not as bad as hurting people. What do you think?"), and *self-defense* (e.g., "A man has the right to kill another man in self-defense") are related to categorizing protest as violence

Table 4-1

What Is Violence?

	Percentage of Respondents Defining Certain Acts as Violence			
	Total sample	*College students*	*White union members*	*Blacks*
Do you think of looting as violence?	85%	76%	91%	74%
Do you think of burglary as violence?	65	47	67	70
Do you think of draft card burning as violence?	58	26	63	51
Do you think of police beating students as violence?	56	79	45	82
Do you think of not letting people have their civil rights as violence?	49	54	40	70
Do you think of student protests as violence?	38	18	43	23
Do you think of police shooting looters as violence?	35	43	23	59
Do you think of sit-ins as violence?	22	4	24	15
Do you think of police stopping to frisk as violence?	16	16	10	34

SOURCE: Blumenthal et al. (1972), pp. 73 and 76.

and police action as nonviolence.[20] Thus, our general values or orientation toward people in general as well as our attitudes towards particular people influence how we perceive and categorize social events.

Similar perceptions surrounded the Kent State shootings. A few days before Kent State, President Nixon expressed his negative attitudes towards demonstrators by calling them "bums." His reaction to the killings was consistent with his attitudes: "This should remind us all once again that when dissent turns to *violence* it invites tragedy."[21] In the President's eyes, the students, but not the National Guard, were violent. However, the mother of one of the victims saw things differently:

> President Nixon wants people to believe Jeff turned to violence. That's not true. What kind of sympathy is this? When four kids are dead he gave no comfort. Nixon acts as if the kids had it coming. But shooting into a crowd of students—*that* is violence. . . . They consider stones threat enough to kill children. I think the violence comes from the government.[22]

The Michigan study and Kent State show that how people perceive social events depends upon their attitudes towards the actors who cause the events. People who are unsympathetic to blacks categorize the events of the 1960s as "crimes or riots" inspired by "outside agitators," "Communists," "radicals," and other undesirable types for the purpose of looting. But people who are sympathetic to blacks and blacks themselves categorize the same stimuli as "protests" backed by the "will of the people" for the purpose of righting wrongs.[23] In short, our attitudes toward people affect our perception of their actions by sensitizing us to their behaviors and by influencing the way we categorize their actions.[24] Violence, like beauty, is in the eye of the beholder.

Along with the effects of familiarity, reinforcement, and attitudes, a person's enduring personality traits may have an impact on how he perceives persons and events.[25] The ego-defense mechanisms of projection and denial may be particularly important here. A person who tends to project his own aggressive tendencies onto others would perceive them as being hostile to him. He might misperceive and miscategorize their behaviors and react aggressively towards them in "self-defense." (For example, the "sniper shot" heard by the National Guardsmen may have been fired accidentally by one of their own men or by a nonstudent. The Guardsmen, perhaps by projecting their own desire to shoot onto the students, interpreted this shot as coming from the students.) At the same time these ego-defense mechanisms enable a person to perceive his own behavior and motives as nonaggressive. He sees the instigation for aggression as coming from others and not from himself. However, for some people, aggression is psychologically threatening regardless of its source. Such people might employ ego defenses (e.g., denial) that would inhibit aggression by blocking aggressive stimuli from awareness.[26] For example, they may dismiss someone's verbal abuse of them as a joke, because recognizing its true aggressive nature would be too psychologically upsetting for them.

Several other personality traits may result in definite "perceptual styles" or ways of perceiving the world. One such style is the person's dependence on the context or field in which a particular stimulus is imbedded.[27] This perceptual style might impair the person's analytic ability to isolate important aspects of stimuli and thereby affect how he reacts to stimuli. Another somewhat dysfunctional perceptual style is the inability to deal with ambiguous or contradictory information (so-called "intolerance of ambiguity"). This perceptual style, which is common to authoritarian or dogmatic personalities, does not allow the person to suspend judgment on ambiguous issues or to tolerate shades of gray in making judgments.[28] Finally, a person's "cognitive complexity" may affect his perception through the number and "width" of his cognitive-perceptual categories. A person with few and broad categories is likely to make fewer distinctions between stimuli and to react to them in more or less the same way.[29] When aroused, for example, such a person is likely to see everyone as either "for him" or "against him" and to act accordingly. In short, perceptual styles may facilitate or inhibit aggression by influencing the individual's ability to perceive and categorize stimuli.

Summary. A variety of momentary and more enduring psychological states and processes influence the perception of social stimuli. These factors influence perception by making individuals more vigilant for particular stimuli and/or by affecting the way individuals categorize stimuli. We argued in the last chapter that even if a tendency to aggress exists in terms of motivation, its expression depends on whether or not there are external cues that may trigger aggressive responses. Obviously, the presence of such cues is detected through perception, and any processes that affect the perception of aggression-instigating or aggression-inhibiting cues are extremely important.

CATEGORIZATION AND STEREOTYPES

In the preceding section we discussed how the use of categories is essential in the recognition and identification of social stimuli. Categories or classes are defined by a set of specific attributes or qualities that an object, person, or event must possess in order to qualify for membership in that category. Take the category "Scotch whiskey." An object needs the following attributes for membership: It must be a liquid of brownish hue, it must be aged about six years or more, it must be imported from Scotland, have a certain alcohol content, and come in a bottle with the label "blended Scotch whiskey." In addition to these "official" attributes, which might be prescribed by a liquor board, Scotch whiskey may have other attributes that we know or infer from past experience or hearsay. Such inferred attributes may include that we feel relaxed after a glass of Scotch, but get drunk and sick after half a bottle. The trouble with these attributes is that they are only probabilistic rather than definite. Some people seem never to get drunk from Scotch even though they consume it in rather remarkable quantities. But Scotch whiskey would still be Scotch whiskey even if it does not make some people drunk, whereas it would not be Scotch if it were concocted in Hoboken. We must differentiate between the defining attributes for a category and those attributes that are commonly thought to be associated with a category because they often have been associated with it in the past.

The same is true for categories of people. The categories of "male" and "female" have certain defining criteria, mostly biological in nature. However, there are many other, primarily social attributes that are commonly thought to be associated with being male or female. For example, in Western cultures a man is supposed to be strong, energetic, independent, aggressive, etc. The fact that many men are weak, lazy, dependent, and very passive does not seem to interfere with the popularly held beliefs about what attributes are associated with being a male. (Perhaps the women's liberation movement will change these popular assumptions about sex roles.)

Social scientists call such popularly held assumptions about the attributes of social categories (i.e., social groups) *stereotypes*. Sex stereotypes refer to general beliefs about what men and women are like and how they ought to behave. Racial stereotypes reflect commonly held assumptions about the kinds of personality traits and behavioral dispositions members of a certain race exhibit. Such assumptions about attributes associated with membership in these social categories may be based on past experience with members of such categories or, more frequently, on information transmitted in socialization of children or by the mass media.

The use of the word "stereotype" often implies that popularly held beliefs about a group of people are always bad or unfavorable and also false. Neither is necessarily true. People usually have favorable stereotypes about the social category they belong to (e.g., "Americans are hard-working, intelligent, and fair") and sometimes even about some they do not belong to (e.g., the "sportsmanship" and "fairness" of the

English and the "efficiency" of the Germans). In addition, there may be stereotypes that are even true *on the average*. Maybe a greater percentage of Germans than French arrive on time for appointments? Since stereotypes can be based on past experience, they may reflect actual characteristics of groups of people. Considered in this perspective, stereotypes are important cognitive "crutches" for our information processing. They are cognitive inference mechanisms that allow us to make complex attributions and decisions on the basis of a few isolated cues. By virtue of identifying the group membership of a person, we quickly "know" a great deal about the person. Just as categorization in general provides perceptual readiness to deal with external stimuli, "accurate" stereotypes would enable us to predict personality traits and behavior dispositions for a person of whom we know little else than his membership in a certain social category.

Unfortunately, the great advantage of stereotypes (i.e., probabilistic inferences on the basis of little evidence) is also their greatest disadvantage. Since little or no proof is required once stereotypes are established, they are difficult to change. In addition, they are very easy and comfortable to use and may prevent people from actively searching for more complete information. In any case, they can only be true for the average or the general case and may be quite wrong in specific cases. However, the biggest problem is that stereotypes often can be quite false. Unfortunately, stereotypes seem to be rarely based on actual correspondence between membership in a social category and possession of specific attributes or dispositions. This seems to be particularly true for the stereotypes that members of one group, race, or nationality hold about members of other groups, races, or nationalities. Social psychologists believe that there is a general tendency for members of a group to maintain inflated positive beliefs about their own group (ingroup) and exaggerated negative beliefs about the members of other groups (outgroups). (See pp. 160–67 for a discussion of ingroups and outgroups.)

This tendency to glorify the ingroup and to derogate the outgroup is well demonstrated by the beliefs of one particular ingroup: Princeton undergraduates. In three studies conducted in 1933, 1951, and 1969, Princeton undergraduates were asked to describe a number of racial and national groups with adjectives selected from a list.[30] The nature of the stereotypes held about the various groups (Germans, English, Turks, Jews, Negroes, etc.) not only changed from 1933 to 1969, but the changes seemed to be related to the political relationships among the various groups. For example, the stereotypes of Germans and Japanese differed markedly depending on whether Germany and Japan were allies or enemies of the United States at the time of the study. This indicates that stereotypes do not depend so much on the actual characteristics of the group (e.g., on its national character) as on the relationship between groups.

The formation of highly negative stereotypes about outgroups is particularly prevalent in times of intergroup conflict. For example, the students at Kent State stereotyped the police and National Guard as "pigs" (i.e., brutal, coarse, and stupid subhuman animals), and the soldiers and police saw the students as "hippie radicals" (i.e., long-haired, dirty, foul-mouthed, sexually permissive, and violent ingrates). In some ways these two stereotypes are mirror images of each other. Both sides see the other as morally wrong, irrational, and dangerous.

Of course, such mirror images are not limited to students and police. During the height of the cold war, an American psychologist travelling in Russia found that many Russians believed that America was an aggressor, exploiter, and deluder of the American people, that the American people did not agree with their government, that American diplomats could not be trusted, and that America's policies were irrational. Sound at all familiar? Just exchange the word "Russian" for "American" and we have the American image of the USSR.[31] More recently, such mirror images of the enemy seem to have played a major role in the Vietnam war. Ralph K. White, a social psychologist, argues

Figure 4-3 These two mirror-image cartoons appeared in American and Soviet newspapers within four days of each other. Each cartoon accuses the other side of spying and of destroying the 1960 Geneva summit conference between Eisenhower and Khrushchev. *Left,* United Press International Photo; *right,* Wide World Photos.

that both Americans and the Vietcong had a "diabolical-enemy" image and a "virile-moral" self-image. Both sides thought the other was an aggressor that had to be stopped to prevent worse things from happening; both thought that the other was conducting a brutal and dirty war of terror, assassination, and torture. At the same time, both parties thought themselves to be virile and moral. They considered themselves to be the powerful, respected, courageous, honorable, and morally good protectors of peace, justice, and democracy.[32]

This example from the Vietnam war makes it clear why stereotypes play a major part in fostering aggression. Exaggerated positive self-images, especially of moral goodness, serve to justify many of our actions. "If I am such a good, law-abiding, morally upright person, anything I do must serve to protect the law, to provide justice, and to uphold the values dear to me." Similarly, the negative beliefs about our enemy justify our aggressing against him. "If he is such a scoundrel, he deserves to be wiped out or, at least, to take a severe beating." In this way stereotypes can serve to facilitate aggressive behavior instigated by anger or other situational factors.[33]

How do such stereotypes get started and how can they be changed? We shall see in later sections and chapters that the mere fact of competing with another person or being in conflict produces hostile attributions about the other's intentions and dispositions, which can develop into rigid negative stereotypes. One reason why this process of negative stereotyping is often irreversible (at least in the short-run) is that a checking of the stereotypical beliefs against reality (i.e., what the other person is really like or intends to do) often becomes impossible because communication breaks down between the persons or groups in conflict. This may lead to what has been called "autistic hostility." Conflict leads to hostility and stereotypes that reduce communication between the groups. This makes reality checking impossible, the stereotypes become more and more hostile, and the chances of communication become less and less.

At this point, we want to focus on a particular aspect of stereotype production and transmission—the role of mass media.

FOCUS
Stereotypes of Heroes and Villains

For a long time the villains in the mass media have been portrayed as dark-haired and dark-eyed, small in stature, and often as members of particular minority groups. Many critics have argued that, by such casting practices, the media produce or, at least, perpetuate stereotypes about the personality, trustworthiness, and moral character of the minority groups used to represent evil characters. A particularly interesting instance of this portrayal of heroes and villains occurred in the German mass media. The Nazi regime specifically used blond, blue-eyed actors to portray heroes in order to glorify its racial ideology. At the same time smallish, dark-haired, and dark-eyed actors were used to portray villains, who represented the inferiority and moral depravity of non-Germanic *Untermenschen*. Do the stereotypes produced by this casting practice still exist in Germany and can they be changed through different mass media content?

In a recent study, twenty-six subscribers to a newsletter of a local television station in Cologne, West Germany, were invited to come to the studio to preview some new TV movies. Upon arrival at the studio, these viewers were told that the station would like to have their opinion of actors who were being considered for major parts in future productions. They were shown slides of several actors and asked to evaluate them in terms of their personality as well as in terms of the roles that they would be suitable to fill. Some of these actors were blond and blue-eyed, while others were dark-haired and dark-eyed. As expected, the dark actors were seen as significantly more wicked, sly, calculating, heartless, amoral, and fraudulent than the blond actors, and they were thought to be much more suitable for roles as swindlers, thieves, pimps, frauds, and imposters. After these initial evaluations, the viewers were shown a number of TV movies in which the traditional casting procedures were reversed (i.e., the heroes in these movies were all short, dark-haired, and dark-eyed actors). After the movies, the subjects were again asked to evaluate some other actors for future productions and they were again shown slides of blond and dark actors. As predicted, there was a change in stereotypes after exposure to these counterstereotypical heroes and villains. Dark actors were seen in much less negative terms and were no longer different from blond actors in terms of their potential for being bad guys.

The same experiment was later conducted with German students, who had not been exposed to the Nazi propaganda. For the students, there was much less difference between the evaluations of the blond and dark actors to begin with. For them, too, there was a small change in the positive direction for the evaluation of the dark actors after they had seen the counterstereotypical films.[34]

Of course, this small experiment does not establish as a fact that mass media can produce as well as change stereotypes. However, a number of other investigators have shown that the mass media portrayal

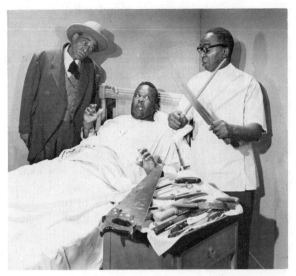

Figure 4-4 Although many Americans enjoyed the "Amos and Andy" television show during the 1950s, the program helped to establish and maintain white stereotypes about black Americans. United Press International photo.

of members of certain social groups, professions, or occupations may be responsible for building up stereotyped thinking in children and for reinforcing and perpetuating stereotyped ideas and incorrect generalizations.[35] For example, a recent study showed that the more frequently blacks were presented in positive roles in the media, the more favorably they were evaluated. Similarly, the more frequently whites were presented in negative roles, the less favorably they were evaluated.[36]

There are some signs that the media in America have become more aware of the powerful influence that their casting procedures may have on stereotypes.[37] There seems to be an effort lately to cast blacks in the roles of heroes and to try to avoid using exclusively Italian actors to portray underworld figures. However, the Saturday morning children's cartoons are another matter. Many of the villains still have slanted eyes or speak with a German or Russian accent.

MAKING INFERENCES
ABOUT CAUSES AND INTENTIONS

Stereotypes, as inferences about the stable attributes or characteristics of a group of people, supply us with an understanding of the causes of a person's behavior. If asked why there are so many Negroes on welfare, we can look to our stereotypes for an answer: "They're lazy and happy-go-lucky, you know." By telling us something about the stereotyped group's personality and behavioral inclinations, stereotypes help us answer one of the basic questions that we face in every social interaction: Why do people act the way they do? Consequently, stereotypes are part of a "naive" or "lay" psychology, which we as laymen use to explain and predict the behavior of others.

Understanding the causes of another's behavior, especially in face-to-face interaction, is necessary if we are to meaningfully interpret his actions and properly respond to them. For example, if someone hits you in the ribs, your response will depend to a great extent upon the perceived cause of the blow. In order to properly respond, you would need to know whether the person is habitually aggressive and prone to doing such things, whether you have angered him and he responded with an impulsive aggressive act, whether he meant it as a friendly poke, or whether it was just an unintentional jab. In short, in deciding upon an appropriate reaction you would go beyond the immediate act (i.e., the jab) and try to infer the causes and intentions that lay behind the behavior. The way that people go about discovering the causes of another's behavior has recently become a major concern of social psychologists, who refer to this area of study as *attribution theory*.

Let us return to our example of someone poking you in the ribs. If we look carefully at the information you would need in order to know how to react, we find that there are two different levels of attribution involved here. First, you need to know the *source* or *cause* of the jab: Did you bump into something or did someone strike you? If someone else is seen as the source, did he do it of his own free will or was he forced to hit you because of circumstances beyond his control? That is, was the cause located in him (i.e., internal) or did it originate in the environment (i.e., external)? Second, you have to ascertain the individual's *intentions:* Did he mean to hit you or someone else? Did he intend for the blow to hurt, or did he mean just to touch you lightly? In short, for you to fully understand someone's behavior, you as the recipient of his actions (i.e., as coactor with him) or as an observer would have to go beyond the immediate behavior and make inferences about the source and intention of his behavior. Once you have done this, you have answered the basic attributional question of "Why did he hit me?"

Source or Cause

In seeking out the sources or causes of another's behavior, we are searching for those relatively stable aspects of the person or the environment that dispose him to act in certain ways. Stable dispositions or in-variances make it possible for us to predict and to control our physical and nonphysical worlds. We recognize the invariances in the physical world rather easily as the size, shape, texture, mass, velocity, etc. of objects, and we turn to them in understanding why objects "behave" as they do. Why does a ball bounce? The reason lies in its shape and elasticity (i.e., its physical invariances or attributes). In the nonphysical world, we turn to enduring characteristics of people (e.g., their person-ality) and of situations (e.g., the difficulty of the task). The major prob-lem facing us as either coactors or observers of someone's behavior is weighing the relative importance of the internal and external causes (i.e., causal factors within the person and within the environment, respec-tively).[38]

How do we go about attributing the cause of a person's behavior to internal and/or external attributes? Harold Kelley, a social psychologist at UCLA, suggests that two different types of situations have to be dis-tinguished. In the first type of situation, we have information about the person based on many different observations of him. In the second, we have information based upon only one observation of his behavior. In our search for the causes of his behavior we can apply the *covariation principle* in the first situation and the *discounting principle* in the second.

Let us first look at the covariation principle. It states that "an effect is attributed to the one of its possible causes with which, over time, it covaries."[39] In other words, when we have information about an effect (i.e., someone's behavior) from several observations, we attribute its origin to the cause that is always present whenever the effect occurs. For example, we observe several small boys playing and notice that Billy frequently comes home with a bloody nose. One possible internal cause for this effect is that Billy is genetically predisposed to nosebleeds. But we note that he never gets them when he plays alone, rather only when he plays with other boys. Since nosebleeds and playing with other boys occur simultaneously (i.e., they covary), this suggests that the cause is not internal, but rather external. The cause probably lies in the other boys (e.g., they hit Billy) or, at least, in Billy's interacting with them (e.g., he is more active when he plays with them than when he is alone).

In the second type of situation, where we have information from only one observation of the effect, we apply the discounting principle: "The role of a given cause in producing a given effect is discounted if other plausible causes are also present."[40] Here Kelley means that we are less sure of the cause of an event if there are several likely causes. To the extent that there are many plausible causes, we cannot confi-dently arrive at an attribution. Let us return to that painful jab in the ribs. Imagine that you are riding on a crowded bus, and suddenly you are hit in the ribs by the guy standing next to you. How should you interpret this? There are several plausible causes, albeit some might be more plausible than others. He might be trying to mug you for your small change, or he may have been pushed into you by the crowd. In this instance, you cannot distinguish between the plausible internal and external causes. Of course, if just you and he were on the bus together, you would be more confident that the cause was internal, especially if the bus were standing still.

Of course, the discounting and covariance principles are not always easily and straightforwardly applied. For one thing, another person's behavior is often the result of both internal and external causes, and it is difficult for us to disentangle their effects. In such cases, the attribution process can become quite complicated.[41] For another thing, human observers are fallible, and there seem to be certain biases that distort the attribution process. For example, people tend to minimize situational factors, while maximizing personal factors. This is especially true when we are trying to ascertain the causes of someone else's behavior. People tend to attribute the causes of their own behavior to situational forces, while attributing the behavior of others in the same situation to personal characteristics.[42] If we hit someone in the ribs, we see the cause lying in the fact that the bus is crowded. But if someone hits us, we tend to see the cause as lying in his aggressive and pushy personality. Similarly, the Kent State students, as observers, attributed the soldiers' firing to their brutality or mental condition ("I thought the soldiers had gone insane. . . ."), while the troopers, as actors, attributed their action to their endangered position ("He [her husband] told me they fired because the students were coming after them, coming for their guns. People are calling my husband a murderer; my husband is not a murderer. He was afraid.")

This situational bias may be due to the different types of information that are available to us as actors and observers. As actors, we know about our personal characteristics, which we carry with us from one situation to the next. We know that we are not the type of guy who goes around slugging other people in the ribs. In addition, our attention is focused on the situation, since it is the new and salient source of information for us. Our personality is a constant factor in our observation of our own behavior, while the situation is a variable factor. In our perception, changes in our behavior are associated (i.e., covary) with changes in the situation. As observers, however, we may see several different people acting in the same situation. Now the situation is constant, while people are the variable factor. Consequently, our attention is drawn away from the situation and is focused upon possible personal attributes that might explain why particular individuals are acting as they do. The question becomes "Among the thirty people on the bus, why did that particular guy hit me in the side?" and the answer becomes "Because he is an aggressive SOB."

Another bias is a tendency to attribute positive, beneficial outcomes to our own efforts and negative, harmful outcomes to other people's.[43] Obviously, such an attribution bias protects us from recognizing bad or undesirable aspects of ourselves. For example, in one study, subjects were required to teach young children some arithmetic materials. For all subjects, the children did poorly on the first set of problems. Then the subjects taught them a second set. For half of the subjects, the students improved their performance on the second problem set, but for the other half of the subjects, they continued to perform poorly. When asked to account for their pupil's performance, the instructor-subjects whose pupil improved credited themselves for his improvement, while those whose pupil performed poorly tended to blame the pupil.[44]

As we hinted earlier, our reaction to a person's behavior depends on whether we attribute the cause to internal or external factors. We may be more likely to respond aggressively to someone when we believe that he personally is the cause of a frustrating or painful experience. However, if we see that the cause lies outside of him and that he has no control over it, then we are less likely to respond aggressively. In this case, we may perceive him merely as a "tool" and not as the cause of the frustration or pain. However, the attributional biases, which we just discussed, tend to focus our attributions upon personal, internal causes rather than on environmental, external causes. Consequently, these biases work in the direction of facilitating aggression.

Intentions

The idea of intention is closely related (although not identical) to the distinction between internal and external causes. This is so because impersonal, environmental causes do not involve intention. We do not speak of a rock as *intending* to roll down the hill and hit us (unless we are paranoid)! Intention implies that a purpose lies behind the activity, and it refers to instances where a person tries to cause a particular effect.[45] When we say, "He intended to hit me," we mean that he had a choice among his behaviors, he had the ability to carry out his act, and he knew what the outcome would be. Similarly, when we say, "He did not intend to hit me," we mean (1) he had no choice, but was forced by circumstances, (2) he meant another effect such as lightly touching us, or (3) he did not realize that a particular effect would result from his action. That is, harming us was an unanticipated effect or an accident (e.g., he intended to leave the bus and while doing so he jabbed us in the ribs). Thus, intention involves our attribution of freedom of choice, ability, and knowledge to the actor.[46]

What factors influence the attribution of intention to a person's behaviors? Of course, we have to compare the importance of internal and external causes. But merely deciding that the cause is internal is not sufficient for attributing intent. However, the perception that the person is "trying" to obtain a goal is crucial to attributing intent. We know a person is "trying" when he works hard (i.e., expends energy), continues at the task over long periods of time and on different occasions, and when he employs various means that all lead to the same end state. We are especially likely to attribute intent when there are plausible reasons for the person's *not* striving for an effect, yet he continues towards the original goal.[47] For example, there might be external causes that would lead us to believe that he would not perform the act (e.g., strong punishment). If he performs the behavior despite these external inhibitors, we are particularly sure that he intended the behavior.

Closely related to this last point is the assumption that people intend to perform behaviors that are beneficial to them. We are more likely to attribute intent to someone when he performs an act that has positive outcomes and less likely when the results are harmful to him. In addition, there is a bias towards attributing intent when we perceive the person's behavior as personally relevant to us.[48] When we are the object of the person's behavior or, at least, when we are affected by him, then we are more likely to see his behavior as intended than when a third person is affected by his performance. Finally, acts that are low in social desirability or are "out of role" for the person are also likely to be considered intended. For example, if a person applies for a job that requires someone who is introverted and the applicant acts in an extroverted manner, we are likely to see his behavior as intended and are likely to believe that he is truly an extrovert.[49]

We can summarize this discussion in an example. Imagine a mystery story where the principal characters are a rich aunt and her poor nephew, who is a policeman. We would know that the nephew intends to murder his aunt when he walks fifty miles to town in a blizzard to buy a gun, a bottle of poison, and several sticks of dynamite and when he employs these weapons against her on several different occasions. Of course, we would be particularly insistent that he is trying to kill his aunt, if we were his aunt!

Holding a person responsible for an event is closely associated with attributing intention to his actions. For example, in assessing criminal responsibility for a deed, the law pays particular attention to whether the accused intended the crime. In our own thinking about responsibility for both good and bad deeds, intention plays an increasingly important role as we become older.[50] Young children blame another child for a bad deed regardless of whether he intended the outcome or not. In addition, children focus upon the seriousness of the event in assigning responsibility. For example, they blame a child who broke an expensive vase more than one who broke a cheap vase. This tendency may not be limited to children alone, however, since there is some evidence that adults blame a person more for a major accident than a minor one.[51]

Another group of studies suggests that we hold others responsible for the bad things in life that happen to them. Subjects in a series of laboratory studies who are forced to watch the suffering of an "innocent victim" or to cause him to suffer by delivering electroshocks tend to derogate the victim, especially when the subjects are helpless to alter the victim's fate. Both observers and perpetrators see the victim as deserving his suffering.[52] Such "blaming the victim" is not limited to "artificial" laboratory settings. Consider the public reaction to the Kent State killings. About 60 percent of the people questioned in a Gallup poll shortly after Kent State blamed the demonstrating students, and only 11 percent blamed the National Guardsmen.[53] Certainly President Nixon expressed similar sentiments in saying, "When dissent turns to violence, it *invites* tragedy." A Kent motel clerk told a *Newsweek* reporter, "You can't really help but kind of think they've been asking for it and finally got it." Thus, while some people expressed regret, most people felt the students got what they had coming.

Consider another instance, this time a 1969 survey of the attitudes of Americans towards poverty and the poor.[54] Over half of the people interviewed saw poverty as the result of some flaw in poor people's personalities (e.g., "they do not work hard enough") and less than a quarter saw structural reasons (e.g., low wages, discrimination) as important in causing poverty.

One possible reason for why an aggressor might derogate his victim is to protect his own positive self-image. Since people find it unpleasant to believe that they would hurt someone unnecessarily, they see their victim as deserving his fate. This view is held by dissonance theorists who argue that the cognitive dissonance aroused by the perception of having committed an act inconsistent with our self-concept will often be reduced by justifying the act through devaluing the victim, minimizing his pain, and believing we were obligated to commit the aggressive act. The dissonance explanation suggests that a person would feel more compelled to derogate his victim the more positive his self-image.[55]

As another explanation for this "blaming the victim," Melvin Lerner suggests that "for their own security, if for no other reason, people want to believe they live in a just world where people get what they deserve. Any evidence of undeserved suffering threatens this belief. The observer then will attempt to reestablish justice. One way of accomplishing this is by acting to compensate the victim; another is by persuading himself that the victim deserved to suffer."[56] While not disagreeing with Lerner's empirical results, other researchers have questioned this explanation and have offered alternatives involving notions of "equity" or "distributive justice."[57]

Conclusion

Although our first reaction to a jab in the ribs may be an almost reflexive response, how we appraise the cause of the jab may either facilitate or inhibit our initial reaction. Throughout our discussion of attribution, we have talked as if the individual consciously and deliberately goes through a complicated weighing and sifting of evidence before reaching a conclusion about the causes of another's behavior. Indeed, we sometimes do this. However, most of the time these processes occur very quickly. We rapidly decide in a semiconscious fashion whether the jab was intended or not, and act accordingly.

Regardless of whether our attributions are the result of a long and deliberate appraisal or of a hasty judgment, our believing that a person intended to harm us probably makes us angry and apt to respond in kind. The attribution of intention means that the frustrator or aggressor is seen as knowing what the consequences of his action would be for us and yet as continuing to pursue them. Thus, his actions are seen as personal attacks against us, and we feel justified in our anger and aggression. Indeed, a few experiments show that perceiving another's aggressive intentions is likely to instigate counteraggression, even if the other person does not carry out his intended aggression.[58] Similarly, if we hold the person responsible for his actions, then it is easier to aggress against him. He is seen as deserving our abuse. In short, the attribution of intention and responsibility to a person for his actions, which have or threaten to harm or frustrate us, directs our aggression against him. Of course, the attribution that the act was unintended mitigates against an aggressive response. For example, we are unlikely to aggress against people who are seen as mentally ill or as physically immature (i.e., children), even though they may frustrate or harm us, because they are not considered to have control over their behavior. This does not necessarily mean we will not be angry, but these attributions may inhibit the direct expression of anger and aggression against the person. He is not seen as responsible for our suffering and, therefore, not deserving of our wrath.

This attribution analysis also helps us to explain why nonarbitrary frustrations are less likely to lead to aggression than are arbitrary frustrations (see pp. 58–63). Nonarbitrary frustrations are often attributed to causes beyond the frustrator's control. Therefore, they are not seen as personal attacks against us and/or they are believed justified. For example, we feel that a policeman is only doing his job when he stops us from driving through a red light. His action may be frustrating, but it is seen as originating in his role rather than in his personality. In addition, we might believe that we have done something to the frustrator (e.g., harmed him) and, therefore, we deserve his attack.[59] Thus, attribution processes may either facilitate or inhibit aggression.

PERCEPTION OF EMOTIONS

In most encounters with other people it is not sufficient to attribute dispositions and intentions to account for their observed behaviors. We also have to be able to infer their present emotional state in order to more completely understand their reaction to a specific situation and to be able to predict what they will do next. Obviously, this information is important in helping us plan our next moves and reactions in the encounter. Consider again our example of someone hitting us in the ribs. Our attribution of the causes of his behavior and the further consequences will probably vary tremendously with the type of emotional expression we see in the perpetrator's face. If he fumes with anger, obviously directed at us, we are much less likely to attribute the jab to external causes, and we will probably prepare to defend ourselves from further aggressive acts. But if we find the person staring pensively off into space, we are much less inclined to attribute his behavior to him personally and to fear further attacks. On the other hand, if the guy is grinning broadly at us, we may infer that he wanted to tease us and we may respond in kind. Consequently, an accurate assessment of the emotional state of our interaction partners will not only enable us to make better sense of the causes and intentions behind their activities, but will also enable us to better adjust our own behavior and plans to the situational contingencies.

Before we turn to a specific examination of the role of emotional expression in instigating and inhibiting aggression, we have to take a closer look at the process whereby the expression of emotional states enables us to infer a person's reaction to a situation or an event and to predict his further behavior. In the last chapter emotion was conceptualized as a cognitive appraisal of a situation or event and the organism's ability to cope with such environmental contingencies (pp. 67–76). In addition, most theorists attribute motivational properties to emotion, indicating that specific emotions can energize specific types of behaviors. The emotion of anger, for example, was conceptualized as a motivational antecedent to aggression. Although the factors that determine whether a person will experience one emotion rather than another are still quite unclear, it seems that three dimensions are involved: (1) the person's appraisal of whether the event is good or bad, or helpful or damaging for his chances of reaching his goals; (2) whether he expected the event or not; and (3) whether he thinks he can cope with the resulting situation or not.

If we know something about the way in which an event affects a person in terms of these three dimensions, we are able to predict to some extent what kind of emotion the person will mostly experience. Of course, this also works backwards. If we know what kind of emotion he is experiencing, we can infer whether the event causing the emotional reaction was appraised as good or bad, whether he expected it, and whether he thinks he can cope with it. This possibility makes the assessment of emotional states a very important part of attributional processes. It supplies us with information about how to chart our own behavior in reaction to the other person's behavior and emotions.

Exactly how do we infer someone else's emotions? Of course, in many situations people let us know quite explicitly how they feel about us, other people, and events. In most languages there is no lack of colorful words for the description of feeling states. Even if people do not explicitly characterize their emotion, their verbal utterances often give many clues about their affective state.[60] A large number of nonverbal indicators of emotion such as facial expression, voice quality, body movement, etc. are even more important than verbal or linguistic cues.[61] Some people even feel that nonverbal signals of affect are more accurate and reliable than verbal cues because in many societies the overt expression of certain affects are discouraged and because we often attempt to hide our emotions from our interaction partners in order to keep them from knowing our true intentions or reactions. However, since we have less control over nonverbal behaviors, they often "leak" our intentions and reactions.[62] Such nonverbal "leakage" of affect may be particularly important in the assessment of emotions directly relevant to aggressive behavior, for in many societies the expression of anger is considered inappropriate and may be repressed in many interactions. Since repressed anger may still lead to more subtle, indirect forms of aggression at a later time, it seems important to be able to infer such emotional states from nonverbal "leakage."

Researchers in the booming field of nonverbal communication have collected a lot of evidence showing that observers can accurately judge many emotions from a number of nonverbal cues. The human face is a primary locus of emotional expression, although it is not the only source of information about emotions. As we saw earlier (pp. 64–66), some theorists assume that the different facial expressions for emotions are genetically and evolutionarily determined, rather than learned. The available evidence shows that observers from very different cultures, ranging from tribes in New Guinea to advanced Western cultures, interpret photographs of facial expressions in very similar terms.[63] Although the evidence is not quite as clear-cut yet for vocal expression, there is little doubt that people can identify emotional states on the basis of vocal cues such as intonation and loudness of voice as well as pauses and rate of speech alone (i.e., without knowing the verbal content of the message).[64] It is quite possible that the vocal communication of affect is also based on culturally universal, innate mechanisms such as relationships between specific physiological arousal patterns and the function of our vocal organs.[65]

Interpersonal attitudes or behavioral dispositions such as dominance or friendliness are often communicated through nonverbal cues. We seem to communicate friendliness by sitting close, leaning forward, smiling, and maintaining eye contact with our interaction partner.[66] Such behavioral dispositions or interpersonal attitudes often transcend particular situations in that they become stable personality traits that predispose a person to act in a particular way across many different situations. Such stable personality characteristics can also be communicated through nonverbal cues such as facial expressions, body posture and gait, and voice quality.[67] Such phenomena have been studied quite extensively in an area with a venerable history in social psychology—person perception. Unfortunately, most of this research is not directly relevant to our present concern. Although we have all heard people being described in terms of having "an aggressive chin" or "an aggressive voice," such phenomena have not been studied very systematically in person perception research. In terms of how nonverbal signals of emotional arousal can serve to instigate or inhibit aggression, we shall focus on one nonverbal phenomenon—eye contact—which has received some attention in terms of its relevance for aggression.

FOCUS
To Stare or Not To Stare

Pulling up to a red traffic light, you notice a young lady on a somewhat dilapidated motorscooter on the inside lane. As soon as you have stopped, this young lady turns her head and starts staring at you with an impassive, neutral expression until the light turns green. What would you do? Chances are that you, like most people, would zoom through the intersection somewhat faster than usual. Actually, this was the result of an interesting field experiment conducted by social psychologist Phoebe Ellsworth and her collaborators.[68] They had both male and female experimenters stare or not stare at male and female drivers in front of red traffic lights both from a motorscooter and from the street corner. It was found that people who were stared at crossed the intersection almost one-and-a-half seconds faster than people who were not stared at. The authors suggest two explanations for this startling result. One possibility is "that gazing at a person's face is a demand for a response and in a situation where there is no appropriate response, tension will be evoked and the subject will be motivated to leave the situation." A second possibility is "that a stare is generally perceived as a signal of hostile intent and elicits avoidance (or counter-attack, in some circumstances)."

The second explanation is very much in line with systematic observations on the role of the stare in animal societies. Ethologists have found persistently that stares are used as signals of threat. Gaze aversion, however, seems to function generally as an appeasement gesture by which the loser in a threat encounter manifests his submission to the winner in order to avoid an actual physical attack. The universal threat value of a stare has been established even for cross-species encounters. The psychologist Ralph Exline had a laboratory assistant direct stares at monkeys in cages. The monkeys responded with excited outbursts, which ended only when the laboratory assistant averted his gaze.[69] In human interaction, a persistent stare also seems to be interpreted as threat and gaze aversion as a sign of submission (as in staring contests among children). Similarly, many ethologists have speculated about the role of gaze aversion as an appeasement gesture in human aggression. Unfortunately, many of these discussions are highly speculative, and little is known about the actual effectiveness of gaze aversion as an inhibitor of aggressive behavior.

This is all the more regrettable because alternative explanations of the function of eye contact and aversion in aggressive encounters are possible. It can be argued that aversion of the eyes "dehumanizes" the victim in an aggressive encounter and makes it easier for the aggressor to treat his victim as an object. Consequently, his inhibitions against hurting another human being are lessened (see the discussion of de-individuation in the following chapter).[70]

These competing predictions on the role of eye contact in aggression were tested by Phoebe Ellsworth and her collaborators in an ambitious laboratory experiment.[71] The design of the experiment closely followed the general type of aggression experiment described on pp. 68–69. We find the usual experimental stooge who angers the subject or does not anger him, after which the subject is given a chance to administer electroshocks to the confederate. The important twist in this study is that the gaze of the victim at the aggressor's face was systematically varied. In one condition, each time after receiving a warning signal that a shock would follow, the victim established eye contact with the subject. In the second condition, the victim glanced at the subject very quickly and then cast his eyes down until the shock was received. In the final experimental condition, the victim sometimes established eye contact and at other times averted his gaze.

The results showed that the eye contact manipulation did not seem to affect those subjects who had not been angered initially by the victim. However, angered subjects gave fewer shocks to victims who consistently looked at them than to victims who averted their gaze. These results seem to represent an inhibition of aggression by eye contact rather than increased aggression due to gaze aversion. These results support neither the "dehumanization" nor the "gaze aversion as appeasement gesture" hypotheses, since in the gaze aversion conditions there was not less aggression. The results may be best explained by the notion that the subjects perceived eye contact as a threat, which served to inhibit further aggression. However, even this explanation is placed in doubt by the fact that those victims who intermittently established eye contact and averted their gaze were shocked more at those times when they established eye contact. The authors decided that the results could be explained overall by assuming that eye contact served as an aversive stimulus or negative reinforcer for the subjects. This led them to shock more in the intermittent eye contact condition in order to force their victim to look away and to shock less in the consistent eye contact condition because the aggressor gave up. The aggressor avoided his victim's gaze altogether by refraining from further attacks.

Obviously, the role of eye contact and gaze aversion in aggression is anything but clear. The effects of eye contact are rendered even more complex by the fact that the interpretation of this nonverbal signal may differ very much from one person to the next. One person may interpret eye contact as a threat, but another may see it as a plea on the part of the victim. Also, eye contact cannot be treated in isolation, since the type of facial expression accompanying eye contact probably has an influence on the inferences about the meaning of eye contact. In addition, it is still not clear whether the interpretation of eye contact as a threat or a plea will lead to an inhibition or further instigation of aggression. For example, when an aggressor perceives eye contact as a threat, it may make him even more angry and lead to further aggression if he thinks he can cope with the threats. But the attribution of threat may inhibit aggression if the aggressor fears retaliation. Similarly, pleading eye contact can instigate further aggression if the aggressor feels the victim deserves punishment or if the pleading by the victim serves as a positive reinforcer. Then again, pleading can inhibit further aggression if it arouses empathy with the victim's suffering as well as guilt or shame in the aggressor.[72]

Pain cues from the victim seem to have both inhibitory and excitatory properties for aggression. A number of studies using college students have shown that pain cues on the part of the victim decrease the strength of aggression, independently of whether the aggressors were angered or not.[73] However, another experiment with juvenile delinquents reported that viewing a movie in which the victim displayed strong pain cues led to more aggression for angered subjects than did viewing a movie in which aggressive behavior was not accompanied by pain cues. These findings were reversed for nonangered juvenile delinquents.[74]

There does not seem to be a simple relationship between pain cues and aggression. Much depends on the nature of these pain cues and how they are interpreted. Are they seen as giving rise to fear or to anger? The significance of pain cues differs very much if we assume from them that our victim is ready to retaliate or is cowering in fear. Another important aspect is the nature of the aggressor's arousal. If he is a sadist or seeks revenge, pain cues may be satisfying to him and may spur him on to even more violent actions. But if the aggressor acts impulsively in the heat of anger, pain cues may dissipate his emotion and make him feel shame or regret. This is most likely when the victim's suffering produces empathy in the aggressor. Such empathy reactions are probably more likely if the aggressor is similar to his victim and has been in similar situations before himself. Little empathy is to be expected if the victim is considered as something less than human, as is often the case in wartime. Finally, whether the person acts aggressively or not would depend on whether pain cues aroused guilt or shame in the aggressor. This depends on the kind of socialization process he has gone through and the degree of internalization of social norms against aggression. Unfortunately, norms may work the other way around. For example, gang members may feel shame if their victim's pain cues inhibit them from further beating a member of a hostile juvenile gang.

This short discussion of the role of the perception of emotion in aggressive encounters could do little more than show the immense complexity of these processes. We can summarize by saying that our inferences of others' emotional states help us to judge how others appraise persons, situations, and events and how they will probably react to these appraisals. Such attributions are made frequently on the basis of nonverbal cues such as facial expression, eye contact, body movement and posture, and voice quality. Whether the perception of emotions instigates or inhibits aggression depends largely on a complex array of factors including our prediction of the possible reaction of the other, our own appraisal of these possible reactions (i.e., are they appropriate to the situation, do they relate positively or negatively to our own goals, can we cope with them?), as well as other variables such as the nature of an aggressor's arousal, his relationship to the victim, the degree to which he experiences empathy, and whether he has been socialized to feel guilty for aggression.

The perception of emotion is an important regulator in aggressive encounters, and if it is impossible to monitor or infer the emotions of others, we are deprived of important signals to the intentions and possible behaviors of other people. Unfortunately, the accurate assessment of emotions becomes difficult in cases of collective behavior like the Kent State shootings. Since there were many people on both sides, it would have been quite impossible to infer the emotions of all of them. In addition, since the Guardsmen were acting under the command of an officer, it would have been his emotions that were particularly important to monitor. However, given the distance between the soldiers and the students and that the troops were wearing gasmasks (see Fig. 4-2), it was impossible for the students to infer the soldiers' emotional state. Similarly, the distances made it difficult for the soldiers to monitor the expressions of different students and may have lessened the inhibitory effects of contact with and pain cues from their victims.

ATTITUDES AND PREJUDICE

So far in our discussion we have focused mainly on the "intellectual" processes of gathering and interpreting information and how these processes can be biased by motivational, experiental, and emotional factors. But people are not just cold data-processing machines. Besides gathering and interpreting information, people also evaluate objects and events. They react emotionally to stimuli and have feelings of liking or disliking. Social psychologists refer to these learned evaluative reactions to objects as *attitudes*. While attitudes are tendencies to evaluate objects or classes of objects on a single dimension such as good-bad, favorable-unfavorable, or positive-negative, they are also thought of as having three components.[75] First, the *affective* component refers to emotional reactions (e.g., anger, hate, love, etc.) as well as verbal statements about affects (e.g., "I get sick to my stomach just thinking about those dirty hippies"). Second, the *cognitive* component consists of beliefs about the characteristics of the attitude-object (e.g., "those troublemakers have long hair, use bad language, and destroy property"). Finally, the *conative* component pertains to tendencies to behave in favorable or unfavorable ways towards the attitude-object, particularly in terms of approaching or avoiding the object (e.g., "one thing they ought to do is, they ought to chase them all out if they don't get their hair cut and cleaned up"). In short, attitudes are emotional reactions to, beliefs about, and behavioral tendencies towards objects or classes of objects.[76]

For our purposes, we may define *prejudice* as a negative attitude toward a person based on his membership in a particular social group.[77] The prejudiced person holds a negative attitude toward another person solely because he is a member of an outgroup. As an attitude, prejudice involves affective reactions to (i.e., disliking), beliefs about (i.e., stereotypes), and behavioral tendencies towards (i.e., discrimination) the attitude-object. In addition, prejudice serves the same psychological functions as other attitudes.[78] In order for a person to receive social approval from his group, he has to espouse its antiblack sentiments.[79] Or, antiblack attitudes may make the exploitation of blacks psychologically easier for an individual. While most sociological theories of prejudice highlight such *adjustive-utilitarian functions* of attitudes, most psychological theories focus on *ego-defensive functions*. Many psychologists see prejudice as the projection of unacceptable impulses onto the members of outgroups. For example, whites see blacks as hypersexual athletes, and this may reflect their fears of their own sexual impulses.[80] Prejudice often serves the *knowledge function* as well by providing people with conspiratorial worldviews. Blacks, Jews, and communists are seen as the sources of all evil in the world, and "if the world were only rid of them, things would be better." Finally, prejudice has *value-expressive functions* in that people can establish a self-identity by expressing their prejudices. In stating their opposition to particular groups of people, they reinforce their own self-concept as a moral and upright citizen.

This functional analysis of prejudice suggests that it may be particularly difficult to change prejudicial attitudes because they serve more than one function. In order for us to change someone's attitudes, we have to supply him with a new attitude that performs the old attitude's function(s) as well as or better than the old attitude. But when the old attitude serves many psychological functions, it is extremely difficult to find a new attitude that will be more "efficient" than the old.

Prejudice is particularly important in the discussion of aggression because it is an attitude shared by large numbers of people and learned as part of the person's socialization. Widespread social consensus gives validity to the individual's prejudice. He believes that his attitudes are right and proper because so many other people think the same as he does on the matter. Of course, consensus implies that he will often have social support if he decides to act out his prejudice (e.g., discriminate). Also, because prejudices are tied to the core cultural values and are learned simultaneously with these values, they take on a moral "givenness." They are felt to be eternal truths about the world and to be utterly natural. Consequently, they may serve as guides to a person's behavior. As a part of the core cultural values, prejudice legitimizes and even demands the selection of particular people as targets for aggression (e.g., "the only good Indian is a dead Indian").

Implicit throughout our discussion of attitudes is the premise that attitudes cause behavior. Behavioral tendencies are assumed to be intimately tied to our attitudes. Knowing how a policeman feels about student demonstrators should tell us something about how he will act when confronted by dissenters. Common wisdom and experience seem to verify this assumption. For example, during the weeks preceding the Kent State incident, government officials across the country expressed hostility towards student demonstrators. Governor Rhodes of Ohio called them worse than "nightriders," "brown shirts," and "communists," and he promised to eradicate them; President Nixon referred to them as "bums"; and Vice President Agnew intoned, "We can, however, afford to separate them [student radicals] from our society with no more regret than we should feel over discarding rotten apples from a barrel."[81] These pronouncements from on high implicitly legitimized and encouraged violence against dissenters. Before and after the shootings at Kent State, similar sentiments were echoed by Guardsmen and civilians alike: "Should have shot 100 of them." "It's a shame it had to take killings to do it, but all those kids were some place they shouldn't have been." "These guys are supposed to be going to college to learn something. What are they doing? Burning down buildings. Locking up teachers. You can't turn on TV without seeing them do something. Shoot." "It's about time we showed the bastards who's in charge."[82] Kent State seems to be one case where actions matched attitudes.

A variety of laboratory studies confirm these impressions about the importance of attitudes in facilitating aggression. These studies show that when a person is reinforced or watches someone else who is reinforced for verbal aggression, he is more likely to later physically aggress (i.e., electroshock) against a victim.[83] For example, in a recent experiment subjects were reinforced for selecting aggressive (e.g., the word "violent"), neutral (e.g., "plastics"), or "helping" (e.g., "cooperation") words before being placed in the usual aggression situation. When tested for aggression, the "aggression word" subjects were more aggressive than either the "neutral" or "helpfulness word" subjects.[84] These studies suggest that the verbalization of hostility, including "innocuous" aggressive jokes, serves as a cue for physical aggression and thereby increases the probability of aggression. In the short run it may be true that "Sticks and stones may break my bones, but names will never hurt me." But, in the long run, words may lead to sticks and stones.

However, experience also tells us that people do not always act in accordance with their sentiments (as, "Don't do as I do, do as I say"). Attitudes are not always good predictors of behavior. A classic example of this is R. T. LaPierre's experience of travelling across the United States in 1933 with a Chinese couple. During their trip, they stopped at 67 hotels and motels and at 184 restaurants and were refused service only once. Six months later, LaPierre sent letters to these same establishments asking them whether they would accept Chinese guests. Only one of the 251 managers answered "yes" (and this response was "accompanied by a chatty letter describing the nice visit she had had with a Chinese gentleman and his sweet wife during the previous summer").[85] Obviously, there was a clear discrepancy between their written attitudes and actual behavior. Two recent reviews of the literature examining the relationship between attitudes and behavior concluded that the evidence for the relationship is extremely weak.[86] These reviewers suggest that even if we know a person is prejudiced against blacks, we cannot predict with certainty how he will actually behave when faced with a black family moving in next door.

There are several possible interpretations of these studies that find a weak or nonexistent relationship between attitudes and actions.[87] First, maybe attitudes really cause behavior, but psychologists have been measuring the attitudes improperly. Attitudes are usually measured via paper-and-pencil tests that tap very broad and general attitudes. For example, albeit an extreme one, a person might be asked to agree or disagree with the statement "I dislike Negroes." That is a very abstract statement, since it is not tied to any particular social relationship or situation (e.g., Negroes as cooks, servants, friends, neighbors, doctors, or relatives). However, behaviors involve actions in very specific situations towards a very specific person. Consequently, there might be too much "slippage" between the general attitude measured and the specific behavior observed.

Second, perhaps psychologists are measuring the wrong attitude. In a particular situation many different attitudes might be causing the person's behavior. Consequently, a measure of prejudice might not relate to behavior because other attitudes are more potent. For example, one of LaPierre's restaurant owners might have served the Chinese couple in order to have avoided an unpleasant "scene." His negative attitude towards creating a scene might have been stronger than his antipathies towards Chinese. In other words, there might be competing motivations or attitudes that take precedence in a situation.[88]

Third, and closely related to the first two points, is the possibility that a person's attitudes are overpowered by the social norms in the situation (i.e., a person's beliefs about how others expect him to behave). A person may refuse service to blacks despite his generally liberal attitudes because he believes that the other whites present would disapprove of nondiscriminatory behavior. Of course, it works the other way around, too. He might refrain from expressing his hostility on account of the prevailing liberal norms[89] (see Chapter 5 for discussion of norms and conformity).

Fourth, we might be measuring the correct attitudes, but people may not be candidly answering our questions. This does not necessarily mean that they are lying. They may misperceive their own feelings in an unconscious attempt to present a favorable image of themselves to the researchers. The overt expression of prejudice is now considered crude, especially among northern college students who are the subjects in most of these studies. In compliance with the prevailing liberal atmosphere, the subjects present themselves as tolerant and unprejudiced. Thus, they may score as "unprejudiced" on the attitude scale, and then their measured attitudes do not predict their behavior when they later discriminate against blacks.

Recent studies suggest that attitudes do predict behavior, but we need subtle and unobtrusive measures and we must consider the specific behavioral situation (e.g., norms, competing motivations, presence of other people).[90] Before ending our discussion of attitudes and prejudice, we should briefly look at another important aspect of the attitude-behavior relationship. Not only may attitudes cause behavior, but the process may also work in reverse. Jabbing someone in the ribs may make us dislike him! Earlier we mentioned that observers and perpetrators of aggressive acts against an innocent victim may end up derogating (i.e., disliking) their victim. Similarly, if we benefit someone whom we feel initially neutral towards, we start to like him as a result of our kind deed. In sum, people may change their attitudes to correspond to their behaviors.[91] However, attitude change following a behavior is not inevitable. It seems to be limited to instances where the actor believes he had a *choice* between various actions (e.g., he could or could not harm a victim). If he perceives that he was "forced" to act as he did either out of fear of punishment or in anticipation of rewards, then his attitudes do not change.

This has important implications for the future performance of a behavior, since we have shown that people tend to act in correspondence with their attitudes. For example, imagine that we neither like nor dislike a person and that we later physically or verbally harm him. Let us further assume that the situation is rather ambiguous and that we feel that our behavior was not constrained by external events (i.e., we had a choice). Consequently, we are likely to derogate and dislike our victim. Our new negative attitude increases the probability that we shall later aggress against him. We dislike him now, so we might go out of our way to injure him in the future!

SUMMARY

Aggression seems to be partially determined by a variety of factors external to the individual's physiology and psychology. That is, environmental events seem to instigate motivational and physiological processes leading up to aggression. Of course, an important aspect of the environment is "other people." In this chapter, and in the following chapter, we ask the social psychological question of what are the factors in human *interaction* that lead to aggression?

As a partial answer to our question, we discussed several social psychological processes involved in our gleaning and interpreting information from our social environment. A common theme to this discussion was the importance of *categorizing* social stimuli. To a great extent, how we react to a person depends upon whether we categorize him and his actions as those of a "friend" or a "foe." Labeling someone or his behaviors as "friendly" inhibits aggression, while categorizing him or his actions as "unfriendly" facilitates aggressive responses.

Under the topic of *social perception,* we saw how the processes of *response salience* and *response disposition* make the perception of aggression-eliciting stimuli more or less likely. For example, a person's momentary need-state may heighten his sensitivity to aggressive cues in the environment. More enduring psychological attitudes (e.g., prejudice) may have similar consequences. We argued in the previous chapter that even if a tendency to aggress exists in terms of motivation, its expression depends on whether or not there are *external cues* that may trigger aggressive responses. Thus, those perceptual processes that increase a person's sensitivity to aggressive cues also increase the likelihood that he will behave aggressively.

Stereotypes refer to culturally based beliefs about the characteristics and behaviors of groups of people. As such, stereotypes provide us with ready-made perceptual categories. When we perceive (i.e., categorize) someone as belonging to a particular group, we immediately ascribe to him a large number of characteristics, which he may or may not actually possess. Since many of these characteristics are evaluative, stereotypes help direct our behavior towards individuals. We are more likely to aggress against negatively stereotyped groups than against positively stereotyped groups.

During our everyday lives, we are constantly faced with the question of "Now, why did he do that?" Obviously, how we answer this question determines to a great extent how we treat a person. *Attribution processes* refer to the ways that we go about understanding the causes of our "co-interactant's" behavior. As such, it is a "lay psychology" (as opposed to a scientific psychology) of human behavior. How we react to a person depends upon whether we see the cause of his behavior as *internal* or *external* and whether we believe he *intended* to behave as he did. To the extent that a person's behavior is seen as internally caused and intended, the more likely we are to hold him *responsible* for his behavior. The more we believe a person is responsible for events that are frustrating and/or harmful to us, the more likely we are to aggress against him.

In order to completely understand another's reactions and to predict how he will behave, we have to make inferences about his *emotions*. A person's emotions are usually inferred from his nonverbal (e.g., facial expressions) as well as verbal behaviors. Once we know a person's emotional state in a particular situation (e.g., fear or anger), we can prepare ourselves for his next behavior (e.g., flight or attack). In addition, our emotional response to an attack against us may influence the attacker's subsequent behavior. Although the evidence is quite mixed at this point, it seems that staring at an aggressor may inhibit further attacks. The picture is even more confusing for the effects of pain cues. Sometimes a victim's expression of pain inhibits further attacks, while in other instances it spurs the attacker on.

In concluding this chapter, we turned to the role of *attitudes* (i.e., evaluative reactions to social stimuli) in aggression. Attitudes are a person's likes and dislikes regarding other people, things, and events. When the attitude-object is an entire social group, then we speak of prejudice. Attitudes and prejudice involve affective reactions to, beliefs about, and behavioral tendencies towards social stimuli. In general, attitudes are part of our psychological coping mechanisms and they enable us to (1) maximize and minimize rewards and punishments, (2) understand and interpret our environment, (3) establish and maintain our self-conceptions, and (4) resist and withstand ego threats. While negative attitudes increase the probability that we shall aggress against a person, they do not automatically lead to overt physical aggression. Many situational factors such as the presence of other people, the prevailing social norms, the consequences of behavior, competing motivations, or other attitudes often inhibit the direct and spontaneous expression of negative (and positive) attitudes. Finally, people may change their attitudes to conform to their behavior. Harming someone may lead to our disliking him and thereby increase the probability that we shall harm him again.

FOOTNOTES

[1] *Newsweek,* May 18, 1970, pp. 31–44; *New York Times Index,* 1970, pp. 996–99; *Life,* vol. 68, no. 18, pp. 31ff.; *Los Angeles Times,* August 5, 1973, p. 1.

[2] Berelson and Steiner (1964), pp. 100–104; Mussen and Rosenzweig (1973), pp. 570–628.

[3] Berelson and Steiner (1964), pp. 104–12; Mussen and Rosenzweig (1973), pp. 585–93.

[4] Bruner (1958).

[5] Bruner (1957).

[6] Secord and Backman (1964), pp. 15–16.

[7] Bruner (1958), pp. 88–92. The so-called "New Look" is now pretty old.

[8] Secord and Backman (1964), pp. 18–22.

[9] Berkowitz and LePage (1967).

[10] Murray (1933). These findings have been confirmed in a later and better-controlled study by Feshbach and Feshbach (1963).

[11] Bagby (1957).

[12] Toch and Schulte (1961).

[13] Secord and Backman (1964), pp. 26–32.

[14] Schafer and Murphy (1943); Secord and Backman (1964), pp. 24–26.

[15] Postman, Bruner, and McGinnies (1948).

[16] Johnson, Thomson, and Frincke (1960).

[17] Allport (1958), p. 133.

[18] For a detailed discussion of this field, see Tajfel (1969), pp. 328–31.

[19] Blumenthal et al. (1972), pp. 71–95.

[20] Blumenthal et al. (1972), pp. 84–87 and 97–133.

[21] *New York Times,* May 5, 1970 (emphasis added).

[22] *Life,* vol. 68, no. 18, p. 34.

[23] Sears and Tomlinson (1968); Turner (1969); Jeffries, Turner, and Morris (1971); Robinson (1970); and Ransford (1972).

[24] Attitudes may also influence social perception through the process of *selective exposure.* People may selectively expose themselves to events and obtain information that supports their attitudes. For example, a prejudiced person might only see and remember the "bad" things blacks do, while not seeing or misperceiving and forgetting all of the "good" actions and qualities of blacks. However, recent research has cast a large shadow of doubt over the validity of the concept of selective exposure. Consequently we shall not pursue this possibility. For a review of the selective exposure literature, see Freedman and Sears (1965).

[25] An overview can be found in Sampson (1971), pp. 177–89.

[26] See Byrne (1964) and Palmer and Altrocchi (1967).

[27] Witkin et al. (1962).

[28] Adorno et al. (1950).

²⁹ Pettigrew (1958).

³⁰ Katz and Braly (1933); Karlins, Coffman, and Walters (1969). See J. Jones (1972) for an excellent short review of the concept of stereotypes.

³¹ Bronfenbrenner (1961); Streufert and Sandler (1971).

³² R. K. White (1966).

³³ For the role of stereotypes and the resulting dehumanization of the enemy in massacres such as My Lai, see Kelman (1973) and Sanford and Comstock (1971).

³⁴ Scherer (1970–71).

³⁵ Maccoby (1964); DeFleur (1964).

³⁶ Perlman and Oskamp (1971).

³⁷ Cox (1969); Kassarjian (1969); Stafford, Birdwell, and vanTassel (1970).

³⁸ Heider (1958), pp. 80–84.

³⁹ Kelley (1973), p. 108. For further discussion, see Kelley (1967) and Kelley (1971), pp. 1–8.

⁴⁰ Kelley (1973), p. 112. Cf. Jones and Davis (1965), pp. 220–37. See Kelley (1967, 1971, 1972) for further discussions.

⁴¹ Kelley (1972).

⁴² Jones and Nisbett (1971).

⁴³ Kelley (1967), pp. 222–23. Cf. Jones and Davis (1965), pp. 237–46.

⁴⁴ Johnson, Feigenbaum, and Weiby (1964).

⁴⁵ Heider (1958), pp. 100–112; Jones and Davis (1965), pp. 220–22.

⁴⁶ Maselli and Altrocchi (1969); Steiner (1970).

⁴⁷ Kelley (1973), pp. 113–15.

⁴⁸ Jones and Davis (1965), pp. 226–27 and 246–49.

⁴⁹ Jones, Davis, and Gergen (1961).

⁵⁰ Heider (1958), pp. 112–14; Shaw and Sulzer (1964); Piaget (1965); and Reisman and Schopler (1973).

⁵¹ This is a rather controversial area of research with studies finding conflicting results: Walster (1966, 1967); Shaver (1970); and Shaw and Skolnick (1971).

⁵² Lerner (1970). Cf. Ryan (1971).

⁵³ *Newsweek*, May 25, 1970, p. 30.

⁵⁴ Feagin (1972).

⁵⁵ Brock and Pallack (1969); Glass and Wood (1969).

⁵⁶ Lerner (1970), p. 208.

⁵⁷ Walster, Berscheid, and Walster (1973). Also see Alderman, Brehm, and Katz (1974) for another explanation.

⁵⁸ Epstein and Taylor (1967); Greenwell and Dengerink (1973).

⁵⁹ Kelley (1971), pp. 14–15. Cf. Jones and Davis (1965), pp. 249–58.

⁶⁰ Davitz (1969).

⁶¹ Scherer (1970); Knapp (1972).

⁶² Ekman and Friesen (1969, 1974).

⁶³ Ekman, Friesen, and Ellsworth (1972); Izard (1971).

⁶⁴ Vetter (1969); Scherer, Koivumaki, and Rosenthal (1972).

⁶⁵ Although there is next to no research evidence on this, it is possible to engage in some interesting speculations: Scherer (1974).

⁶⁶ Mehrabian (1969).

⁶⁷ For example, cross-cultural research has shown that Germans seem to com-

municate dominance through voice quality, while Americans communicate extraversion. See Scherer (1972).

[68] Ellsworth, Carlsmith, and Henson (1972).

[69] Exline and Yellin (1969).

[70] Zimbardo (1969).

[71] Ellsworth and Carlsmith (1973).

[72] Cf. Staub (1971).

[73] Baron (1971*a*, *b*). However, Baron (1974) found the victim's pain cues combined with the aggressor's prior arousal led to increased aggression.

[74] Hartman (1969).

[75] Rosenberg and Hovland (1960); Ostrom (1969).

[76] For recent reviews of attitude research, see McGuire (1969) and Sears and Abeles (1969).

[77] Cf. Allport (1958) for a classic discussion of prejudice and J. Jones (1972) for a recent and excellent review of racism.

[78] Katz (1960).

[79] Pettigrew (1961).

[80] Adorno et al. (1950).

[81] As quoted in the *New York Times,* May 8, 1970.

[82] *New York Times,* May 8, 1970, pp. 16 and 18; *Newsweek,* May 18, 1970, p. 32.

[83] Loew (1967); Gentry (1970); Berkowitz and Holmes (1960).

[84] Parke, Ewall, and Slaby (1972). Cf. Berkowitz (1970) and Berkowitz (1962), pp. 133–62; Genthner and Taylor (1973); Berkowitz and Holmes (1960).

[85] LaPierre (1934).

[86] Wicker (1969); Weitz (1971).

[87] Wicker (1969); Weitz (1971).

[88] Rokeach (1966).

[89] Ajzen and Fishbein (1973).

[90] Cf. Weitz (1971); Sigall and Page (1971).

[91] For discussions of the theoretical issues underlying this process, see R. Brown (1965), pp. 549–609; Bem (1972). For a review of the empirical evidence for observers' and actors' derogation of their victims, see Berscheid and Walster (1969), pp. 14–28.

5 / ONE OF THE GANG

interpersonal factors

It is time that we finally moved outside of the individual's head and looked at the process of social interaction per se. "Cognition," "perception," and "attitude" all refer to processes within the mind of a single individual and, consequently, they rely little upon the nature of social interaction between individuals. While social interaction partly determines and is determined by these psychological processes, we could talk about a person's perceptions, cognitions, attitudes, and behaviors towards a stone just as well as towards another person. However, there are many crucial differences between a stone and a person, one of which is that the other person also has perceptions, cognitions, attitudes, and behaviors. A stone is a constant stimulus, but the other person is a constantly changing stimulus. Thus, interacting with another individual is much more complex, since we have to take into account how he will react to our actions and adjust our behaviors accordingly. In social interaction, one person's behavior serves as the stimulus for the other's behavior, which, in turn, becomes a stimulus for the first person's behavior (*ad infinitum* and possibly *ad nauseam*).

In short, we have to consider more than just intrapersonal processes to understand human behavior and aggression. The core questions for this chapter are, "How does the presence and behavior of other people affect a person's behavior?" "What aspects of social interaction with another person or with a group of people cause aggression?" In attempting to answer these rhetorical questions, we shall look at a few selected topics under the headings of (1) Interpersonal Attraction, (2) Cooperation and Competition, (3) Ingroups and Outgroups, (4) Norms and Conformity, and, finally, (5) Deindividuation.

INTERPERSONAL ATTRACTION

FOCUS
Birds of a Feather Flock Together

Since Aristotle had something to say about almost everything, it is not too surprising that he was one of the first to note that friendship depends partly on similarity between people:

> And they are friends who have come to regard the same things as good and the same things as evil, they who are friends of the same people, and they who are enemies of the same people. . . . We like those who resemble us, and are engaged in the same pursuits. . . . We like those who desire the same things as we, if the case is such that we and they can share the things together. . . .[1]

Following Aristotle's lead, modern psychologists have pointed out that similarity in attitudes leads to liking and dissimilarity leads to hostility.

A large number of correlational studies among preexisting friendship and marital pairs backs up the similarity hypothesis. However, it is impossible to tell from these studies whether people seek out similar others as friends or whether friendship leads to similarity. Theodore Newcomb, a social psychologist at the University of Michigan, established a student boarding house so that he could test the direction of the causal relationship.[2] Newcomb offered rent-free housing to two groups of male transfer students in exchange for their participation in his study. Since the students were initially strangers, Newcomb could watch how they went about making friends. At the time of their arrival, the students answered a variety of attitudinal questionnaires and were assigned roommates. After a time, and at regular intervals throughout the year, Newcomb asked them questions about who their friends were and how much they liked their fellow boarders. Initially, the students named their roommates as friends and attitudinal similarity was not related to friendship. But as time went by and the students had more opportunities to explore the attitudes of the other roomers, the relationship between similarity and friendship became stronger. The students started picking their friends on the basis of attitudinal similarity. New-comb found that attitudinal agreement *prior to* acquaintance predicted interpersonal attraction *after* acquaintance. In addition, the more a man liked someone, the more he perceived that the two of them agreed (regardless of actual agreement). Newcomb's field study showed that actual attitudinal similarity causes liking and that liking causes perceived attitudinal similarity.

A psychologist at the University of Texas, Donn Byrne, has carefully explored the nature of the relationship between similarity and attraction by using experimental laboratory techniques.[3] Byrne's basic technique involves subjects filling out an attitude questionnaire at a first meeting and then presenting them with another person's answers at a second meeting. Byrne systematically manipulates these answers and thereby presents his subjects with a person who is either attitudinally similar or dissimilar. Finally, the subjects indicate how much they think they would like the other person (on the basis of his answers). These studies show a definite linear relationship between attraction and similarity: The greater the number or proportion of similar attitudes, the greater the subject's attraction to the other person.

Although there are occasions when similarity leads to hostility,[4] we can safely say that, in general, similarity causes liking and, in addition, we tend to perceive that liked individuals are similar to ourselves.

Some psychologists have suggested that the similarity-attraction relationship also underlies racial prejudice. Milton Rokeach and his co-workers claim that whites are not prejudiced against blacks because of race per se, but because whites believe blacks hold different attitudes and values.[5] If a religious white were given the choice of interacting with a religious black or an atheistic white, he would select the black. The similarity in attitudes would outweigh race as a determinant of attraction and hostility. Several experiments have confirmed various aspects of this hypothesis. One study showed that whites believe a black stranger is more attitudinally different from them than a white stranger. In addition, prejudiced whites (compared to nonprejudiced whites) perceive a greater difference between their attitudes and those of a black stranger.[6] This study and others also indicate that whites prefer to interact with and to like attitudinally similar blacks over attitudinally dissimilar whites. However, other studies suggest that people give more weight to race than belief as social relationships become more intimate. For very intimate relationships (e.g., marrying versus working together), people are more likely to prefer members of their own race regardless of their beliefs.[7]

The importance of attitudinal similarity may help us understand the National Guardsmen's and the townspeople's hostility towards the Kent State students. In expressing their antipathy towards students, soldiers and civilians often complained about the students' dress, appearance, and their "hippy" life-style. They believed that the students embraced a different set of values and rejected the core American values of the work ethic and the Puritan sexual code. Thus, they disliked the students partially because the students were different from them in values and attitudes.[8]

But why does attitudinal dissimilarity lead to hostility and similarity to attraction? One answer, which may at first seem rather roundabout, is that we like people who reward us and dislike those who punish us. Our feelings are partly determined by whether their behavior is beneficial or harmful.[9] Of course, people do not have to directly reward or punish us in order for us to develop a liking or disliking for them in face-to-face interactions. If they are merely present when we receive a reward, although they did not cause the reward, the reward may become associated with them in our minds through "conditioning." For example, Bob may like John because John always approves of (i.e., rewards) Bob's ideas. Bob may also like Ed, who is always present whenever John rewards Bob, because Ed is associated with pleasant events.[10] In sum, attraction in face-to-face interactions is largely determined by the rewards and punishments that others supply us.

If this is true, and it seems to be so, our question about attraction and similarity becomes, "How is similarity rewarding and dissimilarity punishing?" First, agreement provides us with validation and reassurance about the correctness of our attitudes and beliefs. People learn at an early age that it is important to have correct beliefs and attitudes in order to get along in their environment. Having the wrong attitudes and beliefs can sometimes even be fatal. But how do we know that our attitudes are correct? One way of validating them is by comparing them to those of other people. Since we want to have correct views of the world, it is pleasant (i.e., rewarding) to have our opinions verified. However, dissimilarity in opinions suggests that we are wrong, which is an unpleasant (i.e., punishing) experience. Consequently, it is more rewarding to interact with people who reassure us of the correctness of our attitudes by expressing similar attitudes.[11]

Second, similar attitudes may imply that two people will enjoy performing the same behaviors. If both people like tennis, they will be more likely to play it together and, consequently, to find interacting with each other rewarding. We like similar others because we anticipate engaging in many rewarding activities with them.

Third, we learn through experience that people whom we like tend to reciprocate liking. Thus, when we find that someone is similar to us, we assume that he is likely to like us and, therefore, we like him. We anticipate his liking us and reciprocate the anticipated attitude.

Finally, it is psychologically pleasant (i.e., rewarding) for people to have their "unit relationships" in harmony with their "sentiment relationships." "Unit relationships" refer to the tendency to group objects together into perceptual units (e.g., father and son form a unit), and "sentiment relationships" refer to attitudes. When people perceive that objects are similar to each other, they feel that they "belong together" or form a "unit." Thus, if a person sees that he is similar to another, he feels they form a unit relationship. It is then more pleasant for him to like the other person than to dislike him. However, if he feels they are different, then it is more pleasant to dislike the other, since they do not form a unit relationship.[12]

In summary, interacting with other people leads to our liking them or disliking them to the extent that their behavior is rewarding. Since attitudinal similarity is rewarding, we tend to like people who hold similar attitudes to our own. This is important for aggression because our attitudes towards a person help determine our behavior towards him.[13] As we noted in the preceding chapter, disliking another person makes us suspicious of his actions and quicker to aggress against him. Our discussion also suggests that the separation of ethnic, racial, or social groups fosters hostility, or at least inhibits attraction, by blocking off communication. Without interaction, it is impossible for people to discover that they are basically similar to each other in their values, beliefs, concerns, and experiences. In addition, without communication between people or groups, it is easy for autistic spirals of hostility to develop. It is impossible for people to obtain disconfirming information that might lead to mutual understanding and better relations. Indeed, numerous studies of interracial contact show that equal-status contact reduces prejudice and intergroup hostilities.[14] However, when people are separated, they tend to exaggerate differences, and this increases their hostility and the probability of aggression.

COOPERATION AND COMPETITION

FOCUS
The Robber's Cave

The "good ole summertime" has arrived at last, and parents across the nation quickly pack their kids off to camp with a sigh of relief. For a few summers in the late 1940s and early 1950s, this age-old migration of children was used by the psychologist Muzafer Sherif to study group dynamics.[15] While the boys thought they were only off to a summer of fun and games at the Robber's Cave Camp, they were really part of an elaborate experiment. From the very start, they were hand-picked so that they would be a camp of "typical" American boys. "All were healthy, socially well-adjusted, somewhat above average in intelligence, and from stable, white, Protestant, middle-class homes."

The first time the boys met each other was on the bus to camp. After arrival at camp, they were housed all together as a single, large group, and, naturally, friendships started to develop. However, Sherif divided the boys into two groups so that "best friends" were separated. For the next few weeks, the two new groups had nothing to do with each other. Slowly new friendships developed within each group, and the boys came to see themselves as distinct units. They developed an esprit de corps and chose a name for themselves. One group called itself the Rattlers and the other the Eagles. Now, when asked who their best friends were, Rattlers always chose Rattlers and Eagles chose Eagles.

At this point, the Rattlers and Eagles were brought back together again, but not as a single large group. Sherif arranged for them to compete against each other in a series of baseball games, football games, tug-of-wars, and the like. These games had one important quality in common: There was always a winner and a loser. Both teams could not win. The tournament started with a friendly air of good sportsmanship. But fairly quickly the era of good feelings was replaced with one of hostility. Eagles began to call the Rattlers "stinkers," and the Rattlers called the Eagles "sneaks." Soon "military raids" were carried out against their rivals' cabins, scuffles broke out, and food fights erupted.

While hostility reigned between Rattlers and Eagles, peace and harmony ruled within each group. The boys came to like each other even more and a stronger sense of "we-ness" developed. Morale and cooperation increased within each group as the rivalry between groups became more and more explosive.

After a while, Sherif and his colleagues became concerned about the intense hostility and aggression shown by the campers, and they attempted to turn hostility into friendship. First, they held a "Brotherhood Dinner," where the rivals were to share a special dinner and an evening of fun together. But the Eagles and Rattlers only used the occasion to declare open warfare. Rattlers hurled insults and the Eagles responded with spoonfuls of mashed potatoes. Before long, the counsellors had to forcibly separate the combatants.

Next, Sherif reasoned that if competitive games led to hostility, cooperative activities should lead to attraction. Mysteriously, at this point, a series of "disasters" befell the camp. First, the sole source of water for the entire camp broke down, and Eagles and Rattlers had to join forces to repair the water tank. Then, the food truck refused to start, and Rattlers and Eagles had to push shoulder-to-shoulder for their evening meal. Sherif engineered a series of catastrophes that threatened Eagles and Rattlers alike and that required their joint efforts in overcoming them. Slowly, the series of cooperative acts reduced the hostility between the groups. By the end of the summer, Eagles and Rattlers had forgotten about their previous hostility and counted their former enemies among their best friends. Competition between the groups led to stereotypes, hostility, and aggression, while cooperation resulted in mutual attraction.

Sherif's experiment demonstrates that more than similarity is involved in attraction, hostility, and aggression, for the Rattlers and Eagles were specially selected for similarity in social backgrounds. Naturally, their social backgrounds remained similar throughout the summer, except for their membership in the Rattlers or the Eagles. But membership in the two different groups is not sufficient by itself to cause hostility, since the Rattlers and Eagles changed from mutual antagonism to friendship. The camp's *reward structure* (i.e., how the two groups were interdependent for rewards and punishments) determined whether friendly or hostile relationships prevailed. The series of games established *negative interdependence* between Rattlers and Eagles. Both teams desired the same goal (i.e., victory), but only one of them could attain it and the other one invariably was denied it. Negative interdependence is characterized by *competition* for scarce resources, which leads to exchanging punishments, hostility, and aggression.[16]

While Rattlers and Eagles were negatively interdependent, the members of each group were *positively interdependent*. Each Rattler shared the same goal with every other Rattler: the defeat of the Eagles. In addition, the only way they could achieve this desired end was by working together. Also, if any one Rattler attained his goal, the entire group would simultaneously achieve it. Goal attainment by one did not mean the frustration of another Rattler. Consequently, positive interdependence is characterized by *cooperation*, which leads to exchanging rewards, attraction, and aid.

So long as the reward structure between Rattlers and Eagles favored competition, hostility dominated their interaction. But once the structure was changed to favor cooperation by the introduction of common, superordinant goals, hostility diminished and attraction grew.[17]

Competition engenders hostility and aggression because it is basically frustrating to both parties.[18] When one person obtains the goal that both covet, the other is denied satisfaction. Even though the loser may have worked hard for the goal, another person or group blocks him from achieving it and, to boot, enjoys the goal. In some instances, the frustrated individual may realize that his rival won in a fair contest, and the social norms of "good sportsmanship" may inhibit the direct expression of any hostility or aggression. But the individual may still be disappointed and may aggress against other safer targets or through indirect means. Competition may be somewhat frustrating even for the victor, because it means that he has to engage in greater efforts to attain his goal. Not only must he overcome natural physical obstacles, but he must divert energies to prevent his rival from beating him to the goal. Competition may increase the "costs" of a goal and thereby diminish the goal's worth.

However, some cultures and individuals see competition per se as desirable, and people may gain satisfaction from competing. Rather than decreasing the value of a goal, people may value something more when they have had to fight for it. But to the extent that victory itself becomes a goal, then losing becomes even more frustrating and likely to lead to aggression. Not only is the loser denied the cherished goal, but he also suffers the shame and disgrace of losing ("nobody loves a loser"). Winning and losing become important to people because they are tied up with notions of self-worth and social prestige. The desire to win or the fear of defeat may supplant the original bone of contention as the goal of competition.[19]

This is well demonstrated in a recent experiment in which subjects competed for money in a two-person game under the observation of an audience. For the first ten trials, one subject, who was actually the experimenter's confederate, had the ability to impose monetary fines on the real subject, who was helpless to retaliate. After these ten trials, the real subject was told that the audience believed him to be a "sucker" for allowing his competitor to humiliate him. At this point, the subject was given the ability to retaliate, while his opponent (the confederate) was made helpless (i.e., he no longer had the ability to fine the subject). However, retaliation was not without its costs. In fact, the more the real subject fined his competitor, the less money he could win for himself. Despite this drawback, the subject, who had lost "face" during the earlier part of the experiment, chose to impose fines against his opponent rather than to maximize his monetary winnings. Regaining "face" through making his opponent look foolish to the audience supplanted money as the goal of the competitive game.[20]

Experimental subjects are not the only people who try to "save face" even though it may be extremely costly for them. Westerners have held for a long time that Orientals are particularly concerned about "saving face." However, America's continued involvement in Vietnam may have resulted partly from our desire to "save face." President Nixon frequently announced to the world that he was not going to be the first president to preside over an American defeat. The President exclaimed that America would continue to fight until he achieved "peace with honor." Thus, the American government continued to spend billions of dollars and thousands of American and Vietnamese lives long beyond the point of a possible military victory. Both Presidents Johnson and Nixon seemed to be concerned with how it would look to the rest of the world if America was defeated by tiny North Vietnam. This concern for "saving face," as opposed to cutting losses, probably prolonged the Vietnam war and cost America many lives and millions of dollars.

Thus, the emphasis upon winning may intensify competition and create spirals of rising hostility and aggression. One person punishes his opponent, who loses "face" and attempts to regain status by threatening and punishing the first person. Threats and punishments lead to hostility and to counterthreats and attacks.[21] (We shall return to the role of competition in intergroup conflict in Chapter 8.)

INGROUPS AND OUTGROUPS

If we kept a record of the people with whom we interact during the course of an ordinary day, we would discover that we share some group affiliation with practically all of them. These shared affiliations vary from highly formal groups with written by-laws and organization charts (e.g., businesses, colleges) to very informal groups without written rules and permanent structures (e.g., friendship cliques, ethnic groups). Some groups are extremely large (e.g., the nation) and others are extremely small (e.g., husband and wife). But they all share a common psychological reality for us in that they form part of our self-identity. When we ask ourselves "Who am I?" most of us answer in terms of group memberships: "I am a Protestant, a college student, an American, a woman."[22] In addition, when we are with other members of the group, we recognize our membership and experience a sense of "we-ness." We feel that they and we form a social unit.

This "we-ness" creates an important psychological differentiation in our world, because it divides people into "them" and "us."[23] We either feel attracted towards someone or estranged from him on the basis of his and our group backgrounds. Social scientists speak of this distinction between "us" and "them" in terms of ingroups and outgroups. *Ingroups* are groups to which a person belongs and to which he feels an attachment. Mere physical membership is not sufficient to create an ingroup. A person must also be a member psychologically (i.e., he must identify himself with the group). For example, the famous Swiss psychologist Jean Piaget once asked a seven-year-old Swiss boy where he lived. The boy replied in Geneva and that Geneva was in Switzerland. But when asked, "Are you Swiss?" he answered, "No, I'm Genevese."[24] Of course, *outgroups* are those groups to which a person does not belong *both* physically and psychologically. Whether a group is an ingroup or an outgroup does not depend upon the characteristics of the group. The same group may be an ingroup for some and an outgroup for others. In addition, its status may vary over time and circumstances for the same person. In the United States many white Americans do not feel any "we-ness" with black Americans. But let them meet a black American abroad after months of interacting with "foreigners," and they suddenly feel "kinship." (Well, almost kinship!) Thus, the ingroup versus outgroup distinction is a psychological reality and not a physical reality.

The degree to which a person is attracted to a group and considers himself to be a member depends upon how successful or influential it is in meeting his needs. In short, the more rewards the person receives from membership in the group, the more attracted he is to it and the more likely he will consider himself to be a member.[25] A person may be attracted to a group for a variety of reasons. First of all, membership in the group per se may be rewarding. He may enjoy interacting with its members, gain prestige within the group, enjoy activities that the group pursues (e.g., tennis clubs), etc. Second, membership in the group may help him obtain rewards outside of the group. He may receive respect from nonmembers, make useful business contacts, obtain help for achieving some nongroup goal, etc. Thus, membership in groups is rewarding, and the more rewarding a particular group is, the more positive the person's attitudes towards the group are.

Ingroups and outgroups serve as *reference groups* in that they provide us with norms, values, and beliefs. We look to ingroups as sources of rules for how to behave, and we evaluate others against the standards of our ingroups. To the extent that other people meet these standards, they are considered to be "good" and "desirable." And the major standard for evaluation is that they be similar in behavior, values, and beliefs to our own. In sum, ethnocentrism is closely tied up with the distinction between ingroups and outgroups. The familiar and similar are superior and good; the strange and different are inferior and bad (see the earlier discussion of attraction and similarity).

As we noted earlier, people find belief and attitudinal differences threatening because a major means of validating their opinions is social consensus. The mere existence of other people with contrary beliefs and attitudes challenges the correctness of their own opinions. People defend themselves against this challenge by rejecting and derogating the sources of contrary opinions. If the outgroup is inferior, untrustworthy, and evil, then its opinions need not be taken seriously and pose no threat. Of course, the resulting prejudice against outgroups increases the probability of aggression against them.

This antipathy against outgroups is often encouraged or even created by group leaders as a means of distracting the ingroup's attention away from internal dissatisfactions, of uniting warring factions, and of competing with the outgroup. For example, Hitler skillfully manipulated hostility against Jews to create solidarity amongst the German people. By making manifest latent prejudices, Hitler united conflicting workers and capitalists against a common enemy. By blaming the Jews for internal problems, he offered the German people a simple solution (a "judenfrei" Germany) to their woes and he distracted them from the real causes of their problems and from the true goals of his policies. In addition, Hitler and his backers reaped economic benefits from their Aryanization programs that eliminated Jewish competitors.

Figure 5-1 The Nazis took advantage of existing anti-Semitism to blame Jews for Germany's defeat in World War I and for Germany's economic problems. By scapegoating the Jews, the Nazis were able to unite conflicting social groups against a common enemy. The photograph shows Nazi SA men organizing the first boycott of Jewish stores in Cologne in 1933. United Press International photo.

Of course, such scapegoating of outgroups is not limited to Hitler, Germans, and to the past. Our own American history is replete with instances where leaders have whipped up anti-Negro sentiments as a means for controlling and redirecting the hostilities of "poor whites."[26] More recently, government officials may have used peace demonstrators as scapegoats for their failure to successfully conclude the Vietnam war. They claimed that the antiwar rallies only stiffened the enemy's resistance and undermined the Paris peace talks. However, critics of the Nixon administration contended that the government was attempting to sharpen ingroup and outgroup distinctions in an effort to stifle criticism of government policies.

It would be an error to think that scapegoating occurs only with the premeditated encouragement of leaders. Since existing group norms and beliefs frequently specify outgroups as legitimate and safe targets for aggression, group leaders are only drawing upon preexisting aggressive tendencies. Consequently, people may "spontaneously" scapegoat outgroups without official encouragement by leaders.[27] For example, a few studies show that economic frustrations are correlated with aggression against blacks. Prior to 1930 in the South, low cotton prices were associated with the lynching of blacks. In addition, whites living in poor southern counties were more likely to lynch blacks than whites living in less poor counties.[28] These studies suggest that economic frustrations instigated aggression among whites who were unable to aggress directly against the source of their frustration. Consequently, the whites displaced their aggression and attacked blacks.

Another possibility is that in those periods of economic "bust," blacks became more serious competition for whites for the few existing jobs. Consequently, whites acted to eliminate and/or intimidate the competition. Attacks against outgroup members do not always represent displaced aggression. Frequently, the outgroups may actually be the source of the ingroup's frustration. As we just saw, competition between groups is frustrating and it sharpens ingroup and outgroup distinctions, creates hostility, and fosters aggression (e.g., Rattlers and Eagles, pp. 157–59).

The ingroup versus outgroup dichotomy may facilitate aggression through other means besides the creation of negative attitudes. Group norms may specify, legitimatize, and encourage hostile behaviors against outgroups. Since outgroups possess "aggressive cues," we are more likely to aggress against them than an ingroup member when we are aroused. That is, given the same degree of frustration by an ingroup and an outgroup person, we would be more likely to carry out an aggressive act against the outgroup person. In addition, the ingroup norms create "pressure" towards aggression. Individuals may aggress as a consequence of social norms in an effort to live up to the expectations of their group. Even though they may not feel personally hostile, they may aggress in order to assure social acceptance. Finally, a sense of "we-ness" creates a supportive climate for the expression of hostility. When frustrated, we may feel that we have the support of our group behind us. They will back up our attack, and knowledge of this allows us to overcome internal and external restraints that might otherwise inhibit the direct expression of our anger. For example, in a laboratory experiment, subjects were made to feel that they either constituted an ingroup or had nothing in common. Then, they were insulted by the experimenter and left alone together for a few minutes. Those groups who felt they were an ingroup were more likely to express hostility towards the experimenter than those who believed they had little in common.[29] The feeling of mutual support and attraction enabled them to overcome restraints against expressing hostility.

Aggression is directed not only against members of other groups, but also against members of the ingroup. As we shall see later, groups demand a high degree of conformity to their norms and beliefs, and they are quick to punish nonconformists. Consequently, deviants, people who express opinions or act in ways contrary to prevailing norms, are frequently targets of aggression.

FOCUS
Rejection of Deviants

Stanley Schachter, a social psychologist at Columbia University, demonstrated that groups often reject deviants. Schachter created seven-man groups in which the subjects anticipated returning for frequent discussions. On the first meeting, the subjects were asked to discuss the case of "Johnny Rocco," a juvenile delinquent, and how the authorities should deal with him. After familiarizing themselves with the case, the subjects publicly indicated their preference on a scale varying from a "hard-line" to a "permissive approach." Unbeknownst to the subjects, three members of the group were Schachter's hirelings. Two of them took stands that were widely deviant from the average opinion in the group and the third advocated the average group opinion.

Following the statement of opinions, the group was allowed to engage in a discussion. During the discussion, one of the deviants (the "slider") gradually shifted his opinion until it coincided with the group's opinion. However, the other stooge (the "deviant") held steadfastly to his original, discrepant opinion. The third confederate (the "conformist") continued to express opinions similar to the group's majority. After about forty-five minutes, the experimenter stopped the discussion and steered it towards preparations for the next meeting. He asked the subjects to select some of their group for leadership positions and, under the pretext of having to reduce the size of the group, he asked them to rank everyone according to their preference for remaining in the group.

Schachter's major finding was that people rejected the "deviant," but accepted the "slider" and the "conformist" confederates. The "deviant" was least frequently chosen for leadership positions and most frequently chosen for omission from future discussions. Schachter also found that this tendency was strongest in groups with a strong sense of "we-ness" (i.e., highly cohesive groups). Thus, Schachter's subjects rewarded conformists for agreeing with the prevailing group opinion and punished deviants for their "erroneous" opinions.[30]

Studies by other researchers show that antagonism towards deviants does not stop at merely verbal hostility and rejection. In one series of laboratory experiments, subjects were more likely to punish deviants than nondeviants with electroshocks and they were less likely to reward deviants than nondeviants with money.[31] In addition, other studies suggest that people may even dislike a deviant more than a member of the outgroup.[32] For example, black college students expressed more hostility towards a prosegregation black than towards a white holding similar views.[33] The renegade is often despised more than the enemy.

Observational and experimental evidence tells us that deviants often reciprocate the group's hostility and aggression.[34] History is filled with examples of converts to a new religion who are more repressive against the old religion than those born into the new religion. This is partly because they know what to expect at the hands of their former group. They anticipate mistreatment and know that their fate hinges upon the success of their new group. Also, deviants and converts may hate their old group in an attempt to convince themselves of the correctness of their new and deviant opinions and behaviors. The deviant may feel, in addition, that he must prove himself to his new friends by zealously persecuting his old friends. Thus, dissimilarity in actions and opinions *within* the group as well as *between* groups tends towards mutual hostility and aggression.

The dynamic underlying aggression against deviants is very similar to that underlying aggression against outgroups. If the dissimilarity of the outgroup is threatening to the ingroup's confidence in its norms, beliefs, and behaviors, imagine how much more threatening internal heresy must be! In a way, the outsider can be forgiven for his misguided actions and opinions. He had not had the benefit of being exposed to the "correct" ways of doing things. But the insider who has been exposed to the "truth" and rejects it represents a real danger to the group's self-confidence. People expect those with whom they have "unit relationships" to believe and to behave the same as they do. When deviants do not live up to these expectations, the rest of the group is faced either with reexamining its beliefs and norms (a psychologically painful task) or with rejecting the heresy.

In addition, the deviant threatens not only the group's peace of mind, but its very survival. Widespread deviancy may impair the group's ability to pursue its goals. First, deviant opinions may confuse people as to which goals they should pursue. Without a clear consensus, the group may find it difficult to pursue any goals at all. Second, deviants may not work hard for the group's goals, or they may even sabotage the group's efforts. Third, the deviancy may spread and result in the group's breaking into subgroups. In sum, deviants may threaten the group's ability to obtain its goals and thereby impair its ability to reward its members. This leads to the group's becoming less attractive to members and, ultimately, to the destruction of the group. At the least, members of the group may fear such dire consequences and therefore will attempt to stamp out deviance before it becomes a danger.

NORMS AND CONFORMITY

Group Pressure for Conformity

Our discussion of ingroups and outgroups suggests that both deviants and outgroups are rejected, derogated, and attacked because of their nonconformity to the ingroup's norms. People are expected to live up to the group's standards for appropriate beliefs, feelings, and behaviors. When they violate these normative expectations, group pressure is brought to bear on the deviants to bring them back into line and, if that fails, to expel them from the group. Our earlier discussion also suggests that this normative pressure results from the group's needs to ensure its survival, to obtain its goals, and to validate opinions and beliefs through social consensus. In addition, seemingly nonutilitarian norms for behavior (e.g., dress styles) and beliefs (e.g., patriotism) may develop as means for identifying group members. Consequently, deviation in dress (e.g., the clothing of hippies) may be seen as a desire to disaffiliate oneself from the group and as a rejection of the group's values and norms. Norms also develop for the mundane but important purpose of coordinating and predicting the behavior of other people. When norms exist, people can safely assume that others will behave in accordance with them and, therefore, in predictable ways. They do not have to spend time and energy worrying about how others will behave.[35] There is no need to belabor the point that norms are functional and that deviance is punished.

When we look at the people around us, we notice that they wear the same style clothing, speak the same language, drive on the same side of the street, eat with the same utensils, and do a myriad of other things in the same way. Does this mean that we are all conformists? Most of us would probably disagree with such a verdict and claim that merely following such conventional forms of behavior does not brand a person as a conformist. If conformity is not conventionality, then what is it?

FOCUS
Group Pressure and Action Against a Person

Imagine that you have volunteered to take part in a psychology experiment, have just arrived at the laboratory, and are waiting with three other people (strangers) for the experimenter. The experimenter arrives and explains that the experiment concerns the effects of punishment on learning. One of you will be the pupil or Learner, while the other three will be his teachers. The Learner's task is to learn a list of word pairs (e.g., Boy-Girl). The Teachers will read him the entire list of pairs once, then read him each "stimulus word" (e.g., Boy), and he is to respond with the correct "response word" (e.g., Girl). The three Teachers will have three different, but coordinated, tasks. Teacher 1 will read the word pairs to the Learner, Teacher 2 will indicate whether the Learner's answer is correct, and Teacher 3 will administer the punishment for incorrect answers (i.e., an electroshock). After explaining the experimental procedures to the group, the experimenter assigns each of you a role by drawing slips of paper out of a hat, and you become Teacher 3.

The experimenter takes the Learner into another room and straps him into an "electric chair." Then he returns to explain to you how the shock generator works. It consists of an impressive piece of machinery with a series of 30 levers labeled from 15 to 470 volts and with some verbal designations such as "Slight Shock" and "Danger: Severe Shock." You now learn that all three Teachers, including yourself, can suggest the level of shock the Learner will get for each error. The shock level actually delivered will be the lowest one suggested by any one member of the group of Teachers. Each Teacher will make his suggestions in a specified order, starting with Teacher 1 and ending with you, Teacher

3. This means that you have the final say in determining the level of punishment. If you choose a shock lower than those recommended by Teachers 1 and 2, that is the level you will deliver.

Now, the experiment starts and things run smoothly at first. The Learner makes only a few mistakes, and the other Teachers suggest the lowest shocks. But as time goes on and the Learner makes more mistakes, the other Teachers suggest progressively higher and higher shocks. First 15 volts, then 30, 45, 60, and 75 volts. At 60 volts, the Learner starts to complain. But the Teachers continue to recommend successively stronger shocks. Remember the final say is up to you. Would you go along with the other two Teachers or suggest a different shock level?

Almost all of us would probably answer, "Why, 15 volts, of course! I'm no sadist!" But would we really be able to resist the group's pressure? Stanley Milgram, a social psychologist now at the City University of New York, says "no."

In an experiment at Yale University like the one we just described, Milgram found that most subjects go along with the other Teachers, who are really the experimenter's helpers. The straight line in Figure 5-1 represents the shock level suggested by the experimenter's stooges. Line A indicates the shock levels that the real subjects administered, and line B represents the shocks delivered by subjects in a control condition. These control subjects were alone and performed all three Teacher roles by themselves. Thus, line B is the shock level the subjects gave when they were not influenced by the other Teachers. Figure 5-1 shows that as the stooges suggested progressively stronger shocks, the subjects were influenced to give stronger shocks, although not as strong as the stooges' suggestions. But the subjects administered shocks stronger than those given by the control subjects. In short, the subjects in the group situation behaved differently than they would have had they been alone.[36]

We would all agree that the subjects in Milgram's experiment were conforming. The crucial difference between conventionality and conformity is that the person *changes* his behavior, belief, or opinions in the direction of socially prescribed standards and away from his own initial preferences because of actual or imagined social pressures.[37] The person acts differently in the group than he would have if he were alone. Change, not uniformity in behavior, is the *sine qua non* of conformity.

Is the subject who refused to go along with the other Teachers' recommendations in Milgram's experiment an individualist or a nonconformist? Not necessarily. Even if a person resists the group's pressures

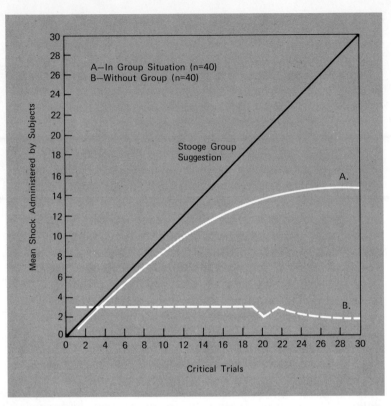

Figure 5-2   Group pressure and action against a person: mean shock levels in experimental and control conditions over 30 critical trials. From S. Milgram, Group pressure and action against a person, *Journal of Abnormal and Social Psychology* 69 (1964): 137–43, figure 1 (data points have been smoothed). Copyright 1964 by the American Psychological Association. Reprinted by permission.

and, in fact, acts diametrically opposed to the group's norms, we cannot say that he is acting independently. First, there is always the possibility that he is conforming to another group's norms and marching to Thoreau's more distant drummer. For example, a Quaker might resist Milgram's stooges because he is conforming to nonviolent religious norms. His behavior is still determined by social norms, albeit those of another group. Second, the person who does just the opposite to the group's demands is likewise still under its influence, so long as his behavior is changed from what it would have been if he were acting alone. Negative group influence or *anticonformity* is not the same as independence. *Independence* refers to behaviors that are neither consistently directed towards (i.e., conformity) nor away from (i.e., anticonformity) group standards. Consequently, we should not think of conformity and independence as forming a single dimension. Perhaps a better way is to conceive of conformity and anticonformity as the poles of a group-dependence dimension and of independence as a second and perpendicular dimension.[38]

Now that we have defined conformity and independence, we are faced with yet another distinction. In Milgram's experiment, we would want to distinguish between (1) subjects who followed the group's suggestions *and* came to agree with them and (2) subjects who followed the group's suggestions *but* privately disagreed with them. Both types of subjects behave publicly in the same manner, but their private beliefs would differ. The distinction is between (1) *private acceptance* and (2) *public compliance*. Unfortunately, most conformity studies deal only with compliance and rarely look at private acceptance. For example, we have no way of knowing in Milgram's experiment whether his subjects changed their attitudes towards electroshocking the Learner. The mean shock levels delivered suggest that their overt behavior is almost a perfect compromise between the group's suggestions and their own inclinations (Figure 5-2). This might imply that their conformity was more like compliance than private acceptance. How can we tell whether a person is complying or privately accepting the group's pressure?

We could always ask him about his private beliefs. But his answer might likewise reflect compliance rather than true conviction, especially if the group were present. *If the group were present. . . .* This phrase suggests an answer to our question. How would he behave if he were removed from the group? The person who is merely complying would probably resort to his initially preferred behavior. Freed from the group's pressure, since the group can no longer monitor and sanction his actions, he should no longer comply. However, the person who privately accepts the group's norms should continue to follow them regardless of the absence or presence of the group. Compliance leads to conformity so long as there is danger of punishment or the desire of rewards that are contingent on conformity, but private acceptance results in conformity because of congruence between the group's and the person's values ("virtue is its own reward").[39]

Milgram's experiment demonstrates rather dramatically that social pressure can force people to engage in aggression when they would ordinarily not do so. Of course, social pressure does not exist only in the laboratory. To some extent, the violence of juvenile gangs reflects conformity pressures, for example. In order to ensure acceptance and to gain prestige in the eyes of their peers, gang members must live up to the gang's violent norms. Group pressures may partially explain why American soldiers massacred unarmed Vietnamese civilians at My Lai and why National Guardsmen shot down students at Kent State. Some of the Guardsmen admitted firing only because their comrades were firing.

Certainly at My Lai, many soldiers complied out of fear of what might happen to them if they refused. In addition, conformity pressures are not limited to people occupying official roles such as soldiers. Members of oppressed minorities, tightly organized revolutionary organizations, labor movements, and terrorist groups, who suspend individual judgment and go along with group demands, are also subject to conformity pressures.[40]

Group pressure is not the sole reason for conforming to a group's norms. As we suggested earlier (pp. 156, 163), other people provide us with information about the world around us. Many of our beliefs that we hold to be factual are actually based on social consensus rather than on empirical verifications. Consequently, we may conform to group standards because they are guides to "correct behavior" and not because we feel forced to go along with the group. This is especially true in ambiguous situations. When in doubt, we turn to others for directions on how to behave.[41] For example, the Kent State Guardsmen may not have felt any pressure to shoot, but fired because the consensus of opinion among the Guardsmen was that their lives were in danger. On the basis of this social reality, which emerged from the chaos and confusion of Kent State, the Guardsmen opened fire. In sum, informational uncertainty as well as group pressure may lead to conformity and aggression.

We should not assume that conformity to norms and to group pressure always has "negative" outcomes. People may refrain from expressing their hostilities and aggressive tendencies because of counterpressures from the group. Nonviolence may even be a group norm, as it is among such religious communities as Quakers. Consequently, normative pressures may inhibit aggression. Group support may also help a person resist other social pressures towards committing a violent act. For example, in another experiment carried out by Stanley Milgram, stooges refused to follow the experimenter's orders to shock the Learner. Thus, rather than encouraging aggression, the group discouraged aggression. The real subjects in this group atmosphere were better able to resist the experimenter than subjects who faced him alone and without allies. Subjects in the group were less violent than subjects who were alone. Thus, group norms and pressures may inhibit aggression as well as facilitate its expression.[42]

Aggressing on Command

Many of the soldiers at My Lai and Kent State fired at unarmed civilians not because they wanted to, but because they were ordered to kill (or, at least, believed an order had been given). As soldiers they had been trained to follow orders without question, even if it meant taking another person's life. In fact, they were taught that their own life depended upon their immediate compliance to a superior officer's commands. Failure to comply might mean death at the hands of the enemy or punishment at the hands of their superiors. Perhaps the most extreme case of "aggression on command" occurred under the Nazis when men killed millions of helpless victims at the orders of legitimate authorities. Many of these men, including Adolf Eichmann, readily admitted that they disliked their work (or some aspects of it), but felt they had to do it because they must follow orders. Of course, we might question whether their statements are merely rationalizations aimed at saving themselves from punishment, but the role of authority in instigating aggression cannot be denied.

In another version of the conformity experiment that we described earlier (pp. 168–69), Milgram has demonstrated that "following orders" is not limited to Nazis, Germans, or soldiers. As in the other experiment, Milgram's subjects were psychologically normal, healthy, everyday run-of-the-mill American males. They varied in occupation from ditchdiggers to college students. In contrast to the previous experiment, the subjects in this experiment were alone with the experimenter, who commanded them to administer electric shocks to a helpless victim. Milgram found that the majority of his subjects followed orders and aggressed against the protesting victim. When questioned after the experiment, the subjects reported that they did not want to hurt the victim, but felt they had no choice. They believed the only action open to them was to follow the experimenter's commands. Few of them felt any guilt for their aggression, for they were "only following orders."[43]

The experimenter's power, and that of leaders in general, is derived from his social position as a legitimate authority. People perceive him as someone who has the right to give commands and to expect that others will obey him. Of course, there are limitations to his rights, but people are not always sure of when his legitimate orders become illegitimate. More generally, the relationship between a leader and follower is one where the leader by definition gives commands and the follower recognizes his right to command. For example, in Milgram's experiment a "good" subject is someone who knows "his place" and follows the experimenter's orders. Following orders is a crucial part of playing the role of subject, soldier, citizen, or student.

In addition to legitimate authority, the leader's power is based upon expertise. The experimenter is seen as a scientist who knows what he is doing and certainly knows more about the experiment than the ignorant subject. The army officer has been trained to lead and knows more about the "big picture" into which the platoon's actions fit. Thus, subjects and soldiers alike defer to the authority's superior knowledge, or

Figure 5-3   *Top left,* shock generator used in the experiments. Fifteen of the 30 switches have already been depressed. *Top right,* learner is strapped into chair and electrodes are attached to his wrist. Electrode paste is applied by the experimenter. Learner provides answers by depressing switches that light up numbers on an answer box. *Bottom left,* subject receives sample shock from the generator. *Bottom right,* subject breaks off experiment. On right, event recorder wired into generator automatically records switches used by the subject. Copyright 1965 by Stanley Milgram. From the film *Obedience,* distributed by the New York University Film Library.

rather to their belief in the authority's superior knowledge, and follow his commands. Many Americans supported the United States' military actions in Southeast Asia for this very reason. They believed that the President and his advisors knew much more than the man-in-the-street about the war and, therefore, such important decisions about bombing or not bombing should be left to the experts. After all, "father knows best."

Finally, authorities or leaders derive power just from the fact that they are in positions of leadership. As part of our childhood socialization, we learn that authorities are to be obeyed and respected. We come to hold them in awe and impute godlike properties to them. Young children believe authorities like the President are infallible, benevolent,

Figure 5-4 The leader's power to command is derived from his ability to reward and to punish, his expertise, and his legitimate claim to leadership. United Press International photo.

powerful, trustworthy, and all-knowing.[44] While we become somewhat more cynical about authorities as we grow older, we still tend to perceive them as benevolent, powerful, and wise leaders who should be obeyed. These generally favorable attitudes towards leaders dispose us to following their orders regardless of their content. Of course, these attitudes are not unshakeable, as recent reactions to the Vietnam war and the Watergate affair show.

The role of the leader in terms of instigating aggressive behavior is not restricted to his commanding particular aggressive actions. The style of leadership may have very strong effects on the type of aggressive behavior shown by group members. For example, one classic study found that children making masks under the direction of an adult leader behaved more aggressively in a social climate characterized by an authoritarian leadership style (i.e., rigid work prescriptions, no explanations of group goals, no group participation in decisions, etc.) as compared to a democratic style where group members were involved in the group's decisions. Thus, the general tone that the leaders set affects the relations between group members in terms of interpersonal aggression.[45]

Yielding to Situational Demands

In recent years, sociologists and social psychologists have repeatedly emphasized the role that situational demands and rules play in our daily interactions. They have pointed out that many situational influences on our behaviors are so routine in nature and so subtle that we do not even realize they exist, even though they have strong and decisive influences on our behavior.[46] Situational pressures can be so strong that "normal" people will do things that they thought they would never even dream of doing. For example, about 98 percent of the people asked how they would behave in the Milgram experimental situations claim they would either resist the experimenter's or the group's pressures. In the actual situation, however, the overwhelming majority comply to the group or the experimenter.

However, not all situational pressures stem from the overt demands that others place upon us. Another important set of situation pressures arises from the demands of the social roles that we occupy. For example, the role of policeman demands that he be aggressive in a number of situations, even though he might be a generally peaceful and friendly guy. The way in which role requirements may transform normal, adjusted college students into brutal, sadistic prison guards was recently demonstrated in a field experiment by a Stanford University psychologist, Philip Zimbardo.[47]

FOCUS
Power, Pathology, and Aggression in a
Simulated Prison

For six days and nights Philip Zimbardo and his co-workers turned the basement of the psychology department at Stanford University into a prison. Student volunteers were randomly assigned to the roles of prisoner or guard, and the prisoners were rounded up in a realistic police raid at their homes, apartments, or dormitories. They were fingerprinted, searched, photographed, and handcuffed by a real Palo Alto police officer before being driven blindfolded to the basement prison. At the prison, the prisoners were forced to wear loosely fitting smocks with just an ID number on the front and back, a chain around one ankle, and a nylon cap over their head. The guards wore a prison uniform consisting of identical khaki shirts and pants, silver reflector sunglasses (which prevented eye contact), billy clubs, whistles, handcuffs, and the keys to the cells. The rules for the prisoners were quite simple and straightforward: e.g., Rule 1: "Prisoners must remain silent during rest periods, after lights out, during meals, and whenever they are outside the prison yard. 2: Prisoners must eat at all mealtimes and only at mealtimes. 3: Prisoners must not move, tamper, deface or damage walls, ceilings, windows, doors or other prison property. . . . 7: Prisoners must address each other by their ID number only. 8: Prisoners must address their guards as Mr. Correctional Officer. . . . 16: Failure to obey any of the above rules may result in punishment."

In this realistic situation, the prisoners quickly experienced the feelings of isolation, powerlessness, frustration, and hopelessness that are typical in real-life prison populations. Even more interesting for the present discussion, the guards took on the behaviors of real-life guards and treated the prisoners in an authoritarian, brutal, and insulting manner. Over a third of the guards were judged as "extremely hostile, arbitrary and cruel in the forms of degradation and humiliation they invented. They appeared to thoroughly enjoy the power they wielded whenever they put on their uniforms and were transformed from their routine everyday existence into guards with virtually total power over other people."[48] Remember the roles of guards and prisoners were randomly assigned. The role of guard "called out" the brutal behavior in the subjects.

Like social norms, roles exert pressures upon people to behave in certain ways. Some of these pressures are external, in the sense that other people expect role incumbents to fulfill their role obligations and reward them accordingly. In addition, the pressures are internal in that roles become part of an individual's self-concept.[49] We know that soldiers are supposed to be "tough" and "brave" and, to the extent that we think of ourselves as soldiers, we try to be "tough" and "brave." Not only do peo-

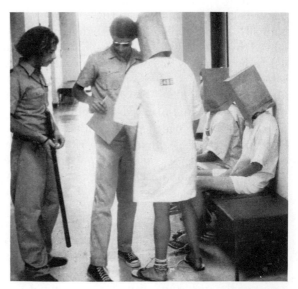

Figure 5-5   Student volunteers participate in randomly assigned roles as prisoners and guards in a six-day-long Stanford University prison study. Dr. Philip Zimbardo.

ple attempt to attain social approval via the correct performance of roles, but they also strive for self-approval in their role performance. The "prison guards" in Zimbardo's experiment may have been brutal or tough because they believed that toughness was an essential aspect of their role.

DEINDIVIDUATION

If you talked to policeman John Doe or to National Guardsman Pete Smith, you would probably find them to be perfectly nice guys and incapable of committing brutal and sadistic acts. Yet, as policemen or National Guardsmen, some John Does and Pete Smiths probably did commit such acts while on duty at the 1968 Chicago Democratic Convention or at Kent State. In part, their aggressiveness is a result of their social role. But also, external restraints against aggression (e.g., social norms or fear of punishment) are frequently weakened when a person carries out aggression that is part of his role. The aggression is legitimate for him, and he may lose sight of the point at which his actions cross over the fine line separating legitimate from illegitimate aggression. In addition, he may not feel responsible for his acts, since he sees himself as being committed to action by "higher-ups."

But beyond these reasons lies another reason why people may commit atrocities when acting as part of a group. The internal restraints that normally keep people from behaving brutally may be reduced or removed by the individual's *anonymity* in a group. Anonymity results when the person is no longer recognizable as an individual. To an outsider, all guards, soldiers, policemen, and rioters lose their individual identity and look alike. This "deindividuation" can result when the identity of an individual is masked by uniforms, gasmasks, sunglasses, or Ku Klux Klan hoods, which prevent others from identifying the individual. Sheer numbers of people may also result in deindividuation, since it becomes difficult for people to pick out any one member of a large crowd. Thus, to the outside observer, they are all the same in their khaki uniforms or in the "faceless crowd."

Similarly, the individual himself may lose his sense of individuality while wearing a uniform or as part of a large group. He sees himself as merely one among thousands and feels anonymous. In his famous book *The Crowd*, LeBon argued that individuals in masses act irresponsibly without fear of consequences because they feel they are anonymous. As a part of the mob, the person feels he cannot be identified and punished for his actions and that the responsibility for his behavior is diffused throughout the entire crowd.[50] William Golding's *Lord of the Flies*

Figure 5-6 Deindividuation results when the identity of an individual is masked as in the case of these Teutonic warriors from the film *Alexander Nevsky*. Deindividuation lessens the restraints against aggression. Compare this photograph to Fig. 4-2. Artkino from Sovfoto.

presents a particularly vivid picture of the conditions fostering anonymity and deindividuation as well as some potential consequences. In his fictional tale, a group of English schoolboys stranded on an isolated island turn into a horde of savage killers.

> The circle became a horseshoe. A thing was crawling out of the forest. It came darkly, uncertainly. The shrill screaming that rose before the beast was like a pain. The beast stumbled into the horseshoe.
> *"Kill the beast! Cut his throat! Spill his blood!"*
> The blue-white scar was constant, the noise unendurable. Simon was crying out something about a dead man on a hill.
> *"Kill the beast! Cut his throat! Spill his blood! Do him in!"*
> The sticks fell and the mouth of the new circle crunched and screamed. The beast was on its knees in the centre, its arms folded over its face. It was crying out against the abominable noise something about a body on the hill. The beast struggled forward, broke the ring and fell over the steep edge of the rock to the sand by the water. At once the crowd surged after it, poured down the rock, leapt on to the beast, screamed, struck, bit, tore. There were no words, and no movements but the tearing of teeth and claws.[51]

Unfortunately, the experimental investigation of deindividuation has been rather slow, and only a few experiments have been carried out. In an early experiment, which was recently replicated, it was found that the more difficulty group members had in identifying who had said what in a discussion, the more likely they were to express hostility.[52] The social psychologist Albert Pepitone of the University of Pennsylvania has pointed out that there is a close relationship between solidarity and co-hesion in a group and the process of deindividuation. He argues that "withdrawal of attention from each other as well as the actual expression of anger or the performance of aggressive acts increase the need for solidarity. At the same time close solidarity helps dissolve the distinction among individuals and allows for the overcoming of restraint."[53]

The most extensive research into the causes and consequences of deindividuation has been carried out by Philip Zimbardo. We have al-ready seen how the process of deindividuation could have played a role in his prison experiment. The guards may have been deindividualized by wearing uniforms and sunglasses and by often acting in groups, which lessened their sense of individuality. In an earlier experiment, Zimbardo showed that aggressive behavior in the usual aggression experiment be-came more severe when the "teacher" wore a hood. Zimbardo concluded that "under conditions specified as de-individuating these sweet normally mild-mannered college girls shocked another girl almost every time they had an opportunity to do so, sometimes for as long as they were allowed, and it did not matter whether or not that that fellow student was a nice girl who didn't deserve to be hurt."[54]

In an effort to analyze the psychological processes that underlie deindividuation, Zimbardo has described this condition by a number of characteristics such as anonymity, diffused or shared responsibility, emo-tional arousal, an expanded sense of the present, sensory input overload, physical involvement in action, reliance upon noncognitive interactions and feedback, novel or unstructured situations, and possibly states of consciousness effected through drugs or lack of sleep.[55] For example, some of these variables may have been acting at Kent State. The Guards-men were rendered anonymous by their uniforms and gasmasks (see Figure 4-2); were under the command of superior officers, which took their sense of individual responsibility away from them; were part of a large group of men acting in a confusing and unstructured situation; were emotionally aroused; were tired from lack of sleep; were perform-ing physical actions under conditions where communication was difficult; and were probably attending more to emotional feedback than to cogni-tive feedback from fellow Guardsmen and students.

According to Zimbardo, these antecedents of deindividuation lead to the following subjective changes: minimization of self-observation and evaluation, and lessening of concern for social evaluation, which leads to a weakening of the controls over behavior based upon guilt, shame, fear, and commitment, which in turn leads to a lower threshold for expressing inhibited behaviors such as aggression. In sum, conditions that lead to deindividuation remove restraints that usually inhibit a person's aggressive behaviors. As an anonymous member of a group or a mob, the person feels that he shares responsibility with others and, therefore, that no one is responsible. He feels secure from reprisal in his anonymity and powerful from his membership in the group. In addition, the lack of individuality in his opponents makes it easier for him to aggress against them. They are seen not as individuals, but rather as objects, and consequently, the restraints against aggression are lessened.[56]

SUMMARY

In this chapter we focused upon the nature of the social relationships between people as potential facilitating or inhibiting forces for aggression. We were concerned less with how people receive and interpret information from their social environment (see Chapter 4) than with the nature of the social environment per se. First, we saw that we like others who reward us and dislike those who punish us. While this is not terribly surprising, it does suggest a nonintuitive relationship between attitudinal similarity and friendship formation. Since similarity is rewarding, we tend to like those who are similar to ourselves, while we dislike those who are dissimilar. In the previous chapter, we saw that negative attitudes towards others facilitate aggression. Therefore, xenophobic reactions (i.e., reactions based on fear of things that are different) to dissimilar others make hostility and aggression more likely.

Second, and more directly to our concern with the nature of social relationships, we noted that how people are interdependent determines the quality of their behaviors towards each other. When people are negatively interdependent, competition, hostility, and aggression result. But when they are positively interdependent, cooperation and "peace and harmony" reign. Thus, the structure of interpersonal relationships may determine whether people exchange rewards or punishments above and beyond people's desires for "peace" or "war." People may be forced by circumstances into a struggle over scarce resources, which leads to hostile attitudes and actions. In addition, individuals may lose sight of their original goals and become obsessed with competition per se. Sometimes we follow irrational courses of action and suffer needless losses in order to "save face" and to defeat our opponent. Competition may lead to a rising spiral of punishments and ever-increasing levels of aggression.

Third, we turned our attention to the fact that most of our daily life occurs within the context of various groups. In general, we tend to classify people by whether they are members of our ingroups or of outgroups. For a variety of reasons, we feel attracted toward the ingroup and either neutral towards or repelled by outgroups. Since there is a general tendency to devalue people who are different, outgroups are often used as scapegoats upon whom we displace our aggression. In addition, competitive relationships between groups may intensify feelings of "us" versus "them" and lead to aggression. We also noted that deviants within groups are frequently the objects of aggression because they are seen as threatening the group's values and survival.

Fourth, we discussed the role of conformity and obedience as contributing factors to aggression. People may aggress against others not out of hatred of the outgroup, but out of love or fear of the ingroup. They may attack others as a means of avoiding punishment or gaining approval from their friends. Thus, aggression may be the result of social pressures to conform to group norms. In addition, people may conform to groups because they use the groups as standards for behavior. Particularly in ambiguous situations we turn to others for cues on how to act. If the rest of the group is attacking another person or group, we may go along as a consequence of our uncertainty about the proper course of action. Both social pressure and informational uncertainty are sources of conformity. Closely related to conformity to groups is obedience to authorities. Authorities are seen as justified in demanding certain behaviors of us, and, consequently, we may commit acts of violence under orders that we would never even consider doing on our own initiative.

Finally, we pointed out that feelings of anonymity and deindividuation may lessen constraints against aggression. As members of a large group (i.e., a mob or an army), people feel they are but one among thousands and they lose their sense of individuality. Being a member of the group makes them feel powerful and beyond punishment for their actions. They feel that they share responsibility with many others and cannot be held accountable. Since many are responsible, none are responsible. In addition, they feel that they are anonymous, that no one will be able to point a finger of guilt at them. Thus, conditions that foster anonymity (e.g., mobs or wearing uniforms) lessen restraints against violence.

In conclusion, this chapter, along with the preceding chapter, has presented a catalogue of social psychological variables affecting aggression. As such these two chapters have not presented theories of aggression, which specify the interrelationships between many variables. This is in sharp contrast to earlier chapters and those following, which focus upon particular theories. Unfortunately, there are no real social psychological theories of aggression. Consequently, we have only suggested some social psychological factors that may facilitate or inhibit aggression, and it remains for future efforts to organize such variables into a coherent theory.

FOOTNOTES

1 Aristotle (1932), pp. 103–5.

2 Newcomb (1961).

3 Byrne (1969).

4 Cf. Taylor and Mettee (1971); Mettee and Wilkins (1972).

5 Rokeach (1960).

6 Byrne and Wong (1962).

7 Silverman (1974); Stein, Hardyck, and Smith (1965); Triandis and Davis (1965).

8 Cf. Lane and Lerner (1970).

9 Berscheid and Walster (1969); Thibaut and Kelley (1959).

10 Lott and Lott (1972).

11 Cf. Festinger (1954); Byrne (1969), pp. 67–85.

12 Heider (1958), pp. 174–217.

13 One recent study failed to find a relationship between belief similarity and counteraggression. While a step in the right direction, this study suffers from a few methodological and conceptual difficulties: Hendrick and Taylor (1971).

14 Allport (1958).

15 Sherif (1956).

16 Deutsch (1962); Gergen (1969), pp. 34–71.

17 Of course, the reward structure does not lead automatically to either co-operation or to competition. For example, even if a person realizes he is positively interdependent with another, he is still faced with the decision of whether he should cooperate. First, does the other person realize the nature of their relationship? Second, can he trust the other person not to exploit him? Third, can they work out a means of cooperating that is mutually satisfactory? These and other issues, including the individual's personality, always make cooperation a problematic outcome. Deutsch (1960, 1962); Kelley and Stahelski (1970).

18 Berkowitz (1962), pp. 177–82.

19 Swingle (1970).

20 B. Brown (1968).

21 Cf. Deutsch and Krauss (1960); Shomer, Davis, and Kelley (1966); Fischer (1969).

22 Gergen (1971).

23 Allport (1958), pp. 28–46.

24 Allport (1958), p. 43.

25 Cartwright and Zander (1960), pp. 69–94.

26 Cantril (1941).

27 Allport (1958), pp. 235–49; Berkowitz (1962), pp. 132–64.

28 Hovland and Sears (1940); Raper (1933).

29 Pepitone and Reichling (1955).

30 Schachter (1951).

31 Freedman and Doob (1968), pp. 72–100.

32 Insko and Robinson (1967); Smith, Williams, and White (1967); Berkowitz (1962), pp. 174–77.

[33] Smith, Williams, and White (1967).

[34] Freedman and Doob (1968).

[35] Thibaut and Kelley (1959), pp. 126–48.

[36] Milgram (1964). Cf. Bordon and Taylor (1973).

[37] Kiesler and Kiesler (1969), p. 2.

[38] Willis (1963, 1965).

[39] Cf. Kelman (1958).

[40] Cf. Sherif (1965); Deutsch and Gerard (1955).

[41] Cf. Festinger (1954); Hyman and Singer (1968).

[42] Milgram (1965). Cf. Asch (1955); Donnerstein and Donnerstein (1973).

[43] Milgram (1963). A filmed version of Professor Milgram's experiments on obedience is distributed by the New York University Film Library, 26 Washington Place, New York, N.Y. 10003. It is available for educational groups.

[44] Hess and Torney (1968).

[45] Lippitt and White (1965).

[46] Cf. Garfinkle (1967).

[47] Zimbardo (1973).

[48] Zimbardo (1973). © 1973 by The New York Times Company. Reprinted by permission.

[49] Gergen (1971).

[50] LeBon (1896).

[51] Golding (1962), pp. 182–83. Reprinted by permission from Coward, McCann & Geoghegan, Inc. and Faber and Faber Ltd.

[52] Festinger, Pepitone, and Newcomb (1952); Cannavale, Scarr, and Pepitone (1970).

[53] Pepitone (1972), p. 28.

[54] Zimbardo (1969).

[55] Zimbardo (1969).

[56] Watson (1973) tested Zimbardo's deindividuation hypothesis by using a cross-cultural survey technique. He found that "killing, torturing, or mutilating the enemy" was more prevalent in societies where warriors were deindividuated by body paint, masks, etc. before going into battle.

6 / THE GRAPES OF WRATH

social structural factors

In previous chapters we searched for the origins of social conflict and violence in the biological and psychological makeup of people. We discussed the role of physiology, drives, learning, perception, attitudes, and social interaction in face-to-face situations. Consequently, we have deliberately minimized the important fact that "man is a political [i.e., social] animal." Like most other primates, human beings are gregarious and live in societies.[1] The complexity of human societies varies from the relatively simple organization of hunting-gathering bands to the highly intricate world of modern industrial and urban nations.[2] Regardless of its complexity, society affects profoundly the individual's behavior. Therefore, to more fully understand our behavior, we must also consider the nature of our society and our position in society.

If biological and psychological agents were the sole or major causes of aggression, we would anticipate few differences in the level of strife present in different societies and within any one society over time.[3] If we compare the criminal homicide rates of modern nations, we immediately notice that there are great differences between nations (Figure 6-1). Although there are many problems and possible biases in using arrest rates as indices of violence,[4] the homicide rate in the United States is between four and eight times greater than the rate of other industrialized countries. In addition, the American rate is increasing faster than

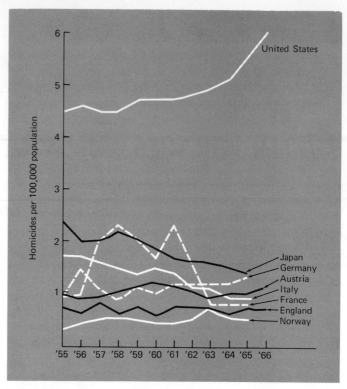

Figure 6-1 Variations in reported homicide offense rates for selected countries. From: Mulvihill and Tumin (1969), p. 118, fig. 50a.

that of other nations.[5] Biological and psychological differences between Americans and foreigners cannot completely account for this because the majority of our ancestors migrated to America from these countries. There are differences not only between societies in violence rates, but also within a particular society. Arrest rates show that a person's chances of either committing violence or being its victim depend greatly upon his social location in American society.[6] Unfortunately, there are no national data on violent crimes broken down by the offender's social class, but a variety of independent studies indicate its importance. For example, in a study of young male delinquents in Philadelphia, the combined arrest rate for criminal homicide, forcible rape, aggravated assault, and robbery was 142 per 1,000 persons for working-class boys and 35 per 1,000 for middle-class boys.[7] Other sources confirm that a disproportionate amount of violent crime is committed by low-income people.[8] These studies and the data reported in Table 6-1 indicate that young working-class, black, and southern males run the greatest risk of both committing and suffering from violence. In short, the incidence of violent crime is not evenly distributed through American society. Certain cate-

Table 6-1

Variations in Reported Arrest Rates for Criminal Homicide
and Four Major Violent Crimes Combined, 1967
(Rates per 100,000 specified population)

		Criminal homicide	*Four major violent crimes combined**
Sex:	Male	15	349
	Female	3	37
Race:	White	3	77
	Black	54	960
Age:†	10–14	1	123
	15–17	10	408
	18–24	18	436
	25+	8	127
Region:	South	9	260††
	West	5	272
	Northeast	4	237
	Northcentral	5	236

* This index consists of the sum of the rates of criminal homicide, forcible rape, aggravated assault, and robbery.
† Based on urban arrest rates for cities with population over 2,500.
†† When robbery rates are excluded from the Four Major Violent Crimes index, the South has the highest violence rate.
SOURCE: Mulvihill and Tumin (1969), Appendices 5–9.

gories of people are more likely to commit violent crime and to be its victims.

Just as societies differ in their rates of interpersonal (i.e., criminal) violence, so are they dissimilar in their rates of intergroup violence (e.g., violent confrontations between different social groups as in communal riots between Muslims and Hindus in India). In a comparative study of the levels of collective violence in 114 nations, Ted Gurr, a political scientist, reported that nonindustrial societies had more violence than industrial countries. In addition, the United States ranked forty-first, indicating that its rate of collective violence is greater than most industrial and nonindustrial countries. In fact, only France and Italy had more intergroup violence than the United States among highly industrialized countries.[9] Thus, nations differ in their rates of interpersonal and intergroup violence, and America is among the more violent countries for both types of violence.

Within the United States, the pattern of intergroup violence has changed in two ways during the past 150 years. First, violence has shifted to different conflicting groups. Early in American history, the conflict was between Protestants and Catholics, slave-staters and free-staters, farmers and manufacturers, settlers and railroad magnates, and workers and capitalists. Now, the conflict pivots mainly around racial groups.[10] Second, the form of intergroup violence has altered. For example, during earlier racial confrontations, white mobs invaded black neighborhoods and did battle with black mobs. These were true communal riots, where members of the two groups fought directly with each other. More recently, the combat is between black civilians and white agents of social control such as the police and the military. The clashes are no longer between black and white mobs.[11]

These variations in both interpersonal and intergroup violence suggest that we should investigate social structural factors as well as biological and psychological determinants. However, in turning to social structure, we are making a subtle shift in the focus of our concern. Previously we had been asking what makes a *particular* person violent. Now we are asking what makes the *rate* of violence differ from one group of people to the next: Why does violence occur more frequently among some categories of people than among others? As we shall see, social structural explanations are not sufficient by themselves to account for the behavior of a particular person in a particular group. But they can explain why some groups as a whole are more violent than others. Social structure may increase the likelihood of a person's performing a violent act by virtue of his group membership, but other factors, such as his personality or the immediate social situation, will determine whether he commits the act. However, our present concern is not in explaining a single person's behavior. Our question is how can we account for the uneven distribution of interpersonal violence and the occurrence of intergroup violence in America?

INTERPERSONAL VIOLENCE

Means and Ends

Social stratification and culture are two components of social structure (i.e., how society is organized) that are particularly important for understanding violence. In most, but not in all societies, people are divided into social categories that command different degrees of respect, power, and privilege. These categories or strata form a systematic hierarchy of ranks ranging from social inferiority at the bottom to social superiority at the top. This hierarchy of invidious comparisons is called the society's *social stratification system*.[12] In actuality, most societies have more than one means of ranking people, though the various systems usually coincide. That is, more than one hierarchy of social prestige commonly exists, but people who are superior in one system tend also to be superior in the others.[13] For example, we can distinguish at least five stratification systems in American society: economic, racial, ethnic-religious, occupational, and educational. Black Americans are usually ranked low on all of these dimensions. They are usually poor, have low-prestige jobs (e.g., unskilled laborers), have little education, belong to low-prestige religious groups (e.g., Baptist as opposed to Episcopalian), and, by virtue of their race, they are considered to be socially inferior to white Americans. Since these different stratification systems tend to order people in the same way, we can speak of only one system of *socioeconomic status* or SES, which we shall think of as a generalized hierarchy of social prestige. We shall use the word "status" to denote a particular position or level in the social prestige hierarchy.

Social stratification systems differ in the ease with which a person can gain in socioeconomic status (upward social mobility) or lose status (downward social mobility). At one extreme, a person is born into a particular stratum and is doomed or blessed with that status for the rest of his life. No matter what he does, it is impossible for him to move upward in the social hierarchy, although it is sometimes possible to move downward. The lines between strata are clearly drawn and movement across them is extremely difficult. In such systems, the person's social status is *ascribed* and based upon criteria over which he has no control (e.g., sex, skin color, family lineage). Social stratification in caste societies, such as India, ancient Rome, and medieval Europe, rely upon ascribed status in ranking people. The *sine qua non* of caste systems is the lack of social mobility.

At the other extreme, a person may move with relative ease up and down in the status hierarchy. He may acquire the criteria of high status such as education, occupation, wealth, proper speech and dress, etc. and thereby be accorded prestige. How far he progresses upward depends upon his native abilities, effort, and luck. However, social mobility is a two-way street. It is also easy for a person to suffer downward mobility through the loss of high-status credentials (e.g., wealth). In opposition to caste systems, upward and downward mobility is frequent in *open-class* systems where status depends upon *achieved* criteria. While no present or past society possesses unlimited or equal opportunities for mobility, modern industrialized societies approach the ideal of open-class systems. In actuality, modern societies contain elements of both caste and class systems. In American society, race is an ascribed status. No matter what a black American does, he is still black and therefore considered to be socially inferior. But, at the same time, a person (be he white or black) can improve his social standing by improving his education, becoming wealthy, and joining the right social clubs. Thus, social stratification in America rests on both ascribed and achieved criteria and contains elements of both caste and class societies.

A person's SES, particularly his social class (i.e., ranking in the economic hierarchy) has a great and lasting influence upon his life. It partially determines whom he will date and marry, the number of children he will have and how long they will live, where he will live and how frequently he will move, his manner of speech and style of dress, whether he will be mentally ill and the type of mental illness he will suffer, his political attitudes and how he will vote, whether he will commit murder or suicide, when he will die and why, and where he will be buried.[14] In addition, his SES affects his ability to influence other people and get them to carry out his wishes.[15] Obviously, the chairman of the board of a multimillion-dollar conglomerate carries more clout than a ditchdigger! Partly because of his social power, people are more likely to treat him with respect and deference. However, power is not the sole reason for receiving reverence. The high-status person has characteristics that most people in society covet, value, and aspire to. Thus, SES determines how a person will live his life, how he will treat others, and how they will treat him.

Culture, another component of social structure, refers to all the knowledge, beliefs, customs, skills, material artifacts, and values that people obtain as members of society. Although many societies share cultural elements, culture is the "distinctive way of life of a group of people, their complete design for living."[16] The society's culture defines how people should live their everyday lives and what makes life worth living. It holds up certain goals as the "good life," the end states that people should value and aspire to obtain. In American society, the good life consists of having a family, a car, a split-level house in the suburbs, a color TV, and leisure time to enjoy the "fruits of our labor." Besides prescribing goals, culture also proscribes (i.e., prohibits) goals. We are told that a life of idleness and debauchery should not be pursued and we are punished for striving toward such proscribed goals.

However, the same goals are not always held out to all people in a society. Depending on their location in the stratification system, people may aim for different goals. Upper-status people may pursue one set of goals, while lower-status people value other goals. The society's culture defines which goals are appropriate for the different social strata. This situation is usually part of a general pattern of divergent values and life-styles associated with each social stratum. In this situation, each stratum is said to have its own *subculture*. For instance, distinctive goals and unique styles of life were prescribed for each of the four major castes of classical Indian society. In contrast to Indian society, many goals are held in common by Americans of all social strata. We are all told to pursue monetary success. However, this does not mean that there are no subcultural differences in American society. A wide variety of evidence suggests that social strata in America have slightly different life-styles, values, beliefs, and rules for behavior. We shall return to this point later.

Besides establishing appropriate goals, cultures also delimit the permitted means for attaining these goals. Cultural rules or *norms* proscribe and prescribe the means a person may employ. Americans are told that honesty, individual effort, education, a steady job, initiative, and perseverance are legitimate means to the "good life," but cheating, robbery, and shady stock deals are prohibited as illegitimate means. Notice that the most efficient and direct means are often illegitimate, while the more tortuous routes are often legitimate. Thus, legitimate means are not always easy to follow. In addition, it is not always clear what the legitimate means are. Different subcultures may define the same means as legitimate or illegitimate. Working-class Americans may believe physical aggression is a legitimate means of getting money, while middle-class norms taboo the use of force. There may also be conflict between the norms within a culture or subculture. For example, the proverb "It is not whether you win or lose that is important, it is how you play the game" contradicts the maxim that "the ends justify the means." Consequently, even if a person wants to conform to norms, it is not always easy because of ambiguities in the rules.

Let us summarize the discussion up to this point. First, we pointed out that societies are stratified. People are ranked in terms of social superiority. A person's location in the stratification system has serious consequences for his life chances (e.g., how much money he will earn, his health, his level of educational attainment), for his social power, and for his social prestige. Next, we stressed that cultures set goals and delimit means. Goals are those things in life that people value, desire, and strive to obtain. Means are the tools and procedures employed to obtain goals. Social norms define which means may be legitimately employed.

Now, how is all of this related to interpersonal violence? The answer to this question starts with another question: What happens when legitimate means to goals are not equally available to all members of society?

FOCUS
Social Structure and Deviance

In America, many of the same cultural goals (particularly monetary success) are set for everyone regardless of his SES. Our culture proclaims that success is open to all and that every man, woman, and child can realize the American dream and change from "rags to riches" like a Horatio Alger character, if he only sells enough newspapers. If a person does not make his fortune, it is his own fault for not trying hard enough. So goes the American creed.

However, the American reality is something else again. Not all Americans have equal access to the culturally sanctioned means of achieving monetary success. For example, high-paying jobs demand high levels of skills, which rest upon many years of education and training. But not everyone can obtain the required college education, since it costs a small fortune. In addition, discrimination blocks the road to success for minority groups.[17] In contrast to working-class and minority people, middle-class people do have the ability to take advantage of the prescribed legitimate means. They have the money to pay for a prestigious college education.

Consequently, the social structure creates a strain between goals and means. Everyone is enjoined to struggle toward the same goals and admonished to use the same legitimate means. But, for lower SES individuals, these means are unavailable. "Ay, there's the rub."

The disjunction between means and goals creates a pressure towards "deviant behavior" (i.e., behavior which violates social norms), with the greatest pressure on those people facing the greatest disjunction. Thus, we expect higher rates of deviance among working-class people. But what types of deviance would occur? Robert Merton, a sociologist at Columbia University, hypothesizes that there are five possible types of reactions or adaptations to this situation, depending on whether the individual continues to accept the cultural goals and/or means or rejects them.[18]

(1) Conformity: In this adaptation, people continue to accept both goals and means. They continue to strive for the prescribed goals and to use culturally sanctioned means.

(2) Innovation: Here, people continue the struggle towards culturally defined success, but reject the means offered them. They turn to alternative, but illegitimate, means. Violence (e.g., armed robbery, mugging) is one innovative technique, but there are many nonviolent means available, too (e.g., forgery, prostitution, numbers rackets).

(3) Ritualism: This involves the rejection of goals, but the retention of means. People give up all hope of attaining the goals, but continue to go through the motions of striving. This adaptation is deviant in the sense that people no longer ascribe to important cultural values.

(4) Retreatism: People may also reject both the goals and means, and, as such, retreatism is the exact opposite of conformity. Mental illness, alcoholism, and drug addiction are examples of retreatism. Violence may accompany this adaptation when alcoholics or drug addicts require money to support their habits and turn to crime to obtain it.

(5) Rebellion: In the last adaptation, cultural means and goals are rejected, but new ones are substituted. It is an attempt to alter society and create a new world, where a new set of goals and means is normative. This course of action may also lead to violence to the degree that it develops into a revolutionary social movement. But, when that occurs, we are no longer talking about interpersonal violence and have moved into the realm of intergroup violence.

According to Merton, deviant behavior results from a strain or pressure created by the social structure. Regardless of their social strata, Americans place a high value on success. For example, over three-quarters of the people interviewed in a small upstate New York town felt that "getting ahead in life" was very important to them. In addition, working-class people were more likely to feel this way and to place a high value on material and economic symbols of success (e.g., home ownership) than were middle-class respondents.[19] However, lower-status and minority people do not have the opportunities to pursue cultural goals of monetary success. As we go down the status hierarchy, a greater proportion of people recognize that chances are limited. They may believe in "equal opportunity" in the abstract, but they also know that a person's social class limits his probability of success. In a study done in Muskegon, Michigan, about three-quarters of the respondents agreed that "there is plenty of opportunity and anyone who works hard can go as far as he wants" (an abstract statement of the American Dream). However, less than half believed that a son of a poor man had the same chance of making the same money as a son of a rich man. Working-class people were less likely to believe this than were middle-class respondents (47 percent versus 57 percent agreeing respectively).[20] Yet, a 1969 national survey shows that the majority of Americans blame poverty on the personal characteristics of the poor (e.g., "they don't work hard enough") rather than on social structural factors (e.g., discrimination, inferior quality school).[21]

Lower SES people are caught in a classic "Catch 22." On the one hand, they are told to strive for monetary success, while, on the other hand, they are denied access to the legitimate means of achieving it. Consequently, they may turn to illegitimate means (e.g., crime) or give up their quest as a way of solving their dilemma.

Thus, Merton's theory helps account for the higher rate of violent and nonviolent crime among working-class as compared to middle-class strata and among minority as compared to majority groups. Since the cultural imperative for monetary success weighs more heavily upon men (i.e., they are supposed to make the fortune), this schema suggests that men feel the strain more than women. Younger people are more likely to be under strain because they are first crashing headlong into reality. Their hopes and dreams are more completely based upon the American Dream and are yet to be tempered by experience. Consequently, they are most likely to find the disjunction between means and goals frustrating. Merton's theory also leads us to expect that deviance rates should be higher in urban areas because of the concentration of minority and working-class people.

Of course, Merton does not suggest that all crime is committed by these types of people. His explanation only claims that the pressure is greater on them, and therefore that a greater proportion of them will become deviant. But what determines the type of deviance that will be most prevalent? Merton's theory suggests that deviance will take particular forms, but it does not offer a way of predicting their relative frequency.

Legitimate and Illegitimate Opportunities

Even if a person wants to "hit it big" by "pulling off a heist," he cannot always do so (and not just because a cop is standing next to him). Suppose young Al Capone wants to "knock off" Tiffany's and "rip off" the Hope diamond. First, he needs help. The job is just too big for one man, so he has to know and recruit accomplices. Second, he cannot just walk into the store unarmed and say "Turn over the loot." He needs a few "rods." But to lay in a supply of rods and ammunition he has to have the right connections with gun merchants. Third, he has to face the possibility that the Hope diamond is safely locked away in a vault and that he can not "persuade" the store manager to open it. Either he needs to have an "inside man" who knows the combination or he needs to know how to "crack" a safe. And for this he needs the appropriate "tools of the trade." Finally, once he has the diamond (and has escaped from the police), he has the problem of disposing of his "hot ice." He needs a "fence." In short, there are many technical obstacles standing in his way

Figure 6-2 According to Merton's theory, when individuals cannot obtain cultural goals through legitimate means, they turn to illegitimate means, such as crime. In these pictures a manager of a shoe store attempted to tackle a shoplifter, and he was in turn attacked by the shoplifter's friends. Wide World Photos.

to success via a life of crime. In many ways, the problems facing a would-be jewel thief are the same as those facing a would-be jeweler. They both need to have the proper connections and the appropriate skills.

Consequently, to understand the occurrence of crime we have to take into account the "opportunities" for deviance available to people.[22] By opportunities, we mean the chances a person has of learning the skills, motivations, beliefs, values, knowledge, and of making contacts with people that will enable him to pursue a "deviant career." People have to learn how not to be law-abiding citizens. They learn criminal motivations and knowledge through the process of *differential association*.[23] In the process of being socialized, people are exposed to both conventional and deviant values, beliefs, and skills. For example, in comparison to nondelinquents, delinquent boys have more frequent and close contacts with delinquent friends and have fewer contacts with adults who support conventional values and who can help them into legitimate careers. Also, members of juvenile gangs and working-class and Negro boys are less likely to believe in the availability of legitimate opportunities, but more likely to believe in the availability of illegitimate means and to approve of these than are nondelinquent, middle-class, and white boys.[24] Depending on whether he is exposed to more conventional or deviant learning situations, the person turns to either legitimate or illegitimate means for achieving success.

However, the opportunities to learn and practice conventional or deviant careers are not evenly distributed throughout society. Middle-class people have greater chances of becoming bankers, jewelers, and accountants, while working-class people have fewer opportunities to pursue these lucrative legitimate careers. However, the opportunities for criminal careers, such as joining the Mafia, are greater for them. But illegitimate opportunities are not equally available to all working-class people. In the United States, organized crime has been dominated by successive ethnic groups that discriminate against others as much as conventional society. The Godfather is not an "equal opportunity employer." Presently organized crime is dominated by Italians, but Irish and East-European Jews have previously held sway.[25] Although many of the Cosa Nostra's activities prosper in black ghettos, blacks have limited access to lucrative criminal occupations because these jobs are reserved for "members of the family." However, these positions may be opening up for blacks as black criminal organizations become more successful and competitive with Italian organizations.[26] Thus, besides being located in legitimate opportunity structures (i.e., the opportunity to employ legitimate means in Merton's schema), people are also located in illegitimate opportunity structures.[27]

As Merton's theory leads us to expect, low-income neighborhoods are high-crime areas.[28] However, these neighborhoods vary "in the extent to which they provide the young with alternative [albeit illegitimate] routes to higher status."[29] At one extreme are neighborhoods providing access to successful criminal careers. These communities are characterized by the presence of criminal role-models, criminal apprenticeship systems, and the integration of criminal and conventional worlds. Young boys growing up in these areas are frequently in contact with successful criminals, who flash "fancy cars and fast women." Just as middle-class children imitate successful adults, lower-class children take successful adult criminals as their role-models. The boys also learn the "tricks of the trade" by associating with older boys who, in turn, associate with adult criminals. Not only do the older boys and adults impart the skills needed for a "life of crime," but they offer moral support by encouraging the younger boys to engage in "on the job training" (e.g., petty thefts). In effect, the boys go through an informal apprenticeship program from which "talent scouts" recruit for the "big time."

In these neighborhoods, the criminal and conventional worlds are not completely isolated from each other. In fact, criminals participate in many conventional institutions such as churches, social clubs, and political organizations, maintain contacts with the "straight world," and also pursue legitimate, "straight" careers. These contacts help them further their illegitimate careers by providing respectability and needed services (e.g., bail bonding, legal aid) and by serving as markets for their criminal services (e.g., disposal of stolen property). Thus, there is a degree of integration between criminals and noncriminals.

Two sociologists, R. A. Cloward and L. E. Ohlin, refer to these neighborhoods as *criminal subcultures*, because they are characterized by a stable, integrated, and organized set of norms and values surrounding criminal and violent activities.[30] While the opportunities for success via legitimate means are few in criminal subcultures, there are many opportunities via illegitimate means. In addition, criminal subcultures tend to channel violence towards instrumental functions (i.e., restrict its use to professional activities) and away from expressive functions (i.e., emotional release through violent outbursts). Young "apprenticed hoods" may be violent in attempting to gain the attention and favor of prestigious higher-ups and because of overconformity to the norms of the group to which they do not yet belong (i.e., organized crime syndicates). But once they are taken into the organization, it exerts control over violence. Like legitimate businesses, organized crime has no use for impulsive and unpredictable individuals, and it tries to control its employees. While violence is used as a tool, it is used with reserve. Consequently, criminal subcultures tend to direct violence towards criminally instrumental activities.[31]

At the other extreme from criminal subculture communities are neighborhoods that do not provide opportunities for either conventional or criminal careers. These communities, characterized by transiency and instability, lack organized criminal activities. Crime takes on the form of individualistic enterprises and is less grandiose. Instead of growing up under the tutelage of "big-time operators," boys maturing in these communities interact with "small-time hoods" and, consequently, do not have access to the esoteric knowledge and skills needed to be a successful criminal.

In reaction to their poor chances of making it big in both the straight and criminal worlds, boys in these neighborhoods turn to expressive violence. A *conflict subculture* develops in which boys gain prestige

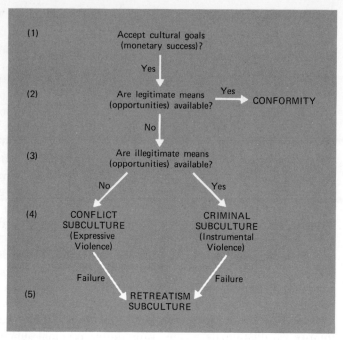

Figure 6-3 A flow chart of Cloward and Ohlin's theory of delinquency.

by establishing a "rep" as a streetfighter. Outside of the criminal and conventional opportunity structures, gang violence flourishes as an expression of frustration and of status striving. While violence in the criminal subculture is a means to an end, in the conflict subculture it is an end in itself. The whole subculture revolves around a mystique of violence.

We can summarize our discussion by using the flow chart shown in Figure 6-3. The steps in the chart represent a time sequence progressing from top to bottom. What happens to people at each level determines their subsequent behavior. The chart starts with Merton's assumption that people are first exposed to and accept the cultural goals and strive towards them regardless of their location in the social stratification system. However, because of their social location, some or many working-class people discover that legitimate means to success are less open to them than to middle-class people. Both strata have internalized the same goals, but the society is so constructed that middle-class people have greater opportunities to achieve these goals via culturally prescribed means. Thus, lower-status people are faced with a conflict between culturally defined goals and means. This conflict predisposes them to illegitimate means (i.e., they seek alternative means of achieving the same goals). At this point, we leave Merton's theory and enter Cloward and Ohlin's model.

Cloward and Ohlin hypothesize that illegitimate opportunity structures exist and that a group's location in them determines the type of deviance that will prevail. Some working-class communities have access to illegitimate means via organized crime and develop criminal subcultures. However, others lack these deviant avenues and develop conflict subcultures. Violence is a part of both subcultures, but in the former it serves instrumental functions and in the latter it performs expressive functions. Instead of equating success with money as the dominant culture and the criminal subculture do, the conflict subculture awards prestige to those who prove themselves "on the field of honor" in gang fights. According to Cloward and Ohlin, high rates of violent crime reflect limited access to both legitimate and illegitimate opportunity structures (levels 3 and 4 in Figure 6-3).

Finally, level 5 introduces a new point. As we all know, not everyone strikes it rich in the conventional world. The same is true in the criminal world; some people just are not good crooks and are failures. Similarly, others cannot make it in the conflict subculture. Perhaps they are not brave or strong enough or have internalized psychological inhibitions against violence and suffer from guilt. In any event, they cannot succeed as streetfighters. Cloward and Ohlin suggest that such "double failures" (i.e., those who cannot succeed in either the legitimate or illegitimate worlds) join *retreatism subcultures* (i.e., become psychotics, alcoholics, drug addicts, hobos, panhandlers, etc.).[32] Of course, this discussion is highly oversimplified. People are not faced with pure choices between "legitimate" and "illegitimate" careers. Many working-class and middle-class people operate in both the straight and criminal worlds by pursuing both types of careers simultaneously or serially.

In terms of our main interest, high rates of interpersonal violence are concentrated in those social strata that have unfavorable locations in both the legitimate and illegitimate opportunity structures.

Subcultures and Violence

As we mentioned earlier, subcultures are variations on a theme of the dominant culture. They form distinctive clusters of values, norms, beliefs, techniques, and artifacts and are associated with particular social aggregates of people. They share many aspects of the dominant "parent" culture, but they also include new elements and/or modifications of old elements. For example, we see many similarities in the way people think and behave that identify northerners and southerners as bearers of a common American culture (as distinct from, say, British or Chinese cultures). However, we also note many differences (e.g., most quickly and easily in language and pronunciation) that give the regions distinctive subcultures. In addition to regional subcultures, there are ethnic,

social class, and, perhaps, occupational subcultures in the United States.
Each of these groups has a style of life that distinguishes it from the
others.

FOCUS
Subculture of Violence

The sociologists Wolfgang and Ferracuti along with others[33] suggest that the high rates of violence among certain groups in society
reflect the existence of subcultures of violence. Violence is "viewed as a
reflection of basic values that stand apart from the dominant, the central, or parent culture."[34] The subculture places a premium on the use of
violence in a wider variety of situations than does the dominant culture.
Growing up in a subculture of violence, individuals learn that violence
is the expected response to certain social interactions and develop
favorable attitudes towards the use of violence. To say that a subculture
of violence exists does not imply that violence is the predominant behavior, but only that it is more frequently "demanded" and employed
than in the dominant culture. In comparison to the dominant culture, nonviolence is the counternorm. The normative response to a slur against one's
parentage may be a challenge to a duel, and the person who fails to
"demand satisfaction" is considered to be a coward and not worthy of
respect. Thus, violence becomes a part of people's lives and is used daily
to solve difficult problems and problem situations. Consequently, people
may use physical force without feeling guilt, for the subculture of
violence supplies moral support for its use.

The high rates of violence among working-class and black young
males may result from subcultures of violence. Some social scientists
claim that the values and norms of the working-class "constitute a distinctive *patterning* of concerns which differ significantly, both in rank
order and weighting from that of American middle-class culture. . . ."[35]
Men are expected to live up to the Bogart image of the strong and silent
type who takes "no guff from nobody."

Many of the facts about interpersonal violence are consistent with
this hypothesis for a working-class subculture of violence. First, interpersonal violence occurs most frequently between intimates. You are
more likely to be hurt or killed by someone you know than by a stranger!
Second, and contrary to popular belief, violence usually occurs among
people of the same race and/or social status. For example, a black is
more likely to kill a fellow black than a white. These two facts suggest

that violence occurs among people who share the same values and norms. Similarly, a third fact, that violence (e.g., homicide) usually occurs in the "heat of passion" (i.e., is not premeditated), points towards interpersonal violence occurring between people who are similarly aroused by social stimuli. Together these facts suggest that the combatants share common values, beliefs, and norms that define the situation as one in which force is the proper response. "Homicide . . . is often a situation not unlike that of confrontation in wartime combat, in which two individuals committed to the value of violence come together and in which chance, prowess, or possession of a particular weapon dictates the identity of the slayer and of the slain."[36]

These facts are suggestive, but is there more direct evidence for group differences in attitudes towards violence? The 1969 national survey of attitudes towards violence, which we discussed in Chapter 4, shows that working-class men are more favorable towards violence than are middle-class men.[37] A national survey carried out in 1968 for the National Commission on the Causes and Prevention of Violence found a few differences by age, sex, and residence in attitudes towards violence and in the actual frequency of physical aggression. Young male residents of metropolitan areas were the highest approvers of violence. There is some evidence that blacks may approve of violence more than whites, but the relationship is weak and not clear-cut. A recent reanalysis of these data found no social class differences in attitudes or actual experience of physical aggression.[38] Finally, another study using the 1968 data failed to find any relationships between general values and aggressive behavior, although it found educational and income differences in these values and in approval of violence (i.e., lower-income and less-educated people approved of violence more than higher-income and better-educated people).[39] Although the picture is not clear-cut, these surveys suggest there are social class differences in the approval of violence.

Besides valuing violence, working-class culture also provides techniques for neutralizing the dominant culture's prohibitions against violence. Since lower-status people are exposed to the dominant culture, they are aware of the middle-class taboos against force and often feel ambivalent or guilty about their behavior. However, by using "techniques of neutralization,"[40] they subtly reinterpret the dominant culture's norms so that they can remain committed to them, but still engage in aggression without guilt. While still supporting the law in the abstract, they learn definitions favorable to violating the law and are provided justifications for their deviance. For example, they deny responsibility for their behavior by blaming "fate," their "bad neighborhood," or their "bad companions." They deny the harmfulness of their behavior by minimizing its consequences (e.g., "It was just a slap" or "I only borrowed the car").

They insist that the injured party deserved punishment or retaliation. They condemn their condemners by seeing them as hypocrites or as impelled by spite. By appealing to each of these rationalizations, they lessen the impact of middle-class norms upon them. They perceive the situation as one where these norms do not apply and as one in which their behavior is justified.

Another subculture of violence in the United States is that of the South, which has been described as "that part of the United States lying below the Smith and Wesson line."[41] Pictures from the Old South of duels, bear baiting, slavery, lynchings, whippings, brawls, and night-riders combine with scenes from the New South of more lynchings, church bombings, assassinations, rampaging mobs, police dogs, and brutal police to form an image of a subculture of violence. This subjective impression is buttressed by a variety of objective facts. For example, 52 percent and 34 percent of southern white and black families own firearms as compared to 27 and 15 percent of nonsouthern white and black families.[42] Also the South has had consistently higher murder and assault rates than the North. The 1967 southern murder rate (9.4 per 100,000 population) and aggravated assault rate (164 per 100,000) were about 200 percent and 143 percent of the nonsouthern homicide (4.6) and assault rates (115).[43] And these higher rates cannot be attributed to socioeconomic and demographic differences between the South and the rest of the nation. When racial composition, median income, urbanization,

Figure 6-4 A variety of impressions and facts suggests that the long tradition of violence in the South reflects a subculture of violence. Wide World Photos.

median number of school years completed, available medical care, and unemployment are taken into account, the difference between regional homicide rates still remains.[44] In addition, the 1969 national survey of American males showed that southerners were more favorably disposed towards violence than non-southerners. (However, the Violence Commission survey found little evidence for a southern culture of violence.)[45] Together these impressions and facts suggest that the long tradition of violence in the South reflects a subculture of violence.

This violent tradition may owe its origins to the long frontier and slavery experiences of the South. In contrast to the North, the South remained a frontier society well past the Civil War. The absence and weakness of organized police forces and the prevalence of weapons made the frontier a dangerous place, where individuals had to defend their rights by the force of arms. Because of the powerlessness of official law-enforcement agencies, citizens often banded together into vigilante committees to protect their mutual rights and to punish outlaws.[46] Thus, southerners learned to rely more heavily upon the "quick draw" and the mob than upon the agents of the law. Since the frontier lasted longer in the South, its effects were greater there than in the North.

The necessity of controlling Negro slaves and the constant fear of slave uprisings also led to an emphasis on force. Numerous local militias were organized to repress actual or imagined slave rebellions, and brutality was the handmaiden of the plantation system. Disobedient and runaway slaves were savagely punished for their transgressions. The Civil War and Reconstruction also had brutalizing effects on the Southern collective psyche. The KKK and other white vigilante groups were organized to insure that blacks would stay "in their place" and that the white southern way of life would prevail. Thus, the frontier and slavery made violence a part of the southern life style, where it was "handed down from father to son along with the old hunting rifle and the family Bible."[47]

In summary, the rate of violence is higher in some social groups than in others because these groups have norms and values that encourage violence. An incident that might seem trivial to a middle-class person is seen as a *causus belli* by a working-class person. A remark about one's parentage may be an insult to both of them, but the working-class subculture requires a physically aggressive response while the middle-class subculture limits the appropriate reaction to a verbal retort. In addition, adherence to subcultural values may make individuals more sensitive to aggressive cues and thus facilitate aggressive responses through the processes of social perception, attribution, conformity, etc., which we discussed in Chapters 4 and 5. Consequently, the group's values and norms make violence a way of life and, as some argue, as "American as cherry pie."

INTERGROUP VIOLENCE

FOCUS
Race Riot in Chicago

In late July of 1919 hundreds of Chicagoans flocked to the shores of Lake Michigan to escape the ninety-degree heat. While swimming, a young Negro boy strayed across the imaginary boundary between the "white" and "colored" beaches and was met with a hail of stones hurled by outraged whites. The boy swam farther from the shore to escape, but tired and drowned before he could safely reach the "colored" beach. When black bystanders demanded the arrests of the stone-throwing whites, a white policeman instead arrested one of them on a minor complaint from a white. The incensed blacks mobbed the policeman, and fighting erupted between blacks and whites. The riot quickly spread to Chicago, where it raged for one week, injured over 200 people, and cost the lives of 15 whites and 23 blacks. Gangs of whites drove through black areas spraying bullets, and blacks sniped from the rooftops. A mob of white soldiers, sailors, and civilians hunted down lone blacks in downtown Chicago, while the police were unable or unwilling to intervene. Not until after Mayor Thompson reluctantly permitted the use of the National Guard was the riot suppressed.[48] Thus, the Chicago riot was an instance of *intergroup violence,* where people attacked others and were in turn attacked primarily because of their membership in social groups.[49]

Intergroup violence is not limited to riotous confrontations between mobs. A single person attacking another is intergroup violence so long as the victim is singled out because of his membership in a particular social group. When Robert Essex, a black, terrorized New Orleans from the top of the burning Howard Johnson Motor Lodge, all fifteen of his victims were selected because of their race. In contrast to this, the only characteristic that Charles Whitman's victims had in common was their misfortune of being in sight when he went on a shooting spree from Austin's Texas Tower.[50] However, most of the dramatic instances of intergroup violence such as lynchings, riots, and rebellions do involve large numbers of people.

In discussing intergroup violence, we shall rely heavily upon Neil Smelser's *value-added theory* of collective behavior.[51] (Collective behavior refers to such phenomena as panics, fads, crazes, riots, social

Figure 6-5 Top, whites cheer after they have set fire to a black residence in Chicago. *Bottom,* under armed guard a black man removes his possessions from his home. Both photos were taken in 1919. United Press International photo.

movements, etc.). The logic of the value-added theory can be best illustrated by the process of converting iron ore into a finished car. The ore is mined, smelted, tempered, shaped, combined with other parts, and painted to produce a particular car. The steps in the process occur in a particular sequence. The ore must be shaped before it is painted, and not vice versa, if we are to end up with a car. Each treatment is a necessary precondition for the following treatment. In addition, as the ore moves through the manufacturing process, the number of potential end-products into which it can be made becomes progressively fewer. Once it is shaped into a car body, it can no longer become an airplane or a spoon (unless the car body is melted and the whole process started over again). However, within the limitations of a car, it still has potentialities in terms of colors and extras. Thus, each stage progressively narrows down the potentialities until only one possible outcome can occur. In order to change the ore into a car, a particular sequence and pattern of activities must take place.

The same logic may be applied to intergroup violence. We start with highly general causal factors that might result in a wide variety of group behaviors. Then, subsequent influences narrow down the potential group behaviors and increase the probability of intergroup violence. For example, industrialization (a general causal factor) may result in religious revivals, political reform movements, communal riots, financial panics, or revolutions (particular group behaviors). However, other variables (e.g., power relationships in the society) make some of these reactions more probable than others. We shall limit our discussion of intergroup violence by considering five different variables as part of the value-added process: (1) structural conduciveness, (2) structural strain, (3) subjective deprivation, (4) generalized beliefs, and (5) agents of social control.

Structural Conduciveness

Under this heading we are referring to social conditions that make possible a given type of intergroup behavior. As an obvious example, two races have to live in close proximity for a race riot to occur. In addition, their relative numbers make a riot, a lynching, a pogrom, or a rebellion more or less probable. When a minority group is hopelessly outnumbered or outgunned, it often passively endures the majority group's terrorism. But when there are enough of them to resist, then communal riots are more probable than pogroms. The relative number of minority to majority group people is conducive to conflict and to the forms it will take. Of course, the mere fact of the two groups living in the same society and their relative numbers is not sufficient to cause intergroup conflict. It only means that the possibility exists and that it is a necessary precondition. As we shall see in Chapter 7, it is this conduciveness that may explain the occurrence of intergroup violence in cities.

Society is divided into many groups by ethnic, religious, economic, and political differences, and these groups are often in competition with each other for economic resources, power, and prestige. (For a more thorough discussion of competition, see pp. 265–67.) Workers struggle with employers over wages, and whites compete with blacks for jobs and housing. Competition is conducive to intergroup violence because it creates lines of division or cleavage within society. Competing groups develop negative stereotypes about each other, perceive the other as threatening and malevolent, and feel they must protect themselves. Thus, violent outbursts follow the lines of cleavage in society and are particularly likely when society is polarized into a few competing camps. As we shall see in Chapter 8, conflict is more intense when many lines of cleavage (e.g., ethnic, religious, economic, political) coincide than when they cross-cut each other.[52]

Another source of structural conduciveness is the availability of channels for expressing grievances.[53] Intergroup violence is more likely when people do not have access to the legitimate avenues of protest. Voting, petition signing, striking, holding mass demonstrations, and initiating court actions are all nonviolent means of drawing attention to a group's complaints. However, powerful groups in society frequently deny less powerful groups access to these means. For example, southern whites disenfranchised blacks as a way of stripping them of political power. However, at the same time, they closed off an avenue of peaceful protest and increased the likelihood of violence. Even when legitimate channels are ostensibly left open, the "power structure" may ignore complaints. Blacks and other powerless groups feel with justification that those in power are not responsive to them. Consequently, they become politically alienated: They have little faith in the normal political process and in politicians and feel powerless or inefficacious.[54] Out of frustration and rage, voiceless groups give voice to their grievances through violence. The "long hot summers" of the late sixties were partially attempts by blacks to draw the attention of whites to their plight.[55] While social cleavages and closed channels of grievance redress are conducive to the occurrence of violence, they do not guarantee its occurrence. They may well exist during periods of turmoil and of peace. For violence to break out, other conditions besides structural conduciveness must be met.

Structural Strain

Structural strain concerns conflicts among values or norms.[56] Ambiguity in values or norms is one source of conflict because people are not certain which values or norms apply in a situation and, therefore, they do not know how they should act. In their uncertainty, they first move in one direction and then in another, never knowing whether they are doing the right thing. Ambiguity in values and/or norms may cause people to experience a sense of "meaninglessness" and "normlessness," two forms of alienation.[57] People may feel that their lives lack direction and that they do not understand what is happening around them. They cannot see the rhyme and reason to daily events, and life becomes a mass of meaningless chaos to them. At the same time, they are confused about the appropriate guiding rules for behavior. They do not know what is expected of them and what norms they should follow in order to avoid social sanctions. Their social world seems normless to them. Consequently, they feel that something is radically wrong with the world and their lives, but they often cannot pinpoint the source of their uneasiness. In such a state of confusion, people readily accept dubious explanations for their sense of malaise that point out other social groups as the sources of evil in the world. As we shall see, these prejudices make intergroup violence more probable.

Besides ambiguity, contradictions in norms and values may exist. Some values or norms tell people to behave in one manner, while others demand different behaviors. Thus, people again are not sure of what is expected of them or what to expect of others. Finally, norms may conflict with values. As we pointed out earlier, the quickest way to monetary success may be a bank robbery, but social norms prohibit this avenue to success. In short, conflicts among values or norms make life unpleasant. As a consequence, people are motivated to seek out the real or imagined causes of their plight and to take appropriate steps to "set the world right."

A major American dilemma is the social position of blacks. White and black Americans are caught between a set of values and norms proclaiming the equality of opportunity for all "regardless of race, religion, or creed" and an opposing set declaring the superiority of the white race over the black race. This contradiction creates guilt in some white Americans, which is sometimes transformed into even more brutal suppression of their fellow Americans. Black Americans are placed in a highly stressful and frustrating situation and often resort to both violent and nonviolent attempts at expressing and eliminating their frustrations.

We stated earlier that social groups compete for economic resources, power, and prestige. Because the superordinate groups receive the "lion's share" by definition, the social stratification system reflects the outcome of this competition. That is, it sets the rules for "cutting up the pie." However, the accommodation is inherently unstable, because groups struggle continuously to protect and enlarge their share, although the intensity of the struggle varies greatly through historical periods. Social strain occurs whenever the system undergoes changes because old values and norms cease to apply and ambiguity and conflict among values or norms are rife as new groups gain ascendancy. Violence usually accompanies the process of change as new stratification systems are created and old ones are destroyed.[58] For example, intergroup violence is more frequent in societies changing from traditional agricultural to modern industrial systems than in either traditional or modern stable societies.[59]

Several sources of structural strain were at work in Chicago prior to the 1919 riot. First, the black population had more than doubled, which increased its potential economic, "military," and political power. Also, the increased population put even more pressure on the already overtaxed housing supply for blacks. Many blacks attempted to move out of the ghetto into traditionally white neighborhoods to escape overcrowding. Second, the war created a rapid expansion in Chicago's industries, but at the same time created a labor shortage by drafting men into the armed forces. In fact, the black migration was spurred by the demand for labor, and many blacks took over jobs that whites had held prior to the war. Third, the companies used blacks as weapons against organized labor. Blacks were hired as strikebreakers and at wages lower than those paid to whites, which gave blacks a competitive edge over whites. Fourth, black troops returning from Europe had been exposed to new values and norms and refused to return to their old subservient roles. Fifth, the rapid industrialization and urbanization of Chicago (and of the rest of the nation) placed values and norms in flux. A new way of life was being created that conflicted with the old rural values and norms.

All of these factors meant an improvement in the life conditions of blacks over what they had known in the South and prior to World War I. However, whites looked upon this with alarm and feared these improvements were made at their expense (as some of them were, e.g., use of blacks as scabs). Violence erupted in Chicago because blacks had challenged the accommodative system by moving into white neighborhoods and jobs and by no longer passively accepting second-class citizenship. Whites reacted to the challenge and attempted to protect their privileges and advantages by violently keeping blacks "in their place."[60]

Subjective Deprivation

Besides causing structural strains, social change may also result in subjective deprivation (i.e., feeling unjustly deprived of power, prestige, or possessions).[61] As changes occur in the social stratification system, subordinate groups feel more acutely that they are not getting their fair share, and superordinate groups fear losing ground to "undeserving upstarts." In general, people believe that their efforts are underrewarded and those of others are overrewarded. In short, both superordinate and subordinate groups feel unjustly deprived. However, social change often means actual improvements in socioeconomic conditions. The change from an agricultural to an industrial society means a higher standard of living for almost everyone. Thus, we have an apparent paradox. Conditions are improving, yet people feel more frustrated and dissatisfied.

Why are people dissatisfied when conditions improve? In other words, why is subjective deprivation associated with improving socioeconomic conditions? One answer is that improvements such as higher wages or removal of segregation barriers raise people's hopes and aspirations for the future. People expect the future to bring even greater benefits. Emile Durkheim, one of the founding fathers of modern sociology, noted that people's aspirations are held in check by society. Social norms put limits upon people's aspirations and desires. However, social change creates ambiguity in norms (i.e., normlessness, or, as Durkheim said, anomie) and therefore takes the lid off aspirations. Desires and aspirations are no longer restrained and are free to rise.[62] As a consequence, expectations for the future often outstrip reality and rise faster than actual improvements, and the gap between what people want and what they get grows continuously. This results in people becoming more and more disappointed and frustrated. The frustration is particularly unbearable if there is a sudden reversal in the trend towards improvement. James Davies, a political scientist, claims that a pattern of rising prosperity followed by a sudden decline in prosperity precedes many instances of social unrest including the French and Russian revolutions. The abrupt reversal causes a sharp increase in the so-called "want-get" gap, and this leads to heightened frustrations and to violence.[63]

This may have also occurred at the time of the 1919 Chicago riot. As we just noted, the war was a boom period for most civilians, and particularly for blacks. Many blacks found it easier to obtain jobs and higher salaries because of the shortage of labor and their immigration to the North. However, with the end of the war, the economy slowed down, jobs became scarcer, and competition became more keen as the troops returned home. The riot occurred during the downward part of the business cycle following the prosperity of the war economy.

A second answer to our rhetorical question lies in what Karl Marx said: "A house may be large or small; as long as the neighboring houses are likewise small, it satisfies all social requirements for a residence. But let there arise next to the little house a palace, and the little house shrinks into a hut."[64] Marx meant that people use others as yardsticks for measuring their socioeconomic circumstances. A person becomes subjectively deprived when he compares himself to others and believes that he unjustly has less than they. The people with whom he compares himself are called his *reference groups,* and they may be friends, relatives, business associates, strangers, or social groups (e.g., racial or ethnic groups or social classes).[65] Of course, whether a person feels deprived or gratified depends upon whom he uses as a reference group. Changes in stratification systems often result in people selecting new reference groups and/or becoming more aware of differences between themselves and their reference groups, which makes them more subjectively deprived. The migration of blacks to the North and the maturation of a generation of northern, urban, and educated blacks has made blacks more likely to compare themselves to whites. Ironically, the improvements in their socioeconomic conditions, which accompanied the northern migration, have made blacks more conscious of how deprived they are in comparison to whites.[66] Thus, the improvements that accompany social change do not always lead to satisfaction, but on the contrary often make people feel more subjectively deprived, dissatisfied, frustrated, and angered. As we saw in Chapter 3, these feelings often lead to aggressive attacks against the perceived frustrators. Consequently, the tensions between groups are heightened, and intergroup violence erupts.

Generalized Beliefs

Generalized beliefs that specify the sources of social strain and offer solutions to the strain are a fourth determinant of intergroup violence. Obviously people must first know what the problem facing them is before they can tackle it. However, the structural strains, which we have been discussing, are extremely complicated and difficult to recognize and understand. People are frequently aware that something is amiss, but they cannot put their finger on what is wrong. In such circumstances, they turn to preexisting generalized beliefs such as prejudices. Prejudices define other people as evil and dangerous and thereby supply us with irrefutable explanations for our problems. "The country is suffering from a depression? It is the fault of those capitalist Jews on Wall Street!" "The country has lost China to the Reds? It is those communist Jews in the State Department!" "The niggers are rioting? Outside communist agitators are to blame!" Besides pointing out the causes of our woes, prejudices offer facile solutions. Since outgroups are evil troublemakers, we simply have to eliminate them to remove the problem. Prejudices offer attractive explanations and solutions that are easy to understand and to act upon. Therefore, when social strains occur, people are quick to focus their anxieties, frustrations, and resulting hostilities upon minorities and other outgroups.[67]

A past history of intergroup violence creates beliefs about the efficacy and inevitability of violence, which makes future turmoil more likely. Countries with high rates of violence during earlier historical periods tend to have high levels of violence in later eras.[68] Violence becomes a tradition and is seen as a normal, if not legitimate, part of social conflict. One coup d'état is followed by others, and coups d'état quickly become routine in the changing of governments. In addition, people expect violence to accompany conflict and believe their opponents will readily use it. Consequently, a self-fulfilling prophecy is created. In self-defense they then engage in "protective reaction strikes" or "beat the other guy to the draw." Traditions of intergroup violence act to increase the likelihood of future violence just as subcultures of violence increase the likelihood of interpersonal violence (pp. 199–203).

Agents of Social Control

Finally, whether violence erupts between conflicting groups often depends upon the agents of social control such as the police, militia, or army. Many communal riots are particularly bloody because the police either passively or actively support one side over the other.[69] For example, during the 1919 Chicago riot, not only did the police precipitate the battle by refusing to arrest the whites responsible for the black youth's death and by arresting blacks instead, but they also gave moral support to white terrorists by turning their backs to the brutality of the white mob. Furthermore, the police arrested three times as many blacks as whites, despite the fact that more blacks than whites had been injured or killed, which suggests that more violence was committed against blacks than against whites. The rioting was controlled only after the National Guard entered the battle and more impartially enforced the law, even to the extent of firing upon whites to protect blacks.

Besides impartiality, decisiveness is often a critical factor. If the police show indecision or unwillingness to use force, then violence is more likely because the antagonists interpret this as weakness or encouragement. The Chicago police vacillated greatly and enforced the laws inconsistently in 1919, while Mayor Thompson hesitated to use the National Guard. Whites correctly interpreted this indecision as tacit support, and blacks realized that they would have to protect themselves. When the militia was finally employed, it acted swiftly and with determination to separate the warring parties.

The amount of force available to the police, relative to that of their opponents, may also determine the course of intergroup violence.[70] Although it is difficult to generalize, an initial showing of superior force seems to squelch disorders. However, the use of force, even superior force, is not without its dangers. The police may create martyrs and mobilize more support for the rioters. Dispersing the crowd may change one big centralized riot into dozens of widely dispersed small riots, making the problem of social control even greater. Also, the police may create a riot out of a peaceful demonstration by employing unnecessary force or by running riot themselves, as they did during the 1968 Democratic Convention in Chicago.

Other dangers arise when the police are not powerful enough to control the disorder. If the police try to separate two embattled groups, insufficient power results in their being ignored or even attacked. If the confrontation is between a group of citizens and the police, insufficient firepower may antagonize the rioters and increase the intensity of the violence. The police may try to control the crowd by attacking it, but quickly find themselves incapable of suppressing the riot and forced to retreat. The attack provokes the crowd, and the retreat proves to the crowd that the police are vulnerable. If the police are incapable of marshaling enough power, a minimal show of force may be better than a half-hearted attempt. (Indeed, a minimal use of force may be best regardless of the force available to the police!) Although not directly related to this point, cross-national studies are suggestive by showing that countries with moderate coercive capabilities (i.e., size of police and military forces relative to the total population) have more intergroup violence than either countries with high or low coercive powers.[71]

Finally, the police themselves may riot or initiate the violence as we just noted.[72] Practically all of the recent urban riots have started with a confrontation between the police and blacks. In addition, most of the deaths and injuries during these disturbances resulted from the action of the police. Police commanders may lose control over their men, and the police then indiscriminately attack rioters and nonrioters alike. Any black is seen as fair game. Often the police overreact and employ overwhelming amounts of firepower (e.g., the 1967 Detroit riot or the 1968 Democratic Convention). In short, the police may be a major contributor to violence during intergroup confrontations.

Structural conduciveness, structural strain, subjective deprivation, generalized beliefs, and agents of social control must act together for intergroup violence to ensue. Structural conduciveness sets the stage for conflict, while structural strain germinates tensions between groups and subjective deprivation results in tensions within individuals. Generalized beliefs focus hostility and anger upon others, and the actions of the agents of social control help determine whether hostile attitudes become hostile actions. Thus, each of the variables in turn shapes the eventual outcome. For example, generalized beliefs other than prejudice might direct people's dissatisfactions away from intergroup hostility. If people

Figure 6-6 Whether violence occurs in crowd situations often depends upon the actions of the police. The violent riots during the 1968 Democratic National Convention were due in large part to the overreaction of the Chicago police. United Press International photo.

believed the anger of the gods was the root of their misfortune, they might turn to peaceful prayers rather than violent attacks on others (so long as the gods' anger was not caused by infidels). In other words, each of the five variables is a necessary, but not sufficient, cause of intergroup violence.

There are a few striking similarities in the hypothesized causes of intergroup and interpersonal violence. Both arguments assume that violence originates in structural strains surrounding the distribution of power, privilege, and possessions. When people cannot obtain culturally prescribed goals because of structural roadblocks, they turn to criminal or political solutions (cf. the discussion of Merton's theory of deviance, pp. 192–94). Criminal responses bypass existing "legitimate" roads to success and substitute illegitimate paths, while leaving the social system unchanged. However, political responses focus on changing the social system. Subordinate groups attempt to alter the distribution of power and goods, and superordinate groups try to maintain it. Regardless of which solution is chosen, violence often results. Simplifying the argument greatly, structural strains lead to frustrations that, in turn, motivate problem-solving behaviors (both rational and emotional reactions to frustration) which are frequently violent.

Although the preceding discussion of violence has relied explicitly on sociological concepts (e.g., social stratification, subcultures), it has implicitly invoked several psychological concepts. Besides employing the psychological concept of frustration, the theories also include assumptions about perception, aspirations, and beliefs. In order for the societal level variables to affect people, individuals must have aspirations for particular goals, perceive the social blocks to success, have beliefs about the cause of the solutions to their frustrations, and have emotional responses. These theories assume that sociological factors operate through psychological constructs. For example, social strain (a sociological concept) is thought to cause subjective deprivation and frustration (psychological concepts) that, in turn, help cause intergroup violence (a sociological concept). As we shall see in Chapter 8, other explanations do not involve such psychological assumptions and seek to explain violence only in terms of sociological concepts.

Before turning to the subject of the next chapter, one interesting question should be asked: How are interpersonal and intergroup violence related? First, it is often difficult to distinguish between the two types of violence, because whether an act is considered to be "criminal" or "political" depends upon our own political outlook. The Czarist government of Russia condemned Stalin as a common bank robber, while his Bolshevik comrades hailed him as a revolutionary hero. The murder of a policeman during a bank robbery may be criminal to some and political to others. Perhaps the best criterion lies within the actor's motivation. But people do not always know or care to admit their true motives. When a demonstrator "trashes" a store and "liberates" the window-display items, is it theft or a blow against the capitalist system? If he answers the latter, is it a rationalization or his true motive? Consequently, the distinction between interpersonal and intergroup violence is rather dubious in some cases.[73]

A more theoretically important aspect of this issue stems from the similarity in the origins of interpersonal and intergroup violence. If both originate in the same frustrations, what determines the type of violence in which people will engage? Do the same or different people commit both types and under what circumstances? What factors determine this? Cloward and Ohlin suggest that working-class boys who desire upward social mobility are prone to intergroup violence, because they see the solution to their dilemma in social change. But, boys who do *not* desire middle-class status seek criminal solutions (i.e., criminal or conflict subcultures).[74] Other possible factors might lie in the existence of "political opportunity structures" (i.e., the availability of social change-oriented groups). When political organizations are active in the community, people are likely to join them. Obviously people turn to other solutions when political organizations are not available. There is some evidence for this in that black crime rates have dropped in a few cities during periods of organized community action for civil rights in those cities.[75] In any event, this is a question in search of an answer.

SUMMARY

Variations in both *interpersonal* and *intergroup* violence rates from one society to another and from one time period to the next suggest that we should look beyond the psychology and physiology of individuals to the *social structure* of whole societies for possible determinants of aggression. In turning to social structural factors, we are shifting our focus away from concern with what makes a particular person aggressive. Now we are focusing on what makes the *rate* of violence greater in one societal group than in another.

Interpersonal violence can be discussed using two aspects of social structure: (1) the social stratification system and (2) subcultural systems. In most societies, people are divided into different social strata that are ranked in terms of social superiority and inferiority. This hierarchy composes the society's *social stratification system*. People's location in the social stratification system has a profound effect upon their lives. Most important (for our purposes), it affects the ease they have in attaining socially prescribed *goals* (e.g., monetary success) through *legitimate means* (e.g., education). In American society, most social groups accept the same goals. But the society is structured in such a manner that not all groups have equal access to the legitimate means of attaining the goals (e.g., discrimination against minorities). Consequently, a *strain* is placed upon some groups to attain the goals through *illegitimate means* (e.g., crime). However, not only may people be blocked from employing legitimate means, but they may also be blocked from employing illegitimate means. Groups outside of both the *legitimate opportunity* and *illegitimate opportunity structures* are particularly likely to be violent.

Subcultures, while sharing some aspects of the dominant culture, form distinctive clusters of values, norms, beliefs, techniques, and artifacts. The high rates of violence among certain groups in American society may reflect *subcultures of violence* whose norms and values encourage violence. The subcultures of the American South and of working-class (particularly male) Americans are possible subcultures of violence.

In the second half of the chapter, we discussed *intergroup violence* (e.g., communal riots) from the perspective of a *value-added theory*. We started with highly general causal factors that might result in a wide variety of group behaviors. Subsequent factors narrow down the potential group behaviors and increase the probability of intergroup violence. Five different variables were considered as part of the value-added process. (1) *Structural conduciveness:* social conditions that make possible a given type of intergroup behavior (e.g., proximity between racial groups and communal riots); (2) *structural strain:* conflicts among values or norms (e.g., racial discrimination versus equality of opportunity norms); (3) *subjective deprivation:* feeling unjustly deprived of power, prestige, or possessions (e.g., rising expectations of black Americans); (4) *generalized beliefs:* beliefs that specify the sources of social strain and offer solutions (e.g., racial prejudices); and (5) *agents of social control:* the actions of the police or military during social unrest (e.g., Chicago police at Democratic Party Convention, 1968). Structural conduciveness sets the stage for conflict, while structural strain germinates tensions between groups and subjective deprivation results in tensions within individuals. Generalized beliefs focus hostility and anger upon others, and the actions of the agents of social control help determine whether hostile attitudes become hostile actions.

FOOTNOTES

[1] DeVore (1965); Southwick (1963).

[2] Lenski (1966).

[3] Of course, this assumes that there are no major biological or psychological differences between races or nationalities or in a particular population over time. This assumption seems tenable in light of existing evidence, especially in terms of particular biological characteristics (e.g., Pettigrew [1964]).

[4] Mulvihill and Tumin (1969), pp. 13–48; Reckless (1967), pp. 73–96; Sutherland and Cressey (1970), pp. 25–47; Wolfgang (1967), pp. 8–14 and 20–36.

[5] Mulvihill and Tumin (1969), pp. 117–20.

[6] Although we present only arrest data, other sources indicate that the perpetrators and victims of violent crime are similar. For example, in a recent study, only 10 percent of the reported criminal homicides crossed racial lines (i.e., where the murderer and his victim were of different races). Similar results were found for rape, assault, and robbery. Criminal violence tends to occur within racial groups rather than between them (Mulvihill and Tumin [1969], pp. 208–15). This partly reflects the fact that criminal violence is more likely to occur between "intimates" than between strangers (Mulvihill and Tumin [1969], pp. 216–20, 514–17, and 941–78; Wolfgang [1966], pp. 203–21). We are more likely to hurt and to be hurt by "the ones we love."

[7] Wolfgang, Figlio, and Sellin (1972).

[8] Wolfgang (1967), pp. 166–70; Reckless (1967), pp. 109–12; Cressey (1964), pp. 62–65.

[9] Gurr (1969), pp. 626–30.

[10] Lipset and Raab (1970). For an overview of violence in Europe, see Tilly (1969).

[11] Waskow (1967); Janowitz (1969); Grimshaw (1969).

[12] For fuller discussions of social stratification, see Lenski (1966), Broom and Selznick (1963), pp. 176–217; Tumin (1970); and Bendix and Lipset (1953).

[13] It is possible for a person to be ranked high on one dimension and low on other dimensions. Such a condition is called "status inconsistency" and is thought to have interesting consequences for a wide variety of social behaviors

(e.g., political beliefs, psychosomatic illnesses). See Lenski (1954) and Petti-grew (1967).

[14] Bendix and Lipset (1953), pp. 271–370; Broom and Selznick (1963), pp. 201–4.

[15] Bendix and Lipset (1953), pp. 129–84 and 596–609; Mills (1956); Dahl (1961).

[16] Kluckholn (1951), p. 86. For a more thorough treatment of culture, see Broom and Selznick (1963), pp. 32–92; or Linton (1936).

[17] Simpson and Yinger (1965), pp. 241–463; Pettigrew (1964).

[18] Adapted with permission of Macmillan Publishing Co., Inc., from *Social Theory and Social Structure* by R. Merton. © Copyright 1957 by The Free Press, a Corporation.

[19] Mizruchi (1964), pp. 68–75. For other studies relating to acceptance of cultural values and aspirations, see Hyman (1953); Simmons and Rosenberg (1971); and G. Lorenz (1972).

[20] Rytina, Form, and Pease (1970). For other studies on the perception of legitimate opportunities, see Mizruchi (1964), pp. 82–87; Short, Rivera, and Tennyson (1965); and Simmons and Rosenberg (1971).

[21] Feagin (1972).

[22] Cloward (1959); Cloward and Ohlin (1960).

[23] Sutherland and Cressey (1970), pp. 75–91; DeFleur and Quinney (1966).

[24] Short and Strodtbeck (1965), pp. 47–76; Short, Rivera, and Tennyson (1965); Jenson (1972); Short (1957); Hindelang (1970); Rivera and Short (1968). See Gibbons (1970) for a review of current theories and research on juvenile delinquency.

[25] Bell (1953).

[26] Mulvihill and Tumin (1969).

[27] This suggests that middle-class people have opportunities to engage in different types of crime than working-class people. For example, middle-class criminals are more likely to be embezzlers and confidence men, while working-class criminals are more likely to be stick-up artists. Sutherland (1940).

[28] Shaw and McKay (1969).

[29] Cloward and Ohlin (1960), p. 153.

[30] Cloward and Ohlin (1960), pp. 161–71.

[31] Cloward and Ohlin (1960), pp. 166–68.

[32] Cloward and Ohlin (1960), pp. 171–78. For a recent review of violent gangs, see Klein (1969), and for a classic discussion of conflict cultures, see Cohen (1955).

[33] Wolfgang and Ferracuti (1967); Cohen (1955); Cohen and Short (1958); see Short (1957) and Wolfgang, Savitz, and Johnston (1962), pp. 211–328, for other readings.

[34] Wolfgang (1967), p. 111.

[35] Miller (1958), p. 6 (emphasis in the original).

[36] Wolfgang (1967), pp. 109–10. Cf. Horowitz and Schwartz (1974).

[37] Blumenthal et al. (1972), pp. 41–71.

[38] Stark and McEnvoy (1970); Erlanger (1972).

[39] Ball-Rokeach (1973).

[40] Stykes and Matza (1957).

[41] H. C. Brearley as quoted by Hackney (1969), p. 506.

[42] Hackney (1969), pp. 518–19.

[43] Mulvihill and Tumin (1969), pp. 69–80.

[44] Hackney (1969), pp. 505–27; Gastil (1971); Pettigrew and Spier (1962).

[45] Blumenthal et al. (1972), pp. 41–71; Stark and McEnvoy (1970).

[46] Graham and Gurr (1969), pp. 101–242.

[47] Hackney (1969), p. 519.

[48] Waskow (1967), pp. 38–59; Demaris (1970), pp. 140–42.

[49] Grimshaw (1970).

[50] *Time*, January 22, 1973, pp. 20–21.

[51] Smelser (1962); Currie and Skolnick (1970).

[52] Smelser (1962), pp. 229–31; Coser (1956), pp. 76–80; Blalock (1970); Bonacich (1972); Simpson and Yinger (1965), pp. 80–108; Dahrendorf (1958); Coleman (1956).

[53] Smelser (1962), pp. 231–40. Cf. Coser (1967), p. 29.

[54] Most of the general studies of political involvement and psychological attitudes towards politics by political scientists fall into the area of political alienation. For examples, see: Almond and Verba (1963); Gamson (1968); Olsen (1965); Aberbach (1970); and Burstein (1972).

[55] Sears and McConahay (1970); Tomlinson (1968); Caplan and Paige (1968); Fogelson (1971).

[56] Smesler (1962), pp. 47–66.

[57] Seeman (1959).

[58] Grimshaw (1970), pp. 18–19; Lieberson (1961); Shibutani and Kwan (1965), pp. 341–71.

[59] Graham and Gurr (1969), pp. 632–80.

[60] Smelser (1962), pp. 242–45.

[61] Gurr (1970), pp. 22–154.

[62] Durkheim (1951), pp. 246–54.

[63] Davies (1969). The rising expectations explanation has not gone unchallenged: Rule and Tilly (1972).

[64] K. Marx (1933), p. 33.

[65] Hyman and Singer (1968).

[66] Pettigrew (1971), pp. 147–65; Abeles (1972, in press).

[67] Smelser (1962).

[68] Graham and Gurr (1969), pp. 605–7; Gurr (1970), pp. 168–77.

[69] G. Marx (1970); Waskow (1967), pp. 38–59; Smelser (1962), pp. 261–68; Kerner (1968), pp. 299–336.

[70] G. Marx (1970); Gurr (1970).

[71] Gurr (1970), pp. 232–73; Graham and Gurr (1969), pp. 608–14.

[72] G. Marx (1970); Ryan (1971), pp. 211–35.

[73] Horowitz and Liebowitz (1967). Cf. Becker (1963).

[74] Cloward and Ohlin (1960), pp. 60–65.

[75] Solomon et al. (1965).

7 / URBAN LIFE AND VIOLENCE

ecological factors

Nowhere is violence a more terrifying threat than in the urban centers of America. Citizens of the large cities bar their doors and windows, exchange accounts of neighborhood muggings in the jocular terms of gallows humor, complain bitterly about the lack of police protection, forego nights on the town and, for some places, days as well, vote over-whelmingly for "law and order" candidates, and speak constantly of their dream of escaping the city to safety. Is this threat real? If so, why?

In the preceding chapters, we examined the ways in which violence may result from the psychological structure of the individual and from the social structure of society. In this chapter, we shall examine the ways in which the physical structure of the individual's environment may determine the chances of violent behavior.

We are intuitively familiar with the influence that the shape and content of physical space has on many of our actions. For instance, there are many acts that we perform only behind closed doors—an isolated, encircled space. Sometimes we may feel free to engage in a personal conversation at a large party, but will cease speaking when so many guests arrive that a circle of people pressing in upon us results. We also often schedule our use of various routes or facilities (e.g., free-ways, stores) as a function of the number of people who are likely to be in that place at a given time. Considerations of the environment such as these (i.e., the shape of the physical space, the number and distribution of persons within it) will determine whether certain behaviors, perhaps violent ones, are performed.

These are called "ecological" factors because they involve the inter-relationship of population and space. *Ecology*, as the term has been used in regard to plant and animal life, generally refers to the processes by which those organisms adapt to each other in a given area. The field of "human ecology" is similar. It has been defined by one of its founders as "the study of the spatial and temporal relations of human beings as affected by the selective, distributive, and accommodative forces of the environment. [It] is fundamentally interested in the effect of *position* . . . upon human institutions and behavior."[1]

In this chapter, we shall examine the ecological approach to violence by narrowing in on one critically important problem: the violence of urban life. The question we shall address is: Why do American cities seem to suffer more violence than do small towns and rural places? It is ecology that defines the city (i.e., the concentration of large numbers of people in a limited space) and thereby makes it an ideal subject for ecological analysis. At the end of the chapter, after examining in detail different explanations for urban violence, we shall turn to a discussion of how the architectural design of physical space may encourage or discourage violent acts.

URBAN VIOLENCE: INDIVIDUAL AND COLLECTIVE

Cities and conflict have been intertwined in at least the American imagination for centuries.[2] One renowned expert on the development of cities has written that the city made violence so normal that "throughout the greater part of history, enslavement, forced labor and destruction have accompanied—and penalized—the growth of urban civilization."[3] In popular opinion, the city has traditionally been the place where the innocent rural youth was morally corrupted and physically assaulted. In America of the 1960s and 1970s, this image has been reinforced by newspaper stories on "crime in the streets" and television films of hostile groups fighting battles at city intersections.

The issue that must be dealt with before proceeding to explanations of this phenomenon is that of whether these images are indeed accurate. Are cities disproportionately the sites of individual, criminal violence? And, are they disproportionately the sites of violent group conflict?

Table 7-1 presents the rates of violent crimes recorded in America in 1970 for each of nine categories of size of city. The statistics strongly

Table 7-1

Rates of Violent Crime by Size of City, 1970

	Offenses Known to Police (per 100,000 inhabitants)			
Size of City	Total violent crime	Criminal homicide*	Forcible rape	Aggravated assault
Over 1,000,000	1,205	18	38	370
500,000–1,000,000	950	18	49	348
250,000–500,000	617	15	30	252
100,000–250,000	450	10	24	218
50,000–100,000	274	5	15	143
25,000–50,000	214	4	11	117
10,000–25,000	159	3	9	105
Under 10,000	141	3	7	108
Rural	102	6	10	74
TOTAL	389	8	20	169

* Excluding manslaughter by negligence.
SOURCE: U.S. Department of Justice (1971), Table 8.

confirm the popular impression: the greater the number of people in a city, the higher its rate of violent crime. In fact, the 26 cities with populations over 500,000 accounted for over half the violent crimes in the nation even though they encompassed less than 20 percent of the population. Since the facts show that the chances of being a victim of violent crime are greatest in our largest cities, it is understandable that urban residents are preoccupied with safety and public order.[4]

Yet, before we proceed to attribute this violence to the nature of urban life, we should be careful to confirm that such criminality is generally an urban phenomenon and not just uniquely so in contemporary America. One way to check on this is to see whether criminal violence is greater in the cities than in the countryside of other nations and in other historical periods.

If we look to foreign experience, we find that *crime* is generally greater in cities, but that this relationship is weak or nonexistent for violent crimes. (It is mostly true for property crimes.)[5] Furthermore, in historical perspective, the image of the city of violence becomes even less distinct. In some historical periods cities were indeed cesspools of murder and mayhem. In other periods, however, cities were rather tranquil.[6] And one careful study of Massachusetts criminal statistics of the nineteenth century actually concluded that urbanization had a "settling" influence and reduced disorder.[7] In fact, there is evidence to suggest that in most places and times (for example, the old American South), violence was a *rural* rather than an urban tradition.[8]

Since violent crime is not always associated with the concentration of people, we shall have to take that into account in attributing today's urban violence to the ecological nature of city life. In any case, it is safe to say that, at least in modern America, criminal violence is more a part of city life than of rural life.

We turn now to collective violence. Television in the 1960s vividly brought home to Americans group conflict in our large cities. Most major American communities were at one time or another reddened by the glare of ghetto fires and the spilled blood of participants in political confrontations: black rioters, white policemen, college students, and, often, bystanders. Cities seem always to have been the scenes of brutal political battle, from the 1770 Boston Massacre to the 1968 Chicago Democratic Convention, from Paris at the fall of the Bastille in 1789 to Paris during the May 1968 student-worker uprisings.

While it is the case that American cities have a long and weighty record of bloody conflicts,[9] how accurate is our impression that collective violence is especially *urban* in character? Historians caution against accepting such conclusions too facilely. In the broad scope of Western history, it has been the rural areas that have provided continuous violent turmoil—food-price riots by farmers, peasant takeovers of absentee landlords' properties, marauding Robin Hood-like bands, and revolts against national authority.[10]

Though this historical perspective casts a shadow of doubt on our image of group conflict as an urban phenomenon, it does not resolve the question of whether such violence is in fact disproportionately city-based. It is not as easy to check this assumption with statistics as it was to check the rates of violent crime. However, some evidence indicates that intergroup conflict may indeed be greater in cities. One study of collective violence in France from 1830 to 1960 showed that the rate of reported disturbances and the proportion of people involved and injured in them was highly associated with the degree of urbanization in the administrative departments of France.[11]

Even if we take as our assumption that the rates of urban group conflict are greater than the rates of rural conflict, we must still recognize other cautions before we assume that collective violence is an ecological phenomenon (i.e., that it is due to the inherent ecological characteristics of the city). We would first have to rule out at least two factors:

(1) Large cities are usually the centers of political power. As a consequence, many battles may be fought there by groups vying for that power and not because of the pressures of urban life. An example

is the civil rights marches that gathered blacks from the rural South to march on capital cities such as Montgomery and Atlanta.[12]

(2) More conflict may arise in cities simply because they have larger numbers of concerned people, thereby increasing the probability that conflict could break out *randomly*. A study of black riots in the 1960s suggests that the chance a city would suffer a major disturbance was simply a function of the number of blacks in the city—not, we may presume, because urban life in some way increased the pressure for violence.[13]

While keeping in mind these sorts of doubts and qualifications, we shall take as given the relationship between urban life and both individual and collective violence. By what principles might we explain such an association?

We shall examine three types of ecological analysis. One argues that the physical crush of people has a direct impact on the biological and psychological functioning of men, driving some to violence. Another argues that the concentration of population sets into motion sociological and psychological processes that weaken the social cohesion of the community and thereby remove the restraints to violence. A third argues that neither of these models is accurate, but rather that cities mean the accumulation of certain types of people and the accentuation within them of the nonecological causes of violence that we discussed in earlier chapters.

THREE THEORIES OF URBAN VIOLENCE

Violence and Crowding

The city is by definition a place of high population density—of crowds—and it is reasonable to begin the search for an explanation of urban violence with this fact. Perhaps the constant assault on the human senses of other people deranges individuals to violence, or perhaps fights for "elbow room" are the inevitable results of having a lot of people in a little space. Consider this as an analogy:

FOCUS
The Behavioral Sink

Life in the city has often been compared to a rat race. John Calhoun, a psychologist at the National Institute of Mental Health, created a real rat race in his laboratory. Intrigued by the effects of overpopulation, Calhoun conducted several experiments with tame Norwegian rats to see how they behaved when allowed to multiply to a point of high population density. Furthermore, he arranged ramps and food troughs in their cages so that large numbers of rats would be packed together into a small area.

Within this environment, Calhoun observed intense viciousness and destructiveness. Fierce and frenzied fighting broke out regularly as rats competed for control of the pen. Having seized control, a rat ruthlessly pursued any other male who tried to enter his territory. His victim, paralyzed with fright, never dared to fight back. Occasionally the dominant rat went berserk, pouncing upon females and juveniles and maliciously attacking the tails of other animals. The ruling rat held sway only until the eruption of another furious battle, at which time another rat would seize control.

There were other instances of abnormal behavior in the teeming pens. A number of passive and disoriented males withdrew permanently from the others, and almost none of the females could complete their pregnancies or care for their litters. Moreover, homosexuality and cannibalism were routine.

In this way, the stress of living under crowded conditions made savage beasts of domesticated rats and intensified many types of pathological behavior—a situation Calhoun termed a "behavioral sink."[14]

Parallels with human behavior are disturbingly plain. While Calhoun's rats fought over their territory, humans also seem to exhibit forms of territorial behavior: Farmers stand with shotguns beside "no trespassing" signs; juvenile gangs conduct "wars" over "turfs"; and we all employ the pointed use of elbows to protect our small corners of buses or subways. Can we, therefore, find one source of human conflict to be the violation of personal space?

Both serious researchers and popular writers have argued that way. One anthropologist has written that "the implosion of the world population into cities everywhere is creating a series of destructive behavioral sinks more lethal than the hydrogen bomb."[15]

The search for evidence for or against this interpretation begins with studies of the animal world, where conflict and violence often involve the issue of physical space. In many species, if one member intrudes upon another's area, a ritualized form of battle will result, with intruder and defender attacking back and forth until, in most cases, the original border is reestablished—usually without any physical harm being inflicted. (See the discussion of ethology in Chapter 2.) Investigators have hypothesized that this "territorial instinct" serves the function of spreading out the species members so that each will have sufficient resources to survive.[16]

But what happens if the animals cannot space themselves out sufficiently and they become crowded? In many cases, physiological changes that reflect stress occur, such as a growth in the adrenal glands. Many of these changes in turn help to slow down population growth.[17] If the population pressure continues to increase, pathologies such as lemmings marching to the sea or "behavioral sinks" may occur.

From these cases of animal behavior derives one theory of urban violence—that it is a "natural" response to "unnatural" densities in our cities. (Sometimes this analogy can be carried to extravagant lengths, as by the biologist who argued that dictatorships were a result of overcrowding.[18] Actually, dictatorships are more common in *less* urbanized nations.)[19]

This theory is not, of course, without its critics, scientists who argue that these analogies from animal behavior to man are essentially invalid. (Again, see discussion in Chapter 2.)

For one, the critics claim that territorial behavior is not universal among animals and is especially unusual among man's closest kin, the apes. Second, in these studies it is often unclear whether fighting occurs because of problems of crowding or because of problems of too few resources. Third, territorial behavior in many animals occurs only at specific times and situations, thereby casting doubt on how "instinctive" it really is. Most important, these social scientists argue that man differs from animals precisely in that his behavior is largely learned and not instinctual. With his ability to learn, man adapts to many vastly different conditions. The density of urban life would be another condition that man the malleable could adapt to—without stress or violence.[20]

Other considerations also cast doubt on the animal analogy. Little if any evidence has been presented of physiological reactions to crowding in comparisons of urban and rural people. Also, we do know that people of different cultures use space and react to density in different ways (e.g., North versus South Americans); and we know that crowding means different things at different times (e.g., at parties versus in bedrooms).[21] Therefore, can territoriality really be a simple, species-wide instinct? Finally, while territorial instincts may arise among animals so as to maximize resources, its existence would not serve the same function for human beings. It is largely by gathering together that man has multiplied his resources manyfold from those found naturally in the world. Cooperation, trade, industry, and specialization have all come with the aggregation of people into tribes, nations, and cities.

Instead of depending on analogies from animal behavior, perhaps one can find studies on human beings that will provide evidence for the

Figure 7-1 People of different cultures use space and react to density in different ways. Westerners would feel crowded in the above scene, while Indians would not be conscious of crowding. Courtesy of Joseph Abeles.

crowding theory. Studies have been made of actual cases of extreme crowding (such as prisoner-of-war camps and bomb shelters). Tensions do arise, personal relationships become strained, and people often come to occupy pieces of territory and defend them as their own.[22] The picture is reminiscent of the familiar World War II submarine movie. However, the striking fact is that withdrawal and passivity are more likely to occur than aggression or violence. People retreat into a corner and stay there. Furthermore, because of the very fact that it took an extreme situation to create the density, it is difficult to know whether any strange behavior should be attributed to the density or the extremity. Finally, since these situations do not usually last very long, we do not know how people might eventually come to adapt to them.

Experimental social psychologists have begun conducting controlled laboratory studies to get at some of these problems, but it is too soon to draw firm conclusions. In one study, students in a crowded laboratory were found to be more irritated and to express more negative feelings than did less crowded students.[23] In other studies, a constant number of undergraduates were placed in rooms of different sizes. In general, no differences were found in the different groups' abilities to work on an assortment of tasks, or on feelings of hostility (though there is some suggestion that males may react negatively to density and females positively).[24]

If we step out of the laboratory into the "real world," it seems clear that overcrowding is related to pathology, including violence. It is those buildings where people are packed many to a room that seem to harbor deviance, disorganization, and violence, which is evidence in support of the crowding theory.[25]

While overcrowding within homes is related to various social and psychological ills, does it *cause* those ills? It must always be kept in mind that people who have no choice but to live in cramped quarters are also disadvantaged in other ways: poverty, extreme youth or old age, and social and physical handicaps of various sorts (not the least of which is racial discrimination). If these factors were ruled out, what could one then say about the effects of crowded quarters?

Research on this issue suggests that overcrowding in housing may contribute to disease[26] and make life less comfortable, private, and enjoyable, but there is little evidence that overcrowding per se generates violence or even hostility (except perhaps under special culturally determined circumstances, such as living closely with nonrelatives).[27] Two investigators in the area of housing have concluded: "There is no body of convincing evidence that crowding in a dwelling unit contributes materially to mental disorder or to emotional instability. Nor is there evidence as yet that crowding interferes with a promotive style of life; that because of crowding, family roles and rituals cannot satisfactorily be carried out; or that the development of infants and children is severely impaired."[28]

Even were we to establish detrimental effects of crowded living quarters that might lead to violence, we would have to be careful about using such facts to explain urban violence. There is a tendency to think "city" and think "tenement" with it. While a recent study suggests that the number of people *per room* is related to social problems such as delinquency, the fact is that the numbers of persons per household and the average number of persons per room tend to be *less* the larger a city is![29] Though there may be thousands of people living beyond a city-dweller's walls, within his apartment or home, he has at least as much space on the average as does his country cousin.

In summation, it is just too simple to say that bringing people together in cities must mean that they will lash out at each other. A few more reflections help confirm this conclusion from the data. Consider Hong Kong where the density of population is over 150 times that of the United States[30] and far greater than that of American cities: There, the homicide rate is one-sixth that of the United States! In other ways as well Hong Kong is hardly a behavioral sink.[31] This is so because, first, "crowding" is a culturally defined fact, not a biological one, and density is interpreted more liberally by Chinese. Second, rules of behavior exist for handling densities without stress.[32] The point is that social and cultural factors are just overwhelmingly more important than this sort of ecological variable.[33]

Consider the increase in violent crime in the last few decades. While the rate of violence has increased in our cities, it has done so at the same time that densities have been *decreasing!* Our cities have been getting larger, but, with suburbanization, less dense.[34] It should be noted that while the population size of a city correlates highly with its violent crime rate, the density of a city does not.[35]

Consider the New York City subway at rush hour. In spite of the fact that everyone's territorial space is being outrageously violated, willful violence is relatively rare, at a rate lower than that for a partially deserted Manhattan street corner at night, or, for that matter, for the homes of the commuters.

Finally, consider the crowd, say, in Times Square on New Year's Eve. It seems to epitomize the city. Yet, the fact is that urbanites spend relatively little of their lifetime in such crowds. Unless he or she uses mass transit, the employed city-dweller will ride to work in a firmly enclosed space, spend eight hours with relatively few co-workers, return home in his moving territory, and remain there in his ever-increasing domicile space.[36] The housewife will encounter crowds even less often. The point is that the city-dweller is not often in the equivalent of "teeming pens."

Even with these serious doubts, we cannot dismiss the crowding theory. (More research is definitely called for.) Obviously, if people had to live at rush-hour densities constantly, *something* drastic would happen. The question is whether the current densities of cities physiologically generate violence and conflict.

More critical, however, is the possibility that the concentration of people may change the ways in which a society is structured and the ways in which people relate to each other. These are sociological effects of crowding and it is to them that we now turn.

The Urban Way of Life

It is a commonplace to hear cities described in the following terms: frenetic, unfriendly, even hostile, inhuman and depersonalizing, concrete "jungles," as well as rat races. These images of urban life are not new. Western culture has been deeply marked by a horror of city life.[37]

The first century A.D. poet, Juvenal, wrote in "Against the City of Rome" that the Eternal City had no place for the honest man, that rights and privileges were expropriated by the immorally spawned wealthy, and that crime in the end erased all gains. He drew this ageless picture:

> *Somebody gives me a shove with an elbow, or a two-by-two scantling,*
> *One clunks my head with a beam, another wacks down with a beer keg.*
> *Mud is thick on my shins, I am trampled by somebody's big feet.*[38]

Two thousand years later, one can easily imagine a similar portrait of most major metropolises.

Yet, paradoxically, our culture has also been infused with another image of cities: as places of free individuals from different worlds who mix in creative exchanges, where civilization and culture grow and thrive, where even the gods choose to dwell.

These contradictory images of the city have stimulated sociologists to attempt to describe what is unique about urban life and urban man and the source of that uniqueness. Studies have been conducted on the growth of cities, on their physical shapes, and on the character of neighborhoods and the character of people within them. Much of the early research pointed toward an understanding of urban life based on the ecology of cities; it held that large numbers in a small area create a population of lonely individuals torn and confused by the many pulls and pressures of urban life. The best explanation of this theory was presented by Louis Wirth.

FOCUS
The Anomic Urbanite

In the first third of the twentieth century, a group of sociologists under the leadership of a former journalist, Robert Park, conducted a large number of important studies of urban life in Chicago. A great deal of this work centered on the social disorganization (delinquency, poverty, transiency, family breakdown) that they found in that rapidly growing metropolis. To a certain extent, this image of Chicago in turmoil formed their image of urban life in general.

One of the leading members of this "Chicago School," Louis Wirth, sought to explain why cities and their residents seemed to exhibit such patterns, patterns best termed as "anomic"—a condition of a people who are without strong social bonds among them and whose norms (rules of behavior) and values carry little moral force.

As Wirth saw it, this urban condition resulted inevitably from the essential nature of the city—a "relatively large, dense and permanent settlement of socially heterogeneous individuals."

Dense heterogeneity means that many different types of people must somehow adapt to living in constant contact and competition. A primary form of adaptation is specialization. There is a physical specialization of space in the form of segregation: Different sorts of neighborhoods ("natural areas") develop (i.e., industrial, residential, commercial). Different ethnic areas develop (i.e., little Italys, Black Belts). There is also a differentiation of functions: Highly specialized jobs, services, and businesses develop as the best way of maximizing production.

On the individual level, people must adapt to being constantly in the company of great numbers of other personalities who exhibit different opinions, appearances, and habits. The basic manner of adapting is to establish distance from other people. One comes to know other people only in "segmental" and "impersonalized" ways. For example, an urbanite knows a store clerk only in his or her role as clerk and not as parent, neighbor, Presbyterian, or citizen. The same is true with fellow bus passengers, workers, or the neighborhood police. An urbanite's relationships with his fellow city-dwellers are in this manner "superficial" and "transitory." This is inevitable, for how can one possibly relate to so many people in a personal way? Intimacy disappears and people can coolly exploit each other.

Similarly, with the great specialization resulting from density, an individual's own identity is fractured: His job is one place, one world; his home is another place and world; leisure-time is yet a third; friends are perhaps a fourth. He is constantly moving from one world to another.

In such a social environment of interpersonal estrangement and personal fragmentation, means must be found to regulate interactions between people. Formal institutions become more important than personal ties: courts and police instead of community pressure; employment agencies in the place of personal contacts; dating services instead of family matchmakers; credit-card businesses instead of personal trust; mass production instead of individual service.

The attitudes that accompany such a formal society are rationality, sophistication, and a blasé perspective. The city-dweller must tolerate differences; he must detach his personality from the onrush of events which surround him. One result is that these detached urbanites can use each other as objects in the most rationally profitable way.

Such a rational and depersonalized life helps keep multitudes of people in some sort of order and cities running. But, a price is paid: anomie. In an estranged environment, where men do not look out for each other, the regulation of people's behavior can at best be haphazard. Where tolerance and rationality about differences are esteemed, fundamental norms and values become questioned, lose their moral power, and are violated. Where man is alone in the crowd, there is no social support or guidance to help him maintain his personality. Where rules rather than social ties maintain order, there is no "sense of community" and that order is a precarious one.

This delicate urban social structure, therefore, constantly shows symptoms of anomie: social disorganization, the breakdown of family and kinship ties, crime, and irrational violence.[39]

We have here an analysis that begins, as did the crowding theory, with population concentration. However, instead of assuming that it operates directly on human behavior, this theory argues that concentration results in types of societies and relationships that release the restraints to violence. The way in which this occurs is twofold, a sociological process and a social psychological one.

On the sociological level, population aggregation sets into motion economic processes of competition and specialization that result in a *differentiated* social structure. In smaller communities, a few basic social units perform a varied number of functions. Kin, the most important group, often work together, are neighbors, are sources of economic assistance, and train children. In large communities, this is specialized: The family is a different group than the work group, neighbors are not related, government adopts welfare functions, and specialized schools train the young.

As the social structure is more diversified, so are the interests and activities of individuals. People working in different places with different groups become more and more dissimilar; their opinions and behaviors diverge. Simultaneously, each individual's time is diversified, spent in different places among different people through the course of the day. Thus, the community is differentiated, people differ from each other, and even individuals' personalities are subdivided.

The critical question sociologists have posed is: How can social order be maintained in this kind of community? In a small community, there is order and stability because people are very much alike and they have the same interests, believe in the same values and rules. This situation has been termed "mechanical solidarity" by the classic French sociologist, Emile Durkheim. In a large community, chaos, lawlessness, and *anomie* are serious threats because people are very different; they do not have the same interests and do not agree on values. Furthermore, the social unity and the many personal ties that made the small community cohesive are gone in the large one, so that the restraints of social opinion and pressure have been lifted.

Figure 7-2 Manhattan street scenes such as this led Stanley Milgram to hypothesize that city-dwellers suffer from urban overload. The Manhattanite must contend not only with many physical stimuli, but he must also face an overload of personal encounters. As a result, he must curtail his "moral and social involvement" with other people. Courtesy of R. Abeles.

The basic way in which such communities maintain order is through "organic solidarity," cooperation that results because people who do different things depend on each other for the products and services they cannot produce. This "solidarity" is maintained by the formal rules and procedures of the marketplace, the courtroom, and the government bureaucracy.

However, organic, formal solidarity is not as effective as solidarity based on personal ties, and so some degree of anomie inevitably results. People are left alone, unsupported and unrestrained, in a society of exploitation, competition, and alienation. Disorder, suicide, and deviance are some of the results. Violence is another.

This is the sociological chain of events that Wirth described. The social psychological process is somewhat different, though related. The argument here is based on the work of a German sociologist, Georg Simmel, who sought to understand the "mental life" in a metropolis. It seemed to him that the immense and varied amounts of events which occur in the city would be so great that a resident would in self-defense have to adapt in certain ways and inevitably be changed in others. He would have to become blasé and indifferent or else be swamped. Even then, he could not avoid becoming sophisticated, rational, and irritated.[40]

A modern variant of the Simmel theory has been presented recently by a resident of the greater New York metropolitan area.

FOCUS
Urban Overload

Stanley Milgram, a social psychologist at the City University of New York, has observed behavior in midtown Manhattan from the vantage point of an office overlooking 42nd Street. From his daily observations, he concluded that the typical city resident is distrusting and rude in his encounters with others and lacks the cheerful helpfulness of his rural cousins. Blasé and uninvolved, the urbanite may not respond even in a critical emergency.

What accounts for the "nightmare quality" of cities—the pushing, the shoving, and the uncaring, impersonal stares?

Milgram attempted to answer these questions by analyzing the psychological impact of "large numbers, high density, and heterogeneity of the population" on the behavior and attitudes of urban residents. Crucial to his explanation is the concept of *overload*. Overload is the result of too many stimuli impinging upon the individual at one time (as in overloading a circuit by trying to draw too much current on it). His mind cannot process them all, nor has he the time or energy to respond to each; he is therefore forced to make selections from among them. The urban resident must contend not only with many physical stimuli (lights, noise, signs, traffic, etc.), but he must also face an overload of personal encounters. As a result, he must curtail his "moral and social involvement" with other people.

Milgram considers many aspects of urban behavior to be essential adaptations to this problem of overload. The harried, impersonal manner of the supermarket clerk towards customers, so different from the casual manner of the country store proprietor, can be explained in this way. The supermarket clerk must serve more people, and so can devote less time to each one. In this way, his indifference is an adaptation to the overload of customers.

Another effect is that city-dwellers are less likely to do favors for strangers. Milgram's graduate students found in one study that a larger percentage of small-town residents permitted a stranger in need to use their telephone than did Manhattan residents. Overload requires that urban residents guard themselves against the entreaties of others. If they were to yield to pleas in a place like New York, they would have little time to do anything else.

Overload explains Milgram's observation that city people are impolite. There is simply no time to interact with or care about everyone, so that, to function at all, one interacts with as few people as possible, and, then, only the most personally important.

These adaptations to overload help account for bystanders' refusals to aid people in distress, as in the infamous case of Katherine Genovese, a woman who was murdered in front of thirty-eight passive witnesses.

Besides blocking inputs, the city-dweller handles the overload problem by devoting less time to each input he does process (being "transitory" and "superficial"), establishing priorities among inputs (like helping "one's own" first), and shifting many of the demands to other parties (e.g., dog-walking services).

In the end, Milgram suggests that "the contrasts between city and rural behavior probably reflect the responses of similar people to very different situations, rather than intrinsic differences between rural personalities and city personalities." Under the impact of the city, we can all be passive bystanders. Though Milgram does not spell it out, violence can be read as one of the outcomes of this process. There is no fellowship to moderate competition and hostility; people do not care enough to restrain others from committing violence; and, the general estrangement reinforces anomie.[41]

The theory, which we have just outlined to explain how urban ecology can lead to conflict and violence, jibes with the oft-heard view that the frenetic pace of cities, the coldness of their people, and their massive incomprehensibility render life there hostile and dangerous. What has social science research to indicate about whether this view of urban life is accurate?

First, we turn to the psychological argument that population concentration leads to psychic overload, strain and stress, and irritability and estrangement. One way we might measure such mental strain is by finding out the degree to which people suffer from stress-related health problems such as tension, inability to sleep, and so on. If the theory is correct, these psychosomatic symptoms should show up more often in urban than in rural people. Sociologist Alex Inkeles investigated this question as part of a large study of modernization in Argentina, Chile, India, Israel, Nigeria, and Bangladesh (then East Pakistan). He found no real differences in stress between people who stayed in rural villages and those who moved to live in the city.[42]

We might also look at the degree to which people suffer psychiatric problems. In the United States at least, urban residents are more likely to undergo psychiatric treatment. However, these statistics are misleading because people in cities are more likely to know of and be able to find psychiatric care, while rural persons are unable to or are more likely to follow the "hide-crazy-Uncle-Charlie-in-the-attic" approach. All in all, it is not clear whether city dwellers are more or less mentally stressed than are rural persons.[43]

What of the estrangement that is suposed to be an adaptation to overload? For a long time, the sociological picture of the city-dweller was that he was indeed personally isolated. But more recent research appears to demonstrate that people in cities have just as many social ties as do non–city-dwellers. Very few urban persons are without close friends and family.[44]

One study compared male residents of Nashville, Tennessee, with similar men in the rural hinterland of the city. The researchers were interested in the question of how much time these men spent with other people and how much of that contact was "primary" (i.e., with family or close friends). Interviewers asked the men to recount exactly how they had spent the previous day. From these "time budgets" it was clear that the city men spent at least as much, if not more, time in primary contacts as did rural (farm and nonfarm) men of the same social class.[45]

More data need to be gathered, but at this time, it is difficult to support the view that city-dwellers are more alone than are non–city-dwellers.

Let us consider the issue of helping people in need. In the last Focus, we reported studies conducted by Milgram's students indicating that city people were less likely to help others than were small-town people. Research on this phenomenon of "prosocial behavior" is relatively new and not fully consistent.[46] For example, in another study, this one conducted on New York City's Lexington Avenue subway run, experimenters faked a collapse as the train was between stations. They sometimes acted as if they were sick, other times as if they were drunk. The researchers wanted to see if and when New Yorkers (that most famous breed of city-dweller) would help. To their amazement, *in virtually every case,* people rushed to help![47]

In this psychological analysis, the life of the urban resident is supposed to be filled with irritation, anxiety, and, generally, melancholy or despair. Is it?

When they are polled, city-dwellers express preferences for life in small towns and the countryside.[48] In one survey, two-thirds of American urbanites wanted to be out of the city within the coming decade.[49] Yet, when attempts are made to measure some general sense of alienation or unhappiness, researchers have generally failed to find consistent urban-rural differences. In fact, the data show, if anything, *less* malaise in cities.[50] For example, in the late 1950s Hadley Cantril conducted a massive international survey in fourteen countries. As part of the survey, people rated themselves on their general situation in life and their hopes for the future. The persistent finding was that urban residents rated themselves better off than did nonurban people.[51]

We have examined some of the predictions of the social psychological part of Wirth's explanation for the conflict and violence of cities. The existing research, though far from conclusive, makes Wirth's hypothesis difficult to accept. What about the sociological side of the theory?

Population size, density, and heterogeneity presumably lead to various forms of differentiation and specialization. Historically, it is true that cities and occupational specialization developed concurrently.[52] It is only when sufficient numbers of customers are present that specialization becomes economical. (Who could survive selling Persian rugs in a hamlet of 500?) In addition, specialization is greater, the larger the size of the city.

In this diversified community, Wirth argued, people's interactions and associations are "formal" and "secondary" rather than informal and primary (e.g., the department store clerk rather than the country store proprietor) and organizations exist in place of small groups and families (i.e., police control in place of neighborhood control). Research here is not very supportive. For one thing, it seems that family and kinship ties persist strongly in cities. This is a finding that has been repeated

Figure 7-3 Contrary to the image of anomic city life, ethnic community life continues to thrive in many American cities. Here Italian-Americans celebrate the festival of Saint Agrippina DiMineo in Boston's North End. Courtesy of the *Boston Globe*.

around the world (as in the examples that follow). Furthermore, it does not appear that urban residents are joiners of formal organizations, after all.[53] Finally, the formal sorts of institutions said to be preeminent in cities turn out not to be all that impersonal.

One case involves social control and police. Presumably, in small towns, control of disorders and quarrels is more often handled by personal contacts (e.g., neighbors stepping in), while in cities it is more often handled bureaucratically, with official rules and regulations. Nevertheless, in one study of the way city police actually work, researchers found that, in regard to juveniles, police usually decided what to do with an apprehended youth on the basis of what the complainant, usually a neighbor, wished—a sort of "community control."[54]

The critical point in Wirth's analysis is that the urban neighborhood is "anomic" (i.e., there is no real community of moral order and social cohesion). In this weakened social body, violence flourishes. Are urban neighborhoods anomic?

FOCUS
Boston's West Enders

In 1958, sociologist Herbert Gans moved into the West End district of Boston. This area, since demolished in an urban renewal project, was a predominantly Italian working-class neighborhood. To an outsider strolling by, the area appeared to be a rapidly deteriorating slum. Yet, though its physical features were poor, Gans found its social life to be rich.

He encountered an urban neighborhood where personal relationships flourished in an atmosphere of solidarity. Get-togethers among friends, he found, were "the vital center of West End life . . . the end for which other everyday activities [were] a means."

These friends, many of them neighbors, gathered often during the week to talk, exchange gossip, and just enjoy each other's company. They might also go out together, inviting single people to join them, because the unmarried were "alone." The West Enders "[did] not like to be alone. . . . [It brought] discomfort and ultimately fear."

Family ties were also close. Grandmothers assisted in the raising of grandchildren and single persons often lived with their relatives. Moreover, kin were always relied upon for advice and assistance.

Central to the nature of this way of life was the assumption that all relationships between people were to be personal ones. Thus, for example, they expected that a policeman would relate to them in terms of the customs and values of the neighborhood, and not in terms of official police rules. They distrusted businessmen who were interested in making profits rather than in making friends.

Such an orientation affected the West Enders' relations to their friends as well as the outside world. People were judged by their conformity and loyalty to group standards—by their fidelity to the expected behaviors of husbands, wives, West Enders, etc. In the End, they were expected to defer their own wishes to those of their peer group.

Thus, Gans found the West End—a deteriorated community in the heart of a metropolis—a neighborhood of close ties and familiarity, where everyone knew "something" about everyone else, so that it was as though they all knew each other, and where life was essentially a group life.[55]

Meanwhile, three thousand miles away. . . .

FOCUS
London's East Enders

In 1955, Michael Young and Peter Willmott conducted a study of the crowded East London tenement district named Bethnal Green.

Much as Gans did, they found that family ties were close and everyone seemed to know everyone else. A spirit of warmth and familiarity pervaded the area. Most people had lived in the borough a long time and shared a background of school or gang or pub with their neighbors. Relatives were apt to live close by. A man had only to "stand at his front door to find someone out of his past who [was] also in his present."

Family relationships were particularly enduring. Brothers and sisters kept in close touch with each other and with their mothers long after they had grown up and established families of their own. Single people rarely lived by themselves; instead they made their homes with either their parents or a married sister or brother. Relatives provided a link with the larger community. A person was friends with his brother's friends and was likely to be acquainted with his uncle's neighbors.

Those who lived on the same street—known as a "turning"—enjoyed a special feeling of community. Each turning made up a sort of village, with its own meeting places, shops, pubs, and occasional parties.

Thus, the Bethnal Greener was surrounded "not only by his own relatives and their acquaintances, but also by his acquaintances and their relatives." This communal nature made the East End a place where "familiarity [bred] content."[56]

To some extent, these studies are limited in their relevance because they deal with working-class communities. The patterns in middle-class areas are somewhat different. Nevertheless, the basic point has been echoed by studies from around the world. Ethnographers have found urban neighborhoods that were real "communities" with a moral order. Often that morality differed from that of other neighborhoods or of the wider society. But a community with unusual values is no less a community *with* values and, if those values have influence, the community cannot be described as anomic. At the same time, researchers have found rural (peasant) communities that seemed anomic or, at least, fraught with hostility and suspicion. These have been described, for example, in France, Italy, and Mexico.[57]

Yet, even if it does not seem that cities are particularly anomic, there remains a problem: Cities *are* especially characterized by *deviance*. As we saw earlier, this is true in terms of crime rates. (For example, in 1970, the burglary rate in cities of over a million was four times the rate in rural areas.)[58] Beyond that, cities are the scenes of a more general sort of deviance, that is, of behaviors that tend to clash with norms and values widely accepted and long-held by the mainstream of the society.

Divorce, illegitimacy, alcoholism, and radical politics all tend to be more frequent in large cities than in small towns.[59] Similarly, in terms of beliefs and values, city-dwellers tend to be less traditional. They are more likely to tolerate premarital sex, favor easing marijuana laws (as well as smoke marijuana), and to be skeptical of religion, among a number of issues.[60] This is, of course, not a hard-and-fast rule, for sometimes rural persons are more deviant.[61] But, in general, rates of deviance increase with community size.

When we speak of deviance in this sense, no negative moral evaluation is implied. Changes, very often ones for the better, begin with new or "deviant" behavior. In this sense, cities are also places of deviance in the form of innovations and of new life-styles. City-dwellers also deviate from the average in terms of being better educated, more informed, and less prejudiced than non–city-dwellers.[62] Deviance cuts two ways (just as conflict does, as we shall see in Chapter 8).

Thus, we arrive at a paradox. The Wirthian theory predicts that cities should suffer more deviance, including its violent forms, than should small communities, and that is true. However, the mechanisms by which it is supposed to occur (via stress, isolation, breakdown of the family, anomie, etc.) are, as far as we now know, not disproportionately present in cities. Wirth's theory is one of the most comprehensive and stimulating in urban sociology and is a source of continuing research. But for our purposes, we should explore yet a third explanation of the relationship between city life and violence.

Figure 7-4   City life makes possible a diversity of cultural groups living in close proximity to each other. Photograph by Maurice Schell.

The Many Urban Cultures

Perhaps the explanation of urban violence and conflict lies not in the physiological effects of crowding, nor in the sociological effects of size, but in the types of cultural groups found in the cities.[63]

Because of the specialized opportunities available there, cities tend to have varied kinds of people. Cities have been historically the recipients of migrant groups from various areas of their hinterlands, leading to large concentrations of people with different traditions and customs. Paris, for example, draws migrants from the Flemish North, the Germanic East, the stoutly Catholic West, Arab North Africa, and the rebellious Southern coast, to mention just a few French cultural regions. Moscow has drawn Westernized persons from the Polish areas, Moslems from the South, Asiatics from the steppes, and Jews from small *shtetls*, among many other ethnicities.

At the same time, minority groups, particularly in the United States, are found to be concentrated in cities and, in contrast to the American conception of the "Melting Pot," these communities persist as meaningful entities for a long time.[64] Even if and when ethnic distinctiveness fades, it does not lead to a common, mass society, but to new groupings based on different criteria (e.g., occupation, incomes, lifestyle, family status, etc.), with their own values and customs.

In addition to ethnic and common-interest groups, cities have historically had specialized communities of other sorts: single men working to send money to families remaining in the villages, transients from small communities whose ties there have been broken, the highly educated (who may provide some sort of "deviance" in the realm of ideas), the power-holders of the society, and so on.

Wirth and his colleagues recognized this diversity of subcultures and argued that the juxtaposition of groups with different beliefs and values meant that all and any norms were weakened (the development of a "relativistic" perspective). How could one expect any values to persist (much less achieve consensus) in a city that puts together the traditionalism of Appalachian whites, the fervent religiosity of older black migrants (and the fervent militancy of their children), the boisterous skepticism of Irish Catholics, the sophisticated agnosticism of university types, the flagrant countervalues of the artistic community, and so on?

The assumption in this section differs from Wirth's. It is that the varied ethnic, religious, professional, and common-interest groups concentrated in the city do maintain their own values and it is these values that determine human behavior in the city (including violent behavior).

Herbert Gans, whose study of Boston's West End we examined earlier, has argued essentially along these lines in an article entitled "Urbanism and Suburbanism as Ways of Life: A Reevaluation of Definitions."[65] Gans argues that Wirth was incorrect in his ecological determinism (i.e., the idea that the place determined the type of people and their behavior). On the contrary, Gans argues that within the same place there are different sorts of people. For example, in the inner city, there are "cosmopolitans" (professionals, intellectuals), the childless (both young couples and old people), the "ethnic villagers" (lower-class but not anomic), the "deprived" (the very poor and handicapped), and the "trapped" (other people who are unable to move out). Gans argues that it is characteristics such as these (class, ethnicity, period in the life-cycle, occupation) that essentially determine behavior (including the behavior of picking a place to live), and it is not place of residence that determines behavior.

Another student of urban life, Oscar Lewis, agreed with this analysis.

FOCUS
The Peasant in Mexico City

The late Oscar Lewis, anthropologist and ethnographer, studied the lives of poor people in cities and villages throughout the world by tape-recording accounts of their life stories. From his observations he came to disagree sharply with the folk-urban anthropological theory which argues that urban and rural living patterns are profoundly different.

Lewis conducted research in Mexico City and the surrounding countryside. Though other anthropologists have reported changes in culture as one travels from primitive villages toward cities, Lewis reported no sweeping behavioral or attitudinal changes in the peasants he studied who had actually moved to the city from the village. Instead, their life-style remained essentially the same, and they adjusted to urban living quite easily. Lewis was especially impressed that family structure and family life remained stable and secure and that kinship ties actually increased in the city.

Lewis did not find the anonymity and impersonality among the urban peasants that the folk-urban theory would have predicted. Nor did he find any conspicuous differences in diet, dress, or in outlook between the city and the countryside. Those who moved to the city became even more intensely Catholic than they had been before and continued to use village remedies and herbs. Furthermore, Lewis notes that "the belief in sorcery and spiritualism [and] the celebration of the Day of the Dead" were just as much a part of life in the city as they were of life in the country.

Lewis's response to the folk-urban theory was to argue that "the city is not the proper unit of comparison or discussion for the study of social life because the variables of number, density, and heterogeneity . . . are not the crucial determinants of social life or personality." On the contrary, Lewis contended, urban social life is not a mass phenomenon. Rather, it is the values and traditions of *small groups* such as families and churches that determine a person's perspective. Thus, through his Catholicism and his neighborhood and family ties, a Mexican peasant, even in the big city, in a certain sense always remained a peasant.[66]

The crux of the Gans-Lewis analysis is that ecological factors are of little importance in explaining urban behavior. What counts is the social characteristics of the groups that make their homes in the city, and, in an anthropological vein, the values of those groups are of paramount importance.

What implications does this view have for explaining urban violence? This theory directs our attention to the nature of the groups in the city. Historically, one prominent part of the urban population has been the communities of refugees from rural poverty. As all people do, the rural poor bring with them the culture, customs, and values of their homes and pass these on to their city-born descendants. In some cases, these cultures merge well with the demands of the new environment; in other cases, there may be harder experiences of adjustment.[67] In certain instances, the traditions brought to the city are heavily laced with violence (e.g., those of peasants from Southern Europe and rural South-erners in the United States).[68] (See the discussion in Chapter 6 on sub-cultures of violence.)

The uniqueness of city life is that these groups are gathered in un-usually large and concentrated numbers. Cultural traditions (in spite of, or, perhaps, partly because of, being under attack in a new place, as im-migrant traditions were in America) are prolonged and intensified in these "ethnic villages."

Part of the explanation being presented here for the high urban rates of individual violence is the migration to and concentration in American cities (partly as historical accidents) of groups that carry with them a tradition of violence. The most notable is that of poor southern, black and white, migrants to the northern cities. The other component of the explanation is that population size encourages the development of another and major "subculture of violence": the criminal community.

Criminal communities flourish in cities, first, because there is a concentration of types of people who contribute to crime. There are, for example, the rich. Without them, burglary and robbery would be far less attractive as occupational specializations. Another market for illegal acts are single men who purchase the services of prostitutes. Similarly, there must be a sizable set of potential drug purchasers (young, "alien-ated" men; life-style experimenters; "bohemians") before pushers will risk handling drugs. In short, crime, like other businesses, requires a "market" of customers or victims for it to flourish (in the same way that exotic restaurants require a sufficiently large number of gourmets in an area before they are feasible). The greater the concentration of certain types of people, then the larger are certain "markets," and the more occupational specialization there is in the field of crime.

This criminal economic sector soon develops a second level or an attached service industry. (After all, criminals are also a market.) Thus, "fences" arise to handle stolen goods; mobsters organize and "police" the business; "bag men" and corrupt politicians provide antilaw insurance, and so on.

Criminal communities are in some ways similar to other urban communities in that they have customs, rules, and values.

FOCUS
The Community of Prostitutes

. . . Prostitutes, in fact, associate almost entirely with other prosti-tutes, pimps, and as Dee (a black streetwalker) puts it, "people in the business, junkies, conmen, people like that."

They have their own favorite spots—several bars in the Times Square area, a couple more elegant establishments uptown for the "mackmen"—the 15 or 20 pimps here who have as many as 15 girls working for them, some as prostitutes, some as shoplifters.

They have their own after-hours bottle clubs, too, and they have decades-old traditions about where to go on a big night out—girl after girl lists the Copacabana as her favorite nightspot.

The biggest night is a championship fight. At the Ali-Frazier fight, Dee was in white satin and feathers. And, even bigger, because it means a whole weekend out of town, is the Kentucky Derby.

They have their own favorite drugs, too—not as much heroin, but cocaine, a strong stimulant that some pimps believe—wishfully—to be an aphrodisiac.

But the girls do not go out for fun very often. Mostly, they spend their free hours at home, pacing with bare feet over the wall-to-wall carpeting that each has installed "to cut down on the noise."

"The worst thing about this life," says Michelle [a "debutante-looking" member of a "stable" of call girls], getting up to turn off her television as a visitor arrives, "is the loneliness."

The girls also suffer under the knowledge they are doing something most people say is immoral. To cope with it, they have developed their own set of mores, and their own vocabulary.

They call themselves "working girls," or, if they are call girls, "courtesans." Their customers are "tricks" and "johns" and "dates." Their work is a "business," or even, to someone like Jackie [a high-class madame], a "social service."

Little Bit [a petite, college junior, Jewish streetwalker] will no longer take her dates to fleabag hotels because when she tried it once, she says, "it made me feel like a whore." Rosie [a policeman's daughter, a streetwalker] will not have an abortion, she says, because "I am a Catholic."

By the prostitutes' code prostitution is moral, while, as Dee phrases it, "what's immoral is giving it away free, sleeping around with anyone." Policemen who lie are also considered as immoral.

Pimps beating girls who hold out money is considered bad, but understandable; hookers beating other hookers, something that the girls say is increasing, is considered bad and unforgivable. Little Bit was robbed by a hooker a few weeks ago. The other girls on her block have not let the responsible girl work their area since.

As for prostitutes robbing their johns, no prostitute will admit to an outsider that she has done such a thing. Those are "tough" girls, they say (they are not really prostitutes, the explanation usually goes), they are crooks posing as prostitutes.[69]

These sorts of criminal communities are particularly prone to violence. For example, during a series of police roundups in midtown Manhattan, 22 percent of the prostitutes were found to have been previously arrested for violent crimes.[70] In a study of murders in Philadelphia, it was discovered that over half of the male murder *victims* had criminal records, most of them for physical offenses.[71]

Two points should be established in more detail: that criminal subcultures are an ecological phenomenon, in that their rise is dependent on the concentration of population; and that much of personal violence can be attributed to cultural milieus.

With regard to the first point, let us emphasize the group nature of crime. Not only do prostitutes have a cultural milieu, which supports them, but so do other criminal ways of life. Youth crime, for example, occurs almost always in a group. Some studies suggest that delinquency is due less to the personal characteristics of the boys involved and more to their local culture. Lower-class neighborhoods that stress values such as toughness and shrewdness above middle-class values of respectability tend to generate crime (see Chapter 6, pp. 198–203). Within the community, these "deviant" values are accepted and defended no matter what the opinion of the wider society.[72]

The importance of the group nature of urban crime is underlined by the evidence that American rural crime tends to be performed by loners and urban crime more often by groups. In the countryside, there simply are not sufficient numbers to create a criminal society.[73] (There are exceptions, of course, like the Sicilian Mafia.)

In this sense, criminal communities can be considered partly ecological in origin. But what evidence is there for the point that individual violence can be traced to such subcultures?

First, in most cases of murder, the victims knew their assailants fairly well. In rape cases, most victims knew their assailants at least casually.[74] Thus, both parties are usually of the same cultural group. Second, murders are usually committed within a general background of criminality and/or violence on the part of *both* murderer and victim.[75] Third, a large proportion of murders turn out to have been precipitated by the victim.[76] The following is an indicative story: "A husband accused his wife of giving money to another man, and while she was making breakfast, he attacked her with a milk bottle, then a brick, and finally a piece of concrete block. Having had a butcher knife in hand, she stabbed him during the fight."[77] (All this contrasts with the popular "crime in the streets" image of anonymous assault.)

There is also evidence of major cultural differences between groups in the frequency of fatal violence. As noted earlier, even such crowded cities as Hong Kong and Tokyo have much lower homicide rates than American small towns. As we saw in Chapter 6, the American South has long had a high rate of murder, and some studies suggest southerners carry this tradition to their new northern homes, where they and their descendants contribute disproportionately to northern violence.[78]

To restate the argument: Particular communities of people (such as the deprived, the professionally deviant, the life-style innovators, the susceptible [the wealthy, the elderly, etc.]) concentrate in cities in such numbers that a criminal, violence-prone community arises. Together with the presence of traditionally violence-prone ethnic groups, this subculture generates the individual violence that marks American cities.

This subcultural interpretation is open to criticism. There is evidence, for example, that lower-class persons (the most frequent enactors of violence) have basically the same values as do middle-class persons.[79] However, the problem comes when lower-class persons attempt to achieve these goals and are frustrated by society's blocks and their own handicaps. One result of this interference can be violent crime (see Chapter 6). The question arises as to why some groups respond to this blockage by violence and others by other ways. Again, the idea that there are *cultural* determinants of this choice seems persuasive.

This subcultural theory would also help explain the predilection cities have for intergroup conflict. Quite simply, cities are unique in that they are where very different groups can come into occasional contact with each other (both positive and negative contact). The rural ancestors of a Chicago black and a Polish-American white, who are now fighting over housing, were thousands of miles apart and neither in conflict with nor aware of each other. Similarly, the descendants of Mexican peasants can now confront Anglos on the streets of Los Angeles daily, instead of only in battles across the Rio Grande. In rural places, the homogeneity of values and life-styles reduces the likelihood of disagreement among organized groups. In the city, because there are many different and distinct subcultures, conflict is more probable. The concentration of these groups in large numbers probably also contributes to the intensity of group conflict (and, thereby, violence). Whereas minorities in a small town may be intimidated, in large cities their numbers (though it may still be a small percentage) may encourage more boldness and more conflict.

We have presented three explanations of the association between urbanism and violence: that it is a natural, almost automatic, response to overcrowding; that it is due to the sociological and psychological ramifications of population size; that it is due to the concentration of particular subpopulations. The evidence we have examined tends to favor the third theory, but it is far from conclusive. A good deal more research needs to be done, both in America and elsewhere, before the debate can be resolved.

NEIGHBORHOOD DIFFERENCES

Any city-dweller knows that there are neighborhoods in which he can walk comfortably and other neighborhoods in which he risks violence. Especially among youth, there are "turfs" set aside for certain groups, usually according to ethnic criteria.[80] For a member of another group to trespass is to risk battle. Whites take chances on Chicago's South Side, as do blacks in some of the city's suburbs.

More commonly, there are dangerous neighborhoods and safe ones in terms of crime rates. Sociologists have found that these neighborhoods tend to show physical deterioration, be overcrowded, and have industry in the area—the image of the slum. Furthermore, the violence-ridden neighborhoods tend to be the same ones no matter which ethnic group inhabits them. The same American neighborhoods have been crime-ridden when inhabited by Irish, Jews, Italians, or Negroes.[81]

This seems to argue for some sort of ecological determinism: Physical space causes behavior. But the paradox is that though the groups that suffered this atmosphere of violence differed in color, language, and religion, at the time they inhabited these neighborhoods they were similar in other ways. Crime-ridden neighborhoods are disproportionately inhabited by persons of low income, broken families, single and unemployed men, and transients.[82] These are characteristics understood to contribute to crime.

What seems to occur is that certain neighborhoods attract particular populations. The most important factor is probably cost of housing.[83] Tenements are all that poor people can afford under present circumstances, which leads to the overcrowding of slums. These deteriorated areas, undesirable for those persons who have the means to live elsewhere, become havens as well for classes of people who "fall out" of society: the transient, the socially or mentally ill, and the professional criminal.[84] As populations with these violence-prone characteristics (of whatever group or race) gather in an area, the forces toward violence accelerate and dangerous neighborhoods develop and persist.

The history of public housing in America is a tragic illustration of the error of assuming that physical characteristics heavily determine crime and social problems in some simple, bad housing–bad behavior manner. Well-intentioned planners saw the correlation of physical deterioration and violence, concluded that the first caused the second, and set about correcting the problem. The results were high-rise apartment buildings, which were physically better than the torn-down tenements. But crime and violence did not abate. It has become clear that a physical location does not alleviate a family's deeper problems of poverty, unemployment, discrimination, and other handicaps.[85]

Finally, as we shall see below, the very design of public housing has often exacerbated the problem of violence.

URBAN DESIGN AND VIOLENCE

Ecological factors may not have the simple effects that have been attributed to them, but there remains the inescapable fact with which we began this chapter: that people operate within a physical space and that inevitably the character and shape of that space will influence behavior. This should be particularly true of specific acts of violence, *not because the nature of the space motivates or drives people to violence,* but, rather, because it may determine whether or not someone will be *able* to commit the act.[86]

The simplest example is the wall. The history of most of the world's cities can be read in the remains of the walls designed to protect their residents from violence, both by armies and individual miscreants. The use of walls to isolate a physical space from potential attackers occurs within cities as well. Courtyards were effectively walled in against intruders in medieval cities as are many new luxury residential complexes in today's American cities—complete with gate, doorman, and closed-circuit television.

The design and layout of streets also has an important effect. Narrow, winding, out-of-the-way streets seem to invite violence. The layout of a city can have an especially important impact on the nature and flow of group violence. The streets of Paris were redesigned during the era of Napoleon III in the form of wide boulevards partly to facilitate the movement of troops into the frequently riotous working-class districts of the city. The layout of streets will help determine how fast crowds can gather and in what directions they can be dispersed. (In this regard, it was noted during the disruptive period at Berkeley in the mid-1960s that one contributing factor to the conflict may have been the fact that the target—the administration building—was located immediately across from the main traffic lanes and gathering-place of students.)

One specific form of interpersonal conflict strongly affected by the shape of physical space is panic. When space is constricted so that safety can be reached only by one or a few channels, a rush may occur which can lead to fighting which exacerbates the danger.[87]

Figure 7-5 "Good design can help prevent crime. . . . Where people are not around in sufficient numbers, violence is an ever present threat." Any predictions about the crime rate in these New York apartment complexes? United Press International photo.

One of the most critical factors in the design of space that affects violence is the degree to which it allows particular points to be seen and traversed by *people*. The greatest safety lies in the presence of others. It is ironic, theories of overcrowding notwithstanding, that a person is far safer from serious acts of violence in a New York subway at rush hour than he would be on a sparsely populated street.

In case after case, the major protective factor is other people. Where people are not around in sufficient numbers, violence is an ever-present threat: lonely streets, back alleys, elevators, and parking structures.[88] Public housing has suffered in this regard because the mammoth apartment structures include miles of "streets" inside buildings, hidden from public view or patrol. These halls, along with hidden stairwells, have become scenes of mugging, rape, and drug addiction. The poor residents then suffer more from the exploitation of the violent few than they did in the smaller though shoddier tenements.

However, good design can help prevent crime. When buildings are constructed so that danger spots such as pathways, stairs, and lobbies are under casual and frequent view, crime is decreased. This can be done, for example, by placing kitchen windows so that they face building entrances or by having elevators visible from the street. Similarly, architectural devices can be used to encourage residents to exercise proprietary guard over building areas. For example, small hallways with only a few apartments in each encourage people to use that space as their own and thus discourage transient malfeasants.[89]

It is the factor of safety in numbers that also explains the importance of lighting as a crime-deterrent. Street lights widen tremendously the range of people who can see and thereby "protect" an area.

The factor of people as a deterrent to violence has been stressed forcefully by one of the major writers on designing the urban environment, Jane Jacobs.

FOCUS
For Safe and Crowded Streets

New York's Greenwich Village exemplifies the urban ideal, contended Jane Jacobs, sociologist and urban planner, in the early 1960s. She argued that busy and well-populated streets which buzz with activity make the area safe and the people secure. But most city streets do not provide much security. In fact, the deserted avenues of most cities are "custom-made for crime."

This crime should not be blamed on the poor or minority groups. The North End of Boston has been known as a slum, yet the director of the local settlement house claimed that there had not been a "single case" of rape, mugging, or child molestation in the previous three decades. He explained that the few times in these thirty years that such attacks were attempted, they had been intercepted by passers-by, by residents observing from windows, or by shopkeepers. Indeed, the profusion of shoppers and businessmen and residents with a clear view of the street provided the North End with ample protection.

Jacobs contrasts this poverty-stricken environment with the "lovely, quiet residential" neighborhood of a friend for whom "the only disturbing sound at night is the occasional scream of someone being mugged."

Constant surveillance guards against such muggings, Jacobs argues, and the basic requirement for such watchfulness is a large number of stores and restaurants and other "public places" along the city streets. Such an arrangement draws many people to the area, and the numerous people provide protection for each other. Nor does it matter that no one knows anyone else. Jacobs tells of one incident in her neighborhood (the Village) that illustrated this point. A man had fallen through a plate glass window, and a woman sitting nearby "snatched the dime from the hand of a stranger who was waiting [for a bus] with his 15¢ fare ready, and raced into a phone booth [to call the hospital]. The stranger raced after her to offer her the nickel, too." Jacobs remarks that no one had ever seen this stranger before the accident, nor has anyone seen him since.

Thus, the safest and best-protected city is the one with busy and crowded streets. Quiet and uniformity are not only not as interesting,

Jacobs maintains, but they also make the people in the area easy prey for muggers, rapists, and criminals of all sorts. A city that functions well has a "*complex* order . . . comparable to an intricate ballet [which] . . . never repeats itself from place to place, and in any one place is always replete with new improvisations."[90]

One can question whether Jacobs' ideas are practical. Considering the many square miles needed to house our urban population, and the economic factors in business location (such as economies of scale served by concentration), it may be impossible to build complete cities of Greenwich Villages. Similarly the recent rise in crime in the Village raises again the greater importance of nonecological variables. Nevertheless, Jacobs has pointed out how the construction of the urban space can affect the likelihood of acts of violence.

In this discussion of design and violence, we have largely focused on deliberate acts of criminal violence by strangers, the sort of violence that has attracted the attention of the American public. Yet this type represents but a portion of the serious incidents of violence occurring daily in our cities. Most violent behaviors are performed by people whom the victim has willingly allowed to occupy the same space as himself or herself (e.g., a spouse, another relative, or a friend).

Until we can understand the forces that lead even intimates to commit violence against each other, shaping our physical space to discourage mayhem can never fully stem the flow of blood currently being shed in our cities.

SUMMARY

Why is there more violence in American cities than in small towns and rural places? Does concentrating a large number of people together in a small area cause violence? In this chapter, we explored three different *ecological* analyses of urban violence. An ecological analysis focuses on the ways in which the physical structure of our environment may determine the occurrence of violence.

Crowding theory hypothesizes that the physical crush of people in cities has a direct impact on the biological and psychological functioning of people, and this leads to violence. While studies using rats show that extreme crowding does lead to many physiological and behavioral abnormalities, there is little evidence that the same thing occurs in human beings. Part of the problem in establishing a relationship between crowding and violence is to show that it is crowding per se and not something else associated with crowding that is the cause of violence. For example, crowding often leads to a scarcity of resources, which may result in conflict and aggression.

The *urban-way-of-life* analysis argues that population density results in types of societies and human relationships that release restraints against violence. This analysis assumes that a sociological process and a social psychological process result in human relationships that are transitory, superficial, segmented, anomic, and impersonal. However, the existing studies fail to show that urbanites suffer the psychological strains or social isolation that this theory leads us to expect.

Our final ecological analysis suggests that violence occurs more frequently in cities because cities make possible *large urban subcultures.* Cities attract and sustain a wide variety of cultural groups. The crux of this argument is that ecological factors per se are of little importance in explaining urban behavior. What counts is the social characteristics of the groups that make their homes in the city. Cities are violent because violent subcultures thrive in the city. The uniqueness of city life is that these groups are gathered in unusually large numbers (e.g., poor migrants, rural southern whites and blacks, criminal communities). In short, this argument states that cities are violent because of the concentration of particular subpopulations in them.

In closing our discussion of ecological factors, we looked at how particular neighborhoods seem to attract particular types of people. For example, violence-ridden neighborhoods in a city tend to be the same ones no matter which ethnic group inhabits them. The same neighborhoods remain crime-ridden through each successive wave of ethnic transition. It seems that certain neighborhoods attract particular populations with violence-prone characteristics: the transient and the poor of whatever group or race. In addition, the design of these neighborhoods (e.g., poor lighting) makes crime and violence likely.

FOOTNOTES

[1] McKenzie (1925). Recently, ecologists have attempted to expand the definition of their field to encompass virtually all of structural sociology. See Hawley (1950) and Duncan and Schnore (1959).

[2] White and White (1962); Strauss (1961).

[3] Mumford (1961), p. 43.

[4] Wilson (1968).

[5] Szabo (1960); Wolfgang (1970); Westergaard (1966); Lodhi and Tilly (1973).

[6] Mulvihill and Tumin (1969), p. 707.

[7] Lane (1969).

8 Lane (1969); Hobsbawn (1959); Hackney (1969); Gastil (1971); Wolfgang and Ferracuti (1967).

9 R. M. Brown (1969).

10 Hobsbawn (1959); Rudé (1964); Tilly (1969); Wolf (1969).

11 Tilly (1974).

12 This is evident in the French data presented by Tilly.

13 Spilerman (1971).

14 Calhoun (1963).

15 Hall (1966). See also Lorenz (1966) and Ardrey (1966).

16 Lorenz (1966).

17 Dubos (1970); Carstairs (1969).

18 Leyhausen (1965).

19 Lipset (1963), chap. 2.

20 Montagu (1968).

21 Hall (1966); Somer (1969); Desor (1971).

22 Somer (1969), pp. 41–42; Carstairs (1969).

23 Griffitt and Veitch (1971).

24 Freedman, Klevansky, and Ehrlich (1971); Freedman et al. (1972). For an extensive discussion of this and other crowding literature, see Fischer, Baldassare, and Ofshe (1974).

25 Mitchell (1971); Michelson (1970); Schorr (1963).

26 Cassel (1972).

27 Mitchell (1971); Schorr (1963); and, maybe, not even then: Anderson (1972).

28 Wilner and Baer as cited by Mitchell (1971), p. 20.

29 Galle, Gove, and McPherson (1971); Fischer (1972a).

30 Davis (1969).

31 Michelson (1970), pp. 154–55; Anderson (1972), pp. 151–75.

32 Anderson (1972).

33 Or, consider Rome: With a population of three million, its murder rate is less than that of Whichita Falls, Texas, which has a population one-thirtieth that of Rome ("Nonviolent cities," *Newsweek*, January 5, 1970, 75:33).

34 Zimmer (1972).

35 Webb (1972).

36 U.S. Bureau of the Census (1971), p. 3. Similarly, the average number of people per housing unit in New York City dropped in the 1960s ("City census finds a rise in housing," *New York Times,* March 11, 1971, p. 29).

37 Howe (1971); Schorske (1963); White and White (1962); Strauss (1961).

38 Juvenal (1958).

39 Paraphrased, by permission, from L. Wirth, Urbanism as a way of life, *American Journal of Sociology* 44 (1938): 3–24. Copyright 1938 by The University of Chicago Press.

40 Simmel (1957).

41 Paraphrased and adapted, by permission, from Milgram (1970). Copyright 1970 by the American Association for the Advancement of Science. A filmed version of Dr. Milgram's article "The Experience of Living in Cities" entitled *The City and the Self* is distributed by Time-Life Films, 43 West 16th Street, New York, N.Y. 10011.

42 Inkeles (1969). American health statistics tell the same story.

43 Freeman and Giovannoni (1969); Dohrenwend and Dohrenwend (1971).

[44] Wellman et al. (1973); Fischer (1972*b*).

[45] Reiss (1959).

[46] Macaulay and Berkowitz (1970).

[47] Piliavin, Rodin, and Piliavin (1969).

[48] "Rural life chosen by most in a poll," *New York Times,* February 9, 1970, p. 95.

[49] Harris (1970).

[50] Killian and Grigg (1962); Sewell and Amend (1943); Inkeles (1969); Fischer (1973*a*, 1973*b*). An Italian poll found respondents to be happier in cities than in the countryside (*New York Times,* January 24, 1971: pp. 31, 33. Part 1).

[51] Cantril (1965).

[52] Gibbs and Martin (1962); Ogburn and Duncan (1967).

[53] Greer (1962).

[54] Black and Reiss (1970).

[55] Herbert J. Gans, *The Urban Villagers: Group and Class in the Life of Italian–Americans* (New York: The Free Press, 1962). Copyright © 1962 by The Free Press of Glencoe, A Division of the Macmillan Company. Reprinted by permission.

[56] Young and Willmott (1957).

[57] Wylie (1964); Foster (1967); Banfield (1958).

[58] U.S. Department of Justice (1971).

[59] Clinard (1964); Berelson and Steiner (1964), p. 609; Lipset (1963).

[60] Fischer (1975*a*).

[61] Abu-Lughod (1964); Szabo (1960), p. 81; Clinard (1964).

[62] Ogburn and Duncan (1967). See Becker and Horowitz (1970) and Fischer (1971).

[63] The assumptions in this argument are given in Fischer (1973*b*).

[64] Glazer and Moynihan (1970).

[65] Gans (1962*b*).

[66] Lewis (1965).

[67] See Handlin (1951, 1969) and Glazer and Moynihan (1970).

[68] Gastil (1971); Hackney (1969). These two have been recently challenged by Loftin and Hill (1973). See also Wolfgang and Ferracuti (1967).

[69] Oelsner (1971). © 1971 by The New York Times Company. Reprinted by permission.

[70] "22% of the Prostitutes Arrested in the City Are Found to Have Records of Violence," *New York Times,* August 17, 1971.

[71] Wolfgang (1966).

[72] Whyte (1955); Liebow (1967); Suttles (1968).

[73] Wilks (1967).

[74] Wilks (1967).

[75] Wolfgang (1966).

[76] Mulvihill and Tumin (1969), pp. 224–29.

[77] Mulvihill and Tumin (1969), p. 225.

[78] Gastil (1971); Pettigrew and Spier (1962); Hoch (1972). In contrast, Loftin and Hill (1973).

[79] E.g., Rainwater (1970). Some recent work, especially Ball-Rokeach (1973), has failed to support a subculture of violence thesis. However, these studies emphasize expressed values. The essence of the culture is the use of violent *means* to obtain common values.

[80] See Suttles (1968), for example.

[81] Shaw and McKay (1969). For a review, see Wilks (1967).

[82] Wilks (1967).

[83] Gans (1962a).

[84] Seeley (1967).

[85] See discussions in books such as Bellush and Hausknecht (1967); Wilson (1966); Rainwater (1970); and Newman (1972).

[86] The discussion in this section is based largely on chap. 16 of Mulvihill and Tumin (1969).

[87] Experiments on panic are reported in a number of places, including Mintz (1951) and Kelley et al. (1965).

[88] See Angel (1968); Newman (1972).

[89] Newman (1972).

[90] Jacobs (1961), chap. 1.

8 / THE PROCESS OF CONFLICT

a systems approach

One of the most common cries of dissidents is the call to smash "The System." Such slogans are often responded to with fatherly admonitions to change "The System" from within. Though the parties engaged in these disputes often talk past each other, they apparently have a common understanding of what they mean by "The System." It seemingly refers to the organization and dynamics of American society. It is, at least according to the dissenters, independent of specific individuals and groups. One can change the man or parties in power, yet "The System" grinds on. It is, according at least to the moderates, something that can change and yet remain the same. Reformers can alter "The System," while still preserving it. For both sides, "The System" is more than the sum of its individuals or groups; it is a whole, living entity, to be protected or to be attacked. This chapter will examine how such a concept, *system,* might yield a further perspective on conflict and violence.

To this point, we have examined aggression among individuals, small groups, organizations, and nations. We have looked at arguments, crime, power struggles, and war, among other violent incidents. The more cases and causes we explore, the more the following sorts of questions arise: "Is conflict in all these instances in some way similar?" and "Are there any general explanations which might apply to these various forms of conflict?" One could, of course, expand a particular explanation, say frustration-aggression, to cover more than individual violence, but experience suggests that the further a specific form of explanation is pushed (say, to war), the less revealing and the more confusing it is.

There exists, however, an approach that is specifically designed for this problem: "general systems theory." The phrase "systems analysis" conjures up a set of fearsome technocratic and mathematical images, but we shall see that it is actually not as complicated nor as mysterious as it sounds. But, first, we must clarify the unique aspects of this approach. The critical idea in systems theory is that, with minor variations, the same basic laws operate at all levels of social organization—among individuals in a couple, groups in a society, or nations in the world. The assumption this idea derives from is that the fundamental dynamics of behavior result from the nature of *relationships among* social units rather than from their *internal traits*. (This assumption is, of course, debatable. But so are the other assumptions we have discussed, such as that there is an "unconscious" or some reality to a "value." The proof of the pudding is whether any insights are derived.)

The system analysis we shall discuss here is intended to suggest a general theory of conflict. It is a perspective on our topic that is radically different from those we have treated before. If it is a useful one, it will yield some novel understandings of why and how conflict arises and is resolved. Before we put it to that test, we should make explicit how its logic differs from previous ones. It does so in essentially two ways: the *level of analysis* and *the form of explanation*.

In Chapters 1 to 7 we focused on *people*, either as individuals or as members of groups. We tried to understand how various forces have influenced people toward violence. We asked, in essence, "Why do people *act* violently?" In this chapter, we shall ask essentially, "Why do societies *have* violence?" Instead of concerning ourselves with *people per se*, we shall be concerned with societies and their parts. We shall not discuss personalities, but institutions of society (e.g., the family, the legal system, the government); not human motivations, but social system needs (e.g., stability, adaptation, resources).

An example may help clarify this viewpoint. When we observe the sadistic policeman in *The French Connection*, Popeye Doyle, bust into a ghetto bar, relieve its black patrons of their illegal drugs, and assault them, we can approach an understanding of the event in two general ways. First, we could try to understand the psychological reasons for the drug addiction, the reasons why Popeye was a policeman, why he was a brutal one, and what led him on this occasion to the bar. Or, we can focus in from a totally different direction: We can try to understand this event as one instance among many of a confrontation between law-enforcement institutions and a powerless, deviant community. We can ask how society comes to produce a class of dependent people, how drug addiction fits into society, and what the police-addict conflict means in terms of the stability and stresses of the society.

The kind of thinking this systems approach entails may seem strange at first: It does not deal with people as individuals, but deals with them instead as units of larger constructs, such as "society," "institutions," "processes." But, for all its immediate strangeness, it suggests some interesting ideas.

The second major analytical difference between this approach and our earlier ones is in its explanation for events. To this point, we have tried to explain conflict and violence in one manner. We have considered particular instances of conflict and violence as events and have searched for their sources. We have looked for the *causes* in the physiology of the brain, in the nature of people's relations to their societies, and in the composition of their social and physical environments. Here, we shall employ a different mode of thinking about conflict. Instead of asking, "*What causes* conflict and violence?" we shall ask, "*How do* conflict and violence *occur?*"

Actually, we think in this manner all the time. For example, when we try to understand *digestion* in the human body, we recognize that we are not asking the same type of question as when we ask what caused a broken leg. In the latter case, we are seeking a specific cause for a specific event. In the case of digestion, we understand that we are talking about a *process,* something that occurs repeatedly in the same *structure* (the body's stomach), something that is preceded by a large number of different events. We know that digestion is just one of a whole chain of processes that are constantly occurring in the body; we know that it is a repeated, patterned, on-going process that is vital to the functioning of the entire organism. It is not a unique or isolated event. Accordingly, it makes more sense to ask, "*How does* digestion *occur?*" than to ask "*What causes* digestion?"[1]

It is in this way that all of us have a grasp of systems analysis: Certain phenomena are best understood as regular processes within a structural whole. For example, digestion, blood circulation, and nerve firings are not unique events. They are processes within the structure of the biological organism. Combustion, water circulation, and lubrication are processes within a mechanical system. Campaigning, voting, and legislating are processes in a political system. We can look at conflict in a similar way.

The discussion of this perspective will differ from earlier discussions in two further ways: (1) We will focus mainly on *conflict.* Violence will be treated as a particularly intense episode during conflict, but it is the latter that needs explaining. (2) Whereas the previous chapters dealt largely with empirical findings, this is an area in which research has lagged far behind theory. So, most of what will be said is theory, not fact. But good theory can point the way to critical facts. Also, a good theoretical perspective will lead us to ask new questions and suggest new answers about conflict. Our inquiry begins with a clarification of the concept "system."

FOCUS
Systems[2]

We can get some intuitive feel for the concept of a "system" when we consider its use in phrases such as "the political system," "the communications system," "the nervous system," etc. What do all these have in common? What is a system?

Let us begin with *elements*. Elements are simply things. They can be material like planets, animal species, body cells, and so on. They can also be abstractions: ideas (in an ideological system), logical propositions (in a mathematical system), or *roles* in a social system.

A Digression: The last example deserves extended comment. When social scientists talk about voters in a political system, producers in an economic system, teachers in an educational system, and so on, they are not talking about concrete people (a John Doe or a Mary Brown). They are referring to *roles*. Sociologists use the concept in a way similar to its use by the theatrical world. A role is a part to be played in specific situations (a "play"). As such, a role cannot refer to a whole individual, but only to part of their *behavior*. Humphrey Bogart was Captain Queeg in *The Caine Mutiny* only part of the time. During his life, he played many other "roles" more of the time—husband, celebrity, etc. Similarly, John Doe plays "voter" only occasionally, and Mary Brown plays "teacher" largely during school hours while playing wife, mother, neighbor, church member, etc. the rest of the time.

Not only do specific roles represent only portions of peoples' activities—many different people can play the same role. A series of great theatre women have played Dolly Levi in *Hello, Dolly*. A large number of men have played the role of President of the United States. Millions of Americans are voters in election years. Many more are fathers, mothers, sons, or daughters. In short, roles are independent of the particular people who play them. So, in any discussion of a social system (economic, political, family, etc.), we are talking of abstractions called roles rather than of particular people.[3]

To return to our main line of discussion: Elements can be material things (like cells) or abstractions (like roles). But to have elements is not enough. A list of unconnected elements forms what physicists call a "heap."[4] Before we can begin to build a system, there must be a *pattern* among the elements. A *structure is a pattern of elements*. It is a non-random or organized aggregate of things. For example, axles, carburetors, pistons, gas tanks, etc. lying on a floor in a pile form a heap. Fit the parts together and you have the *structure* of a car.

So far, we have *structure*. We do not yet have a system, because the structure is static; it does not move nor change. When we dissect a cat, we are able to observe in detail its anatomy—its structure. But we are not observing what we can fully call a cat. What is missing is life, action, movement—*process*. To get a system, one must add process to structure.

A *process is a pattern of events*: an ordered change, movement, growth, etc. The events are not random, but repeated or sequenced in a regular manner, much as things are organized in a structure. The specific impacts that raindrops in a storm make are for all practical purposes random events; the cycle of evaporation, cloud-building, condensation, and rain is a patterned set of events, a process.

A *system is a structure in process*, that is, a pattern of elements undergoing patterned events.[5] Examples: an automobile in motion is a set of elements (pistons, wheels, spark plugs, etc.) in specific processes (ignition, combustion, drive). The human body is a set of elements (heart, lungs, vessels, etc.) undergoing certain processes (respiration, circulation, nervous stimulation, etc.). The same concept can be applied to social phenomena in terms of social systems. Workers, foremen, managers, and secretaries, making products, directing production, making policy, etc., form an organizational system.

This is the basic notion of system that we shall use. Several more terms must be added before we can go ahead and apply it to conflict. *Relationship:* Two elements are said to be related when an event in one occurs with an event in the other. The explosion in the engine precedes the drive of the wheels; the firing of a nerve cell in the brain is associated with the blinking of an eye. It is a pattern of events—a process—that describes the relationships of elements.

Filling out our picture of a system, we now understand it to be a structure of elements related by various processes. An interesting problem arises: In essence, everything is related to everything else. In a universe in which the amount of sugar New Yorkers put in their coffee can affect the political stability of the Philippines, how does one decide what is within a particular system and what is outside of it? That is, what constitutes its *boundary*, the border between what is the system and what is not the system? The best answer to this problem is to say that where we draw the boundary depends on the question we are asking. If we are interested in the political system of the United States and our question is about voting patterns, we may choose to make our boundary so tight as to include only voters, parties, and candidates. But if our question deals with the process of legislating, we might also include lobbying groups and foreign governments. Boundary limits are drawn in relation to one's issue of concern.

We are then led to ask, how is the "inside" of a system related to the "outside"—the *environment*? If there is little relationship between elements inside the system and those outside it, it is said to be a relatively *closed* system. The more it interacts with—is related to—the environment, the more open it is. This relationship refers to the input and output of matter, energy, and information. Example: The body receives matter input (food). Aside from its inefficiency (wastes), the body transforms the matter to energy in terms of heat, motion, and physical change. An example of a relatively closed system is a wind-up doll that will move until it runs down and then stops.

Systems are built in *hierarchies.* That is, systems are the elements of larger systems, in turn the elements of larger ones, and so on. Atoms are parts of molecules are parts of compounds are parts of chemicals are parts of solutions, ad infinitum. It is reminiscent of the line in Thornton Wilder's *Our Town,* where a character discusses a letter addressed "New Hampshire, United States of America, Continent of North America, Western Hemisphere, the earth, the Solar System, the Universe, the Mind of God." In the same way, the social system of American society is made up of institutional systems, like the economy, which are in turn made up of subsystems, like the firm and the household.

Systems are identifiable in the world because they persist over time. Though they are often in the process of forming and breaking down (birth and death), they do maintain themselves. That is, they continue to manifest the characteristic structure and processes that identify them. Maintaining this constancy is called maintaining *equilibrium,* a balance among their elements. For example, a machine must be maintained with a certain amount of energy input and calibration among its parts to function properly and remain an on-going system. When it varies too far from this equilibrium, its processes could cease (i.e., "break down").

A general type of process that helps maintain this equilibrium is called *negative feedback. Feedback* means that outputs of a system at one time determine its inputs at the next. *Negative* means that the result of this process is to return the system back to its original condition. The classic example is that of the thermostat. When its reading is moved by a change in room temperature, the thermostat sends signals to central heating to restore the selected temperature, returning the thermostat to its earlier equilibrium.

But do systems always stay at equilibrium? Don't they change? Indeed, they do. Bodies grow, societies develop, and business firms prosper. The paradox is that *they change and yet they stay the same.* We meet a child after not seeing him or her for a few years, and we note how much he has grown. Yet, we recognize the child as the same person. We describe this phenomenon as a *moving equilibrium.* That is, some aspects of a system change and some remain constant. The child's physical and mental capacities change, while at the same time his general physical and personality configurations remain essentially the same.

While negative feedback mechanisms maintain equilibrium, *positive feedback* provides movement and change. *Positive* does not mean "good"; it means that the result of the feedback is to move the system further in the direction it is going.

In a developing body, growth provides strength which allows for more growth. In a developing society, wealth provides investment capital which helps generate more wealth. The mirror image of this process is the "vicious circle." For example, poverty may breed familial problems which, in turn, breed poverty, and on and on.

The positive feedback effects can dampen out so that the system reaches a new stable equilibrium (as when a person stops growing at about 20), or they can accelerate and oscillate until the system "breaks down" or is radically changed (e.g., the welfare family breaks up).

In this focus, we have introduced a whole series of notions about systems. The final step before going on to conflict is to illustrate these ideas in one major social system: the nuclear family.

We take as our *elements* the following *roles:* father, mother, and children. These elements are found most often together in one regular pattern: one adult male called "father," one adult female called "mother," and one or more "children." This pattern suggests a *structure.* Regular patterns of events—*processes*—occur to this structure, such as what we call homemaking, child-rearing, eating dinner, and emotional interaction. These events *relate* the elements of the structure to each other: mother dresses child; father spanks child; father gives mother money to spend on food for father, mother, and child; father, mother, and child go to grandmother's together; etc. Thus, we have the nuclear family *system.*

We have arbitrarily *bound* this system at the nuclear family (excluding other relatives such as grandparents), but the system does exist within a *hierarchy.* It is part of a larger family network that includes other relatives; it is part of a larger community, and, eventually, a nation. The family system can itself be divided into the husband/wife sub-system, the mother/child subsystem, and the father/child subsystem.

This system is relatively *open*. Resources and influences of all sorts come into it and outputs such as labor, purchasing, and community participation leave it.

Equilibrium is maintained in a number of *negative feedback* ways. If a child is sick—an element fails to perform its function—restoring behavior is called forth: mother nurses child. If the husband/wife subsystem is disrupted by conflict, patterned sets of actions arise to restore the relationship ("kiss and make up"). If child misbehaves, father's response (a pat on the posterior) usually restores equilibrium.

At the same time, the system is in *moving equilibrium*. Children's behaviors, specifically, are expected to change. A child of five performing the behaviors of one of two is punished while performance of a six-year-old's behaviors is rewarded. Thus, there are *positive feedback* mechanisms encouraging maturation in children and inevitably affecting the family structure to the point that children leave the system, reducing it to the husband/wife subsystem.

This example was meant to illustrate a systems approach. While causal analysis asks, "What are the specific causes of these specific events?" (Example: "What caused John Doe to leave his parents' home?"), a systems approach asks, "What is the pattern among these events?" (How do children come to leave their parents' homes?), "Into what larger system does the process fit?" (What do children do after they leave the nuclear family?), and "What function does it serve?" (What does home-leaving mean to the community?). When we perceive the world around us in systems terms, we begin to ask somewhat different questions about what is happening in that world.

As we suggested at the beginning of this discussion, this analysis is by no means mysterious. If we were to walk into a large room on a campus and see events such as an older person talking to a large group of young people who are writing in notebooks, we would not search for a "cause." That would not make too much sense. (Would we say that the speaking caused the note-taking and that the speaking was caused by financial remuneration?) More likely, we would search for a pattern in these events and call it the process of "teaching." We would understand it as part of the higher educational system, its function (or, at least one) being the transferal of information from one element of the system to another. We might even choose to explore this higher education system as an element of the larger social system. This not very mysterious, fancy, or spectacular way of thinking is systems analysis at its essence. As with the man who discovered that he spoke prose, we discover that we do systems analysis all the time.

CONFLICT AS A SYSTEMS PROCESS

Now that we have been introduced to a systems approach and have a language for speaking "systemese," how do we use it to understand conflict and violence? What follows in response is one way of conceptualizing conflict in systems analysis terms—just one among a number of possible ways.[6] The first step is to see conflict in a systems context; that is, to ask, "What is 'conflict' in a system?" Indeed, what *is* conflict?

We shall reach the answer by taking a detour through the idea of *competition.* Competition is a relationship of negative interdependence— where increases in the inputs to one element of a system are associated with decreases of inputs into another. The more customers Hertz has, the fewer Avis has; the more time Veronica spends with Archie, the less she spends with Reggie. According to the model we are presenting, there can be no conflict without such a competitive relationship (see pp. 270– 73).[7]

Conflict is the exchange of negative outputs between elements in a competitive relationship. Whereas competition can occur without any contact between the elements—they are just drawing from the same well —conflict exists when that contact is present. When two business firms are both dependent on the same fixed-size market, they are in competition; but when Avis cars start running Hertz cars off the road, they are in conflict. In an oversimplified way, we can say that conflict differs from competition in that it is direct: one party damages the other directly, rather than only by taking potential resources. Violence is an extreme instance of conflict in that actual bodily or property damage is inflicted on a party.

One proposition that these definitions suggest is this: *Without interdependence, there is no conflict.* That is to say, if elements are not related, are not dependent on each other and/or on the same resources, then competition will not occur and neither will conflict. Sellers of toothpaste and sellers of harvesting machinery will rarely conflict with each other because their markets are quite different. Their degree of interdependency is slight (except as business firms in the same society).

On the other hand, the closer two elements are entwined in the same system, the more dependent they are on the same things—and on each other—then the greater the likelihood of competition and conflict. For example, next-door neighbors may often conflict—over parking spaces, responsibilities for upkeep, etc. In the previous chapter, we pointed out that most violent crimes occur between people who are involved with each other. The point should be stressed: Conflict is more

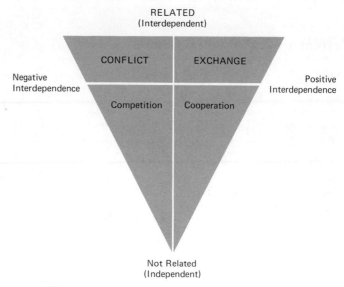

RELATED
(Interdependent)

CONFLICT   EXCHANGE

Negative   Positive
Interdependence   Interdependence

Competition   Cooperation

Not Related
(Independent)

Figure 8-1   Possible relationships between two elements.

likely the more interdependent two elements are. As one writer on violence has put it, "a great deal more fighting occurs between people who
make love than between those who do not. . . ."[8]

However, does not interdependence bring about cooperation as
well as conflict? Could not interdependent elements work together to
maximize rewards? Where do the positive aspects of mutual fate appear?

Figure 8-1 may help clarify the problem. The triangle represents
the area of possible relationships. At the bottom point is the relative
absence of interdependence. In these cases, there can be no competition
and conflict—nor can there be cooperation and exchange. There is no reason for any of these alternatives. (*Cooperation* is defined as a relationship
in which increases in inputs to one element are associated with increases
to the other. By *exchange*, we mean that positive outputs are exchanged.)
As elements become more interdependent, these possibilities emerge, in
that high degrees of interrelatedness may lead to battle or beneficial
trade. Whether one or the other occurs depends on the type of interdependence.

We are led naturally to the next observation: Many relationships
are neither positive nor negative, but a mixture of both. For example,
two business firms may compete over customers but cooperate in ex-
panding the size of the market or in fighting government regulation. Two
nations may be at war, but have a common interest in making sure that
the war does not become nuclear. This sort of relationship has been

termed "mixed-motive"—there are motives both to compete and to co-operate. It has also been termed a "non-zero-sum" game. That is, it is not a "game" in which everything A gets is at the cost of B and vice versa (so that the outcomes to A and B always sum to zero). There are some results that can benefit both parties.

When a relationship has both competitive and cooperative aspects, whether conflict or positive exchange arises depends on the relative weight of the two factors. In a dating couple, he may prefer movies and she plays, and they may dispute the matter (a brief instance of conflict), but on the whole they cooperate to enjoy a good time together. In a war, enemies may agree to release wounded prisoners (a brief outbreak of positive exchange), but the relationship is essentially competitive and conflict is more common.

The way in which a relationship can swing from competition to co-operation was illustrated by the experiment conducted at a boys' camp by Muzafer and Carol Sherif, which we discussed in Chapter 5. When the boys came up at the beginning of camp, they were split into two groups—the Eagles and the Rattlers. These teams were set against each other in sports and other competitions. As one might expect, fights and name-calling were frequent.

Then, on a couple occasions, the Sherifs rigged situations to create positive interdependence. For example, a truck needed to bring food to the hungry campers "broke down." The boys had to work together to overcome the common problem, and the result was cooperation, camaraderie, and good feelings.[9]

Let us review the analysis to this point: We have defined a system as an abstraction meant to capture those things common to small groups, societies, and the international community, as well as physical organisms and organizations. Competition and conflict have been defined in terms of the interdependencies that exist between elements in a system. If conflict arises from the pattern of relationships and inputs within a system, it would be logically consistent to think that the events of that conflict are also patterned, in other words, that they form a *process*. This leads to the central argument of the present chapter, that conflict in social systems is regular and patterned—just as cell growth in an organism or planetary movements in a solar system are patterned. Where does this argument lead us?

TYPES AND NATURAL HISTORIES

If one conceives of conflict as a systems process, one is led immediately to try to *describe* that process. Biologists describe natural processes such as organ growth and decay; a computer engineer can describe the calculation process in an IBM 360. Can social scientists describe the course of conflict in a similar manner? That is, we are asking whether there is a *natural history* of conflict that can be outlined to describe the sequence of events. Perhaps there is one general history of conflict that is applicable to all system levels of hierarchy (individual, group, national), or perhaps there are a number of such natural histories, differing by level or some other factor.

When social scientists have approached this problem, one of their procedures has been to try to distinguish *types* of conflict.[10] For example, one can type conflicts by system level and hypothesize that the natural histories differ accordingly (e.g., that interpersonal conflict follows a different route than does international conflict). Another distinction that has been made is between "realistic" and "nonrealistic" conflict. The first is meant to refer to conflict over material goals, the latter to conflict due to misunderstanding or emotion.[11] Another typology identifies institutionalized and noninstitutionalized conflict. The first is conflict regulated by the system within which it occurs (e.g., a refereed boxing match), the other is uncontrolled (e.g., a barroom brawl).

Perhaps we can arrive at useful typologies if we first try to describe a general natural history of conflict and see how far we can go before we are forced to make distinctions among types. It is that task to which we turn now—a search for a natural history.

We are all familiar with forms of conflict that seem to follow the same rough pattern each time they occur no matter who the specific parties are. Example 1: A parent wants to do one thing; the child, another. Yelling starts. The child breaks out in tears. The parent apologizes and concedes to the child's desires. Example 2: A major-industry labor contract is ending. Labor claims a desperate need for a pay increase; management claims that such an increase will bankrupt it. Negotiations break down. Labor goes on a selective strike; management conducts an industrywide lockout. Labor starts to run out of strike benefits; management faces insolvency. A compromise is reached and production resumes. These conflicts are recognizable, and to these scenarios can be added other familiar ones: the student-administration confrontation; the whiplash victim and the insurance company; the two kids in the schoolyard; the barroom brawl.

These conflicts, experience suggests, tend to follow familiar courses most times they occur, and these patterns seem predictable. They might well be termed "natural histories."

One of the most influential social theories of modern times centers on just such a natural history. Karl Marx's description of the evolution of society is a description of cycles of conflict: "The history of all hitherto existing society is the history of class struggles."[12] In Marx's concep-

tion (which we will grossly simplify here), each period of history witnesses the growth and polarization of two basic classes: the "oppressors"
—those who control the means of production—and the "oppressed"—those
exploited by it. Each epoch experiences the divergence of the ruling class
and a class in opposition. Forces build up until the inevitable revolution
occurs. When the smoke clears, a new economic order is established
under the control of a new class. Once again, divergence and tension
build up between this class and another, and the cycle takes another
turn. This process occurs repeatedly through slave, feudal, and capitalist
society. For Marx, the process was to end after capitalism, because in the
great struggle that was to occur then, the entire society would be polarized into two classes, capitalist and proletariat. When the proletariat
won, there would remain but one class. In this communist, classless society, there could be no controllers and controlled; therefore, no more
class conflict.

Many sociologists disagree with the specifics of Marx's theory, but
for us it is not the economic details but the underlying systems model
that is important. Abstracting Marx into our own terms, he is suggesting
that there is a natural process in societal systems whereby (1) its elements come to be increasingly in competition; (2) they inevitably polarize
into two blocs (or super-elements) that become even more competitive;
(3) conflict continues to break out in increasingly serious battles until
(4) the system breaks down and its elements are reconstructed into a
new, differently organized system; (5) the process begins anew.

This "dialectical" model presents an intriguing hypothesis about the
natural history of conflict. As such, it fits in with some other ideas that
social scientists have had about conflict. For instance, one suggestion is
that "there is a persistent tendency to reduce multiple-party conflict to
two-party conflict via coalitions and blocs."[13] (This recalls the polarization in Marx's theory.)

Other sources of natural histories of conflict are actual accounts of
historical events, such as the following:

FOCUS
The City Mob

The historian E. J. Hobsbawm has drawn attention to common
phenomena in European cities of the nineteenth century: street riots by
large masses of the urban poor.[14]

The appearance of these mobs and the violent course of events
invariably followed a recurrent pattern. When men had jobs and prices
were stable, the mob was silent. Riots occurred only in times of unem-

ployment and rising prices. The poor were barely able to eke out an existence under normal conditions, and unemployment and high prices could destroy them utterly. Hobsbawm describes the riots as "automatic and inevitable reactions" to such conditions.

When the disorders arose, they forced the rulers of the city to improve the lot of the poor, for it was understood that rioting would continue until such steps were taken. The rioters were not attempting to alter the structure of the social system, but merely to achieve certain short-range goals, such as a lowering of prices. Therefore, as soon as the goals were achieved, the violence ceased. Calm prevailed until the position of the poor deteriorated again, at which time the violence resumed. Rioting was such a potent means of pressure that even a brief riot achieved the desired effect. Thus, riots were both "intermittent and short."

Once the European cities had become fully industrialized, riots by the city mob became a thing of the past. But the type of agitation exhibited by the mob existed for a longer time than had any other form of social protest.

Social scientists attempt to gather many such accounts of real-life conflict—whether it is the poor versus the rich, one individual versus another, or countries against countries—in order to develop "models" of social conflict. These models—descriptions and explanations of how the typical conflict proceeds—could be applicable to all these systems levels. Some preliminary theories along this line have appeared in recent years.[15] What we shall do here is describe one such general model, a schematic illustration of which is presented in Figure 8-2.[16]

Stage 1. Precompetition. At this point, the parties have a cooperative relationship or are relatively independent. Examples: a husband and wife in a happy marriage; two fishing fleets in a sea of abundant resources. There is either positive interaction or none at all.

Stage 2. Competition. The system changes (due to internal historical dynamics or to events in its environment) so that the parties are in a competitive relationship. In our examples, the husband advances to a new job that drastically cuts into the time he can spend helping his wife at home; the fecundity of the sea diminishes so that the fishing fleets return partly empty.

Stage 3. Conflict. The parties attack each other. The husband and wife may get into arguments or annoy each other in petty ways; the fishing fleets may sabotage each other's nets.

What has occurred as competition and conflict have intensified is *escalation*. Escalation involves not only an increase in mutual punish-

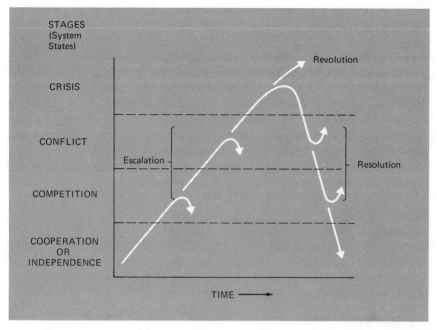

Figure 8-2 A schematic illustration of a natural history model of conflict.

ment but also, in most systems, *polarization.* The relatives and friends of a bickering couple may take sides in the argument; the governments of the two fishing fleets may exchange threats.

There are classic examples of escalation parallel to these two: between families in the case of the clan feud; between nations in the case of arms races and wars. The usual sequence of events (process) is that an action (a shooting or arms purchase) by one party stimulates a reaction by the other, which is in turn reciprocated, and so on, in a spiral. This sort of phenomenon has been called a "Richardson process" after the scientist who demonstrated that relatively simple mathematical formulas for these reactions could describe the arms race that led to World War I.[17]

Escalation is a "positive feedback" process in which each event intensifies its own precursors (see pp. 262–63). Besides these reactions, there are other changes in the system brought about by the conflict which intensify that very conflict. Positive relationships between the sides are destroyed, the damage of battle becomes grounds for further battle (e.g., the United States continued to fight in Vietnam purportedly to retrieve its captured airmen), the most conflict-oriented subelements (e.g., militarists) become dominant in each party, and polarization occurs.[18]

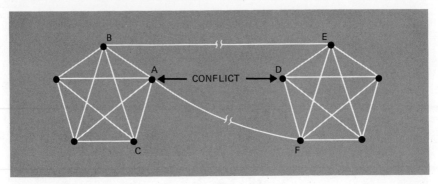

Figure 8-3   An illustration of polarization.

Polarization, the process Marx described, seems pervasive in conflict. As escalation between any two elements proceeds, other elements in the system tend to align on one side or the other, forming conflict blocs (the world wars are easy illustrations). Which bloc an element will be aligned with depends on the number and strength of the positive and negative relationships it has with each element in conflict. An illustration is presented in Figure 8-3.

Points in the figure represent elements (people, groups, nations); lines represent positive relationships. As conflict between *A* and *D* escalates, the positive relationships between *B* and *E* and between *A* and *F* are the most likely to break off and become negative. This is because *E* and *F* are tied most positively via many connections into *D*'s subsystem, while *B* and *C* are tied into *A*'s. The kind of polarization to expect is between the left and right pentagles.[19]

Anthony Oberschall has presented a number of historical cases in which societies undergoing conflict split along lines of previous relationships in just this way.[20] This is one reason (but not the only one) why family members line up together against other families, or neighbors against intruders.

Other case studies also demonstrate the polarization and general escalation process:

FOCUS
Community Conflict

Controversies in American communities are concerned with a wide variety of issues, from desegregation and water fluoridation to campaigns to ban communist books from school libraries. Sociologist James Coleman studied a number of such disputes and outlined the processes that seemed to occur during community conflicts whatever the specific issue at hand.[21]

One pattern typical of community disputes is the shift from specific to general issues. This was very evident in Scarsdale, New York, where a controversy arose over an attempt to purge the school libraries of "communistic" books. In short order, the scope of the conflict was broadened to include the philosophy of the entire educational system.

Along with this movement toward general issues is the appearance of new issues not tied in with the original ones. This was apparent in many controversies surrounding city-manager plans. Over time, these disputes came to embrace ethnic, religious, political, and ideological components as well as the original points of discord.

Accompanying this generalization is a "polarization in social relations." As the dispute proceeds, people tend to dissociate themselves from their acquaintances in the opposing faction. At the same time, contacts within each group thrive (cf. Robber's Cave Focus in Chapter 5).

The formation of partisan organizations is another normal development in community conflicts. In many communities, no organizations exist to forward the positions of each side. As the dispute moves along, new organizations come into being. In addition, existing community groups such as the P.T.A., churches, business associations, and the American Legion begin to choose sides.

In other ways as well—the rise of personal animosities, the emergence of new leaders, and the increasing use of informal, face-to-face communication—there are striking resemblances in the patterns by which community controversies expand.

Thus, polarization further contributes to escalation by changing neutrals into partisans and by eliminating the positive bonds that might restrain the battle. Let's continue now with the natural history of conflict.

Stage 4. "Crisis." This is an ambiguous term and we cannot do much to clarify it, but there appears to be in many conflicts a special period (which may be quite brief in terms of time) when a turn is reached. It is distinguished by a new, intense, and different level of interaction, and it is when violence is most likely to occur. The American Revolutionary War climaxed a period of struggle between the colonists and the British. The impending confrontation of American navy destroyers and missile-carrying Russian freighters was the turning point of the Cuban Missile Crisis of 1962. In terms of the examples we are using, the husband and wife may have a climactic session on the future of their marriage; the navies of the two fishing nations may engage in violent battle.

Stage 5. Resolution—or Revolution. The turning point or period usually means a resolution or a "revolution." The resolution can be immediate (e.g., the husband quits his job; the weaker nation consents to the demands of the stronger), or it can be a gradual deescalation (e.g., the husband and wife try out compromise arrangements; the two countries go through extended negotiations to resolve the fishing dispute), but, in either case, it involves a return to cooperation, or, at least, competition. Another possibility is revolution in the sense that the system is drastically restructured (e.g., the husband and wife break up, thereby destroying that system; the stronger nation conquers and incorporates the weaker, reshaping that system). This latter case, revolution, is rare but important, and we shall devote a section to it later in this chapter.

Though there are various forms of resolution, the most common one is probably *bargaining*—the process by which one or both parties make concessions until such point as the conflict is over. A couple cannot agree on an evening's entertainment, so they go to his restaurant and her movie. ("You've got to give a little, take a little . . . that's the story of, that's the glory of love.") Two Congressional groups are disputing the wording of a bill, so they each surrender a couple of issues to the other. Two nations, after sparring a bit, split disputed territory.

The pervasiveness of this form of conflict resolution in daily life has led to a great deal of study of bargaining behavior. Social psychologists have taken the process into the laboratory and have examined it by using "simulations." That is, subjects are asked to play a game for points or money. Their goal is to reach some sort of agreement in order to gain the most points or money for themselves. These games are constructed so that their logical structure is an analogy to the essential logic of real-life bargaining situations. The closer the logic of the two, the more we can trust what we find in the laboratory to be true of "real life."

The central research question for social psychologists using these laboratory simulations is: Under what conditions will optimal resolutions occur? "Optimal" usually means a result which gives both parties—together—the most they could possibly achieve at the lowest cost in time and travail. The eventual end is to avoid bargaining situations in which conflict prevents the most rational solution or leads the subjects to hurt each other.

In this context, experimenters have described some "natural histories" of bargaining.[22] For example, agreements that end the conflict tend to be made at the very end of the time available for them;[23] there tends to be an alternation in bargaining concessions; and threats and lies tend to be greatest when disagreement is over a very limited resource (when people have their backs against the wall).[24]

Here is a classic type of experimental bargaining study:

FOCUS
The Prisoners' Dilemma

Edward G. Robinson and Humphrey Bogart have just been pulled in by the police as suspects in a bank robbery. They are put in separate cells and each is approached individually by the D.A., who makes the following offer:

"We know you robbed that bank, but we haven't got all the evidence yet," he says. "We can send you both up the river for two years for carrying concealed weapons. But if you turn State's evidence for us and the other guy doesn't, you'll get off scot-free. *He'll* get ten years in the cooler. And if both of you turn State's evidence, you'll each get five years."

This is the prisoners' dilemma. If both keep quiet, they just get two years apiece. That is their best solution to the problem. But each one is tempted to "fink," because he might get no sentence at all. (The other would receive a heavy sentence.) Yet, if both are thinking that way and both "squeal," they each get five years. Furthermore, because they are separated, they cannot communicate to make a deal. Figure 8-4 portrays their dilemma.

This game is one type of conflict-of-interest game that experimental social psychologists have used—after removing the melodrama—to explore patterns of conflict resolution. It is representative of a wide range of "collective choice" conflicts. For example, panics have the same logical structure: If everybody waits patiently before going to the exit door, everybody runs a moderate risk of injury. If everybody *else* waits, but you bolt for the door, you are guaranteed safety. (This is like "squeal-

Bogart

	Keep Mum	Squeal
Keep Mum (Robinson)	Bogart gets −2 yrs. Robinson gets −2 yrs.	Bogart gets 0 yrs. Robinson gets −10 yrs.
Squeal (Robinson)	Bogart gets −10 yrs. Robinson gets 0 yrs.	Bogart gets −5 yrs. Robinson gets −5 yrs.

Robinson

Figure 8-4 The prisoners' dilemma.

ing.") So, often, everybody thinks that way: everybody rushes the exits, and everybody gets hurt.

In the experiments on the prisoners' dilemma, subjects (usually college sophomores) are brought into a laboratory and are introduced to the problem: Trust and cooperate with the other fellow and you might both win moderately—or he might double-cross you. Distrust or try to double-cross him—and risk both losing. (Points or money are used instead of jail sentences.) Subjects are asked to play the game repeatedly, sometimes for hundreds of trials.

One of the results that tends to emerge from the experiments is the "lock-in" effect. After a period of exploring different strategies during which conflict (squealing) will increase, most pairs of players will lock-in on one or another "solution." Either they will tend to cooperate with each other (keep mum) over and over again, or they will defect (squeal) over and over again in an endless cycle of conflict.[25]

This case seems to illustrate the model we outlined. Just as the community conflicts show build-up and polarization, the prisoners' dilemma experiments suggest that, after a period of conflict, parties either resolve the conflict or the system breaks down. (One would expect that,

Figure 8-5 Violence does not always accompany labor disputes because the process of labor-management bargaining has been institutionalized into a set pattern of events. However, violence does sometimes occur as in this case, when two women attempted to drive through a picket line in Naugatuck, Conn. United Press International photo.

if the experimenters had let them, subjects who locked-in on the mutually punishing strategy would have probably just picked up and gone home— destroying that two-person system.) These experimental studies do not stand alone in suggesting a natural history to resolution. We also have case studies of this process:

FOCUS
Labor and Business Bargain

One of the most fascinating aspects of labor and management negotiations is that the two sides almost invariably arrive at an agreement. It is a bit surprising that this should happen with such regularity since the principals start from such flatly contradictory positions. How do they do it again and again? Ann Douglas explored this problem by examining a number of cases of mediation.

Rather than playing down their differences, the disputants accentuate and magnify them. Indeed, they find it advantageous to exploit their conflict. The procedure by which the contenders move from harsh battle to consensus may be understood in terms of three phases.

Phase one consists of ascertaining the limits within which the bargaining will proceed—the most management will give and the least labor will take. For such limits to become clear it is necessary to exhibit "outward signs of deep and irreconcilable cleavage." Disagreement is stressed in the form of long and dogmatic pronouncements for positions that will ultimately be retracted. The discussion, always high-powered and dynamic, at times becomes abusive and rancorous. "Antagonism between the parties is the lifeblood of this stage." These intense exchanges serve the important purpose of "establishing the bargaining range." In addition, they provide some indication as to how stubborn and intractable each side will prove to be in the forthcoming discussion.

Phase two is a search for agreement. Eventually, each side must move toward the position of the other. To do this, each side attempts to assess the firm and the weak points of its opponent. The period is one of "tactical maneuvers, both offensive and defensive, with the parties sparring strenuously back and forth as they jockey for position." Each side seeks to understand the other's real situation so as to be able to carve out a settlement most advantageous for itself. Such understanding develops by way of implicit cues as well as by means of explicit statement and argumentation.

Phase three is the final stage of negotiation, climaxed by an announcement of formal agreement. The problem for each side in this phase is to determine the "irreducible last offer" of its opponent. Each

side will have already said "No" to a number of the opposition's proposals. It is now necessary to distinguish the point beyond which the
opponent refuses to modify his position. When both sides are satisfied
that a continuation of bargaining would not be productive, the negotiations are brought to an end.[26]

We have outlined in the preceding pages a five-stage "natural
history" model of conflict. We make no claim that this model is *the*
model that best describes the course of social conflict. Though the
illustrations are meant to lend plausibility, they do not supply proof of
the model. Instead, the discussion is meant to suggest the kind of theory
to which a systems approach would lead us. Such a theory would be
applicable to all levels of analysis (from persons to countries) and would
help us organize the myriad events that occur in the endless variety of
specific cases of conflict.

Once social scientists develop reasonable natural histories of conflict, more questions will arise. Even if most conflicts do follow such a
general course of events, there will inevitably be variations within the
pattern: Some conflicts never reach a crisis, some are resolved with or
without violence, some lead to revolution rather than resolution, some
extend for long periods of time, etc. We shall then wish to know under
what conditions does the conflict proceed in these different ways. We
might find that the course of conflict will vary by the system level, by
the number of parties involved, or by some other dimension of the
system within which it occurs. (Of course, if there are more variations
to the pattern than there is pattern, we may have to abandon our notion
of conflict as a general process.)

There are already a number of suggestions along this line that are
worthy of research. For example, it has been hypothesized that "the
more integrated into society are parties to conflict, the less likely that
conflict will be violent."[27] (We might translate this into our terms as,
the more numerous and stronger the relationships tying elements in
conflict to other elements in the system, the less likely the conflict will
be violent.) Another hypothesis is that conflict becomes greater the more
equal the parties are in strength.[28] A third, a particularly intriguing one,
is "the larger the number of conflicts in any particular context, the less
likely that any one will become all-inclusive. . . ."[29] This suggests that
the greater the number of conflicts (and/or competitions) which exist in
a system at a time, the less likely it is that any one of them will escalate
and polarize the system—and the less likely it is that there will be
violence.

Let us stop a moment and consider this third hypothesis. At first glance, it seems to contradict common sense for it implies that the more competition and conflict in a system, the more stable it is (the less likely is a breakdown). But the idea begins to look reasonable when we consider the following point: If the elements in a system are involved in many conflicts with other elements, it becomes harder to polarize into blocs of elements. Any two parties that might conceivably unite on one issue will be likely to be in conflict over another issue. Therefore, development of two opposed blocs is unlikely.

We can take as an illustration one frequently recurring dispute in the United States: the issue of trade tariffs. If we make a list of who is involved in the question, it might look something like this:

For Tariffs and Trade Barriers (1)	*Against* (2)	*Essentially Uninvolved* (3)
1. Domestic industries (esp. textiles, shoes, electronics, automobiles) 2. Labor unions 3. Conservatives	1. Import/export industries 2. Consumer groups 3. Foreign policy liberals 4. State Department	1. Civil rights groups 2. National media 3. Church groups 4. Military, etc.

Today tariffs are rarely an issue that tears apart the nation, and one reason for this is that there are other issues in the nation. Among the protariff people, group 1 is often in conflict with group 2, and group 2 is often in conflict with group 3. In the antitariff block, there are divisions between 1 and 2 and between 3 and 4, among others. Thus, the degree of unity is limited on both sides. Similarly, groups now unaligned would be torn if forced to join the battle. For example, civil rights groups are often allied in other conflicts with labor unions and other times with consumer groups. Thus, the intensity of this conflict is minimized by the existence of other conflicts in the system. As one classical sociologist put it, "society is sewn together by conflict."[30]

We have been considering here the conditions that modify the course conflicts take. A critically important condition is *institutionalization*. A conflict is institutionalized if it occurs within a set of rules specifying how, where, and when it will take place. In a sense, the system is protected by sanctions which prevent the conflict from escalating to a point that threatens its existence.[31] For example, the battle over power in the United States is "institutionalized" in the form of a democratic political system. At specified times, people may vie for power, using only acceptable techniques, and, at a specified time, the populace votes to decide the winner and resolve the conflict. Under the institutionalization of labor-management disputes, strikes, picketing, and public appeals are allowed; violence is not. In certain cases, the government may intervene if the conflict threatens the public good by shutting off vital supplies. A third example is a financial dispute over contracts. In such cases there are strictly defined ways of proceeding which are detailed in our law books.

Institutionalization arises because it insures that in most cases (certainly not all) the conflict will follow a specified course and not be destructive to the rest of the system. This has been demonstrated in laboratory studies. Subjects engaged in bargaining will try to adopt rules that will regulate their behavior to minimize the potential damage which they can do to each other.[32]

In which types of conflicts are we likely to find institutionalization? Institutionalization is likely to develop after a kind of conflict has repeatedly erupted and proved destructive. Take, as an example, the area of race relations. The 1960s saw violent clashes in many cities between blacks and police. What emerged as a response in a number of places were procedures for dealing with the outbreaks as they arose, before they escalated to violence. One such mechanism is the "community relations" committee set up to receive immediate notice of problems and to work with all parties for an acceptable solution before rocks start flying.

The history of the labor movement is a classic instance of institutionalization. In England, at the beginning of the Industrial Revolution, there were frequent outbreaks of labor violence. For example, "Luddism" was a movement in which workers destroyed machines that threatened to take their jobs. Through the nineteenth century, workers organized, struck, and agitated for government reform. The disputes were often violent and brutally suppressed by the government.

However, over the course of the nineteenth century, labor unions won grudged legitimacy from government. At the same time, they also moderated their tactics. Gradually, rules developed for handling labor-management disputes through collective bargaining. And workers even came to have their own political party. Employer-employee disputes are now usually handled in routine, nonviolent, legal ways.[33]

The discussion of institutionalization brings us to the consideration of other ways by which resolutions may vary. There is, of course, more than one way to resolve conflict (to slide down the far slope of Figure 8-2). Plaintiff and defendant can settle in or out of court; two children squabbling over a toy can share it or one child can take it from the other; a nation can fight a war to the bitter end or capitulate early in the struggle. One of the tasks for social scientists is to discover when and why one form of resolution occurs rather than another.

For instance, we might suggest the following sort of classification: resolutions vary by (1) whether there is any intervention by other parts of the system, and by (2) how evenly split the resolution is—whether there is a compromise or a clear winner. Intervention of a superordinate element probably depends on the degree of danger the conflict poses to the system as a whole. If the danger is high—say, in the case of serious labor stoppages—institutionalized intervention may arise in the form of arbitration.

The degree of asymmetry that results is probably a function of, among other things, the balance of power between the two parties and the divisibility of the object under dispute. (E.g., money can be split; a person whose affections are being contested cannot.)

An important result of which mode of resolution prevails is that it may determine the likelihood of future conflicts. For example, an institutionalized intervention system might forestall a future conflict by making clear how any such dispute would be resolved. Also, the mode of resolution can affect the viability of the system. If the resolution destroys one party, that element will no longer be able to contribute to the system.

In summary, our argument is that a systems approach interprets conflict as a normal, natural process in human relations. It leads to our searching for a "natural history" of conflict or a model that represents the normal course of conflict in systems of all sorts. We proposed an example of such a model. Once we have a natural history, we are led to ask how and why there are variations in that history. There are a number of hypotheses that can be presented, some of which turn out to be nonintuitive deductions from our systems approach. For example, there is the proposition that a system may be more stable the more conflicts it has. Finally, we pointed to a critical factor in determining the course of conflict—whether it is institutionalized. In the case of institutionalization, we examined the ways in which variations in the nature of a system can shape the history of conflict. We can easily look at the converse—the role of conflict in the history of a system.

THE FUNCTIONS OF CONFLICT

The system perspective suggests that conflict is a natural process in the same sense that a body's reaction to disease is a natural process and that fuel-flow regulation is a natural process in a car. If we pursue the analogy, we can point out that each of these other processes serves a purpose in their respective systems; they serve a *function;* they help keep the system in equilibrium. Does social conflict do the same thing? Indeed, there is good reason to believe that social conflict does serve a function in social systems.

Before going further, two points should be stressed: (1) To say that conflict is functional does not deny that it can at times be *dys*functional

—destructive to the social system. In fact, that may be the case most often. We shall explore a particular case of such dysfunctionality when we treat revolution. (2) By referring to something as *functional,* we do *not* mean *good.* Nor do we mean *bad* when we say *dys*functional. Something that is functional serves to maintain system equilibrium; something that is dysfunctional operates against its viability. Whether they are "good" or "bad" depends on a different set of considerations: one's moral opinions about the system in question. For example, the training of Hitler Youth in Nazi Germany was functional for that system. Nevertheless, most people would agree that it was a morally reprehensible institution, as was the whole system. Civil rights protests in the South were dysfunctional for the social systems of many small southern towns. Yet we would argue that they were morally justified. For this analysis, we shall simply discuss functions in a technical sense—Does it maintain the system?—not in a moral sense.

The argument that conflict can serve a positive function in a system was proposed by the German sociologist Georg Simmel[34] (whom we encountered in the previous chapter). His analysis was expanded upon by the American sociologist, Lewis Coser, in his book, *The Functions of Social Conflict.*[35] We can abstract (with slight modifications) five propositions from Coser's discussion that describe positive functions of conflict.

(1) *Conflict structures a system.* It does so by the polarization of elements into blocs that can persist and operate beyond the conflict. For example, European political parties, though essentially created for conflict, also publish newspapers and provide recreation and social activities for their members. One aspect of this process is that power differentials among these subunits are also established—determining who gets how much of what, and thus saving the system the strain of constant readjustment. The example is the barnyard pecking-order: The initial jousting between a new member and other chickens establishes who is the "pecker" and who is the "peckee." Thereafter, the distribution of food is a settled matter and neither time nor energy need be spent "renegotiating" the matter.

(2) *Many small conflicts make a large destructive conflict less likely.* We discussed part of this argument earlier when we pointed out how having a number of cross-cutting conflicts might prevent one major split from destroying the system.

(3) *Conflicts reinforce the nature of the system.* An obvious case of this is institutionalized conflict. Almost every conflict that proceeds along the institutionalized pattern strengthens that pattern. For example, court cases that are fought by the rules reinforce the legal system. Each labor-management dispute satisfactorily concluded as per National Labor Relations Board rules reinforces the Board. In two other not so obvious ways as well, most conflicts reinforce the system:

Figure 8-6 Battles between neighboring villages in New Guinea help to maintain the structure of the tribal society. The whole culture seems to center around the role of warrior. Despite the fierce appearance of the warriors, the battles usually continue until one or two people are wounded. Consequently, deaths rarely result from such battles. Contemporary Films/McGraw-Hill.

(a) Any conflict over the output of a subsystem strengthens that part of the system. For example, one result of a fierce (but honest) political campaign is to reinforce the power of the voters for whose allegiance the parties are fighting. A labor-management dispute over pay rates strengthens the economic system that produces the profits and pay. (Of course, repeated conflict may end up being destructive.)

(b) Each conflict, especially a regular, institutionalized one, that occurs over routine internal goods is one more conflict that did not occur over the basic structure of the system. When dissidents work "within the system" for votes in political campaigns they forego a struggle over what the political structure of the nation should be. Each time labor fights for bread-and-butter issues, it foregoes a battle over the nature of capitalism itself.

In these ways, many conflicts reinforce the system within which they occur. This is not to say, however, that there are not cases when internal conflict is fought over the character of the system itself or even destroys it.

(4) *Conflicts between systems increase the cohesion of each system.* In the sense that the elements of a system are bound together in co-operative relationship to fight a common foe, the system is stronger. We

are all familiar with the phenomenon of a nation in major war submerging its differences to fight the enemy (the London blitz; Israel in 1967). The new, necessary cooperation overrides the old competitions and conflicts. Science-fiction writers have been fascinated with this phenomenon and have often imagined that if only some extraterrestrial threat to earth could appear (perhaps in the form of a grand deception perpetrated by a band of noble scientists), then the nations of the earth would come together in peace.

(5) *Conflicts help the system adapt to its environment.* During and after the resolution of conflicts, there often arise better arrangements for the system. This is not a very novel notion: The touted advantage of free enterprise is that the process of business competition produces better and cheaper products. Democracy's blessing is thought to be conflict between ideas and political philosophies, wherein the best ideas are supposed to win. Conflict can help rearrange out-of-kilter setups so that they are maximally efficient.[37] Presumably, the battles that are bringing blacks, chicanos, and women into the mainstream of American life will enrich America with a new flow of talent.[38]

FOCUS
Martin Luther King on Constructive Confrontation

During the Spring of 1963, the Rev. Martin Luther King, Jr., led a series of demonstrations in Birmingham, Alabama, as part of the fight against legal discrimination in the South. During that dramatic period—which eventually led to the Civil Rights Act of 1964—the Rev. King was imprisoned. A group of southern clergy published a message criticizing his activities for creating conflict and divisiveness in the South. Dr. King's response, a "Letter from the Birmingham Jail," included the following passage on the role of confrontation in bringing social change. (Note the use of "tension" where we use "conflict.")

> You may well ask: "Why direct action? Why sit-ins, marches and so forth? Isn't negotiation a better path?" You are quite right in calling for negotiation. Indeed, this is the very purpose of direct acton. Nonviolent direct action seeks to create such a crisis and foster such a tension that a community which has constantly refused to negotiate is forced to confront the issue. It seeks so to dramatize the issue that it can no longer be ignored. My citing the creaton of tension as part of the work of the nonviolent-resister may sound rather shocking. But I must confess that I am not afraid of the word "tension." I have earnestly opposed violent tension, but there is a type of constructive, nonviolent tension which is necessary for growth. Just as Socrates felt that it was necessary to create a tension in the mind so that individuals could rise from the bondage of

Figure 8-7   Dr. Martin Luther King, *center,* led about 10,000 civil rights marchers on the last day of their Selma-to-Montgomery march. United Press International photo.

myths and half-truths to the unfettered realm of creative analysis and objective appraisal, so we must see the need for nonviolent gadflies to create the kind of tension in society that will help men rise from the dark depths of prejudice and racism to the majestic heights of understanding and brotherhood.

The purpose of our direct-action program is to create a situation so crisis-packed that it will inevitably open the door to negotiation. I, therefore, concur with you in your call for negotiation. Too long has our beloved Southland been bogged down in a tragic effort to live in monologue rather than dialogue.[39]

To review: The conflict process can serve positive functions in a social system in at least five ways: Conflict can define the internal structure of a system; many small conflicts can forestall one larger destructive one; conflicts can strengthen the structure and processes of the system; intersystem conflict can increase the cohesion of each system; and conflict can generate new solutions for the problem of adaptation.[40]

Violent conflict can also have the side consequence of maintaining the system:

FOCUS
Some Functions of Violence

Writing during a period of great civil disorder in the United States, the sociologist Lewis Coser suggested three positive functions of violence:[41]

1. Violence may serve as a means of achievement for people who can achieve in no other way. If directed against others around them—as is the case of great amounts of interpersonal violence between black males—it may satisfy this need and protect society by directing attention away from the social structure.

2. Violence can signal a danger to the social system; it can reveal severe problems and needs. (This was the case for Hobsbawm's mobs. Also, it is consistent with the fact that black residents in ghettos interpreted the riots of the 1960s as attempts to attract attention to their situation.)

3. Violence can be a catalyst. It can unite people (as did the violence of southern police during civil rights demonstrations); it can bring issues to a climax.

We hope that there may be other ways to achieve these functions of violence. But in modern American society, at least, violence sometimes serves a purpose.

Considerations of the functions of conflict and violence have extended even to war. The anthropologist Andrew Vadya has suggested five functions that war sometimes serves in primitive parts of the world: (1) to reduce inequality between groups (the have-nots take from the haves); (2) to redistribute demographic variables, specifically women (again, the have-nots take from the haves); (3) to reduce population pressure, either by taking new land or losing people; (4) to deter misdeeds—wars can erupt over criminal attacks; (5) to release psychological tension.[42]

As abstract as these hypotheses often are, descriptions by anthropologists in the field support many of them through concrete cases. The distribution of land for Maoris in New Zealand was largely regulated by warfare. When a group had used up its land, it would take land from its neighbor, pushing that group to do the same, until some lineage would get pushed into beginning cultivation of virgin territory.[43] An ethnographer of Morrocan tribes has described how violent blood feuds between these clans sharply defined the units of that society so that they formed very cohesive, organized, and efficient economic and political groups.[44] Among many African tribes, ritualized conflicts help preserve stability by releasing tension and reasserting the basic rules of the societies. For example, ceremonial occasions in which the chief was verbally attacked for not doing his job well worked to reaffirm the basic system—that is, the political arrangements of a chiefdom.[45]

We restate the argument of this section: A systems approach that presents conflict as a normal process will sensitize us to the functions that that process serves in the social system. If the battle of males for a female animal strengthens a species, and if the body produces hormones and enzymes that counteract each other and thereby maintain body functions in balance, then we might also expect the conflict process to contribute positively in human systems.

One of the conclusions of this perspective that conflict is a normal process, following a predictable course, and serving some function, is that we should not expect to easily eliminate conflict from social life. The most that might be done, instead, is to see that the conflict that does occur is resolved without violence and is resolved as quickly and as optimally to all parties as possible. Occasionally, however, peaceful modes of resolution are not achieved. Instead there occurs . . .

REVOLUTION

Of all the instances of violent conflict, few can match the drama and bloodshed of revolution. Fewer still have impacts on the course of history like the "great revolutions"—The American, French, Russian, and Chinese, for examples—have had. Social systems have been turned over—as the word, "revolution," implies—with effects lasting for centuries.

Social scientists have been fascinated by this phenomenon because it is so much the antithesis of social order and cohesion. Numerous theories have been proposed to explain why revolutions occur.[46] Most hypotheses involve theories about individual psychological states—relative deprivation, alienation, loss of trust, and so on. These individual-level phenomena are thought to aggregate and, together with certain social conditions, lead to revolution. We have discussed these sorts of theories earlier, in Chapter 6.

What this section will deal with, albeit briefly, is how the systems approach we have outlined might help our understanding of revolution.[47] The help it might provide is in resolving several difficulties that exist in prevalent theories of revolution: (1) These theories are of revolutions defined after the fact, that is, of successful revolutions. Rarely do they consider failures—situations that had all the preconditions but did not result in a turnover of government.

(2) Social psychological theories of revolution are embarrassed by the fact that relatively few people participate in revolution. If the pre-conditions are society-wide, how can that be the case? Also, how could one predict *who* will participate?

(3) Theories of revolution have been bothered by definitional prob-lems. Are palace coups to be considered revolutions in the same sense that "mass" revolutions are? If so, how can you explain both with the same theory? If not, what are the criteria that distinguish the two cases?

(4) Theories of revolution also are questionable because they are essentially unique theories—models of one specific sort of phenomenon, the great revolt. There is no reason to believe that revolutions, simply be-cause they are important and dramatic, are not in a general class of social conflicts.

(5) Another question arises: Is there such a thing as a nonviolent revolution?

Here is what a systems approach might contribute. First, our defini-tions: "Revolution" refers to the radical altering of a system (as when, for example, a family breadwinner dies). "Political revolution," which is the topic of this section, refers to a major alteration of the system such that different elements in the system come to hold central and dominant power (that is, to allocate inputs). For example, the battle over "taxation without representation" was not resolved within the then existing system. It led to a shift of power from English to Colonial groups in the Ameri-can Revolution.

The key to this systems approach is that political revolution is not a unique phenomenon: Rather, it is a conflict like all other conflicts, dis-tinguished only by the fact that (1) it is not resolved under the current system and (2) the revolution is a political one—control is shifted to other elements within the system.

A description of how a revolution occurs which is consistent with the systems approach of this chapter follows:

First, there exists competition and conflict among social groups within a society. This requires no special explanation; it is a normal process, emerging and resolving under the existing system.

Second, escalation and polarization occur on a large-scale, generally society-wide, level. Earlier, we mentioned how cross-cutting cleavages might suppress conflict. Here, the reverse occurs: A single conflict ex-pands or a number of conflicts merge in such a way that groups with positive internal relationships tend to each be opposed to other such groups. Groups that were tied to both sides are polarized one way or the other. Conflict coalitions are formed.

This division is more likely to occur in a "segmental" society—one in which parts of the nation are separately organized with little inter-connection (as was the case with colonialists and native peoples in Africa). It will also be rapid in these cases because each coalition is al-ready internally organized with common values and authority.[48]

The polarization explains who gets involved. Research indicates that it is neither "the rabble" nor is it the great mass who engage in col-lective violence, but, rather, it is small numbers of members of inte-grated, involved, and "respectable" groups.[49] This follows from our explanation, since it is connected people or groups who are the most likely to get polarized.

Third, the feature critical to political revolution must be present: The government must be involved as a member of one of the conflicting coalitions. Often, the involvement occurs early because the government is central to the conflict (e.g., peasant revolts against higher taxes or con-scription; situations in which the government is economically bound to one conflict group, as in landowner oligarchies). In other cases, govern-ment involvement follows later. It frequently occurs when one party vio-lates institutionalized mechanisms for conflict resolution, compelling intervention against it (e.g., the federal government sent troops to en-force desegregation rulings in the South and to suppress ghetto uprisings in the North).

Fourth, and most important, whether a revolution occurs depends on whether the government wins or loses. In the greatest number of such conflicts—most of which are nonviolent—the government wins. After all, having power is the essence of government.

The notable cases are those in which the government loses and, thereby, power shifts hands. These are revolutions. Whether the govern-ment wins or loses depends largely on strategic factors: firepower, public support, economic strength, foreign allies, etc. Sometimes the "crisis" battle does not last very long because the government was weak ("rotten from within") to begin with—as in the Batista government's fall to Castro, and the fall of the Bourbon king in Paris in 1830. Also, there are occa-sionally nonviolent capitulations.

The major determinant of the government's power is the role of the military (a subelement in the government). Whether the military defects to the other side is probably the key to a revolution's success. Defeating a government's army may be a classic revolution, but it is a rare one.

We should also note the conflict that occurs after the revolution. Often, the change of regime is followed by a "reign of terror." The as-

Figure 8-8 The defection of the military to the side of the rebels is often the crucial turning point in a revolution. Here a column of soldiers demonstrates along Nikolsky Street in Moscow during the October 1917 Socialist Revolution. Novosti from Sovfoto.

sumption of central control by the revolutionary coalition does not mean that the ex-government coalition is vanquished. The battle can continue. Also, when the conflict that united the revolutionary coalition has dissipated, internal schisms may emerge, leading to violent confrontations among the victors.[50]

This systems approach to revolution has been necessarily sketchy, because space does not permit an elaboration. But the discussion may indicate possible solutions to the problems discussed earlier:

(1) A unique theory of revolution is not required—it is simply a part of a general theory of conflict.

(2) Because it does not assume society-wide social psychological states, a systems model can accommodate low levels of participation— and account for who participates.

(3) The coup d'état–general revolution issue is handled this way: If one wishes to examine a situation in fine detail, focusing on the government subsystem, for example, then the shift in power from Generalissimo Numerouno to Generalissimo Numeroduo is in that context a revolution. A broader scope of interest, at the national level, for example, would lead to an interpretation of a coup d'état as simply meaning that power will remain within the military institution of the society. There-

fore, it is not defined as a revolution. It all depends on the investigator's degree of focus.

(4) This sort of theory is not restricted to the societal level. Revolutions as we have described them here can occur within any system level—not only the nation. The processes that lead serfs to overthrow their feudal lord, naval units to mutiny, or countries to revolt are parallel. Understanding each should help understand the other.

(5) Finally, the actual occurrence of violence, though probable if overturn actually occurs, is not necessary to an understanding of revolution.

The topic of revolution is immense. This short section is meant only to illustrate, again, how a systems approach may yield different insights about violent events. In this case, we argue, revolution might best be seen as unresolved conflict that escalates to the point of system destruction and reconstruction (as in Figure 8-2).

CONCLUSIONS

What have we learned? Fundamentally, we have not learned facts so much as a mode of analysis or a perspective. Appreciating different perspectives, different roads to the understanding of conflict and violence, is what this book was about. The understanding of the present chapter was founded on employing a wholistic (and admittedly abstract) model of what society is. It is, metaphorically, an organism with an independent reality and dynamics of its own.

Discussions in the previous chapters oriented us largely toward examining either the internal states (physiology, perceptions, motivations) of actors in conflict or how the environment (other people, society, ecology) affects those internal states. The present perspective directs us away from the actors themselves (be they people, groups, or nations) to examine the nature of their interrelationships. The organization of the system within which the actors operate may be the major determinant of conflict and violence. We have argued that such confrontations have less to do with the desires of people than with the resources available in the environment, the types of interdependencies that exist among the people, or the dynamics of the society in which they live.

Among the points highlighted by the systems perspective are: the importance of interdependence and the nature of that interdependence for conflict; that conflict may follow the same "natural history" and obey the same principles whether it be among individuals or among nations; that social systems may generate conflict out of their own historical dynamics; that cross-cutting conflicts (as well as ties) may inhibit or influence conflict; that conflict arises out of complex settings (i.e., systemic conditions that may determine the occurrence, the escalation, and the resolution of conflict); that an important variation in the conflict process depends on the degree of intervention (institutionalization) imposed by the surrounding system; that conflict is not always pathological, but, rather, a normal and sometimes useful process.

Although all these propositions still require empirical testing, the mode of thinking that they represent should be useful per se. If, upon observing conflict, we are led to ask not only questions about the conditions, feelings, and social traits of the parties, but also questions about the structure within which the parties exist and the processes which they undergo, then the systems analysis has served its purpose.

In this chapter, we stressed the differences between the systems approach and other approaches. This has been emphasized in order to clearly demarcate what is unique about the former. However, this perspective does not really contradict the earlier ones. Actually, they can complement each other.

Take the case of a national, "mass" revolution. When tracing the emergence of competition between groups, we would wish to consider the system changes which led to it and how the existing distribution of values arose. But, also, we would analyze the positions of various groups and individuals within the social structure and their goals and opportunities. It would be important to examine the rise of relative deprivation among the disadvantaged.

As competition shifted to conflict, we could incorporate the psychological concomitants and contributors to the negative exchange—frustration, anger, and scapegoating. The specific way a system polarizes could be explained by the degree of conformity within certain groups, by the alienation of many individuals from social units, and by the effects of ecology on communication among groups, as well as by ties of interdependency.

The battle between the government coalition and its foes will be resolved partly by the weight of public support (determined to some degree by the balance between feelings of legitimacy and those of alienation), the motivations each side can instill in their supporters, and the ecological constraints to both military forces.

The viability of the revolution will be subject partly to how well the victorious coalition can restore and improve the distribution of rewards in the society, the allegiances and conformity it can command, and the extent to which it can forestall or deflect frustrations.

All these forces shape revolutionary conflict and, indeed, all conflict. The relative weights to assign each factor in the dynamics of the entire process are partly known to social science and partly must await the investigations of future social scientists. But taking into account all the variables discussed can only increase our comprehension.

SUMMARY

Throughout the previous chapters we attempted to locate the causes of violence in particular characteristics of people and societies. In this chapter, we shift our perspective by asking *how* does violence occur in society as opposed to why does it occur. In contrast to previous chapters, this final chapter is mainly a theoretical discussion of a particular perspective: *systems analysis*. Violence is seen as a result of *social conflict*, which we defined as the exchange of negative outputs between elements in a competitive relationship. Our central argument is that conflict in social systems is regular and patterned.

Social conflict may be described by a five-stage *natural history*, which we argue is common to all social systems, large or small. Stage 1. *Precompetition:* The parties have a cooperative relationship or are relatively independent. Stage 2. *Competition:* The system changes so that the parties are in a competitive relationship. Stage 3. *Conflict:* The parties attack each other, and escalation and polarization occur. Stage 4. *"Crisis:"* An admittedly vague stage where the conflict emerges at a new, intense, and different level of interaction. It is the time when violence is most likely to occur. Stage 5. *Resolution—or Revolution:* Solutions are found or the system is radically restructured.

A systems analysis perspective suggests that conflict is a natural process and that it serves positive, system-maintaining *functions*. For example, conflicts (1) structure a system, (2) reinforce the nature of the system, and (3) help the system adapt to its environment. Other positive functions are: (4) Many small conflicts make a large destructive conflict less likely, and (5) any conflict over the output of a subsystem strengthens that part of the system. Even violent conflict may have positive functions: Violence (1) may serve as a means of achievement for people who can achieve in no other way, (2) can signal a danger to the social system, and (3) can be a catalyst.

We ended our discussion of social conflict by showing how systems analysis may be used to understand *revolution* and how it may be helpful in summarizing the other causal perspectives discussed in earlier chapters. A major conclusion from the systems analysis approach is that conflict and violence are normal processes, following predictable courses, and serving some system functions. Consequently, we should not expect to be able to totally eliminate conflict and violence. Instead, the most that can be done is to see that the conflicts that occur are resolved without violence as quickly and as equitably as possible.

FOOTNOTES

[1] The distinction we are attempting to draw between causal and systemic explantations is similar to one which Stinchcombe (1968) makes between "demographic" and "functional" explanations.

[2] The conception of a system and of systems analysis as discussed here is indebted to the ideas of Walter Buckley, Kenneth Boulding, Karl Deutsch, David Easton, James Miller, Talcott Parsons, Anatol Rapoport, Herbert Simon, and Evon Vogt, among others. However, the description is ultimately our own, and the cited theorists should not be implicated.

[3] This is, of course, a skimpy introduction to a major topic. A reader new to social science would do well to consult an introductory textbook such as R. Brown (1965) or Broom and Selznik (1963).

[4] Miller (1965).

[5] This definition is not totally satisfying, but no definition seems to be. One author even foregoes a formal definition in favor of using examples. Another states "a whole which functions as a whole by virtue of the interdependence of its parts is called a system" (A. Rapoport, Foreword to Buckley [1969], p. xvii). Others say that "a system is a set of objects together with relationships between the objects and between their attributes" (Hall and Fagen [1969], p. 81). Systems seem to be things people know when they see them, but cannot quite define!

[6] For a discussion of different conceptions of conflict, see Fink (1968).

[7] See Fink (1968) for a list of different distinctions between competition and conflict.

[8] Nieburg (1969), pp. 25–26.

[9] Sherif (1956), pp. 1–6. See discussion in Chapter 5, pp. 157–60.

[10] Mack and Snyder (1957); Fink (1968).

[11] Coser (1956).

[12] Marx and Engels (1970).

[13] Mack and Snyder (1957), p. 231. For studies on coalition formation, see Gamson (1964).

[14] Hobsbawn (1959). See also Rude (1964).

[15] Most notable are Boulding (1962), Rapoport (1960), Dahrendorf (1959), Smelser (1962), and Oberschall (1973). However, none of these has developed testable general systems propositions about conflict. But, then, neither do we.

[16] This model is in many ways similar to one recently forwarded by Kriesberg (1973).

[17] Richardson (1960). See discussions in Boulding (1962) and Rapoport (1960).

[18] Kriesberg (1973), pp. 155–63.

[19] This analysis is similar to that of social psychological balance theory or network graph theory.

[20] Oberschall (1973), chap. 4.

[21] Adapted with permission of Macmillan Publishing Co., Inc. from *Community Conflict* by J. Coleman. Copyright 1957 by The Free Press, a Corporation.

[22] Kelley, Beckman, and Fischer (1967).

[23] Kelley (1966).

[24] Kelley, Beckman, and Fischer (1967).

[25] This report is based essentially on Rapoport and Chammah (1970), but many other studies exist. See also Pilisuk, Kiritz, and Clampitt (1971).

[26] Quotations and paraphrase from "The Peaceful Settlement of Industrial and Intergroup Disputes," by Ann Douglas, *Journal of Conflict Resolution,* vol. 1, no. 1 (March 1957), pp. 69–81, by permission of the publisher, Sage Publication, Inc.

[27] Mack and Snyder (1957), p. 227.

[28] Mack and Snyder (1957), p. 235.

[29] Mack and Snyder (1957), p. 237.

[30] Simmel (1951). Also see Kriesberg (1973), pp. 141–43.

[31] What institutionalization usually means in practice is that there is a third party that will become an ally of an injured party if its opponent violates a rule (e.g., the referee will disqualify a boxer who throws a low blow).

[32] Gruder (1970).

[33] Roberts (1969).

[34] Simmel (1951).

[35] Coser (1956).

[36] Kriesberg (1973), chap. 7.

[37] Nieburg (1969).

[38] Himes (1966).

[39] From pp. 81–82 (hardbound edition), "Letter from Birmingham Jail—April 16, 1963," in *Why We Can't Wait* by Martin Luther King, Jr. Copyright © 1963 by Martin Luther King, Jr. Reprinted by permission of Harper & Row, Publishers, Inc.

[40] Coser (1967).

[41] Coser (1967); cf. Nieburg (1969).

[42] Vadya (1961, 1967).

[43] Vadya (1961).

[44] W. H. Lewis (1961).

[45] Gluckman (1963).

[46] See, among other works, Gurr (1970).

[47] Willer and Zollschan (1965); Rule and Tilly (1972); C. Johnson (1966).

[48] Oberschall (1973), chap. 4.

[49] Oberschall (1973); Rule and Tilly (1972); Rude (1964); Tilly (1969).

[50] Rule and Tilly (1972).

BIBLIOGRAPHY

ABELES, R. P. 1972. Subjective deprivation and black militancy. Ph.D. dissertation, Harvard University.

——. In press. Relative deprivation, rising expectations, and black militancy. *Journal of Social Issues.*

ABERBACH, J. D. 1970. Alienation and political behavior. *American Political Science Review* 54:1199–1219.

ABRAHAMSEN, D. 1970. *Our violent society.* New York: Funk and Wagnalls.

ABU-LUGHOD, J. 1964. Urban-rural differences as a function of the demographic transition: Egyptian data and an analytic model. *American Journal of Sociology* 69:476–90.

ADORNO, T. W.; FRENKEL-BRUNSWICK, E.; LEVINSON, D. J.; and SANFORD, R. N. 1950. *The authoritarian personality.* New York: Harper & Row.

AJZEN, I., and FISHBEIN, M. 1973. Attitudinal and normative variables as predictors of specific behaviors. *Journal of Personality and Social Psychology* 27:41–58.

ALDERMAN, F.; BREHM, S. S.; and KATZ, L. B. 1974. Empathic observation of an innocent victim: The Just World revisited. *Journal of Personality and Social Psychology* 29:342–47.

ALLPORT, G. 1958. *The nature of prejudice.* Garden City, N.Y.: Anchor Books.

ALMOND, G. A., and VERBA, S. 1963. *The civic culture.* Princeton, N.J.: Princeton Univ. Press.

ANDERSON, E. N., JR. 1972. Some Chinese methods of dealing with crowding. *Urban Anthropology* 1:141–50.

ANGEL, S. 1968. *Discouraging crime through city planning.* Working Paper No. 75. Berkeley, California: Institute of Urban and Regional Development, University of California.

ARDREY, R. 1966. *The territorial imperative.* New York: Atheneum.

ARISTOTLE. 1932. *The rhetoric.* New York: Appleton-Century.

ARNOLD, M. 1970. Feelings and emotions. In *The Loyola Symposium.* New York: Academic Press.

ASCH, S. 1955. Opinions and social pressure. *Scientific American* 193(5): 31–35.

AZRIN, N. 1967. Pain and aggression. *Psychology Today* 1(1):27–33.

———; HUTCHINSON, R. R.; and HAKE, D. F. 1966. Extinction induced aggression. *Journal of the Experimental Analysis of Behavior* 9:191–204.

———. 1967. Attack, avoidance and escape reactions to aversive shock. *Journal of the Experimental Analysis of Behavior* 10:131–48.

BAGBY, J. W. 1957. A cross-cultural study of perceptual predominance in binocular rivalry. *Journal of Abnormal and Social Psychology* 54: 331–44.

BAKER, J. W., and SCHAIE, K. W. 1969. Effects of aggressing "alone" or "with another" on physiological and psychological arousal. *Journal of Personality and Social Psychology* 12:80–86.

BAKER, R. K., and BALL, S. J. 1969. *Mass media and violence.* Washington, D.C.: U.S. Government Printing Office.

BALL-ROKEACH, S. J. 1973. Values and violence: A test of the subculture of violence thesis. *American Sociological Review* 38:736–49.

BANDURA, A. 1965. Influence of models' reinforcement contingencies on the acquisition of imitative responses. *Journal of Personality and Social Psychology* 1:589–95.

———. 1973. *Aggression: A social learning analysis.* Englewood Cliffs, N.J.: Prentice-Hall.

———; Ross, D.; and Ross, S. 1963a. Imitation of film-mediated aggressive models. *Journal of Abnormal and Social Psychology* 66:3–11.

———. 1963b. Vicarious reinforcement and imitative learning. *Journal of Abnormal and Social Psychology* 67:601–7.

BANDURA, A., and WALTERS, R. 1964. *Social learning and personality development.* New York: Holt, Rinehart & Winston.

BANFIELD, E. 1958. *The moral basis of a backward society.* New York: Free Press.

BARON, R. A. 1971*a*. Magnitude of victim's pain cues and level of prior anger arousal as determinants of adult aggressive behavior. *Journal of Personality and Social Psychology* 17:236–43.

———. 1971*b*. Aggression as a function of magnitude of victim's pain cues, levels of prior anger arousal, and aggressor-victim similarity. *Journal of Personality and Social Psychology* 18:48–54.

———. 1974. Aggression as a function of victim's pain cues, level of prior anger arousal, and exposure to an aggressive model. *Journal of Personality and Social Psychology* 29:117–24.

BATESON, G. 1941. The frustration-aggression hypothesis and culture. *Psychological Review* 48:350–58.

BECKER, H. S. 1963. *The outsiders.* New York: Free Press.

———, and HOROWITZ, I. L. 1970. The culture of civility. *Transaction* 7:12–20.

BELL, D. 1953. Crime as an American way of life. *The Antioch Review* (summer): 131–54.

BELLUSH, J., and HAUSKNECHT, M., eds. 1967. *Urban renewal: People, politics, and planning.* Garden City, N.Y.: Anchor.

BEM, D. 1972. Self-perception theory. In *Advances in experimental social psychology,* vol. 6, ed. L. Berkowitz, pp. 2–62. New York: Academic Press.

BENDIX, R., and LIPSET, S. M. 1953. *Class, status, and power.* New York: Free Press.

BERELSON, B., and STEINER, G. A. 1964. *Human behavior.* New York: Harcourt, Brace and World.

BERKOWITZ, L. 1962. *Aggression: A social psychological analysis.* New York: McGraw-Hill.

———. 1965. The concept of aggressive drive. In *Advances in experimental social psychology,* vol. 2, L. Berkowitz, ed. New York: Academic Press.

———, ed. 1969. *Roots of aggression.* New York: Atherton Press.

———. 1970. Aggressive humor as a stimulus to aggressive behavior. *Journal of Personality and Social Psychology* 16:710–17.

———. 1971. Experimental investigation of hostility catharsis. In *Dynamics of violence,* ed. J. Fawcett, pp. 139–44. Chicago: American Medical Association.

————. 1973. The case for bottling up rage. *Psychology Today* 7(2):24–31.

————. 1974. Some determinants of impulsive aggression: Role of mediated associations with reinforcement for aggression. *Psychological Review* 81:165–76.

————, and BUCK, R. W. 1967. Impulsive aggression: Reactivity to aggressiveness under emotional arousal. *Journal of Personality* 35:415–24.

BERKOWITZ, L., and HOLMES, D. S. 1960. A further investigation of hostility generalization to disliked objects. *Journal of Personality* 28:427–42.

BERKOWITZ, L., and LePAGE, N. A. 1967. Weapons as aggression-eliciting stimuli. *Journal of Personality and Social Psychology* 7:202–7.

BERKOWITZ, L., and MACAULAY, J. 1971. The contagion of criminal violence. *Sociometry* 34:238–60.

BERSCHEID, E., and WALSTER, E. 1969. *Interpersonal attraction.* Reading, Mass.: Addison-Wesley.

BETTELHEIM, B. 1966. Violence: A neglected mode of behavior. In *Patterns of violence; The Annals of the American Academy of Political and Social Science,* vol. 364, ed. M. E. Wolfgang, pp. 55–56.

BLACK, D. J., and REISS, A. J., JR. 1970. Police control of juveniles. *American Sociological Review* 35:63–77.

BLALOCK, H. M., JR. 1970. *Toward a theory of minority-group relations.* New York: Capricorn Books.

BLUMENTHAL, H.; KAHN, R.; ANDREWS, F.; and HEAD, K. 1972. *Justifying violence: Attitudes of American Men.* Ann Arbor, Mich.: Survey Research Center, Institute for Social Research, University of Michigan.

BOELKINS, R. C., and HEISER, J. F. 1970. Biological bases of aggression. In *Violence and the struggle for existence,* ed. D. N. Daniels, M. F. Gilula, and F. M. Ochberg, pp. 15–52. Boston: Little, Brown.

BOHANAN, P., ed. 1967. *Law and warfare: Studies in the anthropology of conflict.* Garden City, N.Y.: Natural History Press, 1967.

BONACICH, E. 1972. A theory of ethnic antagonism: The split labor market. *American Sociological Review* 37:547–59.

BORDON, J. R., and TAYLOR, S. P. 1974. The social instigation and control of physical aggression. *Journal of Applied Social Psychology* 3:354–61.

BOULDING, K. 1962. *Conflict and defense.* New York: Harper & Row.

BRAMEL, D.; TAUB, B.; and BLUM, B. 1968. An observer's reactions to the suffering of his enemy. *Journal of Personality and Social Psychology* 8:384–92.

BRAMSON, L., and GOETHALS, G. W., eds. 1968. *War*, rev. ed. New York: Basic Books.

BRINTON, C. 1965. *The anatomy of revolution*, rev. and exp. ed. New York: Vintage.

BROCK, T. C., and PALLACK, M. S. 1969. The consequences of choosing to be aggressive. In *The cognitive control of motivation*, ed. P. G. Zimbardo. Glenview, Ill.: Scott, Foresman.

BRONFENBRENNER, U. 1961. The mirror image in Soviet-American relations. *Journal of Social Issues* 17(3):45–56.

BROOM, L., and SELZNIK, P. 1963. *Sociology*. New York: Harper & Row.

BROWN, B. 1968. The effect of need to maintain face on interpersonal bargaining. *Journal of Experimental Social Psychology* 4:107–22.

BROWN, R. 1965. *Social psychology*. New York: Free Press.

BROWN, R. M. 1969. Historical patterns of violence in America. In *Violence in America*, ed. H. D. Graham and T. R. Gurr, pp. 45–83. New York: Bantam Books.

BRUNER, J. 1957. On perceptual readiness. *Psychological Review* 64:123–51.

————. 1958. Social psychology and perception. In *Readings in social psychology*, 3rd ed., ed. E. Macoby, T. M. Newcomb, and E. Hartley, 85–94. New York: Holt, Rinehart, & Winston.

BUCKLEY, W., ed., 1968. *Modern systems research for the behavioral scientist*. Chicago: Aldine.

BURSTEIN, P. 1972. Individual political participation in five nations. *American Journal of Sociology* 77:1087–1110.

BUSS, A. H. 1961. *The psychology of aggression*. New York: Wiley.

————. 1971. Aggression pays. In *The control of aggression and violence*, ed. J. L. Singer, pp. 7–18. New York: Academic Press.

BYRNE, D. 1964. Repression-sensitization as a dimension of personality. In *Progress in experimental personality research*, vol. 1, ed. B. A. Mahler, pp. 170–220. New York: Academic Press.

————. 1969. Attitudes and attraction. In *Advances in experimental social psychology*, vol. 4, ed. L. Berkowitz, pp. 36–90. New York: Academic Press.

————, and WONG, T. J. 1962. Racial prejudice, interpersonal attraction, and assumed dissimilarity of attitudes. *Journal of Abnormal and Social Psychology* 65:246–53.

CALHOUN, J. B. 1963. Population density and social pathology. In *The urban condition*, ed. L. J. Duhl, pp. 33–43. New York: Simon and Schuster.

CANNAVALE, F. J.; SCARR, H. A.; and PEPITONE, A. 1970. Deindividuation in the small group: Further evidence. *Journal of Personality and Social Psychology* 16:141–47.

CANTRIL, H. 1941. *The psychology of social movements.* New York: Wiley.

————. 1965. *The pattern of human concern.* New Brunswick, N.J.: Rutgers Univ. Press.

CAPLAN, N., and PAIGE, J. M. 1968. A study of ghetto rioters. *Scientific American* 219(2):15–21.

CARSTAIRS, G. 1969. Overcrowding and human aggression. In *Violence in America*, ed. H. D. Graham and T. R. Gurr, pp. 751–63.

CARTWRIGHT, D., and ZANDER, A. 1960. *Group dynamics*, 2nd ed. New York: Harper & Row.

CASSEL, J. 1972. Health consequences of population density and crowding. In *People and buildings*, ed. R. Gutman. New York: Basic Books.

CHOROVER, S. L. 1973. Big brother and psychotechnology. *Psychology Today* 7(5):43–54.

————. 1974. Big brother and psychotechnology II: The pacification of the brain. *Psychology Today* 7(12):59–69.

CHRISTIAN, J. J., and DAVIS, D. E. 1964. Endocrines, behavior, and population. *Science* 146:1550–60.

CLARK, K. B. 1971. The pathos of power: A psychological perspective. Paper presented at the American Psychological Association, Washington, D.C.

CLINARD, M. B. 1964. Deviant behavior: Urban-rural contrasts. In *Metropolis: Values in conflict*, ed. C. E. Elias, Jr., J. Gillies, and S. Reimer, pp. 237–44. Belmont, Calif.: Wadsworth.

CLOWARD, R. A. 1959. Illegitimate means, anomie, and deviant behavior. *American Sociological Review* 24:164–76.

————, and OHLIN, L. E. 1960. *Delinquency and opportunity.* New York: Free Press.

COELHO, G. V.; HAMBURG, D. A.; and ADAMS, J. E., eds. In press. *Coping and adaptation: Interdisciplinary perspectives.* New York: Basic Books.

COFER, C. F., and APPLEY, M. H. 1964. *Motivation: Theory and research.* New York: Wiley.

COHEN, A. K. 1955. *Delinquent boys.* New York: Free Press.

——, and SHORT, J. F., JR. 1958. Research in delinquent subcultures. *Journal of Social Issues* 14(3):20–37.

COLEMAN, J. S. 1956. Social cleavage and religious conflict. *Journal of Social Issues* 12(3):44–56.

——. 1957. *Community conflict.* New York: Free Press.

COSER, L. A. 1956. *The functions of social conflict.* New York: Free Press.

——. 1967. *Continuities in the study of social conflict.* New York: Free Press.

COWAN, P., and WALTERS, R. 1963. Studies of reinforcement of aggression: I. Effects of scheduling. *Child Development* 34:543–51.

COX, K. K. 1969. Changes in stereotyping of Negroes and whites in magazine advertisements. *Public Opinion Quarterly* 33:603–6.

CRESSEY, D. R. 1964. *Delinquency, crime and differential association.* The Hague: Martinus Nijhoff.

CURRIE, E., and SKOLNICK, J. H. 1970. A critical note on conceptions of collective behavior. *The Annals of the American Academy of Political and Social Sciences* 391:34–46.

DAHL, R. 1961. *Who governs?* New Haven, Conn.: Yale Univ. Press.

DAHRENDORF, R. 1958. Toward a theory of social conflict. *Journal of Conflict Resolution* 2:170–83.

——. 1959. *Class and class conflict in industrial society.* Stanford, Calif.: Stanford Univ. Press.

DALTON, K. 1961. Menstruation and crime. *British Medical Journal* 1752–53.

——. 1964. *The premenstrual syndrome.* Springfield, Ill.: Charles C. Thomas.

DANIELS, D. N., and GILULA, M. F. 1970. Violence and the struggle for existence. In *Violence and the struggle for existence,* ed. D. N. Daniels, M. F. Gilula, and F. M. Ochburg. Boston: Little, Brown.

——; and OCHBERG, F. M., eds. 1970. *Violence and the struggle for existence.* Boston: Little, Brown.

DARWIN, C. 1872. *Expression of the emotions in man and animals.* London: Murray. Reprinted 1965, Univ. of Chicago Press.

DAVIES, J. C. 1969. The J-curve of rising and declining satisfaction as a cause of some great revolutions and a contained rebellion. In *Violence in America,* ed. H. D. Graham and T. R. Gurr, pp. 690–730. New York: Bantam Books.

——, ed. 1971. *When men revolt and why.* New York: Free Press.

DAVIS, D. E. 1964. The physiological analysis of aggressive behavior. In *Social behavior and organization among vertebrates,* ed. W. Etkin. Chicago: Univ. of Chicago Press.

DAVIS, K. 1969. *World urbanization 1950–1970. Volume I: Basic data for cities, countries, and regions.* Berkeley: Institute of International Studies, University of California.

DAVITZ, J. R. 1969. *The language of emotion.* New York: Academic Press.

DeFLEUR, M. 1964. Occupational roles as portrayed on television. *Public Opinion Quarterly* 28:57–74.

———, and QUINNEY, R. 1966. A reformulation of Sutherland's differential association theory and a strategy for empirical verification. *Journal of Research in Crime and Delinquency* 3:1–22.

DELGADO, J. M. R. 1963. Cerebral heterostimulation in a monkey colony. *Science* 141:161–63.

———. 1966. Aggressive behavior evoked by radio stimulation in monkey colonies. *American Zoologist* 6:669–81.

———. 1967. Aggression and defense under cerebral radio control. In *Brain function,* vol. 5: *Aggression and defense,* ed. C. D. Clemente and D. B. Lindsley. Berkeley: Univ. of California Press.

———. 1969. Offensive-defensive behavior in free monkeys and chimpanzees induced by radio stimulation of the brain. In *Aggressive behavior,* ed. S. Garattini and E. B. Sigg, pp. 109–19. New York: Wiley.

DEMARIS, O. 1970. *America the violent.* Baltimore: Penguin Books.

DESOR, J. A. 1971. Toward a psychological theory of crowding. *Journal of Personality and Social Psychology* 33:444–56.

DEUTSCH, M. 1960. Trust, trustworthiness, and the F-scale. *Journal of Abnormal and Social Psychology* 61:138–40.

———. 1962. Cooperation and trust: Some theoretical notes. In *Nebraska symposium on motivation,* ed. M. R. Jones, pp. 275–319. Lincoln: Univ. of Nebraska Press.

———, and GERARD, H. B. 1955. A study of normative and informative social influence upon individual judgment. *Journal of Abnormal and Social Psychology* 51:629–36.

DEUTSCH, M., and KRAUSS, R. M. 1960. The effect of threat upon interpersonal bargaining. *Journal of Abnormal and Social Psychology* 61:168–75.

DeVORE, I., ed. 1965. *Primate behavior.* New York: Holt, Rinehart & Winston.

DOBZHANSKY, T. 1973. Differences are not deficits. *Psychology Today* 7(7):97–101.

DOHRENWEND, B. P., and DOHRENWEND, B. S. 1971. The prevalence of psychiatric disorders in urban versus rural settings. Paper presented at the Fifth World Congress of Psychiatry, Mexico City.

DOLLARD, J.; DOOB, L.; MILLER, N. E.; MOWRER, O. H.; and SEARS, R. R. 1939. *Frustration and aggression.* New Haven: Yale Univ. Press.

DONNERSTEIN, E., and DONNERSTEIN, M. 1973. Variables in interracial aggression: Potential ingroup censure. *Journal of Personality and Social Psychology* 27:143–50.

DOUGLAS, A. 1957. The peaceful settlement of industrial and intergroup disputes. *Journal of Conflict Resolution* 1:69–81.

DUBOS, R. 1970. The social environment. In *Environmental psychology,* ed. H. M. Proshansky, W. H. Ittelson and L. R. Rivlin, pp. 202–8. New York: Holt, Rinehart & Winton.

DUFFY, E. 1962. *Activation and behavior.* New York: Wiley.

DUNCAN, O. D., and SCHNORE, L. F. 1959. Cultural, behavioral and ecological perspectives in the study of social organization. *American Journal of Sociology* 65:132–46.

DURKHEIM, E. 1951. *Suicide.* New York: Free Press.

EIBL-EIBESFELD, I. 1970. *Ethology: The biology of behavior.* New York: Holt, Rinehart & Winston.

EISENHOWER, M. (Chairman). 1968. *Report of the national commission on the causes and prevention of violence.* Washington, D.C.: U.S. Government Printing Office.

EKMAN, P., and FRIESEN, W. V. 1969. Nonverbal leakage and clues to deception. *Psychiatry* 32:88–106.

———. 1974. Detecting deception from the body or face. *Journal of Personality and Social Psychology* 29:288–98.

———; and ELLSWORTH, P. C. 1972. *Emotion in the human face.* New York: Pergamon.

ELLINWOOD, E. H. 1971. Assault and homicide associated with amphetamine abuse. *American Journal of Psychiatry* 127:1170–75.

ELLSWORTH, P. C., and CARLSMITH, J. M. 1973. Eye contact and gaze aversion in an aggressive encounter. *Journal of Personality and Social Psychology* 28:280–92.

———; and HENSON, A. 1972. The stare as a stimulus to flight in human subjects: A series of field experiments. *Journal of Personality and Social Psychology* 21:302–11.

EPSTEIN, S., and TAYLOR, S. P. 1967. Instigation to aggression as a function of degree of defeat and perceived aggressive intent of the opponent. *Journal of Personality* 35:265–89.

ERLANGER, H. S. 1972. An empirical critique of theories of interpersonal violence. Paper presented at the 67th Annual Meeting of the American Sociological Association.

ERON, L. 1963. Relationship of TV viewing habits and aggressive behavior in children. *Journal of Abnormal and Social Psychology* 67: 193–96.

————; HUESMAN, L. R.; LEFKOWITZ, M. M.; and WALDER, L. O. 1972. Does television violence cause aggression? *American Psychologist* 27:253–63.

EXLINE, R. V., and YELLIN, A. M. 1969. Eye contact as a sign between man and monkey. Paper read at the XIV International Congress of Psychology, London.

FEAGIN, J. R. 1972. God helps those who help themselves. *Psychology Today* 6(6):101ff.

FEIERABEND, I. K.; FEIERABEND, R. L.; and GURR, T. R., eds. 1972. *Anger, violence, and politics.* Englewood Cliffs, N.J.: Prentice-Hall.

FESHBACH, S. 1970. Aggression. In *Carmichael's manual of child psychology,* 3rd ed., ed. P. H. Mussen. New York: Wiley.

————. 1971. Dynamics and mortality of violence and aggression: Some psychological considerations. *American Psychologist* 26:281–92.

————. 1973. Sex and aggression: Some theoretical issues and empirical research. Unpublished paper, University of California, Los Angeles.

————. n.d. The development and regulation of aggression: Some research gaps and a proposed cognitive approach. Unpublished paper, University of California, Los Angeles.

————, and Feshbach, N. 1963. Influence of the stimulus object upon complementary and supplementary projection of fear. *Journal of Abnormal and Social Psychology* 66:498–502.

FESHBACH, S., and SINGER, R. D. 1971. *Television and aggression.* San Francisco: Jossey-Bass.

FESTINGER, L. 1954. A theory of social comparison processes. *Human Relations* 7:117–40.

————; PEPITONE, A.; and NEWCOMB, T. 1952. Some consequences of deindividuation in a group. *Journal of Abnormal and Social Psychology* 47:382–89.

FINK, C. 1968. Some conceptual difficulties in the theory of social conflict. *Journal of Conflict Resolution* 12:412–50.

FISCHER, C. S. 1969. The effects of threat in an incomplete information game. *Sociometry* 32:301–14.

―――. 1971. A research note on urbanism and tolerance. *American Journal of Sociology* 76:847–56.

―――. 1972a. Studies on the social effects of urban life. Ph.D. dissertation, Harvard University.

――― 1972b. Urbanism as a way of life: A review and an agenda. *Sociological Methods and Research* 1(2):187–242.

―――. 1973a. On urban alienations and anomie: Powerlessness and social isolation. *American Sociological Review* 38:311–26.

―――. 1973b. Urban malaise. *Social Forces* 52:221–35.

―――. 1975a. The effect of urban life on traditional values. *Social Forces*.

―――. 1975b. Toward a subcultural theory of urbanism. *American Journal of Sociology*.

―――, BALDASSARE, M., and OFSHE, R. J. 1974. *Crowding studies and urban life: a critical review*. Working paper, Institute of Urban and Regional Development, University of California, Berkeley.

FOGELSON, R. M. 1971. *Violence as protest*. Garden City, N.Y.: Doubleday-Anchor.

FOSTER, G. M. 1967. *Tzintzuntzan: Mexican peasants in a changing world*. Boston: Little, Brown.

FREEDMAN, J. L., and DOOB, A. 1968. *Deviancy: The psychology of being different*. New York: Academic Press.

FREEDMAN, J. L.; KLEVANSKY, S.; and EHRLICH, P. R. 1971. The effect of crowding on human task performance. *Journal of Applied Social Psychology* 1:7–25.

FREEDMAN, J. L.; LEVY, A. S.; BUCHANAN, R. W.; and PRICE, J. 1972. Crowding and human aggressiveness. *Journal of Experimental Social Psychology* 8:528–48.

FREEDMAN, J. L., and SEARS, D. O. 1965. Selective exposure. In *Advances experimental social psychology*, vol. 2, ed. L. Berkowitz, pp. 52–98. New York: Academic Press.

FREEMAN, H. E., and GIOVANNONI, J. M. 1969. Social psychology of mental health. In *The handbook of social psychology*, vol. 5, ed. G. Lindzey and E. Aronson, pp. 660–719. Reading, Mass.: Addison-Wesley.

FREUD, S. 1959. Why war? In *The collected papers of Sigmund Freud*, vol. 5, ed. E. Jones. New York: Basic Books.

FRIED, M.; HARRIS, M.; and MURPHY, R., eds. 1967. *War: The anthropol-*

ogy of armed conflict and aggression. Garden City, N.Y.: Natural History Press.

GALLE, O. R.; GOVE, W. R.; and McPHERSON, J. M. 1971. Population density and pathology. Paper presented at the American Sociological Association, Denver.

GALLUP, G. 1973. *The Gallup opinion index,* Report No. 91, January, pp. 12–15.

GAMSON, W. A. 1964. Experimental studies of coalition formation. In *Advances in experimental social psychology,* vol. 1, ed. L. Berkowitz, pp. 81–110. New York: Academic Press.

———. 1968. *Power and discontent.* Homewood, Ill.: Dorsey.

GANS, H. J. 1962a. *The urban villagers.* New York: Free Press.

———, 1962b. Urbanism and suburbanism as ways of life: A reevaluation of definitions. In *Human behavior and social processes,* ed. A. M. Rose. Boston: Houghton-Mifflin.

GARFINKLE, H. 1967. *Studies in ethnomethodology.* Englewood Cliffs, N.J.: Prentice-Hall.

GASTIL, R. D. 1971. Homicide and a regional culture of violence. *American Sociological Review* 36:412–26.

GEEN, R. G., and O'NEAL, E. C. 1969. Activation of cue-elicited aggression by general arousal. *Journal of Personality and Social Psychology* 11:289–92.

GEEN, R. G., and PIGG, R. 1970. Acquisition of an aggressive response and its generalization to verbal behavior. *Journal of Personality and Social Psychology* 15:165–70.

GEEN, R. G., and STONNER, D. 1971. Effects of aggressiveness habit strength on behavior in the presence of aggression related stimuli. *Journal of Personality and Social Psychology* 17:149–53.

———; KELLEY, D. R. 1974. Aggression anxiety and cognitive appraisal of aggression-threat stimuli. *Journal of Personality and Social Psychology* 29:196–200.

GENTHNER, G. W., and TAYLOR, S. P. 1973. Physical aggression as a function of racial prejudice and the race of the target. *Journal of Personality and Social Psychology* 27:207–10.

GENTRY, W. D. 1970. Effects of frustration, attack, and prior aggressive training on overt aggression and vascular processes. *Journal of Personality and Social Psychology* 16:718–25.

GERBNER, G. 1972. Violence in television drama: Trends and symbolic functions. In *Television and behavior, vol. 1: Content and control,* ed. G. A. Comstock and E. A. Rubinstein, pp. 28–187. Washington, D.C.: U.S. Government Printing Office.

GERGEN, K. 1969. *The psychology of behavior exchange.* Reading, Mass.: Addison-Wesley.

————. 1971. *The concept of self.* New York: Holt, Rinehart & Winston.

GIBBONS, D. C. 1970. *Delinquent behavior.* Englewood Cliffs, N.J.: Prentice-Hall.

GIBBS, J. P., and MARTIN, W. T. 1962. Urbanization, technology, and the division of labor: International patterns. *American Sociological Review* 22:667–77.

GLASS, D. C., and WOOD, J. D. 1969. The control of aggression by self esteem and dissonance. In *The cognitive control of aggression*, ed. P. G. Zimbardo. Glenview, Ill.: Scott, Foresman.

GLAZER, N., and MOYNIHAN, D. P. 1970. *Beyond the melting pot*, rev. ed. Cambridge, Mass.: Massachusetts Institute of Technology Press.

GLUCKMAN, M. 1963. *Custom and conflict in Africa.* Oxford: Basil Blackwell.

GODDARD, G. V. 1964. Functions of the amygdala. *Psychological Bulletin* 62:89–109.

GOLDING, W. 1962. *Lord of the flies.* New York: Coward, McCann and Geoghegan.

GRAHAM, H. D., and GURR, T. R., eds. 1969. *Violence in America.* New York: Bantam Books.

GREEN, J. D.; CLEMENTE, C. D.; and DeGROOT, J. 1957. Rhinencephalic lesions and behavior in cats. *Journal of Comparative Neurology* 108:505–45.

GREENWELL, J., and DENGERINK, H. A. 1973. The role of perceived *vs.* actual attack in human physical aggression. *Journal of Personality and Social Psychology* 26:66–71.

GREER, S. 1962. *The emerging city.* New York: Free Press.

GRIFFITT, W., and VEITCH, R. 1971. Hot and crowded: Influences of population density and temperature on interpersonal affective behavior. *Journal of Personality and Social Psychology* 17:92–98.

GRIMSHAW, A. D., ed. 1969. *Racial violence in America.* Chicago: Aldine.

————. 1970. Interpreting collective violence: An argument for the importance of social structure. *The Annals of the American Academy of Political and Social Sciences* 391:9–20.

GRUDER, C. L. 1970. Social power in interpersonal negotiation. In *The structure of conflict*, ed. P. Swingle, pp. 111–54. New York: Academic Press.

GURR, T. R. 1969. A comparative study of civil strife. In *Violence in*

America, ed. H. D. Graham and T. R. Gurr, pp. 572–632. New York: Bantam Books.

———. 1970. *Why men rebel.* Princeton, N.J.: Princeton Univ. Press.

HACKNEY, S. 1969. Southern violence. In *Violence in America,* ed. H. D. Graham and T. R. Gurr, pp. 505–27. New York: Bantam Books.

HALL, A. D., and FAGEN, R. E. 1969. Definition of system. In *Modern systems research for the social scientist,* ed. W. Buckley, pp. 81–92. Chicago: Aldine.

HALL, E. 1966. *The hidden dimension.* Garden City, N.Y.: Anchor.

HAMBURG, D. A., ed. 1970. *Psychiatry as a behavioral science.* Englewood Cliffs, N.J.: Prentice-Hall.

HANDLIN, O. H. 1951. *The uprooted.* Boston: Little, Brown.

———. 1969. *Boston's immigrants,* rev. and enlarged ed. New York: Atheneum.

HARRIS, L. 1970. A *Life* poll. *Life,* January 9, p. 102.

HARTLEY, R. L. 1964. *The impact of viewing "aggression": Studies and problems of extrapolation.* New York: Columbia Broadcasting System.

HARTMANN, D. P. 1969. Influence of symbolically modelled instrumental aggression and pain cues on aggressive behavior. *Journal of Personality and Social Psychology* 11:280–88.

HARTMANN, H.; KRIS, E.; and LOWENSTEIN, R. 1949. Notes on the theory of aggression. In *The psychoanalytic study of the child,* vol. 3, ed. A. Freud, pp. 9–36. New York: International University Press.

HARTUP, W. W. 1974. Aggression in childhood: Developmental perspectives. *American Psychologist* 29:336–41.

HAWKE, C. C. 1950. Castration and sex crimes. *American Journal of Mental Deficiency* 55: 220–26.

HAWLEY, A. 1950. *Human ecology.* New York: Ronald Press.

HEIDER, F. 1958. *The psychology of interpersonal relations.* New York: Wiley.

HENDRICK, C., and TAYLOR, S. P. 1971. Effects of belief similarity and aggression on attraction and counter-aggression. *Journal of Personality and Social Psychology* 17:342–49.

HERRNSTEIN, R. J. 1973. *I.Q. in the meritocracy.* Boston: Atlantic-Little, Brown.

HESS, R. D., and TORNEY, J. V. 1968. *The development of political attitudes in children.* Garden City, N.Y.: Doubleday-Anchor.

HICKS, D. 1965. Imitation and retention of film-mediated aggressive peer and adult models. *Journal of Personality and Social Psychology* 2:97–100.

HILGARD, E. R. 1948. *Theories of learning.* New York: Appleton-Century-Crofts.

HIMES, J. W. 1966. The functions of racial conflict. *Social Forces* 45:1–10.

HINDE, R. A. 1970. *Animal behavior.* New York: McGraw-Hill.

HINDELANG, M. J. 1970. The commitment of delinquents to their misdeeds. *Social Problems* 17:502–9.

HOBBES, T. 1967. *The leviathan.* London: Oxford Univ. Press.

HOBSBAWM, E. J. 1959. *Primitive rebels.* New York: Norton.

HOCH, I. 1972. Income and city size. *Urban Studies* 9:299–328.

HOKANSON, J. 1970. Psychophysiological evaluation of the catharsis hypothesis. In *The dynamics of aggression,* ed. E. Megargee and J. Hokanson, pp. 74–86. New York: Harper & Row.

HOLDEN, C. 1973. Legitimate therapy or laundered lobotomy? *Science* 179:1109–12.

HOMANS, G. C. 1967. *The nature of social science.* New York: Harcourt, Brace and World.

HOROWITZ, I. L., and LIEBOWITZ, M. 1967. Social deviance and political marginality: Toward a redefinition of the relation between sociology and politics. *Social Problems* 15:280–96.

HOROWITZ, R., and SCHWARTZ, G. 1974. Honor, normative ambiguity and gang violence. *American Sociological Review* 39:238–51.

HOVLAND, C. I., and SEARS, R. R. 1940. Minor studies in aggression: VI. Correlation of lynchings with economic indices. *Journal of Psychology* 9:301–10.

HOWE, I. 1971. The city in literature. *Commentary* 51(5):61–68.

HYMAN, H. H. 1953. The value systems of different classes. In *Class, status and power,* ed. R. Bendix and S. M. Lipset, pp. 426–42. New York: Free Press.

————, and SINGER, E., eds. 1968. *Readings in reference group theory and research.* New York: Free Press.

INKELES, A. 1969. Making men modern: On the causes and consequences of individual change in six developing countries. *American Journal of Sociology* 75:208–25.

INSKO, C. A., and ROBINSON, J. E. 1967. Belief similarity *vs.* race as determinants of reactions to Negroes by Southern white adolescents: A further test of Rokeach's theory. *Journal of Personality and Social Psychology* 7:216–20.

ISAACSON, R. L.; DOUGLAS, R. J.; LUBAR, J. F.; and SCHMALTZ, L. W.

1971. *A primer of physiological psychology.* New York: Harper & Row.

IZARD, C. E. 1971. *The face of emotion.* New York: Appleton-Century-Crofts.

JACOBS, J. 1961. *The death and life of great American cities.* New York: Vintage.

JANOWITZ, M. 1969. Patterns of collective violence. In *Violence in America,* ed. H. D. Graham and T. R. Gurr, pp. 412–43. New York: Bantam Books.

JARVIK, L. F.; KLODIN, V.; and MATSUYAMA, S. S. 1973. Human aggression and the extra Y chromosome: Fact or fantasy? *American Psychologist* 28:674–82.

JEFFRIES, V.; TURNER, R. H.; and MORRIS, R. T. 1971. The public perception of the Watts riot as social protest. *American Sociological Review* 36:443–51.

JENSEN, A. 1973. The differences are real. *Psychology Today* 7(7):80–86.

JENSON, G. F. 1972. Parents, peers, and delinquent action. *American Journal of Sociology* 78:562–75.

JOHNSON, C. 1966. *Revolutionary change.* Boston: Little, Brown.

JOHNSON, R.; THOMSON, C.; and FRINCKE, G. 1960. Word values, word frequency, and visual duration thresholds. *Psychological Review* 67:332–42.

JOHNSON, R. N. 1972. *Aggression in man and animals.* Philadelphia: W. B. Sanders.

JOHNSON, T. J.; FEIGENBAUM, R.; and WEIBY, M. 1964. Some determinants and consequences of the teacher's perception of causation. *Journal of Educational Psychology* 55:237–46.

JONES, E. E., and DAVIS, K. E. 1965. From acts to dispositions: The attribution process in person perception. In *Advances in experimental social psychology,* vol. 2, ed. L. Berkowitz, pp. 220–37. New York: Academic Press.

————; and GERGEN, K. J. 1961. Role playing variations and their informational value for person perception. *Journal of Abnormal and Social Psychology* 63:302–10.

JONES, E. E., and NISBETT, R. E. 1971. *The actor and the observer: Divergent perceptions of the causes of behavior.* New York: General Learning Press.

JONES, J. 1972. *Prejudice and racism.* Reading, Mass.: Addison-Wesley.

JUVENAL. 1958. *The satires of Juvenal,* trans. R. Humphries. Bloomington, Ind.: Indiana Univ. Press.

KAADA, B. 1967. Brain mechanisms related to aggressive behavior. In *Aggression and defense*, ed. D. C. Clemente and D. B. Lindsley. Berkeley: Univ. of California Press.

KARLINS, M.; COFFMAN, T. L.; and WALTERS, G. 1969. Underfading of social stereotypes: Studies in three generations of college students. *Journal of Personality and Social Psychology* 13:1–16.

KASSARJIAN, H. H. 1969. The Negro and American advertising: 1946–1965. *Journal of Marketing Research* 13:29–39.

KATZ, D. 1960. The functional approach to the study of attitudes. *Public Opinion Quarterly* 24:163–77.

———, and BRALY, K. W. 1933. Racial stereotypes of 100 college students. *Journal of Abnormal and Social Psychology* 28:280–90.

KAUFMANN, H. 1970. *Aggression and altruism.* New York: Holt, Rinehart & Winston.

KELLEY, H. H. 1966. A classroom study of dilemmas in interpersonal negotiations. In *Strategic interaction and conflict*, ed. K. Archibald, pp. 49–73. Berkeley: Institute of International Studies.

———. 1967. Attribution theory in social psychology. In *Nebraska symposium on motivation*, ed. D. Levine, pp. 192–238. Lincoln: Univ. of Nebraska Press.

———. 1971. *Attribution in social interaction.* New York: General Learning Press.

———. 1972. *Causal schemata and the attribution process.* New York: General Learning Press.

———. 1973. The process of causal attribution. *American Psychologist* 28:107–28.

———; BECKMAN, L. L.; and FISCHER, C. S. 1967. Negotiating the division of a reward under incomplete information. *Journal of Experimental Social Psychology* 3:361–98.

KELLEY, H. H.; CONDRY, J.; DAHLKE, A.; and HILL, A. 1965. Collective behavior in a simulated panic situation. *Journal of Experimental Social Psychology* 1:20–54.

KELLEY, H. H., and STAHELSKI, A. J. 1970. Errors in perception of intentions in a mixed-motive game. *Journal of Experimental Social Psychology* 6:379–400.

KELMAN, H. 1958. Compliance, identification, and internalization: Three processes of opinion change. *Journal of Conflict Resolution* 2:51–60.

———. 1973. Violence without more restraint: Reflections on the dehumanization of victims and victimizers. *Journal of Social Issues* 29(4):25–62.

KERNER, O. (Chairman). 1968. *Report of the national advisory commission on civil disorders.* New York: Bantam Books.

KESSLER, S., and MOOS, R. H. 1969. XYY chromosome: Premature conclusions. *Science* 165:442.

KIESLER, C., and KIESLER, S. 1969. *Conformity.* Reading, Mass.: Addison-Wesley.

KILLIAN, L., and GRIGG, C. M. 1962. Urbanism, race, and anomie. *American Journal of Sociology* 67:661–65.

KIM, Y. K., and UMBACH, W. 1972. Combined stereotaxic lesions for treatment of behavior disorders and severe pain. Paper presented at the Third World Congress of Psycho-surgery, Cambridge, England, August 14–18.

KING, M. L., JR. 1964. *Why we can't wait.* New York: Signet.

KLAPPER, J. T. 1960. *The effects of mass communication.* New York: Free Press.

————. 1968. The impact of viewing "aggression." In *Violence in the mass media,* ed. O. Larsen, pp. 131–39. New York: Harper & Row.

KLEIN, M. W. 1969. Violence in American juvenile gangs. In *Crimes of violence,* ed. D. J. Mulvihill and M. M. Tumin, pp. 1427–60. Washington, D.C.: U.S. Government Printing Office.

KLUCKHOHN, C. 1951. The study of culture. In *The policy sciences,* ed. D. Lerner and H. D. Lasswell, pp. 86–101. Stanford: Stanford Univ. Press.

KLUEVER, H., and BUCY, P. C. 1937. "Psychic blindness" and other symptoms following bilateral temporal lobectomy in Rhesus monkeys. *American Journal of Physiology* 119:352–53.

KNAPP, M. L. 1972. Nonverbal communication. New York: Holt, Rinehart & Winston.

KRIESBERG, L. 1973. *The sociology of social conflicts.* Englewood Cliffs, N.J.: Prentice-Hall.

LANE, R. 1969. Urbanization and criminal violence in the 19th. century: Massachusetts as a test case. In *Violence in America,* ed. H. D. Graham and T. R. Gurr, pp. 468–84. New York: Bantam Books.

LANE, R. E., and LERNER, M. 1970. Why hard-hats hate hairs. *Psychology Today* 4:45ff.

LAPIERE, R. T. 1934. Attitudes *vs.* actions. *Social Forces* 13:230–37.

LARSEN, O., ed. 1968. *Violence in the mass media.* New York: Harper & Row.

LAZARUS, R. S. 1968. Emotions and adaptation. In *Nebraska symposium on motivation,* ed. W. J. Arnold, pp. 175–270. Lincoln: Univ. of Nebraska Press.

LeBon, G. 1896. *The crowd.* London: Ernest Benn.

LeMaire, L. 1956. Danish experience regarding the castration of sexual offenders. *Journal of Criminal Law and Criminology* 47:294–310.

Lenski, G. 1954. Status crystallization: A nonvertical dimension of social status. *American Sociological Review* 19:405–13.

———. 1966. *Power and privilege.* New York: McGraw-Hill.

Lerner, M. 1970. The desire for justice and the reaction to victims. In *Altruism and helping behavior,* ed. J. Macaulay and L. Berkowitz, pp. 205–29. New York: Academic Press.

Levy, S. G. 1969. A 150-year study of political violence in the United States. In *Violence in America,* ed. H. D. Graham and T. R. Gurr, pp. 84–100. New York: Bantam Books.

Lewis, O. 1965. Further observations on the folk-urban continuum and urbanization with special reference to Mexico City. In *The study of urbanization,* ed. P. H. Hanson and L. Schnore, pp. 491–503. New York: Wiley.

Lewis, W. H. 1961. Feuding and social change in Morocco. *Journal of Conflict Resolution* 5:43–54.

Leyhausen, P. 1965. The communal organization of solitary mammals. *Symposium of the Zoological Society of London* 14:249–63.

Lieberson, S. 1961. A societal theory of race and ethnic relations. *American Sociological Review* 26:902–10.

Liebert, R. M.; Neale, J. M.; and Davidson, E. S. 1973. *The early window.* New York: Pergamon.

Liebow, E. 1967. *Tally's corner.* Boston: Little, Brown.

Linton, R. 1936. *The study of man.* New York: Appleton-Century.

Lippitt, R., and White, R. K. 1965. An experimental study of leadership and group life. In *Basic studies in social psychology,* ed. H. Proshansky and B. Seidenberg, pp. 523–37. New York: Holt, Rinehart & Winston.

Lipset, S. M. 1963. *Political man.* Garden City, N.Y.: Anchor.

———, and Raab, E. 1970. *The politics of unreason.* New York: Harper & Row.

Lodhi, A. Q., and Tilly, C. 1973. Urbanization, crime, and collective violence in 19th. century France. *American Journal of Sociology* 79:296–318.

Loew, C. A. 1967. Acquisition of a hostile attitude and its relationship to aggressive behavior. *Journal of Personality and Social Psychology* 5:335–41.

LOFTIN, C. L., and HILL, R. H. 1973. Regional subculture and homicide. Paper presented at the American Sociological Association, New York.

LOMBROSO, C. 1911. *Crime, its causes and remedies,* trans. H. P. Horton. Boston: Little, Brown.

LORENZ, G. 1972. Aspirations of low-income blacks and whites: A case of reference group process. *American Journal of Sociology* 78:371–98.

LORENZ, K. 1966. *On aggression,* trans. M. K. Wilson. New York: Bantam Books.

LOTT, A. J., and LOTT, B. E. 1972. The power of liking: Consequences of interpersonal attitudes derived from a liberalized view of secondary reinforcement. In *Advances in experimental social psychology,* vol. 6, ed. L. Berkowitz, pp. 109–49. New York: Academic Press.

LÖVAAS, O. 1961. Interaction between verbal and nonverbal behavior. *Child Development* 32:329–36.

MACAULAY, J., and BERKOWITZ, L., eds. 1970. *Altruism and helping behavior.* New York: Academic Press.

MACCOBY, E. E. 1964. Effects of the mass media. In *Review of child development research,* vol. 1, ed. M. Hoffman and L. Hoffman, pp. 323–48. New York: Russell Sage.

McDOUGALL, W. 1960. *An introduction to social psychology.* London: Metheun.

McGUIRE, W. J. 1969. The nature of attitudes and attitude change. In *The handbook of social psychology,* vol. 3, ed. G. Lindzey and E. Aronson, pp. 136–314. Reading, Mass.: Addison-Wesley.

MACK, R. W., and SNYDER, R. C. 1957. The analysis of social conflict—toward an overview and synthesis. *Journal of Conflict Resolution* 1:212–48.

McKENZIE, R. D. 1925. The ecological approach to the study of the human community. In *The city,* ed. R. E. Park and E. W. Burgess. Chicago: Univ. of Chicago Press.

McNEIL, E. B., ed. 1965. *The nature of human conflict.* Englewood Cliffs, N.J.: Prentice-Hall.

MADGE, J. 1965. *The tools of social science.* Garden City, N.Y.: Anchor Books.

MADSEN, K. B. 1959. *Theories of motivation.* Copenhagen: Munksgaard.

MARK, V. H., and ERVIN, F. R. 1970. *Violence and the brain.* New York: Harper & Row.

MARX, G. T. 1970. Civil disorders and agents of social control. *Journal of Social Issues* 26(1):19–57.

MARX, K. 1933. *Wage-labor and capital.* New York: International Publishers.

————, and ENGELS, F. 1970. Manifesto of the Communist Party. In *K. Marx and F. Engels: Selected works.* New York: International Publishers.

MASELLI, M. D., and ALTROCCHI, J. 1969. Attribution of intention. *Psychological Bulletin* 71:445–54.

MAYER, K. B. 1964. *Class and society,* rev. ed. New York: Random House.

MEAD, M., ed. 1961. *Cooperation and competition among primitive peoples,* enlarged ed. Boston: Beacon Press.

MEDVEDEV, Z. A., and MEDVEDEV, R. A. 1971. *A question of madness.* New York: Knopf.

MEHRABIAN, A. 1969. Significance of posture and position in the communication of attitude and status relationships. *Psychological Bulletin* 71:359–72.

MELGES, F. T., and HARRIS, R. F. 1970. Anger and attack: A cybernetic model of violence. In *Violence and the struggle for existence,* ed. D. N. Daniels, M. F. Gilula, and F. M. Ochberg, pp. 97–128. Boston: Little, Brown.

MERTON, R. K. 1957. *Social theory and social structure,* rev. and expanded ed. New York: Free Press.

METTEE, D., and WILKINS, P. 1972. When similarity "hurts": Effects of perceived ability and a humorous blunder on interpersonal attractiveness. *Journal of Personality and Social Psychology* 22:246–58.

MICHELSON, W. 1970. *Man and his urban environment: A sociological approach.* Reading, Mass.: Addison-Wesley.

MILGRAM, S. 1963. Behavioral study of obedience. *Journal of Abnormal and Social Psychology* 67:371–78.

————. 1964. Group pressure and action against a person. *Journal of Abnormal and Social Psychology* 69:137–43.

————. 1965. Liberating effects of group pressure. *Journal of Personality and Social Psychology* 1:127–34.

————. 1970. The experience of living in cities. *Science* 167:1461–68.

MILLER, J. G. 1965. Living systems: Basic concepts. *Behavioral Science* 10:193–237.

MILLER, N. E. 1941. The frustration-aggression hypothesis. *Psychological Review* 48: 337–42.

MILLER, W. B. 1958. Lower class culture as a generating milieu of gang delinquency. *Journal of Social Issues* 14(3):5–19.

MILLS, C. W. 1956. *The power elite.* New York: Oxford Univ. Press.

MILNER, P. M. 1970. *Physiological psychology.* New York: Holt, Rinehart & Winston.

MINTZ, A. 1951. Non-adaptive group behavior. *Journal of Abnormal and Social Psychology* 46:150–59.

MITCHELL, R. E. 1971. Some social implications of high density housing. *American Sociological Review* 36:18–29.

MIZRUCHI, E. H. 1964. *Success and opportunity.* New York: Free Press.

MONTAGU, A., ed. 1968. *Man and aggression.* New York: Oxford Univ. Press.

MOYER, K. E. 1968. Kinds of aggression and their physiological basis. *Communications in Behavioral Biology* 2:65–87.

———. 1971. The physiology of aggression and the implications for aggression control. In *The control of aggression and violence,* ed. J. L. Singer, pp. 61–92. New York: Academic Press.

MULVIHILL, D. J., and TUMIN, M. M. 1969. *Crimes of violence.* Washington, D.C.: U.S. Government Printing Office.

MUMFORD, L. 1961. *The city in history.* New York: Harcourt, Brace and World.

MURRAY, H. A. 1933. The effect of fear upon the estimates of the maliciousness of other personalities. *Journal of Social Psychology* 4:310–29.

MUSSEN, P., and ROSENZWEIG, R. 1973. *Psychology.* Lexington, Mass.: D. C. Heath.

NEWCOMB, T. M. 1961. *The acquaintance process.* New York: Holt, Rinehart & Winston.

NEWMAN, O. 1972. *Defensible space.* New York: Macmillan.

NIEBURG, H. K. 1969. *Political violence: The behavioral process.* New York: St. Martin's Press.

OBERSCHALL, A. 1973. *Social conflict and social movements.* Englewood Cliffs, N.J.: Prentice-Hall.

OELSNER, L. 1971. The world of the city prostitute is a tough and lonely one. *New York Times Magazine,* August 9:31, 33.

OGBURN, W. F., and DUNCAN, O. D. 1967. City size as a sociological variable. In *Urban Sociology,* ed. E. W. Burgess and D. J. Bogue, pp. 58–76. Chicago: Univ. of Chicago Press.

OLSEN, M. E. 1965. Alienation and political opinions. *Public Opinion Quarterly* 29:200–12.

OLWEUS, D. 1972. Personality and aggression. In *Nebraska symposium on motivation*, ed. J. K. Cole and D. D. Jensen, pp. 261–322. Lincoln: Univ. of Nebraska Press.

ORNE, M. 1969. Demand characteristics and the concept of quasi-controls. In *Artifact in behavioral research*, ed. R. Rosenthal and R. Rosnow, pp. 143–79. New York: Academic Press.

OSTROM, T. M. 1969. The relationship between the affective, behavioral, and cognitive components of attitude. *Journal of Experimental Social Psychology* 5:12–30.

PAGE, L., and SCHEIDT, C. 1971. The elusive weapons effect: Demand awareness, evaluation apprehension, and slightly sophisticated subjects. *Journal of Personality and Social Psychology* 20:304–18.

PAIGE, K. E. 1973. Women learn to sing the menstrual blues. *Psychology Today* 7(4):41–6.

PALMER, J., and ALTROCCHI, J. 1967. Attribution of hostile intent as unconscious. *Journal of Personality* 35:164–77.

PANKSEPP, J. 1971. Aggression elicited by electrical stimulation of the hypothalamus in albino rats. *Physiological Behavior* 6:321–29.

PARKE, R. D.; EWALL, W.; and SLABY, R. G. 1972. Hostile and helpful verbalizations as regulators of nonverbal aggression. *Journal of Personality and Social Psychology* 23:243–48.

PARLEE, M. B. 1973. The premenstrual syndrome. *Psychological Bulletin* 80:454–65.

PATTERSON, G.; LITTMAN, R.; and BRICKER, W. 1967. Assertive behavior in children: A step toward a theory of aggression. *Monographs of the Society for Research in Child Development* 32(113).

PEPITONE, A. 1972. The social psychology of violence. *International Journal of Group Tension* 2:19–32.

———, and REICHLING, G. 1955. Group cohesiveness and the expression of hostility. *Human Relations* 8:327–37.

PERLMAN, D., and OSKAMP, S. 1971. The effects of picture content exposure frequency on evaluations of Negroes and whites. *Journal of Experimental Social Psychology* 7:503–14.

PETERFREUND, E., JR., and SCHWARTZ, J. T. 1972. *Information systems and psychoanalysis* (Psychological Issues and Monographs, Nos. 25–26). New York: International University Press.

PETTIGREW, T. F. 1958. The measurement and correlates of category width as a cognitive variable. *Journal of Personality* 26:532–44.

———. 1961. Social psychology and desegregation research. *American Psychologist* 16:105–12.

————. 1964. *A profile of the Negro American*. New York: Van Nostrand.

————. 1964. *A profile of the Negro American*. New York: Van Nostrand.

————. 1967. Social evaluation theory: Convergence and applications. *Nebraska symposium on motivation*, ed., D. Levine, pp. 241–315. Lincoln: Univ. of Nebraska Press.

————. 1971. *Racially separate or together?* New York: McGraw-Hill.

————, and SPIER, R. B. 1962. The ecological structure of Negro homicide. *American Journal of Sociology* 67:621–29.

PIAGET, J. 1965. *The moral judgment of the child*. New York: Free Press.

PILIAVIN, I. M.; RODIN, J.; and PILIAVIN, J. A. 1969. Good Samaritanism: An underground phenomenon? *Journal of Personality and Social Psychology* 13:289–300.

PILISUK, M.; KIRITZ, S.; and CLAMPITT, S. 1971. Undoing deadlocks of distrust. *Journal of Conflict Resolution* 15:81–96.

PLUTCHIK, R. 1962. *The emotions: Facts, theories, and a new model*. New York: Random House.

POSTMAN, L.; BRUNER, J.; and McGINNIES, E. 1948. Personal values as selective factors in perception. *Journal of Abnormal and Social Psychology* 43:142–54.

PRIBRAM, K. H. 1962. Interrelations of psychology and the neurological disciplines. In *Psychology: A study of a science*, vol. 4, ed. S. Koch, pp. 119–57. New York: McGraw-Hill.

PRUITT, D. G., and SNYDER, R. C., eds. 1969. *Theory and research on the causes of war*. Englewood Cliffs, N.J.: Prentice-Hall.

RAINWATER, L. 1970. *Behind ghetto walls*. Chicago: Aldine.

RANSFORD, E. 1972. Blue collar anger: Reactions to students and black protest. *American Sociological Review* 37:333–46.

RAPER, A. F. 1933. *The tragedy of lynching*. Chapel Hill, N.C.: Univ. of North Carolina Press.

RAPOPORT, A. 1960. *Fights, games, and debates*. Ann Arbor: Univ. of Michigan Press.

————. 1969. Foreword. In *Modern systems research for the social scientist*, ed. W. Buckley. Chicago: Aldine.

————, and CHAMMAH, A. M. 1970. *Prisoner's dilemma*. Ann Arbor: Univ. of Michigan Press.

RECKLESS, W. C. 1967. *The crime problem*. New York: Appleton-Century-Crofts.

REDFIELD, R. 1947. The folk society. *American Journal of Sociology* 52: 293–308.

REISMAN, S. R., and SCHOPLER, J. 1973. An analysis of the attribution process and an application to determinants of responsibility. *Journal of Personality and Social Psychology* 25:361–69.

REISS, A. J., JR. 1959. Rural-urban and status differences in interpersonal contacts. *American Journal of Sociology* 65:182–95.

RICHARDSON, L. 1960. *Arms and insecurity*. Pittsburgh: Boxwood.

RIVERA, R. J., and SHORT, J. F., JR. 1968. Significant adults, caretakers, and structures of opportunity. In *Gang delinquency and delinquent subcultures*, ed. J. F. Short, Jr., pp. 209–43. New York: Harper & Row.

ROBERTS, B. C. 1969. On the origins and resolution of English working-class protest. In *Violence in America*, ed. H. D. Graham and T. R. Gurr, pp. 245–80. New York: Bantam Books.

ROBINSON, J. P. 1970. Public reaction to political protest: Chicago 1968. *Public Opinion Quarterly* 34:1–9.

ROKEACH, M. 1960. *The open and closed mind*. New York: Basic Books.

———. 1966. Attitude change and behavior change. *Public Opinion Quarterly* 30:529–48.

ROSENBERG, M. J., and HOVLAND, C. I. 1960. Cognitive, affective, and behavioral components of attitudes. In *Attitude organization and change*, ed. M. J. Rosenberg, C. I. Hovland, M. J. McGuire, R. P. Abelson, and J. W. Brehm, pp. 1–14. New Haven: Yale Univ. Press.

ROSVOLD, M. E.; MIRSKY, A. F.; and PRIBRAM, K. H. 1954. Influences of amygdalectomy on social behavior in monkeys. *Journal of Comparative and Physiological Psychology* 47:173–78.

RUDE, G. 1964. *The crowd in history: 1730–1848*. New York: Wiley.

RULE, B. G., and HEWITT, L. S. 1971. Effects of thwarting on cardiac response and physical aggression. *Journal of Personality and Social Psychology* 19:181–87.

RULE, J., and TILLY, C. 1972. 1830 and the unnatural history of revolution. *Journal of Social Issues* 28(1):49–76.

RYAN, W. 1971. *Blaming the victim*. New York: Vintage Books.

RYTINA, J. H.; FORM, W. H.; and PEASE, J. 1970. Income and stratification ideology: Beliefs about the American opportunity structure. *American Journal of Sociology* 75: 703–16.

SAMPSON, E. E. 1971. *Social psychology and contemporary society*. New York: Wiley.

SANFORD, N., and COMSTOCK, C. 1971. *Sanctions for evil*. San Francisco: Jossey-Bass.

SCHACHTER, S. 1951. Deviation, rejection, and communication. *Journal of Abnormal and Social Psychology* 46:190–207.

————. 1971. Some extraordinary facts about obese humans and rats. *American Psychologist* 26:129–44.

————, and SINGER, J. 1962. Cognitive, social and physiological determinants of emotional state. *Psychological Review* 69:379–99.

SCHAFER, E., and MURPHY, G. 1943. The role of autism in a visual figure-ground relationship. *Journal of Experimental Psychology* 32: 335–43.

SCHERER, K. R. 1970. *Nonverbale Kommunikation*. Hamburg: Buske.

————. 1970–71. Stereotype change following exposure to counter-stereotypical media heroes. *Journal of Broadcasting* 15:91–100.

————. 1972. Judging personality from voice: A cross-cultural approach to an old issue in interpersonal perception. *Journal of Personality* 40:191–210.

————. 1974. Acoustic concomitants of emotional dimensions. In *Readings in nonverbal communication*, ed. S. Weitz, pp. 105–11. New York: Oxford Univ. Press.

————; KOIVUMAKI, J.; and ROSENTHAL, R. 1972. Minimal cues in the vocal communication of affect. *Journal of Psycholinguistic Research* 1:269–85.

SCHORR, A. L. 1963. *Slums and social insecurity*. Washington, D.C.: U.S. Government Printing Office.

SCHORSKE, C. E. 1963. The idea of the city in European thought: Voltaire to Spengler. In *The historian and the city*, ed. O. H. Handlin and J. Burchard, pp. 95–114. Cambridge, Mass.: Massachusetts Institute of Technology Press.

SCHUCK, J., and PISOR, K. 1974. Evaluating an aggression experiment by the use of simulating subjects. *Journal of Personality and Social Psychology* 29:181–87.

SCOTT, J. 1958. *Aggression*. Chicago: Univ. of Chicago Press.

SEARS, D. O., and ABELES, R. P. 1969. Attitudes and opinions. In *Annual review of psychology*, vol. 20, ed. P. H. Mussen and M. R. Rosenzweig, pp. 253–88. Palo Alto, Calif.: Annual Reviews.

SEARS, D. O., and McCONAHAY, J. B. 1970. The politics of discontent: Blocked mechanisms of grievance redress and the psychology of the new urban black man. In *The Los Angeles riots*, ed. N. Cohen, pp. 413–79. Los Angeles: Institute of Government and Public Affairs, University of California.

SEARS, D. O., and TOMLINSON, T. M. 1968. Riot ideology in Los Angeles: A study of Negro attitudes. *Social Science Quarterly* 49:485–503.

SECORD, P. F., and BACKMAN, C. W. 1964. *Social psychology*. New York: McGraw-Hill.

SEELEY, J. R. 1967. The slum: Its nature, use, and users. In *Urban renewal: People, politics, and planning*, ed. J. Bellush and M. Hausknecht, pp. 104–20. Garden City, N.Y.: Anchor.

SEEMAN, M. 1959. On the meaning of alienation. *American Sociological Review* 24:783–91.

SEWELL, W. H., and AMEND, E. E. 1943. The influence of size of home community on attitudes and personality traits. *American Sociological Review* 8:180–84.

SHAVER, K. G. 1970. Defensive attribution: Effects of severity and relevance on the responsibility assigned for an accident. *Journal of Personality and Social Psychology* 14:101–13.

SHAW, C. R., and McKAY, H. D. 1969. *Juvenile delinquency and urban areas*, rev. ed. Chicago: Univ. of Chicago Press.

SHAW, J. I., and SKOLNICK, P. 1971. Attribution of responsibility for a happy accident. *Journal of Personality and Social Psychology* 18:380–84.

SHAW, M. E., and SULZER, J. L. 1964. An empirical test of Heider's levels of attribution of responsibility. *Journal of Abnormal and Social Psychology* 69:39–46.

SHERIF, M. 1956. Experiments in group conflict. *Scientific American* 195(5):54–58.

———. 1965. Formation of social norms: The experimental paradigm. In *Basic studies in social psychology*, ed. H. Proshansky and B. Seidenberg, pp. 461–70. New York: Holt, Rinehart & Winston.

SHIBUTANI, T., and KWAN, K. M. 1965. *Ethnic stratification*. New York: Macmillan.

SHOMER, R. W.; DAVIS, A. H.; and KELLEY, H. H. 1966. Threats and the development of coordination: Further studies of the Deutsch and Krauss trucking game. *Journal of Personality and Social Psychology* 4:119–26.

SHORT, J. F., JR. 1957. Differential association and delinquency. *Social Problems* 4:233–39.

———. 1968. *Gang delinquency and delinquent subcultures*. New York: Harper & Row.

———; RIVERA, R.; and TENNYSON, R. A. 1965. Perceived opportunities, gang membership, and delinquency. *American Sociological Review* 20:56–67.

SHORT, J. F., JR., and STRODTBECK, F. L. 1965. *Group process and gang delinquency*. Chicago: Univ. of Chicago Press.

SIGALL, H., and PAGE, R. 1971. Current stereotypes: A little fading, a little faking. *Journal of Personality and Social Psychology* 18:247–55.

SILVERMAN, B. I. 1974. Consequences, racial discrimination and the principle of belief congruence. *Journal of Personality and Social Psychology* 79:497–508.

SIMMEL, G. 1951. *Conflict*, trans. K. H. Wolff. Glencoe, Ill.: Free Press.

———. 1957. The metropolis and mental life. In *Cities and society*, rev. ed., ed. P. K. Hatt and A. J. Reiss, Jr., pp. 635–46. New York: Free Press.

SIMMONS, R. G., and ROSENBERG, M. 1971. Functions of children's perceptions of the stratification system. *American Sociological Review* 36:235–49.

SIMPSON, G. E., and YINGER, J. M. 1965. *Racial and cultural minorities*, 3rd. ed. New York: Harper & Row.

SINGER, J. L. 1971. The influence of violence portrayed in television or motion pictures upon overt aggressive behavior. In *The control of aggression and violence*, ed. J. L. Singer, pp. 19–60. New York: Academic Press.

SIPES, R. G. 1973. War, sports and aggression: An empirical test of two rival theories. *American Anthropologist* 75:64–86.

SKINNER, B. F. 1953. *Science and human behavior*. New York: Macmillan.

———. 1971. *Beyond freedom and dignity*. New York: Knopf.

SMELSER, N. J. 1962. *Theory of collective behavior*. New York: Free Press.

SMITH, C. R.; WILLIAMS, L.; and WHITE, R. H. 1967. Race, sex, and belief as determinants of friendship acceptance. *Journal of Personality and Social Psychology* 5:127–37.

SOLOMON, F.; WALKER, W. L.; O'CONNOR, G. J.; and FISHMAN, J. R. 1965. Civil rights activity and reduction in crime among Negroes. *Archives of General Psychology* 12:227–36.

SOMER, R. 1969. *Personal space*. Englewood Cliffs, N.J.: Prentice-Hall.

SOUTHWICK, C. H., ed. 1963. *Primate social behavior*. Princeton, N.J.: Van Nostrand.

SPILERMAN, S. 1971. The causes of racial disturbances: Tests of an explanation. *American Sociological Review* 36:427–42.

STAFFORD, J. E.; BIRDWELL, A. E.; and VAN TASSEL, C. E. 1970. Integrated advertising—white backlash? *Journal of Advertising Research* 10: 15–20.

STARK, R., and McENVOY, J., III. 1970. Middle-class violence. *Psychology Today* 4(6):52ff.

STAUB, E. 1971. The learning and unlearning of aggression: The role of anxiety, empathy, efficacy, and prosocial values. In *The control of aggression and violence,* ed. J. L. Singer, pp. 94–124. New York: Academic Press.

STEIN, D. D.; HARDYCK, J. A.; and SMITH, M. B. 1965. Race and belief: An open and shut case. *Journal of Personality and Social Psychology* 1:281–89.

STEINER, I. 1970. Perceived freedom. In *Advances in experimental social psychology,* vol. 5, ed. L. Berkowitz, pp. 187–249. New York: Academic Press.

STINCHCOMBE, A. L. 1968. *Constructing social theories.* New York: Harcourt, Brace and World.

STRAUSS, A. 1961. *Images of the American city.* New York: Free Press of Glencoe.

STREUFERT, S., and SANDLER, S. I. 1971. A laboratory test of the mirror image hypothesis. *Journal of Applied Social Psychology* 1:378–97.

STYKES, G. M., and MATZA, D. 1957. Techniques of neutralization: A theory of delinquency. *American Sociological Review* 22:664–70.

The Surgeon General's Scientific Advisory Committee on Television and Social Behavior. 1972. *Television and growing up.* Washington, D.C.: U.S. Government Printing Office.

SUTHERLAND, E. H. 1940. White collar criminality, *American Sociological Review* 5:1–12.

———, and CRESSEY, D. R. 1970. *Criminology,* 8th ed. Philadelphia: Lippincott.

SUTTLES, G. D. 1968. *The social order of the slum.* Chicago: Univ. of Chicago.

SWEET, W. H.; ERVIN, F. R.; and MARK, V. H. 1969. The relationship of violent behavior to focal cerebral disease. In *Aggressive behavior,* ed. S. Garattini and E. B. Sigg, pp. 336–52. New York: Wiley.

SWINGLE, P. G. 1970. Dangerous games. In *The structure of conflict,* ed. P. G. Swingle, pp. 265–72. New York: Academic Press.

SZABO, D. 1960. *Crimes et villes.* Paris: Cujas.

SZASZ, T. S. 1961. *The myth of mental illness.* New York: Harper & Row.

TAJFEL, H. 1969. Social and cultural factors in perception. In *Handbook of social psychology,* vol. 3, ed. G. Lindzey and E. Aronson, pp. 315–94. Reading, Mass.: Addison-Wesley.

TANNENBAUM, P. H. 1972. Studies in film- and television-mediated arousal and aggression: A progress report. In *Television and social behavior,* vol. 5, ed. G. A. Comstock, E. A. Rubinstein, and J. P.

Murray, pp. 309–50. Washington, D.C.: U.S. Government Printing Office.

TAYLOR, S., and METTEE, D. 1971. When similarity breeds contempt. *Journal of Personality and Social Psychology* 20:75–81.

TEITELBAUM, P. 1967. *Physiological psychology.* Englewood Cliffs, N.J.: Prentice-Hall.

THIBAUT, J. W., and KELLEY, H. H. 1959. *The social psychology of groups.* New York: Wiley.

TILLY, C. 1969. Collective violence in European perspective. In *Violence in America,* ed. H. D. Graham and T. R. Gurr, pp. 4–44. New York: Bantam Books.

———. 1974. The chaos of the living city. In *The urban world,* ed. C. Tilly. Boston: Little, Brown.

TINBERGEN, N. 1969. *The study of instinct.* New York: Oxford Univ. Press.

TOCH, H. H., and SCHULTE, R. 1961. Readiness to perceive violence as a result of police training. *British Journal of Psychology* 52:389–93.

TOMLINSON, T. M. 1968. The development of a riot ideology among urban Negroes. *American Behavioral Scientist* 11:27–31.

TRIANDIS, H. C., and DAVIS, E. E. 1965. Race and belief and determinants of behavioral intentions. *Journal of Personality and Social Psychology* 2:715–25.

TROTTER, S. 1974. Proposed violence center "swirling in controversy." *APA Monitor* 5(4):5.

TUMIN, M. E., ed. 1970. *Readings on social stratification.* Englewood Cliffs, N.J.: Prentice-Hall.

TURNER, R. H. 1969. The public perception of protest. *American Sociological Review* 34:815–31.

ULRICH, R. 1966. Pain as a cause of aggression. *American Zoologist* 6:643–62.

U.S. Bureau of the Census. 1971. *Census of population and housing: 1970. General demographic trends for metropolitan areas, 1960–1970, final report PHC (2)-1.* Washington, D.C.: U.S. Government Printing Office.

U.S. Department of Justice. 1971. *Uniform crime reports—1970.* Washington, D.C.: U.S. Government Printing Office.

VADYA, A. 1961. Expansion and warfare among Swidden agriculturalists. *American Anthropologist* 63:346–58.

———. 1967. Hypotheses about the functions of war. In *War: The anthropology of armed conflict and aggression,* ed. M. Fried, M.

Harris, and R. Murphy, pp. 85–91. Garden City, N.Y.: Natural History Press.

VALENSTEIN, E. S. 1973. *Brain control.* New York: Wiley.

VETTER, H. J. 1969. *Language behavior and communication.* Itasca, Ill.: F. E. Peacock.

WALLACE, C. 1918. Appetites and aversions as constituents of instincts. *Biological Bulletin* 34:91–107.

WALSTER, E. 1966. Assignment of responsibility for an accident. *Journal of Personality and Social Psychology* 3:73–79.

————. 1967. 'Second-guessing' important events. *Human Relations* 20: 239–50.

————; BERSCHEID, E.; and WALSTER, G. W. 1973. New directions in equity research. *Journal of Personality and Social Psychology* 25: 151–76.

WALTERS, R., and BROWN, M. 1963. Studies of reinforcement of aggression: III. Transfer of responses to an interpersonal situation. *Child Development* 34:563–71.

WASKOW, A. I. 1967. *From race riot to sit-in: 1919 and the 1960's.* Garden City, N.Y.: Anchor Books.

WATSON, R. I., JR. 1973. Investigation into deindividuation using a cross-cultural survey technique. *Journal of Personality and Social Psychology* 25:342–45.

WEBB, S. D. 1972. Crime and the division of labor: Testing a Durkheimian model. *American Journal of Sociology* 78:643–56.

WEITZ, S. 1971. Attitude, voice, and behavior: A repressed affect model of interracial interaction. Ph.D. dissertation, Harvard University.

WELLMAN, B.; CRAVEN, P.; WHITAKER, M.; STEVENS, H.; SCHORRER, A.; DUTOIT, S.; and BAKKER, H. 1973. Community ties and support systems. In *The form of cities in central Canada,* ed. L. S. Bourne, R. D. MacKinnon, and J. W. Simmons. Toronto: Univ. of Toronto.

WESTERGAARD, J. H. 1966. *Scandinavian urbanism.* London: Centre for Urban Studies.

WHITE, M., and WHITE L. 1962. *The intellectual versus the city.* New York: Mentor.

WHITE, R. K. 1966. Misperception and the Vietnam War. *Journal of Social Issues* 22(3):1–164.

WHYTE, W. F. 1955. *Street corner society.* Chicago: Univ. of Chicago Press.

WICKER, A. W. 1969. Attitudes *vs.* actions: The relationship of verbal and overt behavioral responses to attitude objects. *Journal of Social Issues* 24(4):41–78.

WILKS, J. A. 1967. Ecological correlates of crime and delinquency. In *Crime and its impact—an assessment*, Task Force Report of the President's Commission on Law Enforcement and Administration of Justice, pp. 138–56. Washington, D.C.: U.S. Government Printing Office.

WILLER, D., and ZOLLSCHAN, G. K. 1964. Prolegomenon to a theory of revolution. In *Explorations in social change*, ed. G. K. Zollschan and W. Hirsch, pp. 125–51. Boston: Houghton-Mifflin.

WILLIS, R. H. 1963. Two dimensions of conformity-nonconformity. *Sociometry* 26:499–513.

———. 1965. Conformity, independence, and anti-conformity. *Human Relations* 18:150–56.

WILSON, J. Q. 1966. *Urban renewal*. Cambridge: Massachusetts Institute of Technology Press.

———. 1968. The urban unease. *The Public Interest* 12:1125–39.

WIRTH, L. 1938. Urbanization as a way of life. *American Journal of Sociology* 44:3–24.

WITKIN, H. A.; DYK, R. B.; FATERSON, H. F.; GOODENOUGH, D. R.; and KAPP, S. A. 1962. *Psychological differentiation: Studies in development*. New York: Wiley.

WOLF, E. R. 1969. *Peasant wars of the twentieth century*. New York: Harper & Row.

WOLFGANG, M. E. 1966. *Patterns in criminal homicide*. New York: Wiley.

———. 1967. *Crimes of violence*. Unpublished manuscript. Department of Sociology, University of Pennsylvania, 1967.

———. 1970. Urban crime. In *The metropolitan enigma*, ed. J. Q. Wilson. Garden City, N.Y.: Anchor.

———, and FERRACUTI, F. 1967. *The subculture of violence*. London: Social Science Paperbacks.

WOLFGANG, M. E.; FIGLIO, R. M.; and SELLIN, T. 1972. *Delinquency in a birth cohort*. Chicago: Univ. of Chicago Press.

WOLFGANG, M. E.; SAVITZ, L.; and JOHNSTON, N., eds. 1962. *The sociology of crime and delinquency*. New York: Wiley.

WYLIE, L. 1964. *Village in the Vaucluse*, 2d ed. New York: Harper & Row.

YOUNG, M., and WILLMOTT, P. 1957. *Family and kinship in East London*. New York: Humanities Press.

ZILLMAN, D. 1971. Excitation transfer in communication-mediated aggressive behavior. *Journal of Experimental Social Psychology* 7:419–34.

ZIMBARDO, P. G. 1969. The human choice: Individuation, reason, and order *vs.* deindividuation, impulse, and chaos. In *Nebraska symposium on motivation,* ed. W. J. Arnold, pp. 237–307. Lincoln: Univ. of Nebraska Press.

———. 1973. A Pirandellian prison. *New York Times,* April 8.

ZIMMER, B. 1972. Urban centrifugal drift. Paper prepared for the Panel on the Significance of Community in the Metropolitan Setting, National Academy of Science.

author index

subject index

Abnormal behavior, 10-11
Adaptation. *See* Coping
Adrenalin, 33
Aggression:
  anthropology of, 5-6, 184 (*n.* 56)
  brain "centers" for, 12-28
  control of, 9-10
  as coping behavior, 64, 72-76, 81
  definition, 2-5
  as disease, 10-11
  ethological theory of, 47-55
  evolutionary functions of, 51-53, 55
  expressive, 197
  fantasy, 4
  fear-induced, 16
  frustration-aggression theory, 57-63, 74
  genetic factors in, 28-30
  hormonal factors in, 32-34, 54
  inhibition of, 19-20, 22-23, 52-54, 60-61, 70, 84, 92-93, 101
  instrumental, 3-4, 36, 58-59, 72, 76, 86-87, 197
  intentionality of, 59, 66
  justification of, 101
  learning theories of, 76, 81-94
  psychoanalytic theory of, 43-47
  subinstincts of, 53-55
  types of, 26

Aggression (*cont.*)
  verbal, 4, 92
  and violence, 4
Aggression machine, 68-69, 87, 97-98
Aggressive behavior:
  completion tendency in, 99
  as functionally autonomous motive, 88-89
  intermittent reinforcement of, 91
  models for, 82-86, 93, 100-101
  punishment of. *See* Punishment
  reinforcement of, 82, 86, 92
  response generalization in, 92
  stimulus discrimination in, 90
  stimulus generalization in, 89-90
  vicarious reinforcement of, 83
Aggressive cues, 57, 60, 70-72, 101, 116, 118
  other person's emotions as, 137-43
  and social norms, 164-65
  weapons, 52-53, 70, 101, 111 (*Fig.* 4-2), 117
Aggressive drive, 44-56, 66
Aggressive energy, 48-50, 54-55
Aggressive targets. *See* Victims
Alcohol, 32
Alienation, 208, 210, 219 (*n.* 54), 236, 230-33. *See also* Anomie